INSIGHT GUIDE

Caribbean

The Lesser Antilles

Part of the Langenscheidt Publishing Group

About This Book

Editorial

Project Editor
Caroline Radula-Scott
Managing Editor
Lesley Gordon
Editorial Director
Brian Bell

Distribution

UK & Ireland
GeoCenter International Ltd
The Viables Centre
Harrow Way
Basingstoke
Hants RG22 4BJ
Fax: (44) 1256-817988

United States
Langenscheidt Publishers, Inc.
46–35 54th Road
Maspeth, NY 11378
Fax: (718) 784-0640

Worldwide
APA Publications GmbH & Co.
Verlag KG (Singapore Branch)
38 Joo Koon Road
Singapore 628990
Tel: (65) 865-1600
Fax: (65) 861-6438

Printing

Insight Print Services (Pte) Ltd
38 Joo Koon Road
Singapore 628990
Tel: (65) 865-1600
Fax: (65) 861-6438

First Edition 1992
Fourth Edition 1999

CONTACTING THE EDITORS
Although every effort is made to provide accurate information in this publication, we live in a fast-changing world and would appreciate it if readers would call our attention to any errors or outdated information that may occur by writing to us at:
Insight Guides, P.O. Box 7910, London SE1 8ZB, England.
Fax: (44 171) 620-1074.
e-mail:
insight@apaguide.demon.co.uk

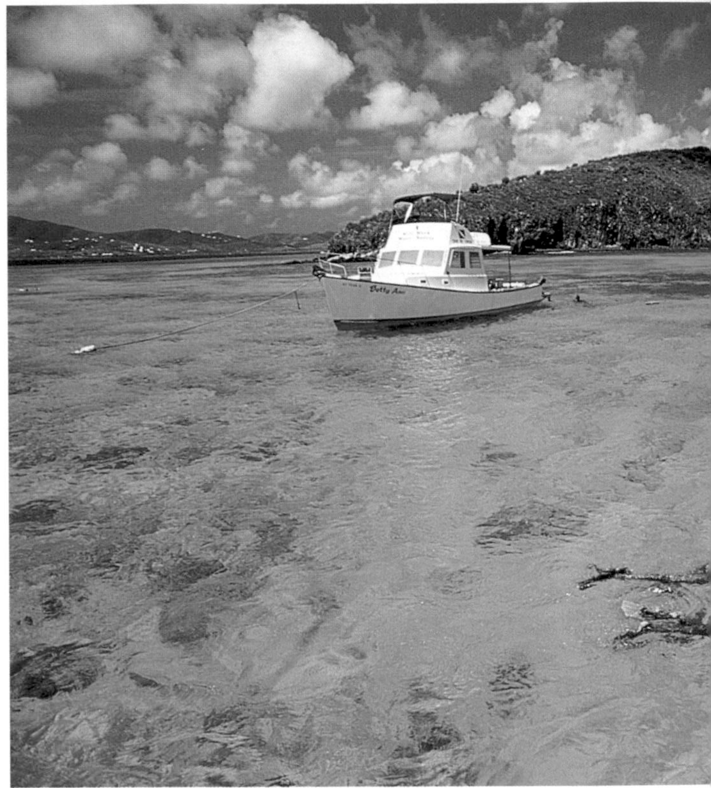

This guidebook combines the interests and enthusiasms of two of the world's best known information providers: Insight Guides, whose titles have set the standard for visual travel guides since 1970, and Discovery Channel, the world's premier source of nonfiction television programming.

The editors of Insight Guides provide both practical advice and general understanding about a destination's history, culture, institutions and people. Discovery Channel and its Web site, www.discovery.com, help millions of viewers explore their world from the comfort of their own home and also encourage them to explore it firsthand.

How to use this book

Insight Guides have a proven formula of informative and well-written text with a fresh photo-journalistic approach.

◆ The first section, with a yellow color bar, covers the region's tumultuous **history** and lively, modern **culture** in authoritative **features**.

◆ The **Places** section, with a blue bar, provides a chapter for each island. Interesting sights, popular beaches, and

nature and marine reserves are cross-referenced by numbers or letters to full-color **maps**.

◆ The **Travel Tips** section at the back includes recommendations on travel, hotels and restaurants. Information can be found quickly by using the index on the back cover flap – a useful bookmark.

◆ **Photographs** are chosen to illustrate the region's beauty as well as convey atmosphere.

The contributors

This new edition was edited by **Caroline Radula-Scott** and builds on the original produced by **David Schwab**. New chapters have been contributed by **Polly Pattullo** and **James Ferguson**, both writers specializing in the Caribbean. Pattullo, whose books include *The Gardens of Dominica*, wrote "Islands in the Sun", chapters on Dominica and Montserrat and the "Insight on..." tropical plants. Ferguson, whose books include the *Traveller's History of the Caribbean*, added to the history section originally written by the late historian **Gordon Lewis**, wrote new chapters on Grenada, island people and literature, updated novelist **Maryse Condé**'s chapter on Guadeloupe, **Neil Bissoondath**'s on Martinique, and contributed to the music chapter originated by Barbadian writer **Michelle Springer**.

"Creole Cuisine" was written by **Sally Miller** who with her husband **Keith Miller**, co-ordinator of much of the book's updating, publish *Ins and Outs of Barbados* and *Barbados in a Nutshell*. Caribbean specialist **Trudie Trox** contributed new chapters on the BVI, Saba and Statia and provided "Insight On..." architecture, diving, boating and Carnival. **Christine Rettenmeier** wrote Trinidad and Tobago and the ABC Islands and **Robert Möginger** Antigua and St Lucia. Contributors also include **Charles Seibert**, **Louisa Campbell**, **Bob Shacochis**, **Larry Breiner**, **David Yeadon**, **Rachel Wilder**, **Dawn King-Steele** and **Pamela Harris**. The Travel Tips section was compiled and edited by **Fiona Duncan** and **Jane Simmonds**. **Adrienne Wyper** proofread the text.

New photographs by **Bob Krist** join the originals taken by **Mitch Epstein** and others.

Map Legend

—··	International Boundary
----	Parish Boundary
—•—	National Park/Reserve
----	Ferry Route
✈ ✈	Airport: International/Regional
🚌	Bus Station
P	Parking
i	Tourist Information
✉	Post Office
✝ ✝ ✝	Church/Ruins
†	Monastery
☪	Mosque
✡	Synagogue
♜ ♜	Castle/Ruins
∴	Archaeological Site
∩	Cave
𝐈	Statue/Monument
★	Place of Interest

The main places of interest in the Places section are coordinated by a number with a full-color map (e.g. ❶), and a symbol at the top of every right-hand page tells you where to find the map.

INSIGHT GUIDE
Caribbean

Contents

Maps

Introduction

History

Features

Dutch-inspired architecture on the ABC Islands

Insight on ...

Information panels

Places

Travel Tips

♦ **Full Travel Tips index is on page 314**

BARBADOS

WELCOME

Stay a while in the sunny Caribbean and you will discover a rainbow of cultures and a rich and exciting history

The Lesser Antilles, from St Thomas in the north to Aruba, off the Venezuelan coast in the south, comprise some of the most magnificently beautiful landscapes on the face of the earth. Within this chain of more than 20 major islands and countless uninhabited cays and islets – known also as the Eastern Caribbean and the West Indies – there seems to be every conceivable shade of blue in the water, every variation of flower, every species of brightly colored bird. The air is balmy and perfumed, the nights are consistently clear, the days are bathed in warm sunshine. Even when it is wet, the rain is warm, refreshing and usually comes in short bursts. Indeed it seems as if everything, the climate, the waters, the land, is unimaginably perfect.

But in some ways such beauty has been a bit of a curse. The world tends to forget that the Lesser Antilles is not one great holiday resort but a collection of small nations and territories struggling to forge economic and political identities; that it possesses both a remarkable and often tragic history, fought over for centuries by warring European countries, and that it has an astonishingly diverse culture – each island proud of its own.

There is a story told by an English historian about discovering a British school in which there were German nuns teaching local children out of an English textbook which they had to explain in Spanish. A wonderful analogy for a history and culture produced by startling combinations. Begin with two remarkable primitive Indian societies, add the influence of the 16th-century gold-seeking Spaniards and their European rivals: the French, English, Dutch, Danes and even the Knights Templars of Malta; add pirates, religious and political refugees, and a huge African slave culture, then stir in Hindus, Jews and Rastafarians and you have the dizzying recipe that makes up these islands.

As these hospitable West Indian isles become more and more accessible, with tourism now the mainstay of their economy, there is a danger that their soul will be submerged in the onslaught of leisure developers. But if you tread carefully you can help preserve the spirit of the Caribbean and all it entails, and because the people are, in general, so open, you can easily explore all its realms; political, religious and cultural. Read on... ❑

PRECEDING PAGES: folk dancers in Tobago; Marigot Bay, St Lucia; messing about in Meads Bay, Anguilla; fun in the sea.
LEFT: a welcoming smile.

ISLANDS IN THE SUN

The rich diversity of these tropical islands is plain to see – from their mountain rainforests to the ocean deep

The islands of the Lesser Antilles form a delicate necklace of coral, basalt and limestone stretching from the Virgin Islands (both British and American) in the north through a 1,500-mile (2,400-km) arc to the three Dutch islands of Aruba, Bonaire and Curaçao off the coast of Venezuela far to the south.

Each small landmass is often within sight of another. So when Amerindians, the earliest people to colonize the Eastern Caribbean, started to move north from South America, they could stand at the northern tip of one island and see – if only as a blurry mauve outline across a truculent channel – the southern tip of the next island. It was an encouragement, perhaps, to move on, to see what new creatures, plants, landscapes, opportunities lay on the horizon.

Each island to its own

The islands of the Eastern Caribbean are physically (and culturally) places of great variety. The images of sparkling white sand, clear turquoise sea and shimmering coconut palms of the travel advertisements do the region a disservice. It is a far richer region than that, with each island's topography reflecting the story of its creation and its history.

From the pristine rainforests of Dominica and St Lucia, where rain pounds the mountain tops with up to 300 in (760 cm) of water annually and tree ferns shimmer in a silver light, to the dry, brittle scrublands of acacia and logwood of St Martin or Barbuda, there seems to be a vegetation for every mood (holiday or otherwise). Even if you stay on only one island, there is often a remarkable range of ecology to be explored: from rainforest canopy to coastal swamp and coral reef.

The flatter islands are less varied and, in many cases, they have been more vulnerable to exploitation. Thus Antigua and Barbados lost their original forest covering to sugar cane plantations, leaving a landscape largely of "bush", with residual corners of sugar cane, cattle raising or vegetable growing.

The ocean and the deep blue sea

Yet wherever you arrive in the Caribbean you are greeted by a sweetness of smell and the breezes of the cooling trade winds. Its tropical climate delivers relatively constant hours of sunshine and a temperature hovering around 80°F (27°C).

The trade winds, which guided the first Europeans to the Caribbean at the end of the 15th century, blow in from the northeast, first over the typically wilder coasts of the wetter windward sides, which are buffeted by the tempestuous Atlantic Ocean, and then across in a more gentle fashion to the tranquil, leeward Caribbean Sea.

The contrast of the two coasts is often striking: with the wilder Atlantic side of most Eastern Caribbean islands having more in common

LEFT: the wild Atlantic coastline of Barbados.
RIGHT: canefields spread across land deforested by the early colonists.

with a Scottish seascape than the gentle white-sand beaches of the hotter and drier Caribbean coast often only a few miles away.

Alive and kicking

With the exception of Barbados, which is perched out on its own, much of the island chain (from Saba to Grenada), was created by volcanic action when the two tectonic plates which sit beneath the "necklace" shifted. The eastward-moving American plate pushed under the westward-moving Caribbean plate and threw up what became this pattern of islands. However, Barbados, to the southeast, was formed by a wedge of sediments pushed up slowly. It is encrusted with the remnants of ancient coral reefs which developed as the water became shallower over the sediments. To the south, Trinidad and Tobago were joined to Venezuela during the ice age when the sea levels were much lower, accounting for the similar fauna and flora on the islands.

Some islands are much older than others: those that have been worn down by erosion, subsided below sea level and then raised up again are the flatter, drier islands of Anguilla, St Martin, Barbuda, and Antigua, on the outside of the volcanic rim.

The geologically younger islands are physically more dramatic, with mountain ranges and steep-sided valleys. Some, such as Montserrat, Guadeloupe, St Vincent, Martinique, have experienced volcanic activity this century – from the devastation of the town of St Pierre in Martinique in 1902, when some 30,000 people were suddenly wiped out, to the most recent activity, which started in 1995 in the Soufrière Hills in the south of Montserrat.

The Montserrat crisis resulted in the "closure" of two thirds of the island, the deaths of 19 people and the evacuation of much of the population. In fact, *soufrière* (from the French word for sulfur) is the name given to volcanoes throughout the region. In St Lucia, for example, the "drive-in volcano", with its moonscape of bubbling mud, mineral pools of boiling water and sulfur springs, is the collapsed rim of a huge old volcano near the southern village of Soufrière.

This dramatic landscape continues underwater where there are mountains, including a submarine volcano just north of Grenada called Kick'

Rip-Roaring Hurricanes

A hurricane blows up when the atmosphere's pressure plunges far lower than that of the surrounding air. Usually spawned in the Atlantic, continuous winds of up to 150 mph (240 kph) blow around the eye, a calm central zone of several miles across where the sky is often blue.

Hurricanes can reach up to 500 miles (800 km) in width and travel northwestwards at 12 to 15 mph (19 to 24 kph), speeding up across land before losing force and dying out. They leave a wake of massive destruction to towns, homes and crops, but loss of life is minimal nowadays as islanders are warned of approaching storms and official hurricane shelters are allocated (*see* Travel Tips).

Lists of hurricane names are drawn up six years in advance in alphabetical order by the National Hurricane Center in Miami. The tradition started during World War II when US servicemen named the storms after their girlfriends. In 1979, concern for equal rights included the use of male names.

Memorable hurricanes have been David (1979), which devastated Dominica, Hugo (1989), which flattened Montserrat, and Luis (1995) which roared through the Leewards with Marilyn hot on his tail.

Em Jenny, caves, lava flows, overhangs, pinnacles, walls, reefs and forests of elkhorn coral.

Volcanoes apart, the threat from hurricanes is a constant feature of life in parts of the Eastern Caribbean, especially in the belt that stretches north from St Lucia to the Virgin Islands. The hurricane season (June too soon, July stand by, August it must, September remember, October all over) interrupts the rainy season, from May to Christmas, often to devastating effect, endangering lives and destroying homes, businesses and crops. The traditional dry season is from around Christmas to May, when water may be in short supply. It is then that the flowering trees and shrubs, like the red-bracted poinsettia, put on their most festive display.

SLY MONGOOSE

The mongoose was introduced in 1870 to control rats and snakes, but it turned out to be a pest itself, plundering birds' nests and now garbage.

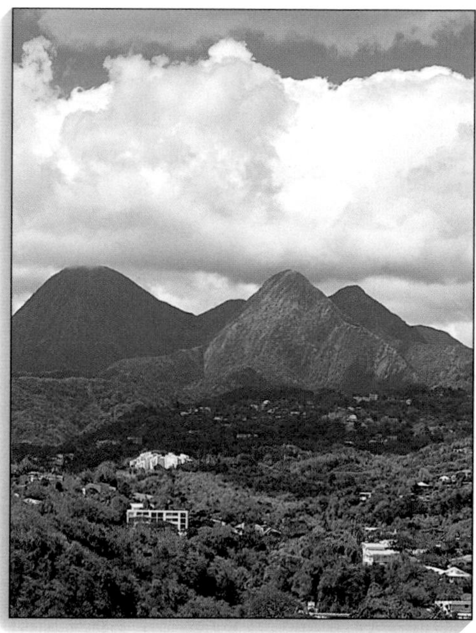

Tropical wildlife

While the flora of the Lesser Antilles is of international importance, the region is less well-endowed with fauna. Many animals, such as the agouti, opossum and the green monkey found in Barbados, Grenada and St Kitts and Nevis, were introduced by man. The mongoose, a creature looking like a large weasel, was brought over to control rats and snakes, but as rats are nocturnal and mongooses aren't, they succeeded in becoming a pest too, plundering birds' nests and rummaging through garbage.

The islands in the middle of the necklace received fewer migrants of both bird and animal life. However, the relative isolation of some of them allowed for the evolution of endemic species: Dominica and Montserrat are the home of a large frog known as mountain chicken, found nowhere else in the world, and Dominica, St Vincent and St Lucia each have their own species of parrot.

While you may not always see a parrot, every day will bring a hummingbird winging its way in a million flutters "to a hibiscus near you". Indeed, birds are a constant presence, although you will have to go to Trinidad (for its 400 species) for the most exotic. Lizards and geckos are everywhere, iguanas are rare (and protected), while the only dangerous snake, the *fer de lance*, is restricted to St Lucia and Martinique.

FAR LEFT: all that is left of an old sugar mill.
ABOVE LEFT: St John's, Antigua, after Hurricane Luis had passed through in 1995.
RIGHT: the volcanic Pitons du Corbet in Martinique.

Linked to the land

These small islands – none of which has a population of more than a million (Trinidad) and some with under 10,000 (Anguilla, Nevis, Saba) – are essentially rural in character. Trinidad's Port of Spain is a modern cosompolitan city, but the capitals of most of the islands are like small market towns in Europe, often picturesque but usually parochial.

While the younger generation is growing up with television (usually American) and the Internet, the sense of national identity remains linked to the land and its usages. This is true whether it is the salt pans on the dry scrub of Anguilla (highest point 213 ft/65 m above sea level) or an acre of hillside in Grenada burgeoning with root vegetables, citrus and mango. And every cultivator will carry a cutlass in the way a city person carries a briefcase. "It's the pen of the farmer," as one islander described it.

The cliché of an earthly paradise is a tempting way to describe some of the still pristine corners of the region. Yet it is a distortion, for its history is of slavery and colonialism. Even now its people are forced by economic poverty to migrate from this "paradise" which cannot support them. This tension between the people and their history is captured in an almost unbearably beautiful way in the works of many Caribbean writers, particularly perhaps in the poetry of Derek Walcott of St Lucia.

To be an Ecotourist...

☛ choose a hotel that is locally owned, employs islanders and uses island products.
☛ go on a whale-watching trip, making the whale an asset to tourism.
☛ leave coral for the fish, don't stand on it and never drop anchor on a reef.
☛ ask people for their permission before taking a photograph of them.
☛ enjoy watersports that don't need a motor.
☛ keep to the trails in rainforests; use a guide.
☛ video or report any pollution you may see from the deck of your cruise ship.

A new money spinner

It is only recently that the economies have shifted away from agriculture to tourism. And it is now the region's greatest money spinner, bringing employment and dollars. Like the first colonizers, who dramatically altered the island hinterlands by clearing the forests – first for tobacco, then coffee and cocoa and then for sugar – the tourist industry has changed the coastlines for ever. The bays where fishermen once pulled in their nets or where colonies of birds nested in mangrove stands now provide for the very different needs of tourists.

The fragile environments of these small islands are, in some cases, in danger of sinking under the weight of the visitors. Local environmental groups are vocal in contesting the destruction of important mangrove stands for hotel building, the damage done to coral reefs by careless tourists and the anchors of cruise ships, plus the cultural threat imposed on small societies by the hordes of holiday makers.

Ecotourism is now the buzz word, and some islands, such as Dominica and Trinidad, which have not developed a "sand, sea and sun" tourism have declared policies for developing a more sustainable tourism.

And visitors, too, are discovering that there is more to the land- and seascapes of the Caribbean than the limited view from a sunbed. Between them, perhaps, the diversity of that island necklace will survive. ❑

LEFT: motmots from Trinidad and Tobago.
RIGHT: whale-watching is popular with ecotourists.

INSVLÆ AMERICANÆ
IN OCEANO SEPTENTRIONALI,
cum Terris adiacentibus.
FLORIDA.
GOLFO DE MEXICO.
NOVÆ HISPANIÆ PARS.
YVCATAN
CVBA
HONDVRAS.
NICARAGVA.
MAR DEL ZVR.
Ampl. Prud. Doct. Viro
D. ALBERTO CONRADI VANDER BVRCH,
I.C. Reip. Amsterdamensis Senatori, Collegii
Scabinorum Præsidi, Societatis Indicæ quæ
ad Occidentem militat assessori, et nuper
ad Magnum Moscoviæ Ducem Legato,
Tabulam hanc inscribit
Gulielmus Blaeu.

MAR DEL
NORT
ESPANOLA
Antillas sive
Camercanæ
Vulgo
Caribes
Insulæ
S. MARTHA
VENEZVELA
CARTAGENA
Milliaria Germanica
Milliaria Hispanica

Decisive Dates

AD 1000–1200 Carib tribes from South America travel north through the Lesser Antilles in dug-out canoes, displacing the resident Arawak Indians.
1493 and 1498 Christopher Columbus is the first European to discover the Eastern Caribbean islands.

Colonizing the islands: 16th and 17th century

European settlers flock to the New World, bringing African slaves to work on their plantations and farms.
1535 Prince Rupert Bay in Dominica is used as a shelter for Spanish treasure ships.

1592 Spanish are first to settle the Eastern Caribbean in Trinidad, building the town of St Joseph. Three years later, Sir Walter Raleigh destroys it.
1623 The English establish their first colony on St Kitts, then Barbados (1625), Antigua (1632), Anguilla (1650) and the British Virgin Islands (1680).
1632 Irish Catholics settle on Montserrat, escaping Protestant persecution on St Kitts.
1635 The French colonize Guadeloupe and Martinique and in 1650 buy Grenada from the Caribs for some hatchets, glass beads and two bottles of brandy.
1634–36 Dutch fleet takes ABC Islands; first Dutch colony on St Eustatius in 1636; Saba (1640).
1648 Treaty of Concordia officially divides St Martin between French (north) and Dutch (south).

Sugar and slavery 1638–1797

Many of the islands had been planted with sugar cane, creating a plantocracy with absentee landowners. Towards the end of the 17th century King Sugar ruled.
1638–1779 Slave trade flourishes in Curaçao, where slaves are sold on to the sugar growing islands.
1675 and 1695 Slave rebellions uncovered in Barbados and the ringleaders executed.
1690 St Kitts and Nevis hit by a severe earthquake and tidal wave wipes out Nevis's capital, Jamestown.
1704 Tobago is declared a neutral island by the European colonizers, and soon becomes a pirate base.
1725 Leprosy epidemic in Guadeloupe leads to the creation of a leper colony on La Désirade close by.
1754 St Thomas, St John and St Croix become a royal colony of Denmark, named the Danish West Indies.
1765 St Vincent Botanical Gardens founded.
1775–83 American Revolution causes famine in British West Indies due to trade embargoes.
1779 Stock Exchange crash in Europe sends sugar industry further into decline.
1780s British introduce nutmeg to Grenada where it becomes a main crop, along with cocoa.
1784 France cedes St Barthélémy to Sweden in exchange for trading rights.
1793 Captain Bligh brings breadfruit plants from Tahiti to St Vincent on *The Bounty*.
1797 Over 5,000 Black Caribs deported from St Vincent after the British quell a revolt.

Reform and rebellion 1802–1902

Throughout the first half of the 19th century there were slave revolts across the Caribbean, demanding liberty.
1802 Spanish Treaty of Amiens gives Trinidad to the British, and Tobago finally ceded to Britain by France.
1816 St Kitts, Nevis, Anguilla and British Virgin Islands administered by British as a single colony.
1816 Easter Rebellion in Barbados of 5,000 slaves led by Bussa demanding freedom.
1828–45 Dutch West Indies governed from Suriname.
1834 Emancipation Act "frees" slaves in British West Indies. The French follow in 1848 and the Dutch in 1863. An "apprenticeship" system is introduced.
1845–1917 Thousands of East Indians arrive in Trinidad to increase the labour force for an indentured period of five years. Many remain.
1848 Slave rebellion in St Croix precipitates their emancipation in the Danish West Indies.
1878 St Barthélemy is given back to France by Sweden.
1888 Tobago amalgamates politically with Trinidad.
1902 Mont Pelée on Martinique erupts, destroying the capital St Pierre and killing 30,000 people. Two days before, La Soufrière on St Vincent erupted, killing 2,000.

GOING INDEPENDENT 1914–83

After the larger British islands became indepedent within the British Commonwealth, the smaller ones followed suit – although not all. The Dutch and French remain with their mother country.

1917 Danish West Indies sold to the United States for $25 million and used as a naval base.

1917–24 Oil refineries built on Curaçao and Aruba.

1946 French islands change their status to *départements* of France, officially becoming regions in 1974.

1951 Universal suffrage granted to British colonies.

1954 Dutch islands granted full autonomy in domestic affairs as part of the Netherlands and in 1986 Aruba is given separate autonomy.

1958 Scotsman Lord Glenconner buys Mustique in the Grenadines, giving HRH Princess Margaret a plot of land as a wedding gift.

1958–62 Formation of the Federation of the British West Indies, which fails when Jamaica and Trinidad and Tobago decide to go it alone.

1966 Barbados is granted independence.

1967 Britain's islands become states in voluntary association with Britain, with internal self-government.

1969 British invasion welcomed by Anguilla, which officially becomes a British Dependent Territory in 1980.

1973 Foundation of CARICOM (Caribbean Community), an organization designed to liberalize movement of trade between member states.

1974 Grenada is first of the Associated States to be granted independence.

1976 Trinidad becomes a republic within the British Commonwealth.

1978 Dominica gains independence and in 1979 St Lucia follows suit.

1979 St Vincent and the Grenadines gain independence and on Good Friday, 13 April, La Soufrière erupts, causing much agricultural damage.

1979 Grenada experiences a bloodless coup by Marxist-Leninists led by Maurice Bishop.

1981 Antigua and Barbuda granted independence as one nation, as are St Kitts and Nevis in 1983.

1983 US and Caribbean forces invade Grenada after the government is overthrown and Bishop murdered.

MODERN TIMES 1983–1998

Corruption and natural disasters create major problems in the region.

1985 Exxon closes oil refinery in Aruba with disastrous effects on the island's economy.

1987 Waters around Saba become a marine park.

1989 and 1995 Hurricane Hugo and then Hurricanes Luis and Marilyn wreak havoc in the Caribbean.

1990 Arms smuggling scandal in Antigua involves Prime Minister's son Vere Bird Jr.

1990 Muslim fundamentalists attempt to overthrow government in Trinidad, killing 23 and injuring 500.

1992 St Lucian writer Derek Walcott wins Nobel Prize for Literature.

1993–95 Operation Dinero off Anguilla traps international drug traffickers, money launderers and arms dealers.

1994 Tropical Storm Debbie hits the Caribbean, dumping 26 in (66 cm) of rain on St Lucia in just seven hours. In contrast, Guadeloupe is declared a disaster zone after the worst drought for 30 years.

1994 General election called in St Kitts and Nevis after politicians exposed in corruption scandal.

1995 First prime minister of East Indian descent, Basdeo Panday, is elected in Trinidad.

1995–98 Volcanic activity on Montserrat culminates in three eruptions in 1997, killing 19 people and destroying Plymouth, the capital. The island remains on Red Alert in 1998.

1998 Caribbean Forum, chaired by British Foreign Secretary Robin Cook, promises help with cracking down on drug trafficking.

July 1998 Residents of British Dependent Territories (to be renamed British Overseas Territories) are promised British citizenship. ❑

LEFT: slaves celebrate their freedom.
RIGHT: flag of the Republic of Trinidad and Tobago.

THE COLONIAL PERIOD

When Christopher Columbus came upon the islands of the West Indies, he threw names at many of them as he sailed past. The colonists arrived 100 years later

Accounts by Spanish historians and other European travelers tell of a vibrant Indian civilization which existed before the arrival of Columbus at the end of the 15th century. In fact, most of what is known about the Indians comes from these accounts and archeological excavations.

However, such observations have to be read with care because, with the single exception of the Dominican monk, Bartolomé de Las Casas (1474–1566), the defender of the Indians in the early 16th century, they were filled with the *hubris* of a European man who saw the native inhabitants as savage children hardly fit for missionary enterprise. Alternatively, some of the accounts presented the inhabitants of this new world in Utopian terms, in contrast to the decadence of European life. Beatriz Pastor, in *Discurso narrativo de la Conquista de América,* has shown how these psychologically conditioned responses oscillated between two opposite pictures: savage cannibalism or romantic primitivism. European visitors saw what they wanted to see.

Arawaks and Caribs

The Indians mainly comprised two completely different races, Arawaks and Caribs, both originating from South America. The Arawaks are believed to have settled on the islands at around the time of Christ or earlier and lived in fishing and agricultural communities of a quite sophisticated character. Ruled by a chieftain, *cacique,* they possessed their own system of laws and government, based on patriarchical lineage. Their ceremonial grounds indicate complicated games and their boat-building technology was advanced, enabling them to travel great distances.

The more warlike Caribs (*see page 213*) ventured northwards through the islands about 1,000 years later, killing the Arawak men and taking their women. Word went round amongst the conquering Europeans that the Caribs ate their captives, giving us the word cannibal.

Much of this Indian civilization disappeared under the pressures of European conquest and colonization. English and French soldiers and settlers undertook what were in effect genocidal wars against the native populations of the islands during the 16th and 17th centuries. Today, only a handful of the descendant Caribs exist on a reservation in Dominica.

There were two general consequences of the Indian presence on the islands. The first was the growth of a European Utopian literature. European writers, using the travelers' accounts, invented the fiction of a natural, idyllic life situated in an imaginary island in the Antilles or the South Seas. Daniel Defoe's *Robinson Crusoe* (1719) is the best-known example. The second was the refusal of the Indians to become enslaved; few Caribs were prepared to play Man Friday to the white man's Crusoe. Thus the colonizers turned to Africa for labor.

LEFT: portrayal of early tribal life in the Caribbean.
RIGHT: a Romantic interpretation of Christopher Columbus.

Colonial rivalry

The 16th, 17th and 18th centuries were the major formative period of the Lesser Antilles, marked, successively, by war and rivalry between European nations, the establishment of settlements and colonies and introduction of a sugar economy, the organization of the slave trade, the implantation of chattel slavery, the rise of white superiority and slave rebellions.

The early Spanish claim to the West Indies was rapidly challenged by its European rivals – England, France, Denmark and Holland. The Spanish hegemony was anchored mainly in the Greater Antilles – Cuba, Hispaniola and Puerto Rico – where there was real treasure, although there was a brief Spanish episode in Trinidad.

Because they were the first ports of arrival for the invading European fleets the Lesser Antilles bore the brunt of the inter-state rivalry. It was a period of almost uninterrupted insecurity for the region, when the political ownership of any island could suddenly change. The native populations could wake up on any morning to discover that they had a set of new masters. West Indian historian and politician, Dr. Eric Williams, called it a condition of "in betweenity". The island of St Croix (now part of the US Virgin Islands), for example, changed sovereignty at least seven times in a period of less than 100 years, including a brief rule by the Knights Templars of Malta.

The European powers saw their new tropical possessions as an opportunity for enriching the emergent state systems of post-Reformation Europe, both Catholic and Protestant. And they wanted to weaken Spain's influence in the New World. Through much of the 16th century Spain had dominated the high seas plying to and from the Caribbean with treasure. In an attempt to break their monopoly, Sir Francis Drake had become the first official pirate, reaping the rewards for Elizabeth I.

BUCCANEERING SPIRIT

"If our number is small, our hearts are great; and the fewer persons we are, the more union, and the better shares we shall have in the spoil." Henry Morgan told his men after a pirate raid in 1668 yielding a booty of 250,000 "pieces of eight".

Pirates and buccaneers

European chancelleries and war ministries continued to use their pirates and buccaneers – fugitives from justice of all nationalities – to harass the Spaniards in the 17th century. Sir Henry Morgan (1635–88) started his infamous career as a British licensed privateer. Dutchman Esquemiling wrote *The Buccaneers and*

Marooners of America in 1674: "...from the very beginning of their conquests in America, both English, French, Dutch, Portuguese, Swedes, Danes, Courlanders, and all other nations that navigate the ocean, have frequented the West Indies, and filled them with their robberies and assaults."

The European governments eventually agreed to dispense with these motley forces because they were becoming too much of a nuisance to their own ships. Governor Woodes Rogers' suppression of the pirate stronghold in New Providence in the Bahamas in 1722 finally marked the end of piracy.

Stretched like a line of watchdogs across the route between Spain and her seaborne New World empire, the islands were perfectly positioned for the establishment of naval stations, like Nelson's Dockyard in Antigua. Indeed, if, as the saying goes, the Battle of Waterloo (1815) was won on the playing fields of Eton, then it is equally true to say that the Battle of Trafalgar (1805) was won in the naval stations of the Lesser Antilles.

Some of the most decisive battles were fought here, most notably when Admiral Rodney destroyed the French fleet in the Battle of the Saints off the Windwards in 1782. He then destroyed the commercial port of St Eustatius, which had become a supply center of arms for the anti-English forces in the American Revolutionary War. Even today, Statians remember Rodney's sack of their island, known as the Golden Rock, just as Southerners remember Sherman's burning of Atlanta in the American Civil War.

Naval warfare

By 1700, the four great powers of Caribbean economic and military aggression – France, Holland, Spain, and Great Britain – had established flourishing island colonies when the Atlantic seaboard colonies of Massachusetts and Virginia were hardly beyond their first stages of settlement. The colonization of the islands and Spanish Main produced cities rivalling those of Europe in size and magnificence.

The governments of both the mother country and local colony were forced, often at ruinous expense, to build defenses, such as the Brimstone Hill fortifications on St Kitts, against such calamities. For the small town populations of the time, life must have been marginal and precarious. St Croix alone, the island center of the

LEFT: battleships – a constant sight around the islands during the 1700s.
ABOVE: the colonial good life portrayed in an 18th-century cartoon.

Danish West Indies, was occupied in the year of 1650 by three different European war parties.

Such warfare continued right into the period of the Napoleonic Wars, when the political map of the region was eventually settled by the 1815 Treaty of Vienna.

Profits of paradise

However, the history of the New World, called the Enterprise of the Indies, was not just war. War was simply the prelude to trade. Once the European powers had more or less settled their respective "spheres of influence" – Trinidad, for example, was finally ceded to Britain in the 1802 Treaty of Amiens that ended the Seven Year War – the Lesser Antilles settled down to its socio-economic-cultural development as peripheral economies of the European states.

That meant the development of sugar as a staple crop and the sugar plantation economy, supported by the slave trade, which lasted nearly 400 years, from 1500 to 1860, supplying a large and cheap labor force capable of doing heavy unremitting work under brutalizing tropical conditions.

ADVENTURERS ALL

Every sort of European adventurer – Welsh Royalist, Dutch Jew, Cromwell's transported prisoner, Puritan merchant, Catholic friar – ventured to the Antilles eager for a share of the legendary spoils of the New World, free from class restrictions.

Island patterns

From north to south these islands shared a common pattern of colonialism and slavery deriving prosperity from the sugar economy, either producing sugar or developing as commercial trade centers. For example, in the north, St Thomas, under Danish rule, developed as an important commercial trade center as it was too hilly for sugar, while St Croix, while ruled by the Danes, developed as a sugar plantation economy. Of course, there were differences between the individual islands. For instance, Barbados was English and Guadeloupe French. In the south, Trinidad emerged as a Franco-Hispanic Catholic society while Tobago became an English-speaking Protestant society of small farmers and fishing folk. Antigua became a sugar colony while mountainous Dominica had little to do but develop an infant lumber industry. In the French Antilles, Martinique early on developed a small creole middle class of professional elite, while Guadeloupe remained mainly peasant. This distinction survives even to the present day.

In the Dutch Antilles, Curaçao became another

commercial trade center as it was too arid for sugar, while Bonaire developed a small salt-pond industry and became a prison for rebellious slaves. Even the Lilliputian islands of Anguilla, Barbuda and the Grenadines, as dependent wards of large sugar islands, were affected by the sugar economy.

The slave trade

As a consequence of the Europeans' seemingly insatiable taste for sugar, the islands, with few exceptions, became arrival ports and slave markets. And the triangular trade, between the African trading posts, the European middle-passage ports and the Antilles, laid the foundations of slavery as a domestic institution. Richard Ligon described in his book *A True and Exact History of the Island of Barbados* (1657) how the smallholdings of the early lower-class white immigrants were replaced with large-scale sugar plantations.

Later, the British dramatist and politician Richard Sheridan's study of the rise of the colonial gentry in 18th-century Antigua showed how no entrepreneur in that society could hope to survive unless he was also a planter-merchant.

The entire house of Antillean society was built over this slave basement. It became a strange melting pot of white colonists, black slaves, indentured servants, freed Indians, Catholics, Protestants, heretics, Jews, transported political prisoners, felons, "poor whites", all mingled in a fascinating exoticism under tropical skies. It was a *picaroon* world of all colors and creeds, slowly learning to co-exist with each other.

Naturally enough, it was a society of ranking status in three tiers, composed of upper-class whites, mulattos or freed persons of color – the consequence of the Antillean miscegenative habits – and slaves at the bottom of the pile.

LEFT: a working plantation showing the main house, mill, slave huts, slaves and owner.
ABOVE: Caribbean market in the 19th century.

White plantocracy

Each group had its own pride and prejudices. In turn, they saw the group of "free coloreds" as social upstarts, presumptuously claiming to be "white when in fact they were black." As a class, the white plantocracy was arrogant, racist, and socially gross. In fact, much of its own ancestry in the islands was suspect: the 18th-century, Jesuit traveler Père Labat noted in Martinique that his slave owner neighbors were originally engaged servants. These observations hardly made Labat popular in those old creole communities and explains why, after some 14 years, he was recalled by his superiors and never allowed to return.

The islands at this time were overcrowded not only with African slaves, but also with the white riffraff of Europe who hoped to become plantation owners and escape their lowly origins. Their skin color gave them a new status in the islands; and their sexual irresponsibility showed how they used it to unscrupulously advance their careers. In this

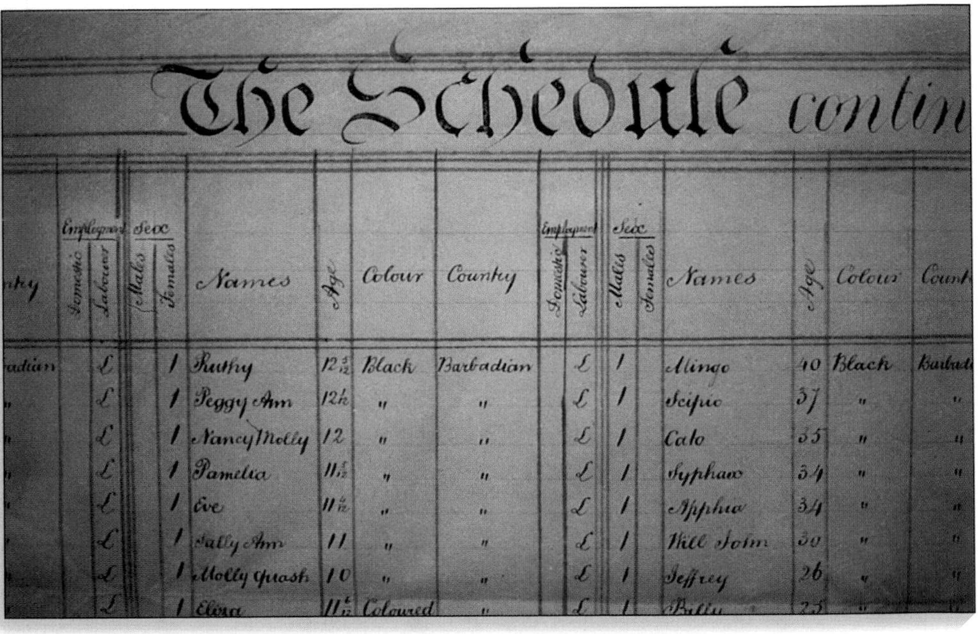

...ntry	Domestic	Labourer	Males	Females	Names	Age	Colour	Country	Domestic	Labourer	Males	Females	Names	Age	Colour	Count...
...adian		L		1	Ruthy	12 5/12	Black	Barbadian		L	1		Alingo	40	Black	Barbadi...
"		L		1	Peggy Ann	12 1/12	"	"		L	1		Scipio	37	"	"
"		L		1	Nancy Molly	12	"	"		L	1		Cato	35	"	"
"		L		1	Pamelia	11 5/12	"	"		L	1		Syphax	34	"	"
"		L		1	Eve	11 6/12	"	"		L	1		Apphia	34	"	"
"		L		1	Sally Ann	11	"	"		L	1		Will John	30	"	"
"		L		1	Molly Quash	10	"	"		L	1		Jeffrey	26	"	"
		L		1	Elvira	11 6/12	Coloured	"		L	1		[illegible]	25	"	

sense, the social history of the islands during this period is in part the sexual exploitation of the black women by the white plantation males, whether overseers, accountants, indentured servants, or even masters. Better, after all, to be a *grand seigneur* in Martinique than a lowly serf in Provence.

Most of the slave-owning class were vulgar to a degree and they lived in continuous fear of slave rebellion. Danish Virgin Islands Governor Gardelin's slave mandate of 1733 was typical in its severity of punishments for slaves guilty of bad behavior, not to mention slaves guilty of rebellious behavior. In the French Antilles the official Code Noir of 1785 reflected the negrophobia of the time, listing some 128 grades of color, by which every person in the colony was awarded a status.

ABSENTEE OWNERS

Plantation profits were sent to the absentee owners in England, who wasted them on a lifestyle of such prodigality that it disgusted even 18th-century observers.

Few visitors failed to note the ostentatious display of wealth and the extravagant style of entertainment practised by the planters, one of the causes of their perennial indebtedness.

Absenteeism was endemic and plantation profits were sent to the owners in England, who wasted them on a lifestyle of prodigality that disgusted even 18th-century observers.

Gens de couleur

A history of interracial breeding produced the second group in Antillean society, the "free coloreds" or *gens de couleur*. They were a highly significant group, in part because they occupied a marginal position between the whites and the slaves. Also, their numbers were growing rapidly while the numbers of whites tended to decline. After all, it was a rare white person who did not father colored children, except for the descendents of the Scottish-Irish "poor whites" of the 17th century, known today as "Redlegs" in Barbados.

The history, then, of the Antilles during much of this period was the story of this mulatto group's struggle for social status and for political and civil rights. The first breakthrough in political rights occurred in the late 18th century in Antigua, when free persons of mixed race possessing the necessary property qualifications were allowed to vote at elections.

Social respectability

This long drawn-out rise of the people of color was important for two reasons. In the first place, though hardly a revolutionary movement, it did revolutionize society. Like the whites, the mulattoes had important interests in slave holding. They resented their own subordination, but did not resist the social structure of which it was a part. They needed the white group as a role model in their search for social respectability, and the whites needed them as allies against slave unrest and, even worse, slave rebellion. The coloreds also had to stay on good terms with the white governments, both local and abroad, in order to gain concessions for themselves.

A typical example was the remarkable royal edict of 1831 in the Danish Virgin Isands, permitting the legal registration of colored persons as white citizens on the basis of good conduct and social standing. The coloreds responded to those concessions by developing their own extravagant life style – wearing precious stones and silk stockings, holding masked balls, and adopting the use of ceremonial gunfire at funerals – which the government tried to curb.

Social snobbery thus supplanted common racial brotherhood, and the Antillean free coloreds, at least in this formative 18th century period, became known as a group given more to lavish social display than to mental activity and academia. Lafcadio Hearn wrote in his book on Martinique, although it applied to all the islands. "Travellers of the 18th century were confounded by the luxury of dress and jewelry displayed by swarthy beauties in St Pierre. It was a public scandal to European eyes."

LEFT: a register listing slaves with age and race.
ABOVE LEFT: a British emancipation society's view of the horrors of slavery.
ABOVE RIGHT: mulattoes enjoying a dance.

The slave population

The slaves generally came from West Africa. Philip Curtin, in his definitive book, *The African Slave Trade*, estimated that from its beginnings in the early 16th century to its termination in the 19th century, some 12 million Africans were brought to the New World by means of the triangular trade. They arrived as unnamed chattel slaves, later to be renamed by their slave owners and masters, which accounts for the Europeanized names of their descendants.

The present-day reversion to African names is a phenomenon of the 20th century, since the Black Power movement began to influence black communities in the US, Europe and the Caribbean in the 1960s and 1970s. The loss of name was, in a psychological sense, important because it was a part of the total loss of liberty that deprived the African of his right to be regarded as a human being, never mind an equal.

RESISTANCE

As a form of rebellion, slaves retained a way of life – in dance, music, and religion – that endured alongside the life of the white minority population.

African traditions

Yet there was play as well as gruelling work. "Every people," wrote the political writer Edmund Burke (1729–97), "must have some compensation for its slavery." And so, from the very beginning, the slaves brought with them their traditions of song and dance. Music played a very large part in their lives; a music that emerged out of a blending and meeting of both the imported European musical forms and the various African song and dance formulations. These encounters gave rise to completely new, exciting forms of dance and music which became uniquely Antillean.

A similar process of creolisation took place, during this early formative period, with language. In the New World setting – planter, overseer, slave, with all of their respective duties and obligations – had to learn to understand each other. The problem was solved, *ad hoc*, by the invention of creole *patois*, which differed between islands.

Slave rebellion

The habit of what was called in the French islands *petit marronage* – of running away from the estate for short periods of time to visit a woman friend, or attend a prohibited church meeting, or just simply to feel a taste of freedom – often escalated into rebellion.

Such rebellious attempts, all crushed with severe cruelty, occurred regularly, but most notably in St John in the Danish West Indies in 1733, Antigua in 1736, St Croix in 1759, Grenada in 1795, and Barbados in 1816.

Certainly they showed that slaves had a capacity for insurrectionary leadership. There were leaders like Tackey and Tomboy in Antigua, who planned to kill all the whites, and set up an Ashanti-type black kingdom on the island. Nanny Grigg, in Barbados, told her followers, according to the official record, that the only way to get freedom was to fight for it. Then there was Daaga, who led, although after Emancipation, a brief mutiny of the 1st West India Regiment in Trinidad in 1837. He told his interrogators, on the eve of his execution, that the seeds of the mutiny had been sown on the passage from Africa.

Two other forces helped destroy the slavery system in the 19th century. First, the economic factor: slave labor was more costly and less efficient than free wage labor, an over supply of sugar led to catastrophic drops in world prices, and the West Indian planters lost their privileged position in the British market as the world free-trade policies were established. Second, the influence of the British religious-humanitarian movement, led by William Wilberforce (1759–1833) and Thomas Clarkson (1760–1846), that finally convinced public opinion of the un-Christian character of the system. ❑

Chains of Slavery

For 300 years, slaves arrived in the West Indies in their thousands. They landed from ships in which they had been literally packed together like sardines in the hold for the months-long voyage from West Africa, each of them chained down to prevent rebellion or suicide.

Conditions in the ships were just sufficient to keep them alive, although many died on the journey known as the Middle Passage. Those that became ill with diseases that rampaged through the holds, such as smallpox and dysentery, were thrown overboard. That so many survived is due to the slave traders choosing only the strong, healthiest looking men, whom their African chiefs traded for metals, guns, ammunitions, trinkets and cloth.

Once off the ships in the Caribbean, in trading islands such as Curaçao and St Thomas, the slaves were sold to plantation owners. They became property – part chattel, part real estate – that could be sold or traded against debts.

On the plantations living conditions were abysmal. Slaves were housed in floorless huts, with barely enough food to keep them working for 12 hours a day, six days a week. Historian Karl Watson has written that slaves in Barbados started their day at half-past five, when the plantation bell summoned them to assemble in the main estate yard to receive instructions. After being given hot ginger tea, they were divided up into gangs of 20 to 60 and sent out to dig cane holes, to manure, or to cut and crop mature cane under a burning sun until dark.

The work discipline was relentless as John Luffman reported in the 1780s: "The negroes are under the inspection of white overseers...subordinate to these overseers are drivers, commonly called dog-drivers, who are mostly black or mulatto fellows of the worst dispositions; and these men are furnished with whips which, while on duty, they are obliged, on pain of severe punishment, to have with them, and are authorized to flog wherever they see the least relaxation from labor; nor is it a consideration with them, whether it proceeds from idleness or inability, paying, at the same time, little or no regard to age or sex."

The slaves were given their food weekly. A typical weekly ration consisted of 28 lbs (13 kg) of yams or potatoes, 10 pints (5 liters) of corn, 8 oz (225 g) of fish and $1^3/_4$ pints (1 liter) of molasses. The yearly ration of clothing would have been a jacket, shirt, pair of trousers and cap for a man and a jacket, gown, petticoat and cap for a woman.

The slaves that acquired skills fared better than the field workers, sometimes becoming overseers of other slaves – many rebellions were thwarted through slaves telling on each other – cattle keepers, carpenters, blacksmiths and tailors. Domestic slaves – maids, cooks and butlers – were also more trusted and better treated than field workers.

However, the white owners generally regarded their slaves as lazy, irresponsible, grossly sexualist, potentially rebellious, and rationally inferior.

And in many cases with good reason, because often the only way slaves could resist was through quiet, covert protest such as malingering, feigning illness, working slowly, sabotaging property, and even poisoning their masters.

Certain defense mechanisms evolved to make life tolerable. They disguised their feelings and adopted exaggerated attitudes of deference to the point of pretending to be the stupid black person in which the white mentality believed. They also preserved their African culture through music and religion, much to the annoyance of their owners.

Resistance showed that slavery could only be maintained by force, a proposition which Europeans found objectionable in the early 19th century. ❑

LEFT: runaway slave, or maroon, with musket.
RIGHT: slaves toiling on a sugar plantation.

ROADS TO INDEPENDENCE AND BEYOND

As the freed slaves struggled for survival, many of the colonies sought independence. Now, with the decline of island agriculture, tourism is the major breadwinner

With slavery finally abolished – in the British islands in 1834, the French islands in 1848, and the Dutch islands in 1863 – the post-Emancipation period began. This lasted until the vast social and political changes unleashed by the World War II (1939–45) started the ball rolling towards most of the islands being given independence.

The freed slaves, permitted for the first time to develop an independent economic life, and previously denied land of their own, started buying up parts of abandoned estates, fought for the use of Crown lands, and organized networks of staple crop production and sales outlets in the towns. They were joined by thousands of East Indian indentured contract workers brought to parts of the region from Asia between 1838 and 1917 to work on the labor-starved plantations.

New Caribbean farmers

Over the decades the emancipated slaves became the nutmeg farmers of Grenada, the fishermen-farmers of Antigua and Barbuda, the small banana growers in St Lucia, the small sugar producers of St Croix, the small cocoa farmers of Trinidad, and the market women, or "higglers," became the mainstay of the developing town market economy.

Much of what they produced were cash crops, destined for sale in the local market or even for sale abroad. They were peasants in the sense that their lifestyle, with all of its old kinship patterns of family, was rural; but their economic values were capitalist. They operated, often with characteristic shrewdness, as sellers and buyers in a free-market island economy. As a class, however, they were stratified like all classes, for there were at once the rich farmers and the poor farmers, as is still the case today.

At the same time, an urban work force evolved in the more thriving centers of trade and commerce, like St Thomas, Fort-de-France, Bridgetown, Port of Spain and Willamsted. In the 1900s another work force developed around the oil refineries in Trinidad, Curaçao and Aruba, and around the transatlantic banana companies like the Geest group in St Lucia.

With the oil companies came a full-scale process of industrial and financial capitalism resulting in technological dependency, the growing separation between the European and colonial economies, with an increasing imbalance of trade between the two, external ownership and control, the influx of foreign managerial personnel, and a system in which the West Indian colonies sold cheap and bought dear. In effect, they produced what they did not consume, and consumed what they did not produce.

PRECEDING PAGES: workers load the sugar cane train in Guadeloupe in around 1900.
LEFT: a young indentured laborer from India who came to Trinidad in the 19th century.
RIGHT: breaking cocoa during harvest.

Breakdown of colonial rule

Between the two world wars, the native workers served as a dependent, low-paid docile labor force for industry, commerce, and agriculture. Conditions that were bad enough in the 1920s were made worse by the onset of the Depression. The British colonies became known as the "slums of the empire" with a declining sugar industry supporting an estate labor force by means of an exploitative task-work system.

In St Kitts and St Vincent, the wage level had barely advanced beyond the daily shilling rate introduced after Emancipation a century earlier. There was gross malnutrition and chronic sickness in the population; a housing situation characterized by decrepit, verminous and unsanitary conditions, and a working class, when it had work, in a state of economic servitude to a well-organized employer class. The defense mechanisms of a strong trade union movement were stultified by the existence of punitive legislation.

Such conditions led to the labor riots that swept through the English-speaking islands between 1935 and 1938 and to bloody encounters between workers and police, especially in Barbados and Trinidad.

These riots, plus the findings of the British

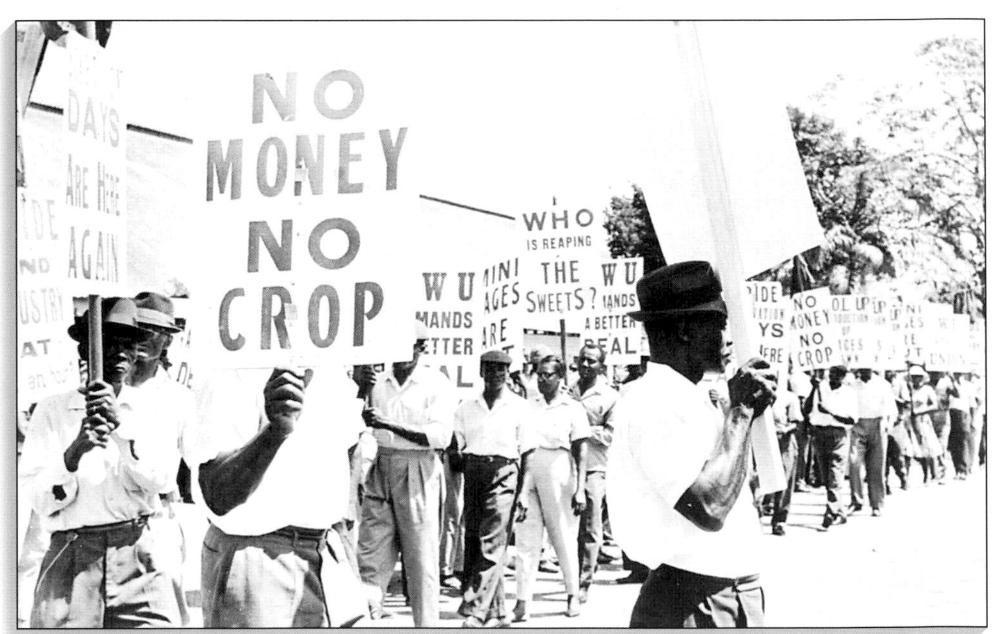

PRIDE AND PREJUDICES

By the start of the 20th century, the economic power of the white population had weakened, but whiteness was still regarded as the ideal image. In contrast to America, which classified itself by a simple black-white caste system, in the Antilles the classification system was more a subtle "shade" prejudice.

Social status depended upon fine degrees of skin color with wealth and income a factor. Whereas in US society money talked, in Antillean society, money whitened. This led to evasive habits of identity, summed up by the Martiniquan phrase, *peau noir, masque blanc* (black skin, white mask). The whites retained their identity by marrying only within their own racial group.

Today, the prejudices relate more to ethnicity in as far as the "native" US Virgin Islanders look down on the immigrants from the Leeward Islands. Trinidadians regard Grenadian immigrants as "small islanders" and the East Indians and creole blacks retain stereotyped images of each other. The French and Dutch islands are experiencing a new white immigrant in big business or government, prone through ignorance to alienating the locals.

However, the Antilleans with all their differences still manage to lead a harmonious existence together.

Royal Commission of 1938, helped to further the formation of new worker movements, which led to the creation of new political parties seeking first, internal self-government and, second, independence.

Some of the new leaders, like Grantley Adams (1898–1971) in Barbados, were black middle-class lawyers. Most were grassroots leaders, such as Vere Bird in Antigua, Uriah Butler in Trinidad, Robert Bradshaw in St Kitts, Eric Gairy in Grenada, among others. Since they were all greatly influenced by the politics of the British Labour Party, the parties they founded were also, in the main, called Labour parties.

Trinidad and Tobago were immediately granted independence within the British Commonwealth (1962) and were soon followed by Barbados in November 1966. But the end of the Federation had left the smaller Leeward and Windward islands out in the cold. As a result, in 1967, the British government took the opportunity to change their constitutional status to "associated states"; a status that gave them the right to internal self-government but left the jurisdiction of foreign affairs and defense in the hands of London civil servants and politicians.

Through the creation of these states, some islands such as St Kitts, Nevis and Anguilla were lumped together as one. Anguilla took exception, breaking away in 1969 and demanding to be returned to British jurisidiction, and it remains so to this day.

Winding road to independence

It was not a straightforward march towards independence. Initially a movement, led by Grantley Adams, favoring a federation between the islands, culminated in the short-lived West Indies Federation of 1958–62.

That experiment broke up mainly because Jamaica and Trinidad were not prepared to sacrifice any of their sovereignty to a central federal government. Nor did they want federal taxation.

LEFT: farm workers on strike in the 1940s.
ABOVE LEFT: historian Dr Eric Williams, the first Prime Minister of Trinidad and Tobago in 1962.
ABOVE RIGHT: Sir Grantley Adams, social reformer.

One by one, the British islands gained independence within the British Commonwealth, but without any great enthusiasm to begin with. Grenada was the first in 1974, followed by Dominica in 1978, St Lucia and St Vincent and the Grenadines in 1979, Antigua and Barbuda in 1981, and St Kitts and Nevis in 1983. Nevis made an attempt at secession from St Kitts in August 1998, but failed when only 62 percent, instead of the two-thirds necessary, voted in favor in a referendum. However, Montserrat,

Turks and Caicos, Cayman Islands and British Virgin Islands have clung to the Crown, and are known as Britain's Overseas Territories. To paraphrase Shakespeare: "Some states are born independent, some achieve independence, and some have independence thrust upon them."

Dutch and French loyalties

Political and constitutional developments were different in both the French and the Netherlands Antilles. After the abolition of slavery, these islands never questioned loyalty to the Dutch Crown or to the French Republic.

With the arrival of the oil companies, political and union leaders in the Netherlands Antilles became more involved in their relationships with them than with the Hague. There was, however, the same old inequity of power between the mother country and the colony, but it was an imbalance alleviated by the innovative Dutch Kingdom Statute of 1954, which gave the colonies direct representation in the Dutch cabinet and parliament as an autonomous state.

However, a strong separatist movement grew up in Aruba and the island finally broke away in 1986, forming its own parliamentary democracy with a status equal to the rest of the Netherland Antilles. In 1993, Aruba shelved its plans for independence scheduled for 1996.

The French Antilles have also been marked by a close relationship with France. The *loi cadre* passed by the Paris National Assembly in 1946 established the islands as overseas departments, *départements d'outre-mer* (DOM) – with St Barthélemy and St Martin joining up with Guadeloupe to share equal status with Martinique. This gave the islanders all the rights of French citizens and equal representation in national politics with economic support from France, which has tempered the development of significant separatist movements. In 1974 their status improved when they became a *région* giving them more administrative power.

New nations

The new nation states saw the rise of a new and more modern government. Local trained civil servants replaced the colonial "expatriate" administrative staff. Also, there was the increasing involvement of the state in the economic sectors. Some industries were nationalized, and governments became majority shareholders in others. For example, in Trinidad, thanks to the oil boom of the 1970s, the government became involved in oil, gas, fertilizer, airlines, shipping, telecommunications, banking and finance, food manufacturing, and hotels. Such changes in the nature of the Caribbean reflected and expressed wider socio-economic-cultural changes.

With the growth of industrialization and modernization – electronics in Barbados, oil refining in St Croix – came the expansion of the tourist industry. Many of the new states acquired their own national airlines – an insignia of national pride – like British West Indian Airways (BWIA) in Trinidad and the Leeward Islands Air Transport (LIAT). New education systems were founded, like the regional University of the West Indies (UWI) with main campuses in Jamaica, Trinidad and Barbados. Privately owned condominiums, tracts of middle-class housing, and public housing projects were also built. But modernity had its price as it caused a vast movement of rural depopulation with people flocking to the towns in search of a better standard of living.

PEDAL POWER

"The small Antillean countries have become bicycle economies with Cadillac tastes."
– W.H. BRAMBLE, CHIEF MINISTER OF MONTSERRAT (1961–1970)

Americanization has also been a major factor in the modernization of the Caribbean. The American influence has permeated the region, particularly the English-speaking islands, not only in obvious economic fashion but also in the more subtle and pervasive social and cultural fashion. The modern and sometimes luxurious US-style shopping malls and supermarkets that have appeared on the islands everywhere, usually next to the cruise ship docks, have helped Americanize practically every aspect of life in the Caribbean – dress habits, food tastes, speech mannerisms and language, entertainment modes, social relationships and even moral values. American radio and television add to this saturation of transmitted American-style attitudes and behavior patterns.

LEFT: Antigua and Barbuda celebrate independence.
ABOVE: one of LIAT's island-hopping planes.

Fresh challenges

Like their sister islands further north, the Lesser Antilles are facing the grave problems often linked with modern life. On some islands money and politics have mixed to encourage an element of government corruption: an ex-prime minister of Dominica has been convicted of a plot (backed by South Africa), to overthrow the elected government of his successor; a top cabinet minister in Trinidad had to flee to Panama after being accused of making money on a racecourse complex project; and a leading member of Antigua's ruling family, the Birds, has been embroiled in gun running and drug dealing.

The money involved in such scandals often

originates from international drug rings, arms merchants and organized crime syndicates. Thus, the small island politician is entrapped in a world of high-stakes intrigue which he is ill-equipped to deal with.

Private lives, public secrets

Admittedly, there have been political leaders of high caliber, such as Grantley Adams and Errol Barrow in Barbados and Dr Eric Williams and A.N.R. Robinson in Trinidad and Tobago. But in the small islands, the politician can manipulate a system in which personal charisma is sometimes more important than ideology. Power can be obtained by a system in which votes are exchanged for favors and thus an elaborate network of family, friends and job-holders is held together by patronage. Since government is the main emloyer, the plums are jobs in the local civil service.

It is a kind of market square politics that emphasizes crowd oratory. In this kind of political arena, private lives, become public secrets. In Trinidad it is called *picong*, *mauvais langue,* robber talk. To listen to its most skilled practitioners at a West Indian political meeting is to understand the West Indian gift for talk, its spirit of ribald irreverence, its street defiance of the high and mighty, which is all pulled together in the famous Trinidadian calypso form.

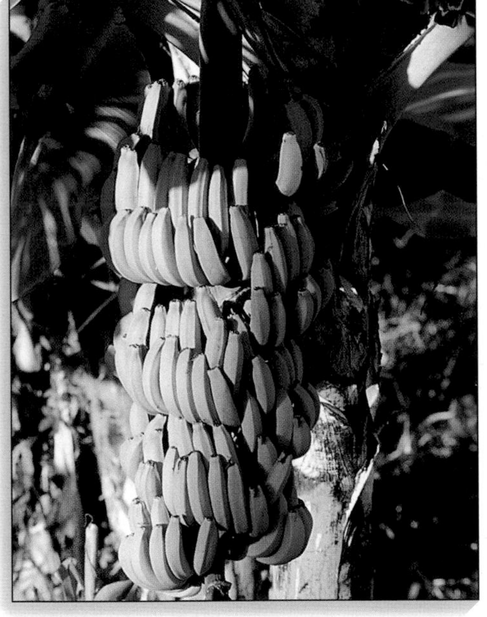

GREEN GOLD

Bananas are the perfect crop for the small Caribbean farmer. They take only six months to grow, are happy on steep hillsides and fruit all year round, providing a steady cash income.

Even a hurricane is not a disaster, as bananas can be quickly replanted and harvested. So it is little wonder that they have been celebrated as the farmer's "green gold".

However, now that the Caribbean banana industry is under threat, experts are warning that some small farmers are turning to another green gold – marijuana.

The effects of big business

With economic development, a new, affluent middle class has emerged; and the basic standards of living, in housing, education and health, has improved immeasurably. But consumerist tastes have evolved through American movies, television and tourism, which can hardly be satisfied in these underdeveloped societies. It has generated expectations that cannot be realized.

As a 1960s Montserrat chief minister, W.H. Bramble, once put it, the small Antillean countries have become bicycle economies with Cadillac tastes; and Errol Barrow, the first prime minister of an independent Barbados, reiterated that the high cost of living was not the problem but the cost of high living. Absolute standards of life have improved, but the gap between rich and poor still grows.

This is not helped by the tourist industry. From the Virgins to the ABC islands, the landscape is dotted with luxury resorts owned by overseas hotel chains offering all-inclusive holidays where everything can be paid for at home, meaning little revenue goes into the island pockets. At the same time, they drain local agriculture, because the average worker prefers to be a maid or a bartender in the hotels rather than remain on the land.

Worst of all, development by import capital has greatly increased the structural dependency of the region's economy upon international capital from multinational companies. Some of them seek cheap labor, others – like the pharmaceutical companies – freedom from environmental legislation at home. Others – especially in high finance – set up offshore operations for worldwide business. These situations become vulnerable and hazardous when a small island becomes host to a single industry. In 1984, for example, major oil companies, such as Exxon, evacuated Aruba and Curaçao one by one, temporarily devastating the islands' economies.

SUGAR FREE

The advent of sugar substitutes in Europe and North America has meant that "King Sugar" no longer rules the Caribbean.

The present situation

The 1990s have not been kind to the region's beleagured small-island economies. Traditional export crops are increasingly threatened by competition from other parts of the world, while attempts to industrialize out of dependency on farming have run into trouble. The sugar industry, now confined to Barbados, Trinidad and St Kitts, is living on borrowed time, propped up by artificially high prices paid by the European Union (EU) to former colonies. These subsidies will eventually disappear as the EU reforms its Common Agricultural Policy. Also, changing dietary habits and the advent of sugar substitutes in the West has meant that "King Sugar" no longer rules.

Even more of a blow to small farmers is the crisis surrounding the region's banana industry. Since the 1950s, smallholders in St Lucia, Dominica, St Vincent and Grenada have been guaranteed a market and more or less stable prices thanks to preferential treatment offered by Britain and then the EU. Complaints by US banana companies and Latin American producers that the EU discriminated against them led to a World Trade Organization (WTO) ruling, in the late 1990s, that the EU system was illegal. Local growers fear that they cannot compete without protection against the big growers of Ecuador or Costa Rica. What will happen to the 50,000 small farmers when the banana boat stops calling?

The arrival of the North American Free Trade Agreement (NAFTA) between the US, Canada and Mexico in 1994 created another cloud on the horizon. Caribbean islands producing garments and electrical components for the US market suddenly found themselves in direct competition with low-wage Mexico. As a result, factories have closed and jobs have been lost as offshore manufacturers head for Tijuana and other border towns – which leaves a booming tourist industry as a "last resort". ❑

LEFT: green gold of the Caribbean.
ABOVE: tourism is booming.

R
R

R

A CARIBBEAN BLEND

The culture of the Lesser Antilles is bursting with vitality, all due to the spicy mix of people living here that the French call "créolité"

Almost everyone in the Caribbean islands is, in some sense, a stranger. Not just the tourists, of course, or the wealthy expatriate communities, European and North American, who have opted for a tropical idyll. But the "locals" who, although they and their forefathers may have been born in the Caribbean, are likely to have their roots in an entirely different continent.

The modern-day Caribbean is peopled by the descendants of African slaves, Indian and Chinese laborers, European colonists and Middle Eastern traders. Even the indigenous Caribs originated from the great rivers and deltas of the South American mainland.

Many of today's people have ancestors who arrived in chains after being crammed into suffocating ships for weeks on end. The great majority came against their will, snatched from another life and transplanted, like much of the flora and fauna of the West Indies, into a strange new world.

And yet their descendants have stayed and many have prospered. Slavery continues to cast a shadow over the region and is held responsible for all manner of economic and social problems, but the contemporary Caribbean wastes little time on nursing historic grudges. On the contrary, a strong and positive sense of identity, both national and regional, has grown out of past injustices, and most people look forward rather than back to a tortured history.

Creole mix

Caribbean societies are by their very nature a mix of different people and cultures. The word creole, originally referring to a European-descended settler born in the Americas, has come to signify this combination of cultural influences, blended into a distinctive whole. Languages, cooking, clothing and architecture all carry the term, which, as in New Orleans, implies a highly spiced or highly colored fusion of ingredients.

The European factor

European influence has marked the Caribbean since the first Spanish expeditions, but in the Eastern Caribbean the dominant nations were Britain, France and, to a lesser degree, Holland. Their imprint is still clearly to be seen in the cricket pitches of Barbados, the haute cuisine of Martinique and in the gabled warehouses of Curaçao. But with the exception of a handful of left-over colonial outposts, the days of European rule are long gone, and it would be hard to see in any Caribbean territory a miniature imitation of the old metropoles.

Europeanness has merged into Africanness, the set of languages, customs and beliefs that came to the Caribbean with the millions of slaves across the "middle passage". Surviving the culture shock of slavery and the imposition

PRECEDING PAGES: it's carnival time in St Lucia; whiling away the hours.
LEFT: making music.
RIGHT: a winning smile.

of colonial values, African influence is stubbornly omnipresent: in rural housing, agricultural techniques, food, music and dance. In modern town centers, with air-conditioned malls and fast food outlets, this heritage is not so obvious, but in fishing villages or farming communities up in the mountains it is unmistakable.

Asian influences

Add to this the sights, sounds and flavors of the Indian subcontinent, characterized by Hindu temples and prayer flags, tassa drums and local variants on curry, and the creole mix begins to take shape. Other ingredients are important too; more recent migrants from China, from Madeira and from Africa have preserved elements of their culture, and few islands are without an influential group of Syrian or Lebanese-descended people. But perhaps most important is the constant contact with North America and its cultural exports, eagerly appreciated by most locals, especially the young.

In the French islands they have a word for it: *créolité*. It is what sets Caribbean people apart from other cultures, what makes island life distinctive and unique. It also implies that blending process, that ability to absorb influences and shape them into something different

WORDS OF WISDOM

In Barbados, general conversation is peppered with wise old sayings especially in the rural areas. Here are a few:

- *Hansome don' put in pot* – sustained effort is needed to achieve anything worthwhile.
- *News don' lack a carrier* – there is always someone to pass on gossip.
- *Two smart rats can' live in de same hole* – two tricksters won't get on together.
- *Goat head every day better than cow head every Sunday* – it is better to be treated reasonably well all the time than have first class treatment some of the time.
- *Head en' mek fuh hat alone* – use common sense.
- *Pretty-pretty things does fool li'l children* – superficial things impress superficial and naive people.
- *Ole stick o' fire don' tek long to ketch back up* – old love affairs can soon be revived.
- *A eyeful en' a bellyful* – just because you can see it, it doesn't mean you can have it (said by women to men).
- *De higher de monkey climb, de more 'e show 'e tail* – the more you show off, the more exposed your faults are.
- *De las' calf kill de cow* – taking the same risk too often can have disastrous consequences.
- *Fisherman never say dat 'e fish stink* – people never give bad reports about themselves.

– it's a dynamic process, one that never stops still, and one that perhaps accounts for the bursting vitality of the region's culture.

Creole tongue

Creole languages are widely spoken across the Caribbean and are a complex cocktail of linguistic elements. In Martinique and Guadeloupe (and to a lesser degree, St Lucia, Dominica, Grenada and Trinidad), French provides the basis for the local creole. But don't expect to understand it even if your French is fluent. Added to the old colonial language are traces of English, Spanish and, above all, African vocabulary.

Creole was spoken among slaves from widely differing backgrounds in Africa and so combines a multitude of different linguistic sources. Guadeloupean creole, for instance, contains the English-descended *kònbif* (corned beef) and *djòb* (job) as well as such African-inspired words as *koukou-djèdjè* (hide and seek) and *zanba* (devil).

Without doubt, the most eclectic creole is papiamento, spoken in some of the Dutch islands, but principally Curaçao. From there it spread more widely throughout the region via the men from many different islands who worked in the oil refineries. This language has had a magpie tendency to take words from wherever it could: Dutch, English, Spanish, Portuguese and some African sources. The result is baffling when heard but strangely familiar when seen in written form, especially if you know some Spanish. *Pan* means bread and *awa* means water (*pan* and *agua* in Spanish), while *kaya* is not far from *calle* (street) or *aki* from *acqui* (here). The English speaker may recognize *motosaikel* (motorcycle).

PAPIAMENTO

The common language of the ABC Islanders, *papiamento* – a combination of dialects rolled into one with no fixed spelling – is used for debates in parliament, books and newspapers.

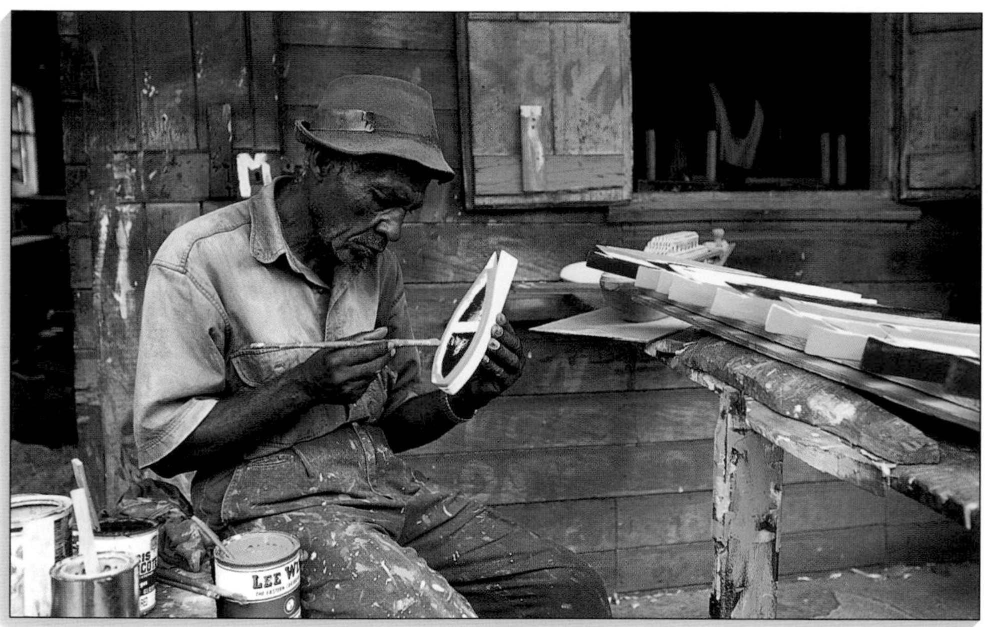

LEFT: making friends in St John.
ABOVE: a model boat craftsman in St Lucia.

A choice of worship

If linguistic ingenuity is a characteristic of Caribbean societies, then so too is religious feeling. Driving through small villages in Barbados or Antigua you'd be excused for thinking that churches outnumbered potential parishioners. The profusion of church groups throughout the region is nothing short of spectacular, ranging from established Anglicans and Roman Catholics to the new generation of Pentecostals and other evangelical sects. Church-going on a Sunday morning is a serious business, as you'll soon notice from the sheer activity on country roads and village streets as people in their Sunday best head for their chosen service.

Religion, like language, is a living example of creole adaptability. The slave owners may have only half-heartedly imposed Christianity on their slaves, but they responded enthusiastically, soon creating an independent tradition of preaching and self-help. Many social institutions – youth clubs, credit schemes, educational facilities – are intimately linked to the churches.

FOLK BELIEFS

Duppies, or ghosts, are kept out of the house at night by sand left on the doorstep as, before entering, it must count every grain – an impossible task before dawn.

But Caribbean people have also given Christianity their own emphases and influences; in some cases religious practices from Africa were mixed in with the teachings of the testaments to produce local faiths. Trinidad's Shango, for instance, is a cult made up of African traditions blended with elements of Roman Catholic and Baptist Christianity.

In other cases, African belief systems have remained more or less unadulterated. *Obeah*, a form of sorcery originating in West African folklore, is still widely believed in throughout the islands, although few people will admit to it. Similar to Haitian voodoo practices, it can involve the use of magic spells and exotic potions either to cause harm to others or to seek cures for all sorts of problems. The obeahman or obeahwoman is still a figure who merits some considerable respect, not to say fear, in the community.

Back to Africa

Although originating in Jamaica, Rastafarianism has spread throughout the Lesser Antilles and is typical of the synthetic development of religious ideas. A mix of literal Old Testament reading and African mysticism, it seeks to right the wrongs suffered by black people across the world by reuniting them in the promised land of Ethiopia. Ras Tafari was the name of the late Emperor Haile Selassie (1892–1974) who is revered as a god by members of the movement. Not all of its adherents believe in a real return to Africa, but most are attracted by a lifestyle that is both rebellious towards authority and stringently devout to their cause.

The Indo-Caribbeans are also in evidence through their religion. In islands such as Trinidad and Guadeloupe, where indentured immigration was greatest after abolition, the landscape is dotted with Hindu temples, adorned with images of Krishna, Shiva or Rama. Prayer flags flap limply outside village houses or amidst clumps of banana or bamboo, and Indian communities celebrate religious feast days, such as *Phagwa* and *Diwali*, with traditional music and dancing.

LIFE IN THE SLOW LANE

Creole culture values freedom above all else – and freedom includes the right to live life at your own pace.

Living in harmony

It is a tribute to local tolerance that such a heady mix of religious faiths has rarely produced friction between differing practitioners. The established churches used to campaign against African religion, denigrating it as "superstition" or "black magic", but that is largely a thing of the past. The new US-inspired evangelicals may be inclined to preach against obeah and its ilk, but their message is not widely followed.

This tolerance extends to many walks of life and may explain why the Eastern Caribbean islands, although poor and deprived by some definitions, have not witnessed the social strife that experts predicted in the transition towards independence. It is dangerous to generalize and stereotypes can be condescending, even when well-intentioned.

Yet terms like "laid-back", known as "liming" on the islands, contain a grain of truth about local attitudes to life and personal relations, suggesting with some accuracy a general distaste for unnecessary stress and conflict. Some tourists have difficulty in adjusting to the slower pace of life in the Caribbean, detecting idleness in a measured approach to work in a tropical climate. The problem is largely theirs and their irritation is an unfortunate and mostly futile waste of energy. In the Caribbean, to be in a hurry is not necessarily considered a desirable attribute.

If the historically mixed people of the islands exhibit a common characteristic, it is probably this refusal to be hurried from a positive appreciation of life as it comes. Creole culture values freedom above all else – and freedom includes the right to live life at your own pace. Tolerance and respect for others are widely appreciated qualities, perhaps born from an innate understanding of how life once was without them. And they are readily extended to strangers, for here everybody knows what it is like to be a stranger. ❑

LEFT: dressed up for church.
ABOVE: looking cool in St Vincent.

BARBAD
miles long and a smile

AND THE BEAT GOES ON

Caribbean music never stands still and the eastern islands, where fusion is a way of life, are fast earning a reputation as the music mecca of the world

Think of Caribbean music, and what do you come up with? Reggae would be an obvious first choice. Almost everybody can recognize the sound that took the world by storm in the 1970s with artists like Bob Marley and Peter Tosh and which is still a force to be reckoned with. And then what? Salsa became a phenomenon in the 1990s, with Cubans, Puerto Ricans and mainland Latin Americans setting the pace. Then there's calypso and steelband, the infectious good-time music that seems to evoke the region in its every note.

But these three totally different types of music are just the tip of an ever-growing musical iceberg. Leaving aside the bigger islands, such as Jamaica, Cuba and Puerto Rico, even the smaller territories of the Lesser Antilles reveal an extraordinary diversity of styles and sounds that literally stretches from A to Z. In between Trinidad's aguinaldo and Martinique's zouk you'll find genres such as bélè (French islands), jing ping (Dominica), raggasoca (Barbados) and tambu (Dutch islands). And that's not to mention bouyon, parang and soukous.

Medley of influences

This baffling array of musical forms is testimony to the creativity and individuality of each Caribbean island. It also reminds us of the many different influences – linguistic as well as musical – which have left their mark on the region. European colonizers from Britain, France and Spain brought their music and instruments with them, recalled today in dances such as the *quadrille* of Martinique and Guadeloupe. From Africa came the drum-based rhythms and tradition of collective participation that underlie almost all contemporary styles in the region. Indian migrants contributed distinctive instruments and harmonies, especially in multicultural Trinidad. More recently, American jazz, rock 'n' roll and rap have been incorporated and adapted into local forms, together with everything else from Latin brass sections to country and western.

Caribbean music never stands still. Constantly borrowing and developing, it keeps pace with technological advances while remaining rooted in age-old traditions. In a region where so many cultural influences, good and bad, have been absorbed, fusion is a way of life. No wonder that the Caribbean is fast earning a reputation as the music mecca of the world.

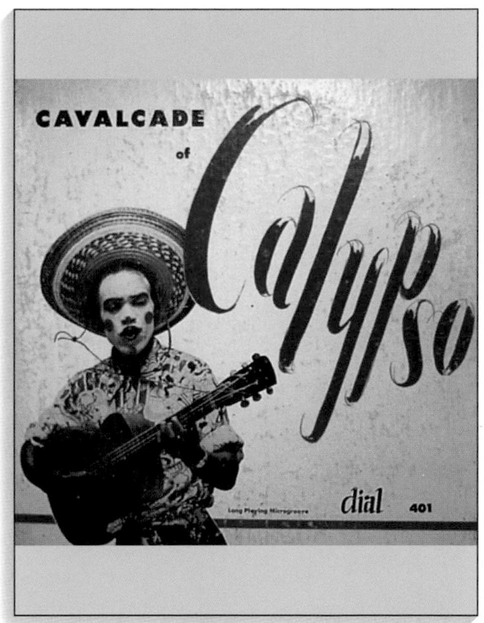

PRECEDING PAGES: making music in Trinidad
LEFT: in with the swing.
RIGHT: a calypso record sleeve from the 1950s.

Steel pan – a by-product of oil

You'll hear steel pan throughout the region, but Trinidad claims not just to have invented it, but to be world leader in playing it. There are still arguments over who it was who first realized the musical potential of a discarded oil drum in the 1930s. But there is no dispute that rhythm and percussion were already well established on the island. Predecessors included the tamboo bamboo orchestras, which beat bamboo tubes with sticks (used instead of drums banned by the British colonials as they thought it would encourage rioting) at folk dances, funeral wakes and, of course, Carnival. Other percussionists resorted to biscuit tins, dustbins and kitchen pots until the imported oil drum, a feature of Trinidad's booming petroleum industry, was converted into the versatile instrument we know today.

To begin with, steel pan and its players suffered a serious image problem. Associated with the slum areas of Port of Spain and tainted by regular violence between competing bands and their over-enthusiastic supporters, the music was considered rough and disreputable by respectable Trinidadians. Its reputation worsened as gangs formed around the bands to fight turf battles among themselves and against the police. It was only with the advent of corporate sponsorship and the commercialization of Carnival that the violence subsided. With the threat of companies withdrawing band sponsorship, peace broke out and has remained in force to the present day.

Calypso – voice of the people

The calypsonian was – and still is – the people's orator. In post-Emancipation times, as people

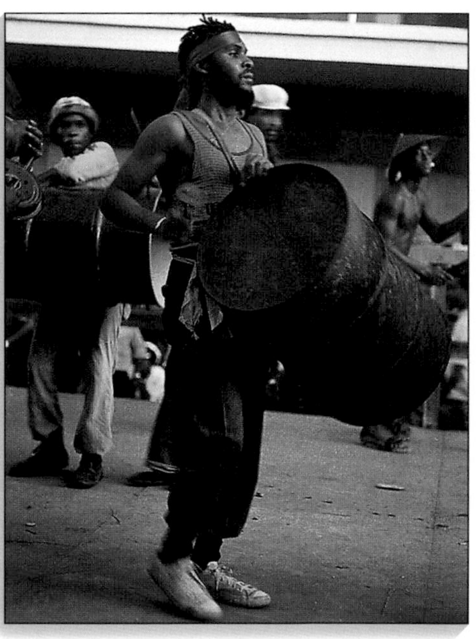

flocked to the city in search of jobs and away from the plantation, the calypsonian took on the traditional role of the chantwell, the improvising vocalist who used to sing boasting and comic songs during rural stick-fighting sessions. His function involved the dissemination of gossip, the spreading of news and the mocking of those in authority. His performances took place in special tents, in front of discerning audiences who judged the artist's topicality and originality.

Today, little has changed, although there are female performers, and subjects such as feminism and gay rights provide up-to-date inspiration. The calypsonian's armoury con-

PARANG – A CHRISTMAS TRADITION

The build-up to Christmas in Trinidad wouldn't be the same without the Afro-Spanish tradition known as parang (from the Spanish *parar*, meaning "to stop at" or "put up at somebody's house"). The music is named after the roving performers who would move from house to house at the festive season with violins, cuartos, mandolins, guitars and maracas, along with the African-descended box drum and box bass.

Deeply traditional in form, the styles include Spanish names such as *aguinaldo*, *galerón* or *paseo* and are largely descended from the carol singing of 18th and 19th-century Spanish settlers.

tains spontaneous improvisation, wit and picong (biting, literally piquant, observations). His (or her) songs may be narrative, oratorical or extemporaneous, but it's likely they'll focus on sex, scandal and what is known as "bacchanal".

Calypso is part of Trinidad's cultural lifeblood, which permeates through the whole of the Caribbean, and the climax comes each year at Carnival – or Crop Over in Barbados – which provides the background for fierce competition, lucrative prizes and front page headlines. Trinidad's hall of greats contains performers with grandiose names such as Roaring Lion, Attila the Hun and Lord Kitchener. The Mighty Sparrow is a Grenadian by birth, while Arrow, the singer of the worldwide hit *Hot Hot Hot*, is from Montserrat.

A CALYPSONIAN IS...

"...not only an articulator of the population, he is also a fount of public opinion. He expresses the mood of the people, the beliefs of the people."
– MIGHTY CHALKDUST, Trinidadian teacher

That song, in fact, is actually more soca than calypso, a faster-paced, dance-oriented style that has evolved from the fusion of *so*ul and *ca*lypso and is extremely popular across the Eastern Caribbean as youth music with attitude.

And the musical evolution continues to gain momentum with the creation of raggasoca, the fusion of Jamaican-style reggae with soca that has also taken the region by storm. This hybrid currently rules in Barbados and Trinidad and Tobago and dominates the radio airwaves and Carnival.

Ceremonial tuk

One thriving aspect of Barbados's annual Crop Over festival (historically held to mark the end of the cane-cutting season) is the tuk band. These percussive outfits are believed to date from as far back as the 17th century and later accompanied the island's local friendly societies, known as "landships", in ceremonies and outings. They are also thought to have modeled themselves on the marching bands of 18th-century British regiments.

Today's tuk band is made up of bass, snare and kettle drums, a penny whistle or flute and usually a triangle. Despite what might seem at first to be a limited musical range, the bands' versatility is amazing and is often shown off in a wide repertoire of songs, covering the spectrum from European classical pieces to Negro

FAR LEFT: Barbadian calypsonian Red Plastic Bag.
LEFT: old oil drums are still used as steel pans.
ABOVE: horns add a soca beat to a Carnival band.

spirituals and current *Billboard* (Top Ten) hits.

But it is always the performance of original, Caribbean-flavored material that brings out the best in the musicians, and thanks to the efforts of calypsonian Wayne "Poonka" Willcock and his group Ruk-a-Tuk International, tuk music is staging something of a comeback in the mushrooming local festivals.

Begin the beguine...

The earliest authentic style to have come from Martinique and Guadeloupe is generally agreed to be the beguine, its bolero rhythm a firm favorite among dance orchestras from the 1930s to the 1950s. Over the following two decades, the French Antillean soundscape underwent significant changes due to migration and freshly imported influences. An important new ingredient was brought by Haitian immigrants in the form of kadans or "cadence", a subtle blend of musical accents, syncopation and instrumental colour derived from Haiti's mini-jazz ensembles (featuring brass, lead and bass guitar, bell and drums).

From kadans evolved zouk in the 1980s, a genre which was less a fad than a true phenomenon, reaching beyond the confines of the Caribbean to touch the continents of Africa,

Round-up of Music Festivals

With music playing such a major role in the region, more and more islands are staging music festivals in addition to the musical events and calypso competitions during Carnival (*see pages 282–83*):

January Barbados Jazz Festival, St Croix Blues Festival; St Barths Music Festival (classic, folk, jazz);

March St Patrick's Day Festival, St Croix;

April Holders Season, Barbados (opera);

May St Lucia Jazz Festival; Big Drum Festival, Union Island; Gospel Fest, Barbados; Curaçao Jazz Festival; Curaçao Merengue Festival; Rapso Month, Trinidad; Spice Jazz Festival, Grenada;

June St Kitts Music Festival; Aruba Jazz and Latin American Music Festival;

July BVI Summer Festival (calypso);

August Curaçao Salsa Festival; Pic-o-De-Crop Calypso Finals, Barbados;

October St Croix Jazz and Caribbean Music Festival; Antigua Jazz Festival; World Creole Music Festival, Dominica;

November Curaçao Golden Artists Music Festival; International Jazz Festival, Martinique (biennial); Guadeloupe Creole Music Festival;

December St Lucia Country Music Festival; Carriacou Parang Festival, Grenada.

America and Europe. Zouk trailblazers were the Guadeloupean band Kassav, whose founders, Pierre-Edouard Décimus and Jacob Devarieux, captured the festive mood and euphoria that marked the local *vidé* (spontaneous street carnival parade) and integrated old-style rhythmic dance elements into a modern good-time sound.

The success of Kassav and others marked the entry of French Caribbean music into the international marketplace. It also offered an original, rather than borrowed, model, including a long overdue emphasis on women's voices, that appeals not only to the Caribbean as a whole, but to aficionados of dance music from further afield.

Ringbang

More of a style of living than a type of music, Ringbang, endorsed by the Mighty Gabby, encompasses all Caribbean music with the rhythm not the melody as its focus.

Sandwiched between French/Creole-speaking Martinique and Guadeloupe, the island of Dominica has long been influenced culturally and musically by the two French *départements*. But even if its rhythms are similar to those of its Gallic neighbors, there has still been room for considerable innovation. Dominican soukous, for instance, is characterized by its rhythmic dynamism, a driving bass guitar and lightning fast guitar licks. And the Windward Caribbean Kulture (WCK Band) specializes in bouyon, an eclectic mix of cadence-lypso (itself a fusion) and traditional jing ping. The end result being a compelling cocktail of pulsating drums *à la digital* and keyboards.

Jazz fusions

The Afro-American art form of jazz has also found a home in the Caribbean, to be mixed into the melting-pot of influences. Some 30 jazz festivals take place in the region each year, while local musicians have tirelessly experimented with a variety of fusions which embrace New Orleans rhythms and their own distinctively Caribbean flavors.

Notable jazz exponents from the Lesser Antilles to be seen at all the festivals are St Lucia's Arthur François with his zouk crossover, Barbadian saxophonist Arturo Tappin who merges jazz with reggae, "Professor" Ken Philmore (Trinidad) who plays steel pan jazz, Nicholas Brancker (Barbados) and his funk/jazz and Trinidadians David Rudder and Clive Xanda who perform jazz-inspired calypso music. ❑

Left: Monty Alexander is popular at jazz festivals.

Above: Kassav, a Guadeloupean zouk band, has found international success.

PASSION AND POETRY

The Lesser Antilles has a rich literary tradition – albeit a relatively young one, because for centuries stories and poems were passed down by word of mouth

*"Love for an island is the sternest passion:
pulsing beyond the blood through roots
and loam"* – Phyllis Allfrey, Dominica

The islands of the Eastern Caribbean inspire passion and poetry in equal measure. And in impressive quantity. Few parts of the world can have produced so many top-class writers from so small a population. Although many of them today live in self-imposed exile, the landscapes, language and people of the islands fill their work with the unmistakable flavor of their home.

Yet literature is a relatively late arrival in the Caribbean. The great Barbadian novelist George Lamming was guilty of only slight exaggeration when he said in the 1960s that Caribbean writing was just 20 years old. However, there has, of course, always been plenty written about the region – from the 17th century, priests, merchants and other itinerant observers sent back their impressions of island life to be replaced in the 19th century by travel writers who invariably made their trip "down the islands" with a book in mind.

Early storytellers

But literature by local people was for a long time in short supply. Slavery, illiteracy and constant inter-colonial warfare were not ideal conditions for a thriving literary culture, while most slave owners or landlords were hardly bookish by inclination. Significantly, one of the earliest examples of Caribbean poetry is *Barbados* (1754) in which Nathaniel Weekes offers useful, if unromantic, advice to the island's planters:

*"To urge the Glory of your Cane's success,
Rich be your Soil, and well manur'd with Dung,
Or, Planters! what will your Labours yield?"*

The culture of the slaves was oral rather than written, and their tales, riddles and proverbs were handed down by storytellers in spoken form. Since slave-owning societies actively discouraged the formal education of the black majority, it was hardly surprising that few books were read, let alone written.

Even after Emancipation, the Lesser Antilles lagged behind larger territories like Cuba or

Haiti in literary output. The small islands lacked publishers, bookshops and libraries and, above all, a reading public. Amidst widespread poverty and lack of education, only occasional clerics or dilettantes put pen to paper, but their poetry tended to be little more than tropical adaptations of well-worn European conventions.

One remarkable exception to the rule was John Jacob Thomas, a self-educated black Trinidadian. In 1888, Thomas read *The English in the West Indies*, which was a study of British colonialism in the Caribbean by the eminent Oxford professor, James Anthony Froude. Incensed by Froude's patronizing and prejudiced view of black society, Thomas wrote

LEFT: Nobel Prize-winner Derek Walcott.
RIGHT: George Lamming explored his Barbadian childhood in *In the Castle of my Skin.*

a devastating riposte, *Froudacity: West Indian Fables Explained* (1889), in which he accused the pompous professor of "fatuity" and "skinpride".

On the literary map

Several factors coalesced in the 1940s and 1950s to put the region on the literary map. World War II and the immediate post-war years witnessed a massive increase in migration and mobility as islanders seized work opportunities in Europe and the US. Young men like Lamming and Trinidadians V.S. Naipaul

and Samuel Selvon found themselves in London, exposed to a range of new influences. It may have been cold and hostile (as comically described in Selvon's masterpiece, *The Lonely Londoners*, 1956), but it had publishers and literary reviews eager for fresh material.

Other would-be writers from the English-speaking islands went to New York or Montreal, while those from Martinique and Guadeloupe revelled in the cultural ferment of post-war Paris. From these experiences of self-imposed exile emerged some of the enduring themes of Caribbean literature: rootlessness, nostalgia, the bitter-sweet reality of returning home.

This period was also one of political and cultural revaluation as the islands moved towards independence or greater autonomy, creating a sense of nationalism, of regional identity, long suppressed by colonialism. Fast disappearing were the days when schoolchildren would have to write essays entitled *A Winter's Day*, and writers began to find a distinctive, Caribbean voice. Often this voice was satirical, mocking the colonial system and values which had dominated for centuries. The title of Barbadian Austin Clarke's memoir, *Growing Up Stupid Under the Union Jack* (1980) is typical of the anti-colonial genre.

GUADELOUPE

"And yet it was a land of verdant hills and clear waters, beneath a sun every day more radiant."
– SIMONE SCHWARZ-BART *(Between Two Worlds)*

Home-grown talent

As writers and intellectuals reassessed their mixed cultural heritage, the beginnings of a local literary establishment emerged. Most early authors were published in London or New York, but a handful of literary journals such as *Bim*, founded in Barbados in 1942, began to publish the work of home-grown talent. Along with improved communications, this encouraged a new generation of writers to go into print.

The 1950s was the decade in which Caribbean literature finally established itself overseas. Three novels created international reputations for their authors and set out some of the principal themes and attitudes which were to follow in much more fiction. Lamming's *In the Castle of My Skin* (1953) explored the decline of British colonialism in Barbados and the awakening of new aspirations within a small rural community. Selvon's *The Lonely Londoners* (1956) followed a group of Trinidadian emigrants to Britain and the ensuing culture shock they endured. Naipaul's *The Mystic Masseur* (1957) painted a bitter-sweet picture of incompetence and pretentiousness in colonial Trinidad. Each novel, in its own way, dissected the legacy of British rule and the question of contemporary Caribbean identity.

The smaller English-speaking territories started producing top-rank literature in the 1970s and 1980s with work by Derek Walcott (St Lucia), Jamaica Kincaid (Antigua) and Caryl Phillips (St Kitts). Today, almost every island, however small its population, can claim at least one internationally recognized writer.

Official recognition came in the 1990s for

two authors, whose work is rooted in the region. In 1992, Derek Walcott received the Nobel Prize for Literature, in tribute to his long and productive career as a poet and playwright. In 1990, his magnificent *Omeros*, a reworking of the Homeric legend amidst a fishing community in St Lucia, had confirmed his status as one of the world's leading poets. The previous year, the Martinican novelist Patrick Chamoiseau had won the Prix Goncourt for his complex novel *Texaco*, a sought-after sign of approval from the Parisian intellectual establishment.

Vibrant French literary scene

The literary productivity of two of the French overseas regions – Martinique and Guadeloupe – is as impressive as that of their Anglophone neighbors. The white Guadeloupean poet Saint-John Perse won the Nobel Prize for Literature in 1960 (although it is generally known he disliked his island of birth), while Martinique's Aimé Césaire wrote the trail-blazing surrealist epic, *Return to My Native Land* in 1939.

Nowadays, thanks to first-world levels of education and opportunity, the two islands enjoy a vibrant literary scene which is taken more and more seriously by the big Parisian publishers. Interestingly, many of the most prominent novelists from Martinique and Guadeloupe are women, who mix specifically female themes into the wider theme of French/Caribbean identity – Maryse Condé, Simone Schwarz-Bart and Gisèle Pineau are three of the better known.

Influences from abroad

It is difficult to generalize about common themes in the region's writing, but certain preoccupations do recur. Many Caribbean authors continue to examine the relationship, both positive and negative, between the islands and the old European powers.

The influence of the US, from tourists to CNN, is another widespread motif as writers struggle to define what is culturally distinctive about their homelands. In this context, language itself is an important issue, and many authors are keen to highlight the richness of local Creole or patois. In the French islands, in particular, writers such as Chamoiseau and Raphaël Confiant have championed their expressive creole against the dominance of "official" French.

The modern Caribbean writer is above all aware of the fragility of his or her island home in an age of mass tourism and rampant development. In accepting his Nobel Prize, Walcott spoke of a way of life threatened by such progress: "How quickly it could all disappear! And how it is beginning to drive us further into where we hope are inpenetrable places, green secrets at the end of bad roads, headlands where the next view is not of a hotel but of some long beach without a figure and the hanging question of some fisherman's smoke at its far end." ❑

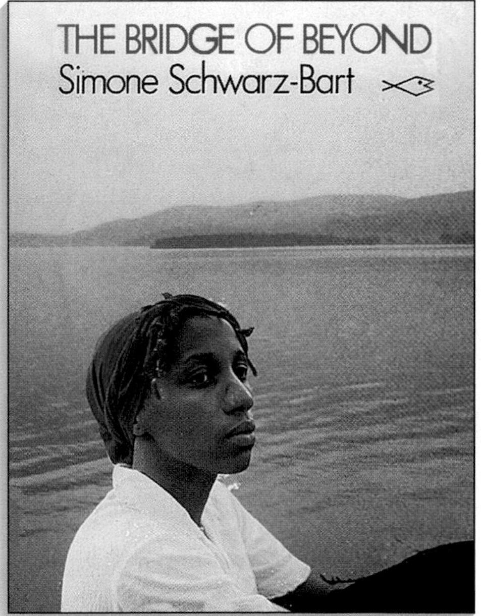

LEFT: Trinidad's V.S. Naipaul wrote from London.
RIGHT: Simone Schwarz-Bart uses female themes.

TWO OF A KIND

The small, mountainous island of Dominica is the birthplace of two celebrated novelists, both women from white families.

After a notoriously Bohemian career in 1930s Europe, Jean Rhys disappeared until her book *Wide Sargasso Sea* (1966) became a cult classic. Its eerie atmosphere of tropical menace and madness bears some resemblance to the decadent island world described in *The Orchid House* (1953) by Phyllis Allfrey. Although of the same generation, the two women never met (Rhys only returned to Dominica once) but they corresponded extensively.

FREEDOM SOCIETY
HAND$
OFF
OUR
BUTT$

Heineken

Creole Cuisine

Between American fast-food joints and the international haute cuisine of the big hotels there is the delicious food of the Caribbean to be enjoyed

As the word creole generally means "born in the islands but originating from the outside world", it seems an appropriate collective name for the region's home cooking, given its history. However, despite the common thread uniting the creole cuisine of the islands, the miles of water that separate them, along with their diverse historic influences from the outside world, ensure that the food of each one is usually quite distinct and often unique.

The common thread is provided by the region's rich Amerindian and African heritage; the readily available fresh produce of the fertile land, with its year-round growing season; and the abundance of superb seafood from the surrounding Caribbean Sea and Atlantic Ocean. Meanwhile, the wonderful variation within the styles of cuisine has been created by the diversity of the European countries that colonized the islands, the introduction of indentured labour from the east, and the wide range of differing topography throughout the region.

Fresh from land and sea

When the settlers started arriving, there was already some wild game on the islands, such as agouti, iguana, deer, hogs, land tortoises and guinea pigs, and they added chickens, cattle, sheep and pigs. Today, people in the country are still happy to run a small farm or raise their "stocks" on whatever pasture is available. On land the swamps and rivers can supply crabs and crayfish, but the best and most plentiful source of protein is the fish and other seafood which abounds in the surrounding ocean.

Caribbean seafood can be rated as some of the best in the world. As a result of the generally short distance from the sea to the table, it is served particularly fresh, contributing to its intense flavor. Grouper, barracuda, kingfish, swordfish, sea bream, jacks, parrotfish, snapper, tuna, albacor, bonito and dolphin are the names of fish most heard of in these islands. Dolphin is an ugly, scaly fish not to be confused with the mammal which is known as a porpoise, often also referred to as a dolphin, and a role model for *Flipper*. Flying fish are only widely served in Barbados, where the intricate skill of deboning them has been perfected and passed on down the generations.

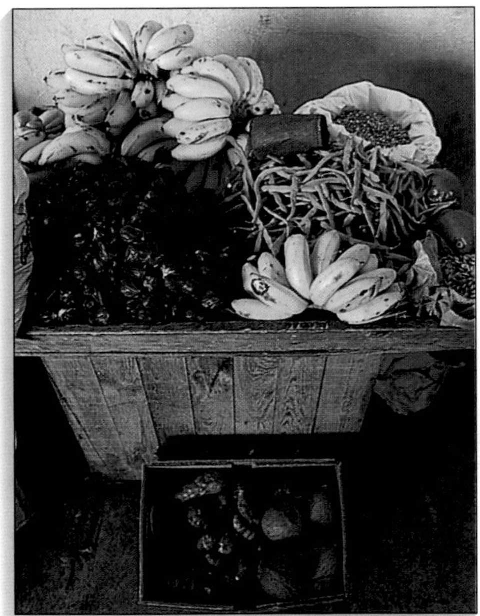

The Caribbean waters also contain plenty of sea crab, spiny lobster, conch (sometimes called lambis) with their large beautiful shells, sea egg (sea urchin), octopus and, in the south, very large shrimp, also referred to as "giant prawns". The end result of this exciting array of fresh ingredients, prepared in a variety of tantalizing ways, is an exotic culinary extravaganza.

A culinary legacy

Foods that can be traced back to the Amerindians, are still found throughout the islands. Pepperpot stew, a mixture of meats, vegetables and hot peppers, cooked in black cassava juice, a

Preceding Pages: flying fish for lunch.
Left: pick up a lobster in Grand Case, St Martin.
Right: fresh island produce goes into the best meals.

natural preservative, was originally a means of preserving the hunter's bountiful catch. Once brought to the boil daily, it will not go off. Even in this day and age, some establishments and households keep a pepperpot on the stove for months, in a traditional pottery *coneree*, adding in fresh ingredients as required. Pepperpot soup, freshly made with vegetables, such as okra, pumpkin and yam, has only been slightly modified since the Amerindian days with the introduction of imported salt meat.

Another favourite of the Amerindians, and still a popular snack, was roasted corn. The husk is removed and the corn is cooked over an open fire until it is completely black. It was in fact these highly self-sufficient people who gave the world the barbecue, derived from their word *barbacoa* meaning cooking over a fire.

The Amerindians also made delicious bread from cassava and corn. Fresh bread made with bran and wheat flour is the most common staple and can be smelled baking in the early morning in virtually every village and town.

An African inheritance

The African slaves were given by their masters rations of rice, imported salt cod, salt meat, and dried peas and beans on which to feed and

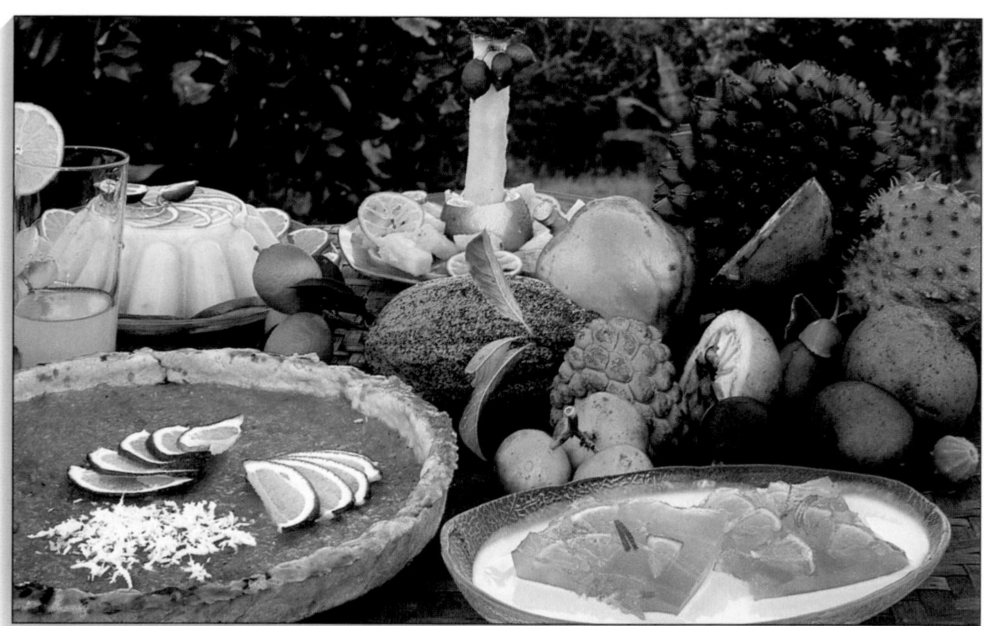

nourish themselves. They were also given small plots of land to grow produce to supplement their meagre fare. From this paltry larder came the basis of the delicious food served today. Every island has its own recipe for rice and peas, which is usually made with salt beef or pork and fresh herbs such as shallots and thyme. Fish cakes consisting of salt fish, flour, a variety of pepper and herbs, dipped in batter and deep fried, have an irresistible aroma.

To season their food, slaves grew thyme, marjoram, mint, sage, rosemary, shallots and peppers. Today, every island has its own "seasoning" made from finely chopped herbs, onions, garlic and pepper; and each one offers

A Fair Exchange

In the early days of colonization and exploration, there was a tremendous exchange of horticulture and agriculture around the world. While the Caribbean gave the world the pineapple, pepper, cashew, avocado, runner bean, potato, sweet potato and tomato, to name some of the more famous produce indigenous to the region, the outside world returned the favor with many of the fruits, vegetables and herbs that are now frequently associated with this area – such as mango, lime, orange, banana, coffee, sugar cane, pigeon pea, yam, okra, nutmeg, cinnamon, clove, ginger, shallots, thyme, parsley and coconuts.

its own version of a fiercely hot pepper sauce, which should be sampled very cautiously.

Chicken, roasted, fried or stewed; roast pork, garlic pork, pickled pig's head, tail and trotters, pork stew, whole suckling pig roasted on a spit and ham has always been popular weekend and celebration fare – not a piece of the pig is spared. All the islands prepare variations of black pudding made from pigs intestine stuffed with the blood mixed with sweet potato and seasoning.

GRAPEFRUIT

Although most citrus came from the Pacific region, the grapefruit was conceived in Barbados in the 18th century. It is a cross between a sweet orange and a large, bitter citrus fruit called a shaddock, brought over from Polynesia by a Captain Shaddock.

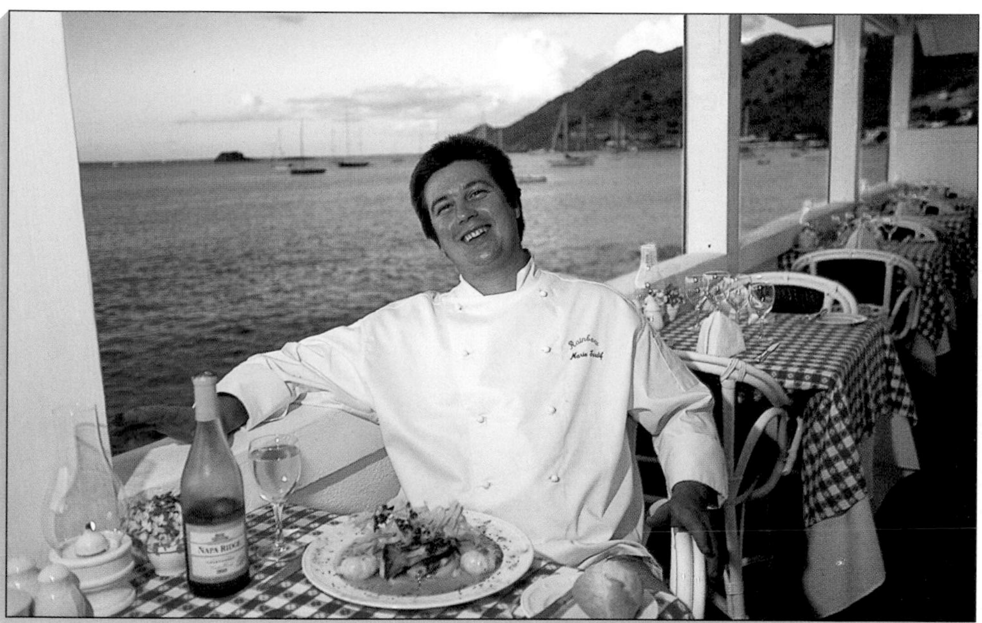

One pot cook ups

With most of the cooking being done over an open fire, usually with only one pot, many recipes developed for "one pot meals" which included a large variety of tasty soups such as split pea soup, callaloo soup made from eddoe leaves and crab, pumpkin soup, fish soup, peanut soup, and a "big soup" that you can stand the spoon up in, made with an assortment of root crops and fresh vegetables. Other one pot meals known as cook ups are based on a starch such as rice or yam, to which is added any vegetables, seasonings, fish, meat or chicken that the cook can find to make a tasty and nutritious meal. As a result of the ingenius use of herbs and spices, stews in the Caribbean tend to be full of flavor.

An interesting observation about Caribbean cuisine is that the Amerindians, when first encountered by Europeans, were preparing many foods in exactly the same way as some West Africans thousands of miles across the Atlantic Ocean. For example, cou-cou or fungi – ground corn, boiled up with okras and mashed into a thick paste – is an indigenous dish of both the Caribbean and Africa. Still enjoyed today, it's usually served with a pungent salt fish, fresh fish or beef stew.

LEFT: limes are an important ingredient in these dishes. **ABOVE:** with a restaurant by the sea, a chef has no problem wondering what to cook.

Caribbean sweet tooth

Since the 17th century when the European settlers set about planting sugar cane, the Caribbean people have developed a very "sweet tooth" blending the sought-after resulting product with island fruits to create such delicacies as tamarind balls, guava cheese, coconut sugar cakes, toolum, comforts and shaddock rind –

unique candies that have been prepared for generations of children. The preserves of lime and orange marmalade, guava jelly, nutmeg jelly, chutney and fruit jams are of a very high quality because the golden crystals of Caribbean sugar are bursting with tangy flavors.

Traditional desserts tend to come from a combination of British heritage and Caribbean style: bread 'n' butter pudding, rich fruit cake laced with rum, banana and coconut bread, jam puffs, chocolate pudding and coconut turnovers. And restaurants everywhere include their own versions of the delicious coconut pie on their dessert menu.

REFRESHING DRINKS

The abundance of fruit on the islands means that fresh fruit juices are served everywhere: guava, mango and soursop are some of the most exotic. Mauby is a bitter-sweet drink made from tree bark, and sorrel is a traditional Christmas drink created from the dried bright red blossom of a type of hibiscus.

European flavors

The islands generally have a very separate and distinct cuisine from each other, depending on who they were colonized by. The French brought their *pâtisserie* (pastries), stuffed crab back, tomato and herb fish stews reminiscent of Provence, escargots in garlic, and frogs' legs (coyly called mountain chicken in Dominica),

Jug Jug, a Christmas dish of pigeon peas, guinea corn flour, salt meat and herbs, and a corruption of the Scottish dish haggis, was introduced to Barbados by the Scots when they were exiled there after the Monmouth Rebellion of 1685.

The Spanish, left Trinidad a delicious legacy of their favorite dishes: *pastelles* (meat and grated corn steamed in a banana leaf), *escoviche* (pickled fish), *buljol* (salt fish, tomato, lime, pepper, garlic and avocado), to name just a few. In later years, Indian and Chinese food was introduced to Trinidad by large numbers of immigrants from Asia, and the roti – a thick curry wrapped in a chapati – is now sold throughout the region, keeping the American burger joints on their toes. Trinidadian Chinese cooking has also evolved into a new and delicious style, modified by the use of different ingredients.

The Dutch islands enjoy an Indonesian flavor to their dishes due to the Netherlands' connections with the Far East. So the food of the Caribbean is as diverse as the origins of its people – a multitude of exotic flavors, all drawn from the sun blessed, fertile land, the bountiful seas and the creative genius of generations of multi-ethnic cooks and chefs. ❑

Yo ho ho

Rum has long been associated with pirates, smugglers and sailors and featured in many a classic "Boys' Own" adventure story as barrels of the liquid gold were rolled on to British shores by the light of the full moon – duty free.

It didn't take long to discover that a forceful fiery liquor could be produced from sugar cane and in Barbados in the 1640s, the first batches of locally distilled spirits were introduced or rather experienced! Referred to as "kill-devil" by the English Royalist refugee Richard Ligon in *A True and Exact History of the Island of Barbados* in 1657, the drink was strong and barely fit to drink; those who imbibed it quickly felt its effects, as Ligon wrote, "It lays them to sleep on the ground."

Or, too much of it ended in a "rumbullion", an old English word for a noisy brawl – hence the name rum. Another early visitor to Barbados wrote that "the chiefe fudling they make on the Island is Rumbullion, alias Kill Divill, and this is made of sugarcanes distilled, a hot, hellish and terrible liquor."

Rum is actually made from molasses, the thick, black treacle left after the juice from the sugar cane has crystalized. Spring water – in Barbados it is filtered through coral rock – is then added and it is left to ferment. After distilling, more fresh water is added to what is now a colorless liquid of almost 95 percent alcohol and it is poured into oak barrels to slowly mature; the best rum is stored for at least seven years. The golden color develops from the secret ingredients added by the master blender, which may include vanilla, almond extract, caramel or older types of rum combined with the smoked interior of the barrel. It remains colorless when kept for a short time in stainless steel barrels.

Many of the islands have their own rum factories with their own brand that they are fiercely proud of, for example, Barbados, where it all began, has Mount Gay and Cockspur; Trinidad has Old Oak and Vat 19, and Martinique produces several including Trois Rivières and St Clément.

For sailors in the British Royal Navy, rum was an important ingredient in their daily rations – it helped keep them upright in stormy seas and raised morale. But they were mighty upset in 1731 when Admiral Vernon ordered that the spirit be diluted with water. This concoction was disparagingly called a "grog" after the admiral whose nickname had been Old Grog because he always wore a cloak of a coarse material called grogram.

Since then rum has been diluted with a wide variety of juices and mixers creating wonderful cocktails and punches that are sipped in beach bars, by swimming pools and on verandahs all over the Caribbean. The word punch originates from India, another of Britain's former colonies: the Indian word *panch* means five for the drink's five ingredients: "*One of sour* (lime juice)*/two of sweet* (sugar syrup)*/three of strong* (rum)*/four of weak* (water)*/five dashes of* (Angostura) *bitters and nutmeg spice/serve well chilled with lots of ice.*"

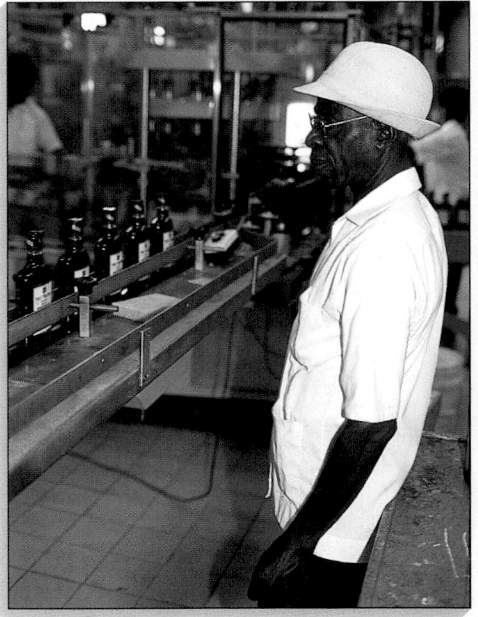

In the rum shops on islands such as Trinidad and Barbados (where you will find one on almost every corner) rum is drunk neat or "on the rocks". A rum shop is not merely a bar; it is a village store, a community center, an arena for fiercely competitive domino-playing, a place where tongues are loosened, politics discussed and rumors spread. "Man, leh we fire one on that!" is the exhortation prompted by a happy event.

It is still largely the province of men: "Men in de rum shop; women in de church," so the saying goes. And Lord Byron may have been thinking along the same lines when he wrote, *"There's nought no doubt so much the spirit calms/as rum and true religion."* ❑

LEFT: Sea eggs, or urchins are a Caribbean delicacy.
RIGHT: bottling the liquid gold.

GINGERBREAD AND BALLAST BRICK

Caribbean architecture reveals influences from the Arawaks, Africa and the European colonizers, from simple Kunuku cottages to Great Houses

When Columbus hit upon the West Indies at the end of the 15th century, the dwellings he found there were nothing compared to what he was used to in Europe, and he wrote to a friend that the " [Indians] *live in rocks and mountains, without fixed settlements, and not like ourselves.*" In fact Arawaks and Caribs slept in round or oval-shaped huts built of sticks and covered with a conical roof made of palms or grass from swamps.

The first Europeans left on islands to set up trading posts, and then the settlers, copied these Indian shelters, but soon introduced wall construction with wooden beams and shingles for the roofs. However, even after Emancipation the slaves rarely built with stone, and single-roomed thatched houses with walls of clay and straw were still in use in the 20th century.

A MEDLEY OF STYLES

When the sugar trade to Europe started, many ships brought huge amounts of red brick and stone in their hulls as ballast. And wealthy planters and merchants on islands like Barbados or Antigua built their Great Houses with it. In Statia's heyday ballast was used for the warehouses on the waterfront. Several styles developed, the Spanish adopting Moorish traditions, while the French introduced cast iron and, later, the American invention of mechanical saws gave rise to the intricate wooden lacework – gingerbread – on many façades.

▷ MAGNIFICENCE
Stollmeyer's Castle (1904) is one of the "Magnificent Seven" examples of architectural opulence in Port of Spain, and was inspired by Scottish and German castles.

▷ THE GREAT HOUSE
Planters modeled their homes on European styles adapting them to suit the climate, with thick walls, shutters and verandahs.

△ ADMIRAL'S RETREAT
The two-storey verandah on this naval retreat (1855) in Nelson's Dockyard, Antigua, still provides shade and protection from heavy rain.

△ COLONIAL STYLE
Many hotels, such as Divi Little Bay in St Maarten, are being built with a colonial touch and traditional decor in an attempt to complement their tropical surroundings.

▷ GINGERBREAD TRIM
At the beginning of the 20th century, English, American and Dutch-influenced islands decorated façades with delicately sawn wooden lacework.

KUNUKU
'ew of these traditional
e-room farmhouses with
ry thick walls of clay and
t grass. A thatched roof
n still be seen in Curaçao.

▷ SEA BREEZES
The clever construction of houses on hills to harness the cooling trade winds through airy verandahs and Italian shutters makes modern air conditioning superfluous.

▽ NOTHING BUT THE BEST
Dining tables made of large pieces of mahogany were the pride of wealthy planters and often sat 30, laid with English silverware and bone china, for dinner.

CHATTEL HOUSES: MOBILE HOMES

For the black population of Barbados, mobility was once essential to survival. After Emancipation the planters had to employ labor and, still wanting to control the freed slaves, allowed them to establish small settlements on their land. This made the workers dependent on their employer's good will and they were rapidly chased off the land if there were any problems. So the chattel house was developed: a small wooden "sleeping box" easy to dismantle and take along on a cart to another plantation.

Supported by big rocks or concrete blocks so that rainwater can pass underneath, the one-room house with an optional partition inside is made up of wooden planks fixed to a framework. Makeshift steps lead up to the only door opening on to the family's living space. Here parents and children, and often grandparents as well, used to sleep in one room. The cooking was done outside, as was any entertaining of neighbors and friends.

This nucleus of a family home – with one or two extensions – is still a common sight in Barbados, especially in the more remote country districts, and only a few years ago a whole village moved from a hilltop to a valley, where running water was available.

PLACES

A detailed guide to the entire Lesser Antilles, with principal sites clearly cross-referenced by number to the maps

At one time just getting to these tropical islands was an adventure, now the adventure can start on arrival. Whether you are cruising "down the islands" on an ocean liner, sailing between them on a yacht or you have picked out one or two just to spend some time relaxing on, there is plenty to explore – under the sea, on the coasts, in the rainforests of the mountainous interiors and around the streets of their tiny capitals.

Each island has a character of its own and conveys a different mood. With tourism the mainstay of their economies, their natural assets are available, sometimes controversially, for the benefit of the visitor. St John is peaceful and dedicated to nature, whereas St Thomas only a few miles away is bustling and vigorous. Miniscule St Barths is as chic as the Left Bank in Paris; Barbados is as English as they come upholding the tradition of afternoon tea. Tiny St Martin, ruled peacefully by two European nations, offers a frenetic nightlife on one side of the border in contrast to gourmet dining and quiet beaches on the other. Trinidad is host to the greatest street party on earth as is St Lucia to a major music festival and Barbados to a season of opera. Aruba extends a welcoming arm to gamblers.

The surrounding warm waters provide perfect conditions for sailing, all kinds of watersports, from windsurfing off the Atlantic shores to waterskiing in the calm Caribbean bays, and diving around the dramatic coral reefs and shipwrecks.

The terrain is equally diverse. One island has a salt lake, another a pitch lake and mountainous, rainforested Dominica has a boiling lake. What tiny and steeply vertical Saba lacks in beaches it makes up for in underwater scenery, whereas flat and arid Anguilla has an astonishing number of beaches.

Quite simply, you never know what to expect, not only from island to island, but past the next bend on their narrow roads. And that is one of the true pleasures of the Lesser Antilles. ❑

PRECEDING PAGES: farmers in Guadeloupe; relax with Diamond Rock in the background; enjoy a Caribbean picnic on the beach.
LEFT: the calm and charm of Cinnamon Bay, US Virgin Islands.

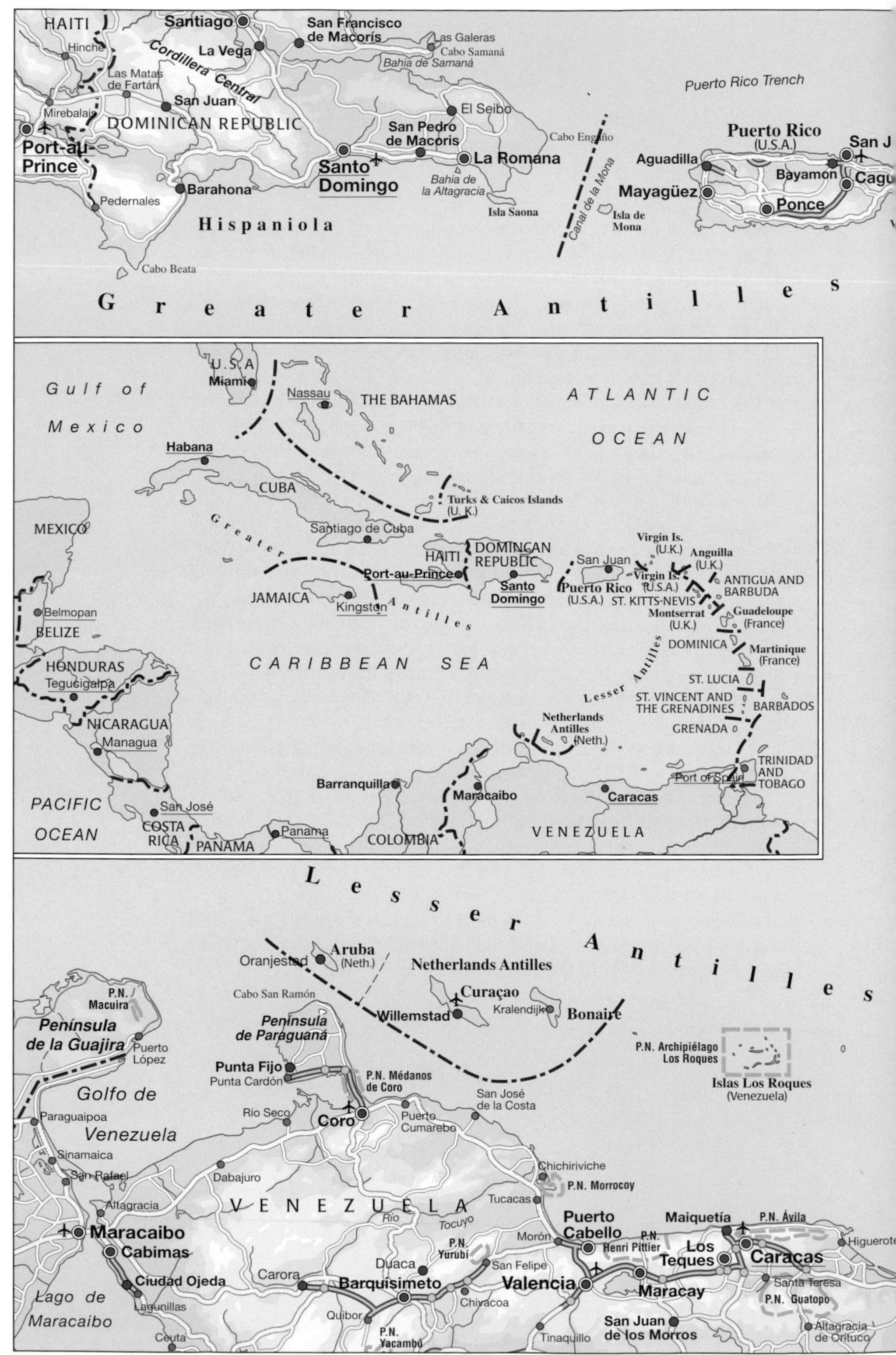
HAITI
Santiago
San Francisco de Macorís
Las Galeras
Cabo Samaná
Bahía de Samaná
Hinche
La Vega
Cordillera Central
Las Matas de Fartán
San Juan
Puerto Rico Trench
Mirebalais
DOMINICAN REPUBLIC
El Seibo
Port-au-Prince
San Pedro de Macorís
Cabo Engaño
Puerto Rico (U.S.A.)
San J
Santo Domingo
La Romana
Aguadilla
Bayamón
Cagu
Barahona
Bahía de la Altagracia
Canal de la Mona
Mayagüez
Pedernales
Isla Saona
Isla de Mona
Ponce
Hispaniola
Cabo Beata
Greater Antilles
U.S.A
Miami
Gulf of Mexico
Nassau
THE BAHAMAS
ATLANTIC OCEAN
Habana
CUBA
Turks & Caicos Islands (U.K.)
MEXICO
Santiago de Cuba
Greater Antilles
HAITI
DOMINICAN REPUBLIC
Virgin Is. (U.K.)
Anguilla (U.K.)
San Juan
Port-au-Prince
Virgin Is. (U.S.A.)
ANTIGUA AND BARBUDA
JAMAICA
Kingston
Santo Domingo
Puerto Rico (U.S.A.)
ST. KITTS-NEVIS
Montserrat (U.K.)
Guadeloupe (France)
Belmopan
BELIZE
DOMINICA
Martinique (France)
HONDURAS
Tegucigalpa
CARIBBEAN SEA
ST. LUCIA
Lesser Antilles
ST. VINCENT AND THE GRENADINES
BARBADOS
NICARAGUA
Netherlands Antilles (Neth.)
GRENADA
Managua
TRINIDAD AND TOBAGO
Port of Spain
Barranquilla
Maracaibo
Caracas
PACIFIC OCEAN
San José
COSTA RICA
Panama
PANAMA
COLOMBIA
VENEZUELA
Lesser Antilles
Aruba (Neth.)
Oranjestad
Netherlands Antilles
P.N. Macuira
Cabo San Ramón
Curaçao
Península de la Guajira
Península de Paraguaná
Willemstad
Kralendijk
Bonaire
Puerto López
P.N. Archipiélago Los Roques
Punta Fijo
Punta Cardón
P.N. Médanos de Coro
Islas Los Roques (Venezuela)
Golfo de Venezuela
San José de la Costa
Paraguaipoa
Río Seco
Coro
Puerto Cumarebo
Sinamaica
San Rafael
Dabajuro
Chichiriviche
P.N. Morrocoy
Altagracia
VENEZUELA
Tucacas
Río Tocuyo
Puerto Cabello
Maiquetía
P.N. Ávila
Maracaibo
Cabimas
P.N. Yurubí
Morón
P.N. Henri Pittier
Los Teques
Caracas
Higuerote
Duaca
San Felipe
Ciudad Ojeda
Carora
Barquisimeto
Valencia
Maracay
Santa Teresa
Lago de Maracaibo
Lagunillas
Chivacoa
P.N. Guatopo
Quibor
San Juan de los Morros
Altagracia de Orituco
Ceuta
P.N. Yacambú
Tinaquillo

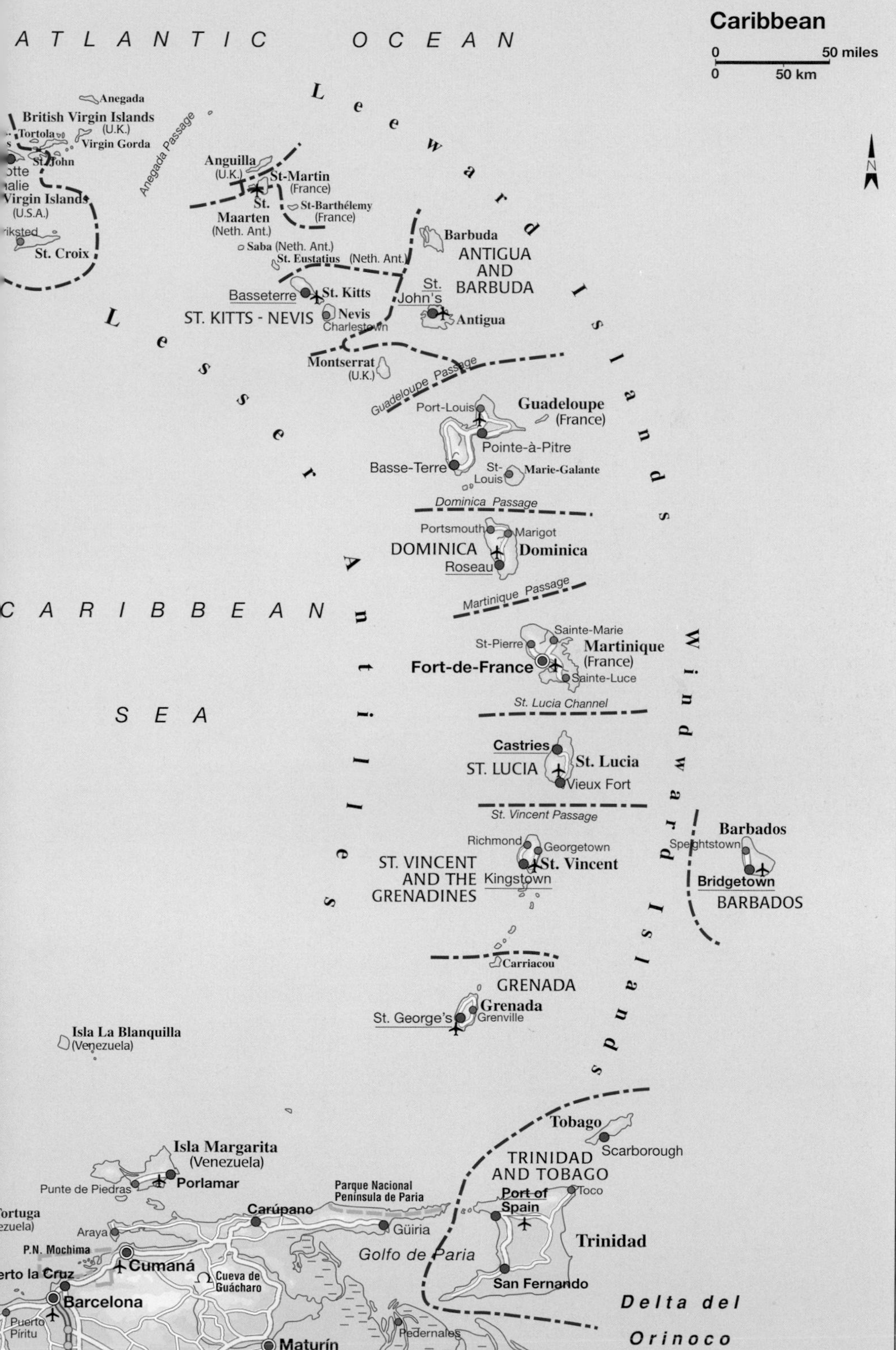
Caribbean
0 50 miles
0 50 km
ATLANTIC OCEAN
CARIBBEAN SEA
Leeward Islands
Lesser Antilles
Windward Islands
Anegada
British Virgin Islands (U.K.)
Tortola
Virgin Gorda
St. John
Virgin Islands (U.S.A.)
St. Croix
Anegada Passage
Anguilla (U.K.)
St-Martin (France)
St. Maarten (Neth. Ant.)
St-Barthélemy (France)
Saba (Neth. Ant.)
St. Eustatius (Neth. Ant.)
Barbuda
ANTIGUA AND BARBUDA
St. John's
Antigua
Basseterre
St. Kitts
Nevis
Charlestown
ST. KITTS - NEVIS
Montserrat (U.K.)
Guadeloupe Passage
Port-Louis
Guadeloupe (France)
Pointe-à-Pitre
Basse-Terre
St-Louis
Marie-Galante
Dominica Passage
Portsmouth
Marigot
DOMINICA
Dominica
Roseau
Martinique Passage
Sainte-Marie
St-Pierre
Martinique (France)
Fort-de-France
Sainte-Luce
St. Lucia Channel
Castries
St. Lucia
ST. LUCIA
Vieux Fort
St. Vincent Passage
Richmond
Georgetown
St. Vincent
Kingstown
ST. VINCENT AND THE GRENADINES
Barbados
Speightstown
Bridgetown
BARBADOS
Carriacou
GRENADA
Grenada
St. George's
Grenville
Isla La Blanquilla (Venezuela)
Tobago
Scarborough
TRINIDAD AND TOBAGO
Port of Spain
Toco
Trinidad
San Fernando
Isla Margarita (Venezuela)
Punte de Piedras
Porlamar
Parque Nacional Peninsula de Paria
Carúpano
Güiria
Araya
P.N. Mochima
Cumaná
Golfo de Paria
Cueva de Guácharo
Barcelona
Puerto Piritu
Maturín
Pedernales
Delta del Orinoco

THE US VIRGIN ISLANDS

Cruising, sailing, diving, beautiful beaches, and a national park teeming with wildlife – the US Virgin Islands, or USVI, have them all, just shared between St Thomas, St John and St Croix

Map on page 92–93

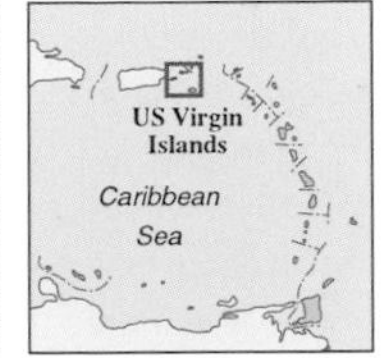

Green volcanic islands peer from the never-ending blues of the Caribbean for as far as the eye can see, their submerged feet concealing a vast underwater landscape. No one knows for certain how many islands there are but Christopher Columbus on his second voyage of discovery in 1493 felt there were too many to count and named them after the 11,000 martyred virgins in the legend of St Ursula. However many there are, the United States of America has 68 of them, amounting to 136 sq. miles (352 sq. km) and Britain has around 60 (*see pages 104–113*).

Situated at the top of the Lesser Antilles chain, only three of the USVI are inhabited: St Thomas (pop. 51,000) is the most developed and can have up to eight cruise ships visiting on some days; neighboring St John (pop. 3,500) is the smallest and least developed, as it is mainly taken up by a national park; St Croix (pop. 49,000), 40 miles (64 km) to the southwest, is the largest of the three but is more tranquil than St Thomas. When sugar cane production bowed out of the economy in the 1960s, the US started developing the islands' potential as a "holiday paradise" for Americans, and today more than 2 million visitors descend on them every year, most of them arriving by cruise ship or under sail – only just over a third fly in in the conventional way.

PRECEDING PAGES: sunset on Cruz Bay. **LEFT:** Magen's Bay, a popular beach. **BELOW:** out for the night in St Thomas.

St Thomas, with USVI capital Charlotte Amalie, is the recipient of the largest proportion of holidaymakers and there is very little of the island left that hasn't been built on which gives it rather a crowded feel: the airport runway juts out into the sea – there is no other place for it – a paved stretch of landfill which jumbo jets have to negotiate like aircraft carriers.

In September 1995, Hurricane Marilyn hit the islands with such a force that it took many resorts, particularly in St Thomas, almost a year to get back on their feet again.

A thriving Danish colony

Columbus met with a hail of arrows on his visit to the Virgin Islands and as a result of such Carib ferocity, no European settlement was established until the 17th century when the Danes took control of St Thomas and St John.

St Croix, on the other hand, was settled first by the Dutch and English in around 1625, then by the Spanish in 1650, followed briefly by the Knights Templars of Malta under the sovereignty of France. Finally in 1733, St Croix was sold to Denmark, and the Danish West Indies officially became a colony in 1754.

The colony thrived with sugar growing on St Croix and a roaring slave trade in St Thomas, also an important stopping-off port for ships after crossing the Atlantic. However, as a result of the abolition of

US Virgin Islanders waved goodbye to the "last vestiges of Danish colonialism" in 1993 when their government bought the West Indian Company (WICO), including a cruise ship dock and Havensight Shopping Mall in St Thomas, for US$54 million. Denmark had hung on to the company when selling the colony to the US in 1917.

slavery, the drop in the price of sugar and the technological advances in shipping making it no longer necessary for ships to stop off at St Thomas, by the beginning of the 20th century, the economy had gone into decline.

Meanwhile the USA had been eyeing up the colony, anxious to protect the Caribbean and the newly opened Panama Canal (1914) from the Germans, and bought the islands from Denmark for US$25 million in 1917. They were then ruled by the US Navy until 1931 when a civil government was established. The inhabitants were given US citizenship a year later but they still don't have the right to vote in presidential elections: the status of the USVI is as an unincorporated territory with a non-voting delegate in the House of Representatives. The government is structured like the US Federal Government with three branches – executive, legislative and judicial.

After World War II, the islands were neglected until American conflict with Cuba sent tourists looking for new white beaches, coral reefs and azure waters. The construction industry boomed, labor had to be imported from other Caribbean islands and at the same time new industrial centers opened up on St Croix. Now the USVI offers the highest standard of living in the West Indies, although new resentments have emerged between the islanders and immigrants providing cheap labor and US continentals going for the top jobs.

St Thomas – a popular island

The main island of St Thomas is often called "Rock City" because it is essentially one big mountain – its highest point being 1,550 ft (470 m) – with one main town, Charlotte Amalie, the capital of the USVI, on its central south shore. The remainder of the island's coastline is a garland of beach resorts around a wooded interior of private homes – bright red, corrugated tin roofed eyries set into the steep hillsides. If you stay at any one resort beach too long, you begin to feel like you're on your back in one of those fancy hotel lobby ashtrays, with the insignia impressed in the perfect white sand. In the end, it's that sense of confinement that compels you to move about and discover what a diversified place the 32-sq. mile (83-sq. km) island St Thomas really is.

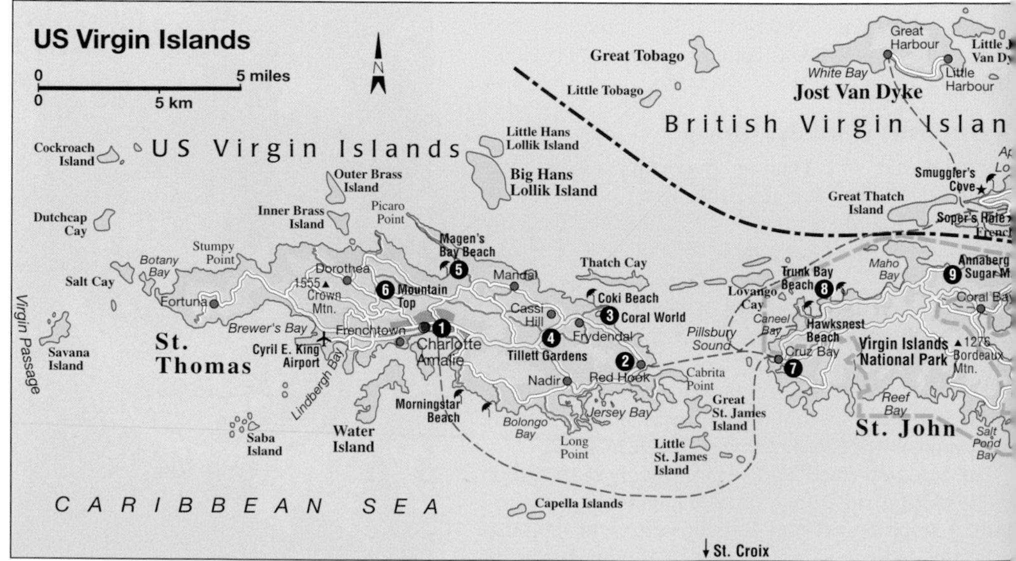

Charlotte Amalie – a shoppers' paradise

Built by the Danes on the south coast of St Thomas and named after the Queen of Denmark in 1692, **Charlotte Amalie** (pronounced Ah-mahl-ya) ❶, the capital of all the USVI, is a bustling, congested town set round an equally bustling and congested harbor. Tax-free shopping is the name of the game here, and you can wander along the narrow streets lined with old Danish shipping warehouses all converted into shops and restaurants. Brightly painted houses with filigree balconies give the downtown area the feel of the New Orleans French Quarter. All the streets retain their Danish names displayed on corner buildings – Kongens Gade (King's Street), Dronningens Gade (Queen's Street), which is also called Main Street, and so on. These names and driving on the left are the two Danish traditions that the US has preserved.

Two blocks north of Main Street along Raadets Gade, you come to **Crystal Gade** and one of the oldest synagogues still in use in the western hemisphere. The present hurricane-proof building with an original sand floor dates from 1833 although its Hebrew congregation was formed by Sephardic Jews from Amsterdam and London in 1796. The adjacent **Weibel Museum** (open Mon–Fri; free) charts the history of St Thomas Jews.

An American paradise and a high crime rate often go hand in hand. Here it is unsafe to walk in Charlotte Amalie at night or go to remote beaches alone. Never leave any valuables unattended on the beach.

Wandering eastwards along the waterfront you can see the lines of docked boats, sleek yachts and sailboats with names like *Windjammer* or *Kon Tiki* in the harbor. St Thomas hosts the Rolex Regatta every Easter week, and in 2000, the USVI is competing in the Americas Cup for the first time; the yachting world is buzzing with anticipation – sailing gets into your blood on these islands. The ferry that runs every two hours to St John waits here alongside the inter-island cargo ships: oafish, round-bellied boats with smoke stacks and circular windows; rusted hulls and lamp-lit, lived-in cabins furnished with little cooking stoves, clothes-strewn bunk beds and radios. Each has a backboard hanging off the side rail, listing their destinations: "Accepting cargo for St Martin, Dominica, St Lucia and St Kitts."

Behind the wharf is the red-painted **Fort Christian** constructed in 1672 by Dutch settlers and one of the oldest American buildings. Among many uses, it

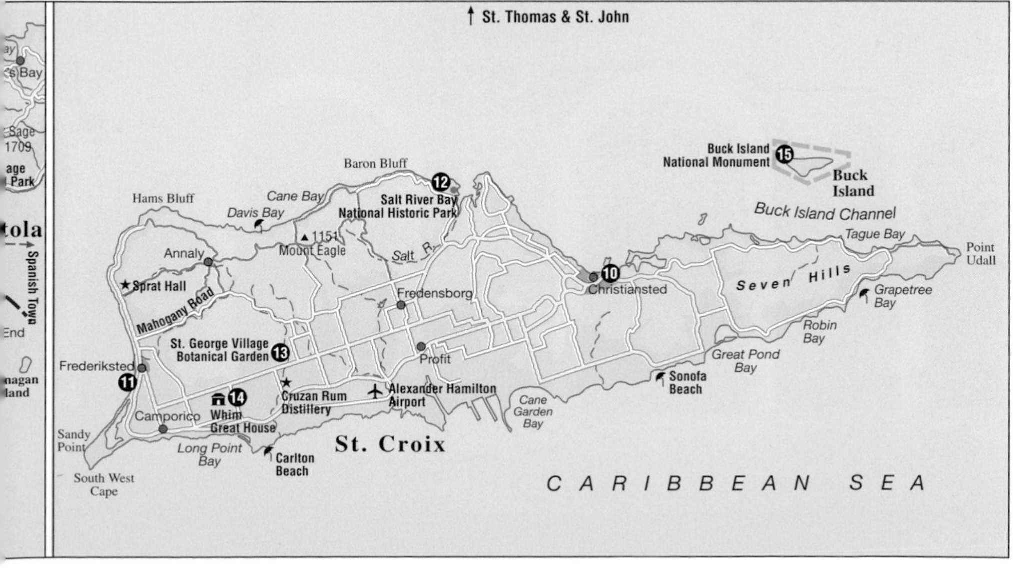

Feel the power of the wind in the sails of a catamaran or trimaran on a day, half-day or sunset cruise – picnic and snorkeling gear provided. Call 775-9500 or 775-2584.

served as a prison with the last prisoner leaving in 1982. Now the dungeon houses the **Virgin Islands Museum** (open Mon–Fri; donations welcome) displaying Amerindian artefacts, local history and colonial furniture. On Government Hill above the fort is the **Seven Arches Museum** (open Tues–Sat; entrance fee), a striking example of classic Danish West Indian architecture, with a flower-filled courtyard where you can relax with your free drink.

To the yachting havens of the east

To break into the open country outside Charlotte Amalie might take you some time. Traffic jams are a constant factor in the town. But they are peculiarly "island" traffic jams – not so much the result of too many cars as they are of a relaxed attitude of locals who come upon a friend for a chat through the car window. Once outside of town, the roads twist and tumble drastically, and seem to want to pull you seaward to the little lanes that lead off to yet another posh resort. As you drive, you'll get two views of the island. At first, it's an extension of America; a nice little island dream that the large continent is having. After a while, you have the pleasant realization that it's a place unto itself, completely dependent upon tourism – the only vital industry, besides rum-making, left to these islands.

Leaving the town along the Waterfront you quickly come to **Havensight Mall** another major shopping center where the cruise ships dock. Denmark owned all this until 1993. From **Yacht Haven Marina** you can charter a yacht for the day, go light tackle fishing, or deep-sea fishing for blue marlin – St Thomas is often referred to as the Blue Marlin Capital of the World – take a seaplane to St Croix or explore spectacular reefs in the Atlantis Submarine. Past the

BELOW: a stroll past Fort Christian.

urn-offs to the dazzling **Morningstar Beach** (where the people dazzle as well) nd the idyllic **Secret Harbour**, after half an hour you come to **Red Hook** ❷, at East End, and the **American Yacht Harbor** offering more sailing of all sorts and choice of ferries running regularly to neighboring islands. Don't forget, the British Virgin Islands are another country and so passports or, for US and Canadian citizens, birth or citizen certificates or voter's registration cards need to be hown. There is a plethora of beautiful islands out there and you can explore hem at speed but not in peace by renting a power boat from the marina.

Map on page 92–93

Coral World – an underwater experience

A fascinating underwater observatory in which you the visitor become the contained curiosity, and the fish the passing curios, **Coral World** ❸ (open daily; ntrance fee), 20 minutes northeast from Charlotte Amalie at Coki Point, eopened to the public after being badly damaged by Hurricane Marilyn in 995. The marine complex includes an underwater observation tower, an aquarum and colossal tanks featuring exotic reef life in one and sharks and other redators in another.

And if that inspires you to swim down there among the exotic fish, the Orange Cup corals and the colorful sponges in the underwater gardens off **Coki Beach**, Coki Beach Dive Club offers beginners' courses close by, with practice dives on he shallow reefs between St Thomas and St John. Many of the 15 dive companies on the island also give lessons in underwater photography.

On the road back to the capital (a 20-minute drive away) lies **Tillett Gardens** ❹, n old Danish farm that was converted into an arts and crafts center in 1959. Outbuildings scattered around the grounds hold an art gallery, with local artists'

At Eunice's Terrace, close to Coral World on the east coast, you can enjoy creole cooking such as Gutu, a sweet, steamed white fish, with fungi – a grit-like mixture of yellow cornmeal, okra and butter – on an open wooden deck on stilts above nothing but jungle brush. The Clintons ate here in 1997.

BELOW: a birthday picnic on the beach.

A St Thomas pipe smoker.

work for sale, and screen-printing and crafts studios, and you can combine a vis with lunch in the pretty garden restaurant. During the winter season, the garde provide the setting for a series of chamber music concerts and three times year, the Arts Alive Arts and Crafts Festival is held here.

Back on the coast road, continue west for another 3 miles (5 km) or more, pa the spectacular cliffside 18-hole **Mahogany Run Golf Course**, and you reac **Magen's Bay Beach** ❺ (entrance fee), a sheltered horseshoe bay voted "one c the 10 most beautiful beaches in the world" by *National Geographic.* All the fu of the beach can be had here on this mile-long stretch of sand that is perfect fc children. Follow the marked trail to **Little Magen's Bay** for official sunbathin in the nude – but don't get burnt. The picturesque Route 35 back to Charlott Amalie passes **Drake's Seat**, literally a concrete bench in a layby which i believed to be the spot used by Sir Francis Drake as his lookout.

For more views and the "world's best banana daiquiris" **Mountain Top** ❻ the highest viewpoint on the island, nearly 2 miles (3 km) from the capita offers more duty-free shopping. Two islanders wait up here all day with tw flower head-dressed donkeys, so you can take what they insist is a once-in-a-life time photograph. Instead, most people train their cameras on the view; th almost perverse beauty of Magen's Bay – a bright green teardrop of calm pro tected waters in a shell of white sand – toward St John and the British Virgi Islands. Winding your way back down to Charlotte Amalie as evening falls the boat lights in St Thomas Harbor look like felled constellations bobbing o the water. Island nightlife then kicks into gear as revellers gather to dance in th bayside bars around **Frenchtown** and the former World War II Sub Base to th west of the harbor – away from downtown which is not a safe place at night.

BELOW: preparing the pool before a wedding party.

WEDDINGS IN PARADISE

The USVI has become a prime spot in which to ge married. After all, what could be more romantic than wedding ceremony on a white sandy beach or in an exoti tropical garden? What could be more original than tyin the knot under the sea in a coral garden or on top of mountain with a spectacular panorama as a backdrop? O course you can get married the traditional way in a church or at any time of day from sunrise to sunset – or how abou chartering a luxurious yacht for you and your guests? Th choice of settings in the USVI is endless.

As the islands are an American Territory, US marriage laws still apply, so there is just an eight-day waiting perioc after the Territorial Court of your chosen island has receivec your application. Then, with the help of the tourist office, which has long lists of addresses and telephone numbers, you can contact the army of wedding consultants, planners, florists and photographers necessary to achieve the "wedding of your dreams".

Weddings are big business here and yacht charterers are used to working with wedding planners to enable a trouble-fee ceremony and reception on the sea, even providing diving gear if desired. And you won't have to go far for your honeymoon – that can be laid on too.

St John – a nature island

The ferry from Red Hook on St Thomas to St John takes you right across Pillsbury Sound into Cruz Bay in just 20 minutes. Essentially, St John's fate was sealed by the Caribbean itself, which lapped up enough of the island's coastline to render it a mere charm, larger than an atoll but not so large that one man couldn't buy up most of it, as Laurence Rockefeller did in the 1950s. He then deeded what amounts to about two thirds of the 28 sq. mile (70 sq. km) mountainous island to the National Park Service. There are no high-rise hotels here and a four-wheel drive is the best mode of transport. If you are over just for the day, taxis offer a two-hour trip around the island.

The main town of St John, **Cruz Bay** ❼ is rather like a little town in Cape Cod: people come in to meet a friend at the ferry, pick up their mail, get some groceries, and then retreat back into the woods. The town square, opposite the ferry dock, is a raised curb bordering a patch of grass. To one side there is a fenced-in mound (either it's a sacred Arawak Indian mound, or the town statue only works part time). Taxi drivers mill about and there are T-shirt shops, moped rental shops, open food stands, bars and restaurants. To the right is **Wharfside Village**, a beachfront shopping mall with a working spice factory. The road to the left goes to **Mongoose Junction**, another mall a few minutes' walk away, and the **National Park Visitors' Center**. Nothing is too far away in Cruz Bay.

Map on page 92–93

Beautiful Northshore Road

Things seem pretty clear-cut on St John. People come here to hide away and feel good; businessmen falling off sailboards, college girls sneaking through the woods to isolated arches of white sand so they can get all-over tans (Solomon

BELOW: a bird's eye view of St John.

Bay is an unofficial nudist beach). The **Northshore Road** follows the lus green coastline through the park to beach after beach of soft, white sand. A **Caneel Bay**, a few minutes drive outside town, the rich and famous enjoy goin without their luxuries in the hotel on the beach. Created by Rockefeller in 195 as an "ecoresort", it is basic living here.

Hawksnest Beach in the next bay is another dream of a beach, popular wit locals and film-makers alike and at **Trunk Bay Beach** ❽, the cream of th crop (so it does get crowded), snorkelers can follow the well-marked, 650-f (200-m) long National Park Underwater Trail. Around the corner are two camp-grounds: Cinnamon Bay, run by the National Park Service, offers "the simpl life" in canvas tents on the beach backed by tropical vegetation and a little fur-ther on Maho Bay concentrates on de luxe camping with all mod cons.

Park trails and sugar mill ruins

There are 22 hiking trails in the National Park and many of them start from the Northshore Road. From Leinster Bay, just past Maho Bay, you can take a 30-minute walking tour of the **Annaberg Historic Sugar Mill Ruins** ❾, wher there are the barest remains of old slave quarters and villages. The morta between the stones of the buildings is made of flour, molasses and sea shells, sc you've essentially got very old, hard cakes in front of you. The trail back to the parking lot is lined with small, low growing, fern-like plants known locally as *greeche greeche.* As if bearing some long held grudge, the plant's tiny leaves retract and fold up at the touch of a human hand.

The walking tours with rangers through the park are an eye opener, especially if you're curious about the indigenous flora (there are 800 varieties of plants and

BELOW: a colorful shop in St John.

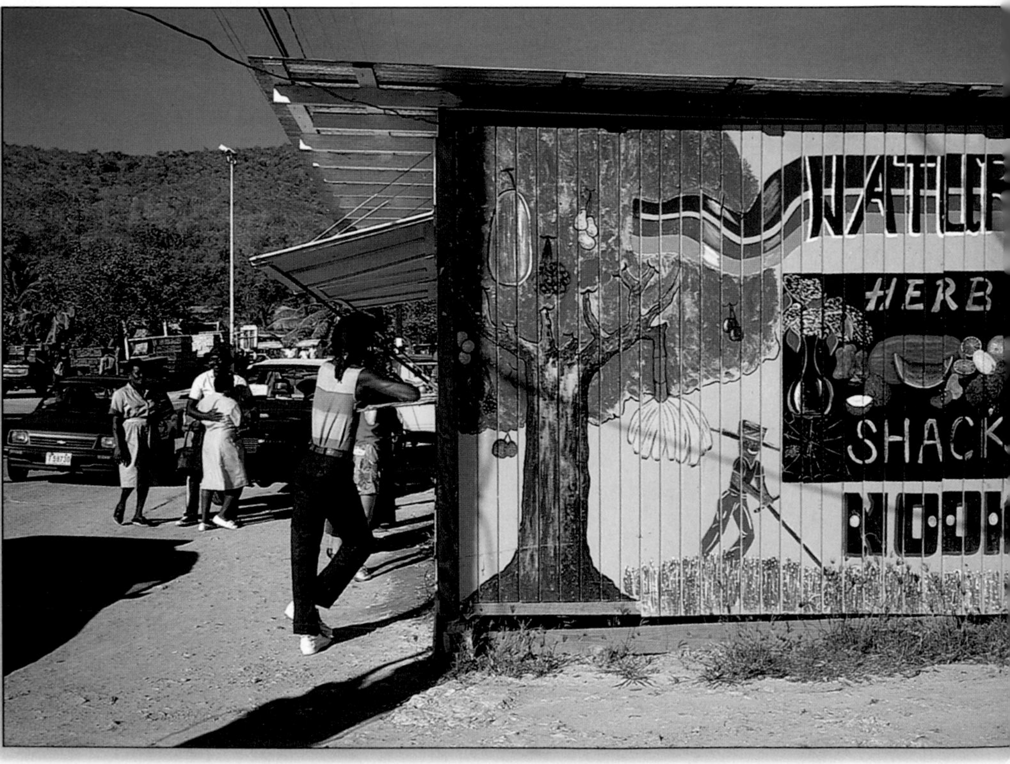

60 species of birds) and its various medicinal uses. On the 3-mile (5-km) **Reef Bay Trail** (reservations at the Visitors' Center), you see a sugar mill ruin and petroglyphs (prehistoric stone pictures) and have a boat ride back to Cruz Bay.

St Croix – an island with a difference

A sea plane – "It's fun to land on water" says the sign at the St Thomas terminal – takes you to St Croix (pronounced Croy as in toy), 40 miles (65 km) to the south of St Thomas. As you go through the main town of Christiansted to your hotel, condo or villa, you'll get a notion of just how different St Croix is from St Thomas. For one thing, it takes longer to get around, and from east to west there is a dramatic change in the landscape – from low, grassy seaside hills that are reminiscent of Cornwall, England, to lush rainforests. Nearly 20 miles (33 km) long and with 84 sq. miles (210 sq. km), St Croix has room for changing climates; it's drier in the east and prone to drifting mists over the west end.

Bush teas are drinks made with medicinal plants from recipes handed down over the centuries. Many are still used for minor ailments: mango tea is taken for arthritis, soursop for insomnia, limebush for an upset stomach, and guava for coughs.

In the bars you'll hear many conversations comparing one island to another, declaring what one has over the other. You hear a lot of that from the resident aliens who make up one third of the population here – those from other Caribbean islands who've migrated to the USVI to find work and who are known as *garotes*, after a local bird that flies from island to island, and North Americans, called Continentals, who have made their home here. They say how they want to keep St Croix quiet and modest, not like St Thomas.

Christiansted – a Danish preserve

You can feel the Danish influence everywhere, especially in the main town of **Christiansted** ⑩, in the northeast, where the cream-colored buildings are made of bricks that the Danish ships brought over as ballast. Somehow, the Danes perfected a weighty architecture that barely interrupts the air. Christiansted is a town built to house its offshore breezes, with overhanging balconies and cool arcades, and walking along the streets you feel like one of those figures in a Chagall painting, too light, always floating up out of the frame.

Many of the red-roofed buildings constructed in the properous years of the 18th century by rich merchants have been restored and the harbor front is now a historic site along with the majestic and colonial **Government House** on King Street where you can visit the ballroom, gardens and the Court of Justice (open daily; free). In the square on the waterfront, the **Old Danish Scale House**, where sugar and molasses was weighed before being shipped out, serves as a visitors' center. Close by, **Fort Christiansvaern** (open Mon–Sat; entrance fee, which includes Steeple Building) built by the Danes in 1774, has been well preserved by the National Parks Service and you can see the dungeons and punishment cells plus an exhibit on how to fire a cannon. Across Hospital Street, the **Steeple Building** (open Mon–Fri; closed 12–1pm; entrance fee includes admission to the fort) originally built as a Lutheran church in 1753, is now a museum of the island's early history. Since its deconsecration in 1831, the building has also been a bakery, school and hospital. Behind the Boardwalk where the sea

BELOW: the perfect spot for a chat.

Once a private club for wealthy planters, Pink Fancy, in Prince Street, Christiansted, was opened as a hotel in 1948 by the Ziegfeld Follies star Jane Gottlieb whose guests included the writers and artists of the day. Built round a 1780 Danish town house, the hotel is now one of St Croix's historic landmarks.

plane checks in, **King's Alley Walk**, developed after the 1995 hurricanes, penetrates a fascinating maze of arcades and alleys lined with shops, restaurants and bars. Several times a year, whether it needs it or not, shopping is actively encouraged with "Jump Up" when bands play in the streets, Mokojumbie dancers (stilt walkers) dance away evil spirits and a party atmosphere pervades.

In tiny **Frederiksted** ⓫, 17 miles (27 km) away on the west coast, a small network of shops greets the cruise ships as they dock at the modern 1,500-ft (450 m) pier built after the old one was destroyed by Hurricane Hugo in 1989. This fortified town is not a stranger to disaster, as 100 years earlier it had been gutted by a fire and the islanders rebuilt it in wood…!

Every plantation tells a story

If St Thomas is "Rock City", then St Croix might be considered its pastoral suburb. The island's expansiveness, its largely undeveloped inner landscape of old sugar plantations – with names like *Jealously*, *Upper* and *Lower Love* (names the Danish plantation owners gave as tributes, of sorts, to their different island mistresses, which makes you wonder about the plots called *Bold Slob* and *Barren Spot*) – all give the place a provincial feel. Many of the sugar mills have been restored as private homes.

Traveling northwest out of Christiansted for 4 miles (6 km), you reach **Salt River Bay** ⓬, where Columbus landed looking for fresh water (he found hostile Carib Indians instead) and which is now a National Park. **Northshore Road** runs along many of the island's beautiful beaches. Unprotected by reefs, the surfing is good off these shores and divers love the drop-off wall at Cane Bay. Heading south on Route 69 past the **Carambola Golf Course**, Robert Trent

BELOW: Mahogany Run Golf Course – beautifully positioned.

ones's pride and joy, you reach **Mahogany Road**, which leads west through the eart of the rainforest – a rich, bowered darkness with vines hanging from giant nahogany trees, kapoks and the tidbit, also called the mother-in-law tongue or the way its long seed castings rattle in the wind.

On the way to Frederiksted, on Route 70, a collection of over 1,000 species of tropical and exotic flowering trees, vines and shrubs can be seen flourishing among the ruins of a 19th-century plantation village in 16 beautiful acres 6.5 ha) at **St George Village Botanical Garden** ⓭ (open daily Nov–May; losed Sun and Mon June–Oct; entrance fee). Two miles (3 km) further on daily ife on one of the island's 400 plantations during Danish rule is portrayed at the arefully restored **Whim Great House** ⓮ (open Mon–Sat; entrance fee).

An underwater park

Buck Island National Monument ⓯ covers around 850 acres (340 ha) of dry and, crystal clear water and barrier reef just off St Croix's northeast shore. There's a nice stretch of beach to the west that boaters like to dinghy up to vhere there are changing facilities and picnic tables – charter a boat (there are lenty on offer) and it comes ready equipped with lunch, snorkeling and diving gear – and two underwater trails provide a series of little white arrows on submerged headstones and an occasional sign warning you not to touch anything; he coral is very brittle. It is kind of a sunken china shop out there – the delicately designed fish float free from the coral shelves, and the sea's most exotic and psychedelic renderings pass you by like a pre-arranged fashion show: the dusky damselfish, the redbanded parrotfish, the yellowhead wrasses and the ookdown moonfish – you can just check them off in your program. ❑

Guided nature horse-rides are arranged from the stables at Sprat Hall Plantation just north of Frederiksted (tel: 772-2880). For the more hearty, the Tropical Mountain Bike Tour heads up through lush rainforest (tel: 772-2343).

BELOW: youths with attitude.

NOTICE
OVAL OF SAND
BEACH IS PROHIBITED
VIOLATORS WILL
OURCES
EALTH

THE BRITISH VIRGIN ISLANDS

Once a pirates' refuge, today the crystal clear waters that wash the white powdery beaches of this peaceful archipelago are a mecca for sailors and divers

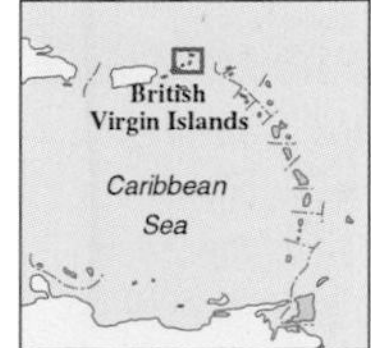

Only a few miles away from the glitz of the US Virgin Islands, the BVI, as the British Virgin Islands are affectionately referred to, are more like a "land that time forgot". On the main islands of Tortola, Virgin Gorda, ost Van Dyke and Anegada, out on a limb to the north, there are no high-rise evelopments, flashy hotels or casinos and most of the other 50-plus islands are ninhabited. For a long time, they managed to evade the whirlwind of change hat enveloped most of the Lesser Antilles and are now capitalizing on their simle treasures: a pleasant, gentle citizenry and long, unspoiled beaches of powery white sand bordering clear seas that give new meaning to the word blue.

Here, all the action takes place above and beneath the surface of the water: ailors love the warm breezes that blow them from island to island where they an sample the secret coves only accessible by sea, and divers have a rich underorld of reefs to explore. This natural wealth forms the basis of the islands' conomy and upmarket resorts have developed around marinas offering yacht nd hotel accommodation combined – it's the yachties the Government wants) attract, along with those seeking somewhere quiet and beautiful to escape to. Jp on the mountain slopes, hairy lianas (vines) hang from ancient mahogany ees in snatches of remaining forest.

PRECEDING PAGES: beach at the Baths, Virgin Gorda.
LEFT: a seagrape tree hangs over a quiet beach.
BELOW: a friendly conversation.

All the islands are of volcanic origin apart from negada, a flat coral and limestone atoll 30 miles (48 m) northeast of the largest island Tortola (21 sq. iiles/55 sq. km). Both Tortola and Virgin Gorda, 14 iiles (20 km) away, rise steeply from the sea, each ith a volcanic peak – Tortola's Mount Sage is 1,760 (540 m) and Gorda Peak is 1,360 ft (415 m). With oastlines only 3 miles (5 km) apart at their furthest oint, getting anywhere in a hurry on Tortola is imposible. Some of the roads are easily on a par with lpine passes in Europe with altitude differences of early 1,000 ft (300 m) within a couple of miles. The sphalt road encompassing most of Tortola was only ompleted towards the end of the 1980s; before then, nyone from Sea Cow Bay in the south who wanted to o to Cane Garden Bay in the north went by donkey.

irate haunts

hristopher Columbus may not have been all that npressed by these seemingly haphazardly located olcanic rocks when he discovered them in November 493. Who was looking for good beaches at that time? iold was what he was after, and there wasn't any. he predominantly steep terrain of Tortola provided ie English with a handful of plantations later on, and iere were enough fish in the sea to keep the slaves ell fed. To protect the plantations and settlements om the incursions of pirates, forts were built along

Mrs Scatcliffe fills her verandah in Carrot Bay every night with people eager to feast on her papaya soup, home-made coconut bread, chicken in coconut milk and soursop sherbert.

Tortola's south coast. One famous pirate dropped anchor here on numerou occasions: Sir Francis Drake, for whom the strait between Tortola and the south ern islands is named. His fleet was based in the area from 1568 to 1595 to kee the Spanish and Dutch in check, which also entitled them to plunder their golc Sometimes the forces of nature helped by dashing the ships on to the reefs nort of Anegada – more than 300 vessels lie on the seabed here. Other pirates roame the southern islands feeding the imagination of story-tellers for years to come

The BVI have been in British hands since 1666 and today are mainly self-gov erning as a British Overseas Territory.

Road Town – the capital on Tortola

The new yachting harbor, built around the artificial moles of Wickhams Cay and 2, and the attractive marina beneath the renovated walls of the Fort Bur Hotel to the southwest have given **Road Town** ❶ a bustling maritime charac ter – "road" is the nautical name for a protected and safe place to drop ancho The paved roads are never busy here and rush hour is an alien concept but, th same, Waterfront Drive on the landfill area seems to be widened more each yea

On picturesque **Main Street**, once the waterfront road, the typical West India style wooden houses are being carefully restored, and banks, insurance com panies and souvenir shops are mushrooming here and on **Wickhams Cay** acros Waterfront Drive. Palm trees and shrubs are taking a while to grow on this bar ren area of reclaimed land, and new structures such as the Government Build ing are coming in for quite a bit of stick. Caribbean T-shirts emblazoned wit tropical patterns dangle from stalls in the **Crafts Market** close by, alongsid colorful fish mobiles, napkin rings, and other delightfully impractical items

BELOW: hula at playtime in Tortola.

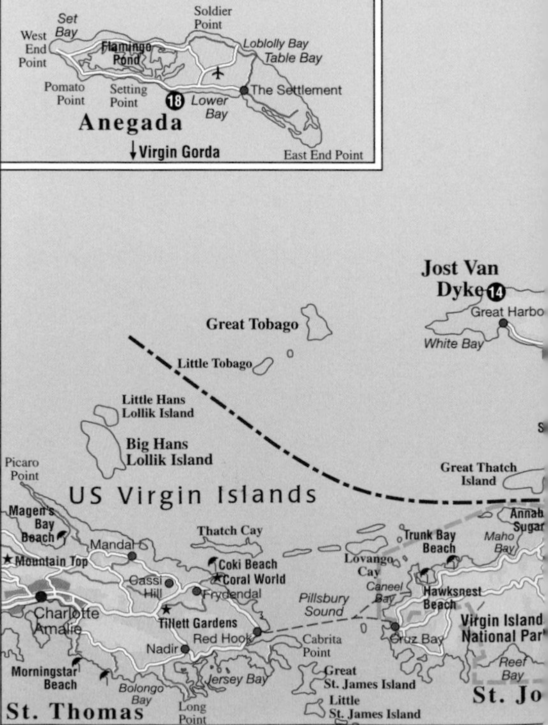

Near the **ferry docks** a few minutes' walk southwards – where boats leave regularly for other islands including St Thomas and St John (*see pages 90–101*) – **Pusser's Co. Store & Pub**, an attractive gingerbread-style house that's hard to miss, has all the atmosphere of a British harbor pub. This is the place to try the Admiralty Rum, or Pusser's Painkiller, a notorious rum cocktail, and listen to maritime yarns. Through a door, Pusser's store (branches in Soper's Hole, Marina Cay and Leverick Bay) provides items with a nautical flavor.

Behind, the **Virgin Islands Folk Museum** (irregular opening hours; entrance fee) documents the colonial era alongside marine exhibits and Amerindian artefacts inside a typical old West Indian wooden building. At the bottom of Main Street, fronted by some spectacular flamboyant trees, the classical green-shuttered **Government House** overlooks the harbor with a pompous air.

To the north of the town, next to the police station, the **J.R. O'Neal Botanic Gardens** (open daily; donations welcome), with an avenue of palm trees, beautifully portrays the various vegetation zones of the islands and includes an orchid house, fern house and medicinal herb garden.

Map on pages 106–7

Great Thatch island off the western end of Tortola is being developed by the BVI Government as a national park "in keeping with our unspoilt destination promotion."

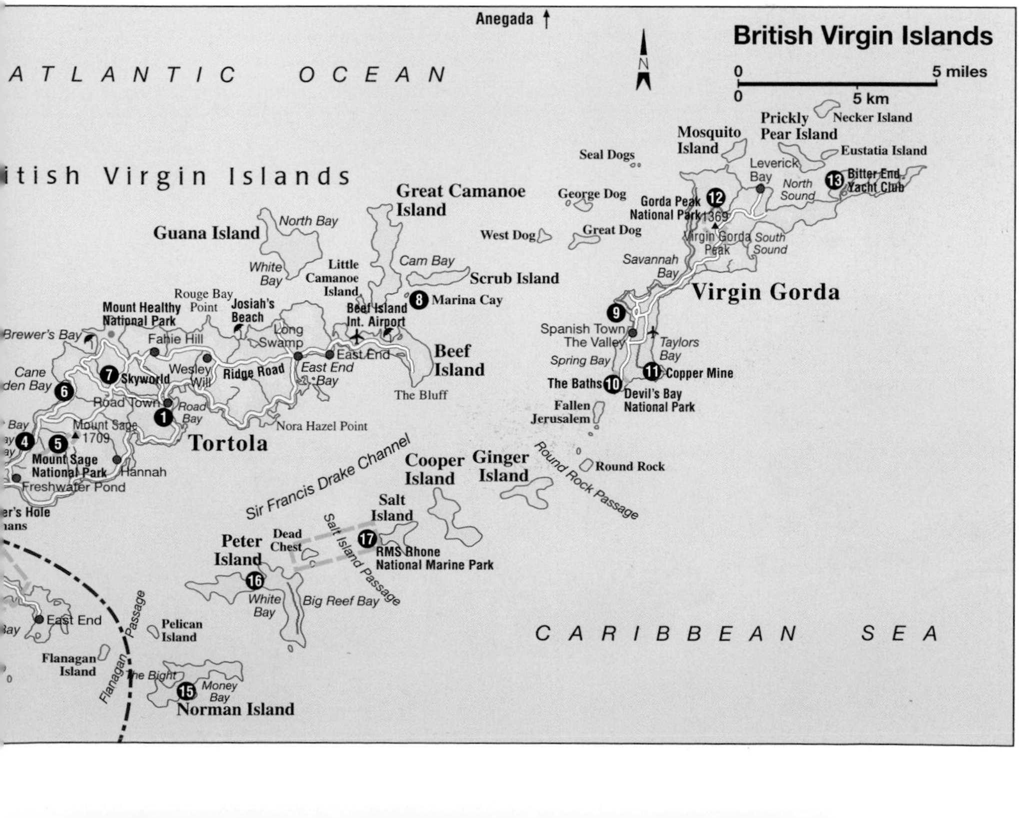

Tortola's West End

Winter in the BVI means only a few hours of rain every now and then. It never gets cold or unpleasant; big warm raindrops fall on to the hot ground, and the sun's rays appear from time to time through dramatic cloud formations. Then in summer the islands look very exotic and green. Bougainvillea covers the houses with its magnificent blossoms, and the gardens are full of bright red hibiscus. The marina at **Soper's Hole** ❷ on Frenchman's Cay, 8 miles (13 km) west of Road Town, Pusser's Bar, the yacht charter buildings, the galleries and the

British Virgin Islands

shops all combine with the surrounding countryside to create a magnificently colorful scene, especially just before sunset. Ferries to the US Virgin Islands and Jost Van Dyke (*see page 112*), 5 miles (8 km) away, leave from beside the **Jolly Roger Inn**, where two friendly women cook delicious Caribbean food.

Since all the beaches in the BVI are public, you're certain to find a quiet spot near the elegant hotels in **Long Bay** at the end of the steep road over Zion Hill. The bumpy track westwards past Belmont leads to **Smugglers Cove ❸**, a delightful sandy inlet with guaranteed sunshine until evening and wonderful snorkeling. Around to the west, dramatic rocks rise from the sea at **Steele Point** and smart villas decorate the steep slope behind.

Trophies and shells

When Hurricane Luis passed this way in 1995, it seems to have had something of an effect on **Bomba's Shack**, in **Apple Bay ❹**. A venue popular with locals, yachties and surfers jumping the waves in the bay, a few more oddities were added to the collection of trophies plastered over the ramshackle walls: an ancient bra, a pennant from New Zealand, T-shirts and other flotsam, many bearing personal dedications to the shack's owner. This place has become a real institution and one of the best-known nightspots in the BVI – the "full moon parties" and weekly reggae nights are quite an experience: hips sway amidst the barbecue smoke, and the fun spills out on to the road.

At the other end, in **Carrot Bay**, a more traditional collection can be seen at the North Shore Shell Museum Bar & Restaurant where after a drink or a meal of cracked conch, grilled lobster and good West Indian cooking you can see exhibits of local crafts alongside the countless shells.

ABOVE: a colorful spice shop on Soper's Hole Wharf.
BELOW: Bomba's Shack – *the* nightspot in the BVI.

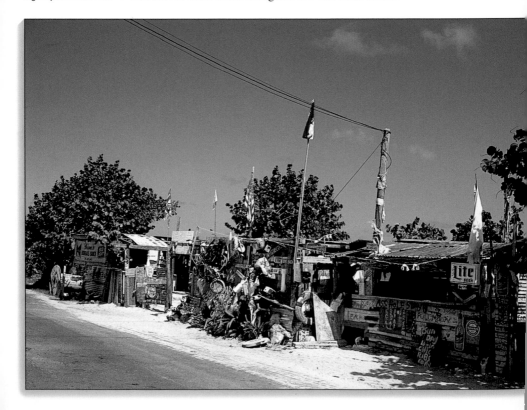

Panoramic hairpins around Mount Sage

The coast road winds up from Carrot Bay along spectacular Windy Ridge towards Cane Garden Bay and branches off into **Mount Sage National Park ❺**, a protected area of tropical forest spared from clearance in the plantation era. Giant mahogany trees with complex roots cling on to the rockface of the 1,709-ft (521 m) **Mount Sage**, and lianas, moss and numerous orchids leech moisture from tree trunks and hollows; tree frogs start their chorus just before sunset. As water takes longer to seep through volcanic rock than through limestone, the vegetation grows profusely here on an annual rainfall of less than 12 in (300 mm).

Rum plays a major role in the BVI, but much of it actually comes from other islands. There was once a total of seven family-run firms producing the "liquid gold" in **Cane Garden Bay ❻** and now you can only see the fine Arundel Cane Rum being produced at the 200-year-old **Callwood Distillery** (open Mon–Fri; free). The secret of the rum's high quality, according to owner Michael Callwood, is that it is made from the sugar cane juice rather than molasses left behind in the sugar refining process (*see page 75*).

The gently curving bay in front is one of the Virgin Islands' top beaches: deckchairs and sunshades are for rent, yachts move slowly past buoys on the turquoise sea, all types of watersports are on offer and calypso bands strike up outside the bars just before sunset. **Brewer's Bay** further north is far more provincial: the sand is much darker, and don't be surprised to see the odd cow walking across it. The roads around here are very steep and signposts point to the ultimate viewing spot at **Skyworld ❼** on Ridge Road where there is a 360-degree panoramic view of Road Town, surrounding islands and the rolling hills to the east. A perfect place for a picnic before hitting the challenging mountain

The best surfing can be experienced from November along Tortola's north coast at Apple Bay, the eastern end of Cane Garden Bay and Josiah's Bay.

BELOW: walkers in Mount Sage National Park.

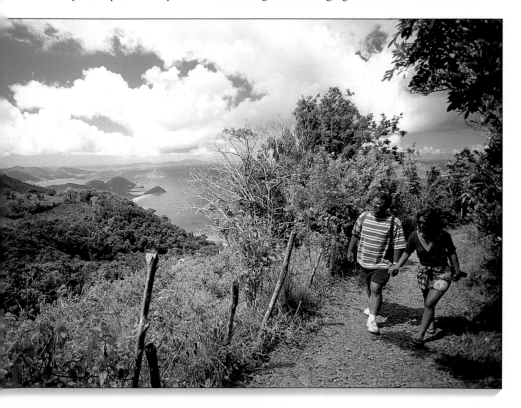

Windsurfers from all over the world flock to Tortola at the end of June for the annual week-long Bacardi HIHO regatta which involves races between islands and accommodation for participants on large yachts.

road once more to Long Swamp and East End, 7 miles (11 km) away. From the turn steeply northwards and over the summit to the new Lambert Beach Reso where, with a drink on the terrace, you can gaze in wonder at the creamy whit beach edged by palms and ancient seagrapes around **Elizabeth Bay**.

From **Beef Island**, connected to East End by the Queen Elizabeth Bridge, th tiny 6-acre (2 ha) island of **Marina Cay ❽**, only slightly higher than the sur rounding coral, looks as if it could easily disappear under a large wave. Free fe ries ply to and from the island, five minutes away, around 10 times a day from **Trellis Bay**, just east of the airport and a popular windsurfing spot. Once owne by the author Robb White who used it as the setting for his book *Our Virgin Isl* and the film version *Two On The Isle* with Sidney Poitier in the 1950s, Marin Cay is now a private resort belonging to Pusser's and offers a wide variety c watersports such as snorkeling, underwater safaris, kayaking, deep-sea fishing

The fat Virgin and her giant "marbles"

If Columbus had been thinking of St Ursula and her 11,000 virgins when h named this archipelago, why should a granite island have been named Virgi Gorda (fat virgin)? Speculation abounds, one notion being that, from afar, th 10-mile (16 km) long island looks like a reclining woman with a protrudin stomach. **Spanish Town ❾**, also known as The Valley, is the main town o Virgin Gorda and until 1741 was the capital of the entire group of islands. Th houses are dotted across various parks and gardens, and souvenir hunters wil find a handful of colorful boutiques near the modern and well-equipped **Yach Harbour**, south of the ferry dock.

From here taxis can take you across the southern part of the island past huge rounded granite blocks looking like giant marbles scattered all over the place to **The Baths ❿**, where the house-high boulders have formed natural grottoes and pools perfect for swimming and snorkeling. There's an easy trail between them with ladders and bridges over the tricky parts. Geologists refer to this phenomenon, which is part of the **Devil's Bay National Park**, as "woolsack weathering" – long ago, a thick layer of soil covered the stone, and acids from the humus gradually worked their way into hairline fissures in the rock wearing it away. As the topsoil gradually disappeared, wind, heat and salt particles continued to erode the rough granite so that some look as if their shells are about to break.

BELOW: a beach-front police station.

Noticing that the granite southeastern coast of Virgin Gorda was similar to that of Cornwall, where copper mining was a lucrative industry in the early 19th century, the British speculated that there must be some copper here too. They were right and Cornish miners worked the **Copper Mine ⓫**, not far out of Spanish Town, for around 30 years. The chimney of the old mine, ruins of old stone buildings, a copper ore pit and remains of a smelting furnace can all still be seen.

Yachting in the north

Because of all the attention given to the southern bays, the north tends to get overlooked. Anyone with a boat will find this hard to fathom, because some of the

nest beaches on Virgin Gorda are here. Just 5 minutes north of Spanish Town es **Little Dix Bay** where in 1964, after his success with Caneel Bay Resort in t John (*see page 97*), Laurence Rockefeller opened the BVI's first hotel, geared xpressly towards family holidays, and put Virgin Gorda on the map.

At the narrowest point of the island, less than 980 ft (300 m) of land separate ıe spray-covered coast to the east from gorgeous **Savannah Bay**. On weekdays ıis coastline is like one long private beach – all yours. The road continues orth, branching off to **Gorda Peak** ⓬ (1,369 ft/417 m), a national park where ıe views from the observation point, reached after a short walk through some rotected mahogany forest, are quite dizzying. Then it's downhill all the way to ıe happy and colorful Pusser's hotel at **Leverick Bay**.

The North Sound Express launch stops off at the hotel on its 45-minute jour-ey eastwards from Tortola (depending on the currents) across the unspoiled eep water of the North Sound to the **Bitter End Yacht Club** ⓭ at John)'Point. Here the yachties rule and the beach and watersports facilities are we-inspiring. Instead of staying in any of the discreet-looking villas on the illside or beach, you can spend your holiday on one of their 30-ft (9 m) yachts. ;itter End is well known for its food too: the chef, Angus Bowen, won the gold ıedal in the *1997 Taste of the Caribbean* cookery contest in Puerto Rico ɔgether with Earl Williams from the Biras Creek Hotel (also on North Sound) nd Alson Pont from the Peter Island Resort (*see page 112*).

On the northeastern edge of North Sound lies **Prickly Pear Island** which as a beautiful long white beach at **Vixen Point** and a small beach bar and vatersports center. No ferries stop here, so the most idyllic way to get there is ınder your own sail.

Sailing and windsurfing courses for all ages are available from the Nick Trotter Sailing School at Bitter End Yacht Club (tel: 494-2745) and you can learn about live-aboard cruising with the Offshore Sailing School (tel: 494-5119).

BELOW: a beach hut at Biras Creek.

Foxy's reputation stretches far and wide. At his beach bar on Jost Van Dyke he always has a typically local song on his lips and his weekend parties are legendary with sailors.

Jost Van Dyke – a tranquil retreat

The moment the speedboat to **Jost Van Dyke** ⓮ from Soper's Hole has docked all the passengers disappear into Great Harbor except for the tourists, who stand gazing around them in astonishment. Time seems to stand still here: a handful of houses in a bay, and green hills under a scorching sun – indeed, electricity was only brought to the island in 1991. A few people stand in front of the Customs House, and goats graze peacefully in the cemetery. A pink sign bears the words "water-taxi" together with a phone number. What on earth do people spend their time doing here? Some, such as Foxy in his beach bar, have become storytellers (*see left*).

The water-taxi quickly takes you westward round to White Bay where you have to paddle barefoot through the waves to the beach. Trousers and dress hems get wet, but dry out again almost as quickly while you're lying in the hammocks among the palm trees at the aptly named Soggy Dollar Bar. Every day feels like Sunday here. The atmosphere is perfect, and so romantic that it is almost a cliché: palm and seagrape trees, ultra-fine sand, gentle hills on the southern horizon, and all of it at the place where a painkiller (Pusser's Painkiller) was supposed to have been invented. What ailments needed to be cured in this paradise? Surely it can only have been the pain of having to leave.

Treasure islands

Forming the southern edge of the Sir Francis Drake Channel, south of Tortola are a collection of tiny islands that provided perfect hiding places for pirates and inspired romantically inclined 19th-century authors such as Robert Louis Stevenson (1850–1894). This Scottish novelist and poet is supposed to have chosen the uninhabited **Norman Island** ⓯ as the location for his *Treasure Island* (1883) and treasure hunters have done a great deal of digging ever since, to no avail. The real treasures, however, are under the water around the reefs of the protected bay known as **The Bight** which are bountiful in colorful fish; the caves along the rocky west coast, reached by boat, offer snorkelers a magnificent show. When it's time to come up for air, drinks and Caribbean food are served up by the galley team on the *William Thornton II*, a replica of an old Baltic trading vessel, in The Bight. More underwater caves and reefs give divers and photographers a fascinating few hours around **Pelican Island** and the pinnacles of rock called **The Indians**.

BELOW: yachties meet up on the beach.

Despite the name, **Deadman's Bay** on the north coast of **Peter Island** ⓰ is often ranked as one of the top romantic beaches in the world – a white sand beach fringed with palm trees and lapped by a gentle turquoise sea has to be irresistible. Cacti and enormous agaves cover the island, owned by the environmentally conscious Peter Island Resort. Gold medal winning chef Alson Pont's Caribbean specialties can be sampled at the beach restaurant.

With a view of **Dead Chest**, where the pirate Blackbeard is said to have left 15 sailors to die – "*15 men on a dead man's chest/ Yo ho ho and a bottle of rum*" – the diving boats set off towards the buoys surrounding the *RMS Rhone* in the **Rhone Marine Park** ⓱. In

367, this 320-ft (100 m) long Royal Mail vessel sank just to the west of **Salt land** during a hurricane. One passenger and 20 crew members were rescued d to thank the Salt Island rescuers, Queen Victoria gave them ownership ghts to it in return for one English pound of salt a year. Several of the boats that ke divers out to explore the colonies of coral and sponge fore and aft of this ip – which lies 70 ft (20 m) below the surface and has an amazingly large pro-eller almost 20 ft (6 m) across – dock at Salt Island. In between dives, the two derly men who still gather salt to send to the Queen, demonstrate how it is pro-uced and relate their life stories over refreshments.

negada – an island of beaches and wrecks

he flat island of **Anegada** ⓲ at 11 by 3 miles (17 by 5 km) is easy to overlook: s highest point being a mere 28 ft (9 m). But, with a continuous white beach om the Anegada Reef Hotel in the south, round West End along the north hore, where turtles nest, to East End, it would be a mistake if you did. However, ivers and snorkelers will be disappointed, as the surrounding reefs responsible or 300 shipwrecks and magical scenery are closed while a marine park and oorings are established to counteract the damage already caused by count-ss yacht anchors. But fishermen still go out and provide the hotel with the best obster in the BVI – it's also a top spot for bone fishing (a form of fly-fishing).

Two short strips of tarmac meet up in **The Settlement**, where most of the 300 strong population live. The controversial decision to introduce flamingos to the agoon in 1992 proved a success when wild ones joined them and they reared ome young. Anyone just here for one day would do well to hire a jeep and isit **Loblolly Bay**, on the north coast, which is flanked by two bars. ❑

British entrepreneur and head of the Virgin empire Richard Branson couldn't resist the idea of owning a Virgin Island and his 64-acre (32 ha) Necker Island, north-east of Virgin Gorda is available to rent – at a price.

BELOW: romantic Deadman's Bay.

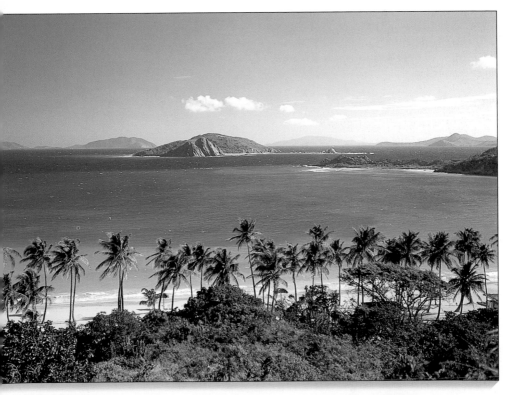

LIFE ON THE OCEAN WAVE

The steady northeasterly trade winds which carried Columbus into the New World have made the Caribbean one of the top sailing destinations

The image of sailboats cruising in the gentle waters around the Grenadines seems like a dream – quiet sand-fringed bays below rolling hills, rustic harbor towns and lively beach bars. Visitors from all over the world flock to the Caribbean harbors during winter months with their own boats, but the international yacht charters also have a growing clientele in Europe, renting large yachts with a skipper and a crew. The old English seafaring tradition has influenced regatta competitions in the British Virgin Islands and in Antigua, with its annual Sailing Week at the end of April, preceded by the Antigua Classic Yacht Regatta, when beautiful schooners, ketches and sloops built as early as 1909 race off the southern coast of the island at English Harbour. Many yacht clubs on the bigger islands organize inter-island races which attract a more local crowd.

ISLAND HOPPING

Sailing during the night and funfilled days spent on different islands: cruises on the luxurious all-inclusive waterhotels are big business. Cruise liners mainly begin their routes in Miami, and offer guests 24-hour entertainment with a break during the day to explore an island or shop in the tax-free malls which are popping up all over the Caribbean. Some cruise lines offer thematic holidays such as those for gay travelers or even romantic novelists.

▷ REGATTAS
The annual Antigua Sailing Week in April is one of the world's top five regattas, with five days of tough international competition and two days of harbor fun.

△ SEE THE SEA
Charter a yacht for a day, a week or a month – fully staffed with a crew including a cook to provide culinary delights at sea. Alternatively, join the crew yourself.

△ FLOATING HOTELS
Columbus's ship, the *Santa Maria* appears a nutshell compared to the cruise liners which carry one thousand or more people.

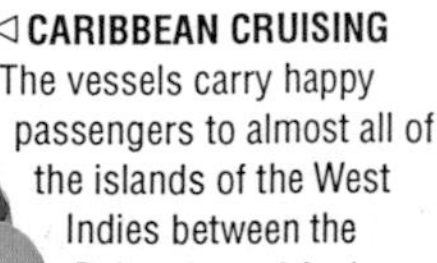

◁ CARIBBEAN CRUISING
The vessels carry happy passengers to almost all of the islands of the West Indies between the Bahamas and Aruba.

ITS ALL IN THE GAME

When visiting the Carib Territory in Dominica you'll see large wooden canoes carved out of one tree trunk just like those of the Arawak fishermen. The Indians were clever fishermen using spears to kill the fish or by throwing branches of *matapisca* – the Papiamento name for *Jacquinia* tree – into the sea, which would slightly paralyse even big fish, but didn't harm man.
Today, big game fishing enthusiasts fight tuna, marlins and wahoo while strapped to comfortable seats on motor boats. Equipped with special rods, private charter boats offer day trips on many of the islands, but it is better to book from home. Smaller companies also provide angling gear, but the tale of the red snapper or grouper that got away is up to you.

BARE BOATING
ıchts are usually chartered ır a week or two allowing ·chorage in remote rquoise-colored bays.

TRIMMING
'hen racing, the highly ·chnical, state of the art ıchts still require the skills ḟ a good crew for a good ım of the fibreglass sails.

HARD ON THE WIND
hough mostly gentle the aribbean sea can be a reat challenge even to xperienced skippers when ·opical storms build up.

◁ PIRATE STYLE
Potent rum cocktails, food galore, music and lots of fun are guaranteed on the Jolly Roger party boat cruises.

▷ WINDSURFING
Aruba and the British Virgin Islands are top with international windsurfing buffs.

ANGUILLA

Romantic, long white sandy beaches, a few exclusive hotels and a feeling of seclusion are the assets of this small British outpost, where the strong-minded people are welcoming and courteous

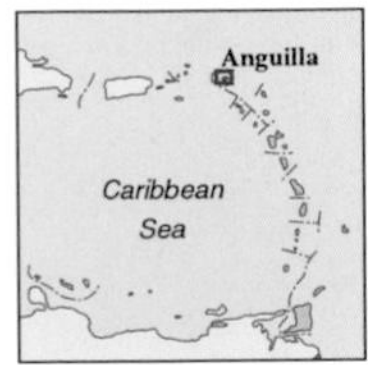

The low coral island of Anguilla sits at the top of the Leeward Islands chain, a serene, remote place of empty beaches with powdery white sand, untouched cays and reefs, adrift in the wide blue sea. Nothing much hapens now on this tiny British territory, far from the mainstream of a busy world. nd this tranquility is the island's main asset. Since it stood up and flexed its uscle against its governing partners St Kitts and Nevis in the late 1960s, nguilla seems content to retain its sleepy character, proud and protective of its 2 miles (19 km) of well-kept beaches, crystalline waters and exquisite coral efs teeming with a wide variety of marine life – a magnet for sun worshippers, atersports enthusiasts (but no jet skis!) and divers alike.

At 16 miles (26 km) long, 3 miles (5 km) wide, Anguilla (Spanish for eel) is one f the drier islands, covered in tangled vegetation and low tough scrub, foraged y hundreds of goats. Trees have never really been a feature here, especially after e ones they had were uprooted by Hurricane Luis in 1995 (a disaster the landers have put behind them), but now due to a concerted effort by a band of nguillians to beautify the island, they are shooting up all over the island. Topoil is scarce on this flat island, and only a few acres are fertile enough to support ome hardy crops: pigeon peas, cassava, yams, corn and tropical fruits. However, modern technology, in the form of hydroponic griculture, has permitted a small new industry, growng vegetables for the local market as well as for the estaurants of St Martin (*see pages 127–34*), 5 miles 8 km) to the south.

PRECEDING PAGES: at the end of the race. **LEFT:** Sandy Island before Hurricane Luis blew the palm trees away. **BELOW:** a simple church with style.

A quirky history

This impoverished land endowed Anguilla with a ocial history that, like its political history, is quirky. rcheological digs have unearthed evidence of merindian presence on the island dating from 300BC, centuries before the Arawaks are believed o have settled the Caribbean chain at around the time f Christ. Remains from Arawak villages have also een discovered at Rendezvous Bay, Sandy Ground nd Island Harbour, making Anguilla one of the most rcheologically interesting places in the Caribbean. By the time the first British settlers had arrived in 650, the Arawaks had disappeared.

The colonizers tried to plant tobacco and, later, ugar. Because of the dry climate and poor soil, these ash crops never took root and neither did plantations or slavery. Still, slaves were duly imported, although hey were freed long before Emancipation in 1834, s beleagured planters could barely feed themselves.

Thus, Anguilla's barren land left its people free of he scars of slavery, evolving into an extraordinarily egalitarian and color-blind society, where everybody

Goats roam everywhere.

owned their land and helped each other through the frequent droughts and hı ricanes, and to overcome the lack of fresh water and arable soil. Neverthele: one resource, besides characters, was left to the Anguillians – the sea. Unli other West Indians, landlocked by the success of plantations, Anguillians becaı expert boatbuilders, sailors and fishermen.

Up in arms

Such strength of character, sense of community and loyalty, however, we severely tried when in 1967, against the Anguillians' wishes, Britain, in ; attempt to disperse its dependencies, made Anguilla and the much-resented Kitts and Nevis 70 miles (110 km) away an Associated State. More autonon was directed from St Kitts, sparking the Anguilla Revolution (*see page 122*

Today, contentedly one of Britain's few remaining Overseas Territorie Anguilla's local government handles almost all domestic affairs, while a Britis governor takes care of the civil service, police, judiciary and foreign affair

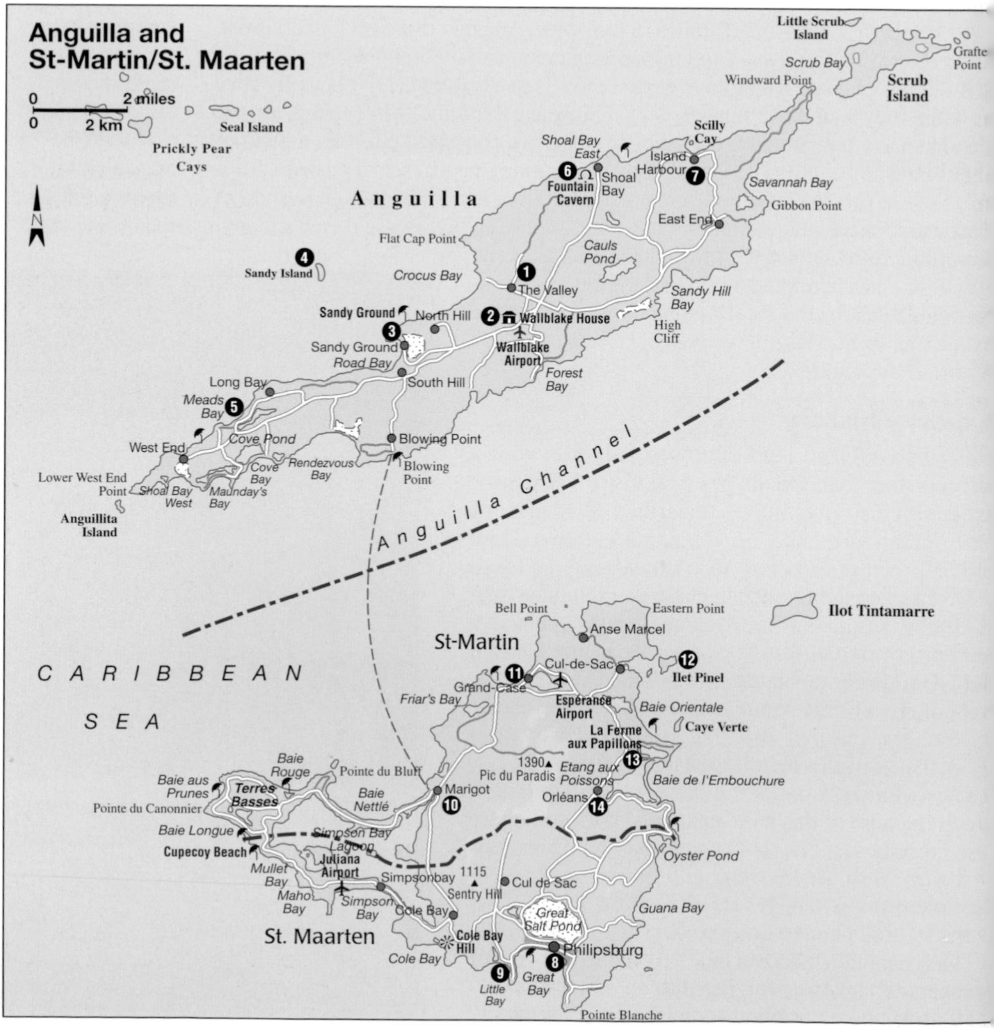

Anguilla and St-Martin/St. Maarten

0 2 miles
0 2 km

Anguilla
Little Scrub Island
Scrub Bay
Scrub Island
Grafte Point
Windward Point
Seal Island
Prickly Pear Cays
Scilly Cay
Shoal Bay East
Island Harbour
Shoal Bay
Fountain Cavern
Savannah Bay
Gibbon Point
East End
Flat Cap Point
Cauls Pond
Sandy Island
Crocus Bay
The Valley
Sandy Hill Bay
Sandy Ground
North Hill
Wallblake House
High Cliff
Sandy Ground Road Bay
Wallblake Airport
Forest Bay
Long Bay
South Hill
Meads Bay
Cove Pond
Blowing Point
West End
Rendezvous Bay
Cove Bay
Lower West End Point
Shoal Bay West
Maunday's Bay
Anguillita Island
Anguilla Channel
CARIBBEAN SEA
Bell Point
Eastern Point
Ilot Tintamarre
Anse Marcel
St-Martin
Cul-de-Sac
Ilet Pinel
Grand-Case
Friar's Bay
Espérance Airport
Baie Orientale
La Ferme aux Papillons
Caye Verte
Baie Rouge
Pointe du Bluff
1390 Pic du Paradis
Etang aux Poissons
Baie aus Prunes
Terres Basses
Baie Nettlé
Marigot
Baie de l'Embouchure
Pointe du Canonnier
Orléans
Baie Longue
Simpson Bay Lagoon
Cupecoy Beach
Juliana Airport
Oyster Pond
Mullet Bay
Simpsonbay
1115 Sentry Hill
Cul de Sac
Maho Bay
Simpson Bay
Cole Bay
Guana Bay
Great Salt Pond
St. Maarten
Cole Bay Hill
Philipsburg
Cole Bay
Great Bay
Little Bay
Pointe Blanche

Tasteful tourism

Much of Anguilla's charm lies in what it lacks. No jetport means no mass market package tours. Wallblake Airstrip can only take small, island-hopping planes. Arrivals are usually by sea at **Blowing Point**, on the south coast, on swift ferries from Marigot in St Martin, just 20 minutes away). Not many people, only around 11,000 full-time residents, means courtesy reigns. Everybody knows one another and cars don't pass each other without a nod, a wave or a honk. There are no casinos, scarcely any crime and the Church – Methodist, Anglican, Baptist and Seventh Day Adventist – is still the center of Anguillian life.

The islanders, as a whole, have adopted a tasteful approach to tourism restricting development to small, expensive resort-hotels, such as the exclusive Cap Juluca at Maunday's Bay (with a prize-winning chef) and Malliouhana (the Arawak name for the island) in Meads Bay, two of the Caribbean's most costly hotels. Moreover, they seem deeply committed to protecting their natural assets, introducing measures to assure the conservation of the island's fragile ecology, curtailing such potentially disastrous practices as sand mining for construction, and enforcing strict regulations to protect the marine environment.

Map on page 120

When a major cruise line proposed to develop a cay as an island getaway for its passengers, the Anguillian owners of the land turned down the deal, worth millions of dollars, preferring to preserve the unspoilt islet for their children.

The Valley – a growing capital

Since the island has been reaping the financial rewards of tourism and a thriving offshore finance sector, **The Valley** (pop. 500) ❶ has recently grown from a few houses on a country crossroads to a small commercial center with new banks, business places and even a shopping mall. Although the shopping is minimal, young women dress fashionably off the racks of the Parisian boutiques on St Martin, and everyone gets their American, left-hand-drive cars here, too, even though driving is on the left.

In a private home on the road to Crocus Bay is the **National Museum** (open Mon–Fri; free) jointly set up by the Anguilla National Trust and the Anguilla Archaeological & Historical Society with natural history displays, Ameridindian artefacts and historical exhibits up to the Revolution. The National Trust plays a leading role in island conservation creating wildlife protection schemes and youth programs such as an Adopt-A-Beach scheme. The Archaeological & Historical Society (tel: 497 5297) gives tours of the old buildings every Tuesday at 10am.

Heading south out of The Valley towards Sandy Ground, you come to **Wallblake House** ❷ (reopening in 1999 after renovation). Built in 1787, it is the oldest plantation house on the island. Cut stone had to be hauled across the island from the East End or Scrub Island and burnt coral, shells and molasses were mixed into the mortar. The house is home to the Roman Catholic priest of **St Gerard's**, the tiny modern chapel next door with walls of open stonework, through which the trade winds whistle into Mass.

A succession of Magistrate-Doctors, representing the British Crown, used to live in **Old House**, built in around 1800, further along the road. The two-storey wooden structure has been restored and painted apple-green. Now an art gallery with a restaurant, it serves local dishes and bread baked in the original brick oven.

BELOW: rough-housing on the beach.

The beautifully designed Anguillian postage stamps are very collectable. Issues such as Corals of Anguilla, Iguanas and Fountain Cavern commemorative are on display at the Philatelic Bureau in The Valley Post Office (open Mon–Fri, free).

A salty heritage

Anguilla was once famous for its salt which was mined from saline ponds dc ted around the island. They are home to a wide variety of birdlife, visiting ar resident, such as the great blue heron and white-cheeked pintail. The last bag salt was processed at Road Pond in **Sandy Ground** ❸ in 1985, and at the nort ern end of the bay, which sweeps round in a horsheshoe of white sand, the min museum in **The Pumphouse Bar**, once the old salt factory, documents the stor of salt "picking". A few doors away **Johnno's** is said to be one of the best beac bars in the Caribbean, and literally jumps to live music at the weekends.

From Sandy Ground it's a five-minute boat ride (from the pier; on the hou 10am–3pm) to **Sandy Island** ❹, a veritable desert island of sand – with a beac bar! Not long ago it was covered with palm trees but they were all blown off b Hurricane Luis. The surrounding coral reef offers fascinating snorkeling, an further out to sea divers can explore the spectacular underwater canyon by **Prick Pear Cays** another short boat ride away.

Beautiful beaches

Many people come to Anguilla just for the beaches and continuing around th west coast are plenty of uncrowded long stretches of perfect, white sand. **Mead Bay** ❺, 3 miles (5 km) along from Sandy Ground is one of the trendiest, attrac ing film stars and the super rich, while **Shoal Bay West** on the other side of We End Point is more remote. Sheltered **Rendezvous Bay** on the south coast look over to St Martin and offers good windsurfing.

However, one of the reputedly best beaches of the Caribbean is **Shoal Ba East**, 3 miles (5 km) north of The Valley – a perfect spot for swimming, snor

BELOW: Meads Bay beach in front of the Malliouhana.

"WE WANT ENGLAND!"

Animosity began between St Kitts and Anguilla after 182 when Britain incorporated the two islands with Nevis int one colony. The Anguillians resented the St Kitts governmer which treated them as country bumpkins and did little to hel them through some lengthy droughts.

Several pleas to London for direct British rule were ignore and the situation finally came to a head in 1967 when Britai tried to join the three islands together permanently as a Associated State of St Kitts-Nevis-Anguilla. Anguillians rebelle saying, "We don't want statehood, we want England", sent th 13-strong St Kittitian policemen adrift in a boat and mounte an 18-man attack on St Kitts, which, in fact, fizzled out.

Until then, Anguilla had been poor and undeveloped wit inadequate public and health facilities, such as no electrici or piped water, and high unemployment.

The St Kitts administration still didn't help and Britai remained blind to their plight, so the Anguillians took over the own management. Finally, in March 1969, 400 British para troopers, marines and policemen invaded Anguilla to a grea welcome, and established it back in the arms of Mothe England.

Today, the Revolution remains a crucial part of the islander psyche and they celebrate the anniversary every year.

Map on page 120

eling and relaxing. Nearby, centuries before Columbus, Amerindians used to ome to the **Fountain Cavern** ❻ to perform religious rites to their god Johacu ;iver of cassava). A natural spring in a large underground cavern, this is an nportant archeological site where magnificently preserved petroglyphs have een found alongside a 2,000-year-old stalagtite carved into a head (of Johacu) t the top. Closed to the public at the moment, the cavern and the area around are being developed by a subsidiary of the Anguilla National Trust into the sland's first National Park, with plans for an interpretive center, museum and asy access into the cave.

ailing – the national passion

sland Harbour ❼, 3 miles (8 km) to the north, is a pretty working fishing vil-ıge where brightly painted, prosperous-looking fishing boats neatly line the each. Fishing off Anguilla has always been a booming business where sweet nd luscious spiny lobsters are so plentiful they are exported to St Martin, Puerto ico and St Thomas. After the day's catch, sacks of them are spilled on to the and for prospective buyers. But apparently their taste is a mystery to the fish-rmen, most of whom are Seventh Day Adventists forbidden to eat shellfish.

Now powered by outboard motor, the fishing fleet once flourished under sail hen the fishermen would race home from their grounds 30 miles (50 km) out ɔ sea. Consequently, racing became a passion and today, the traditional wooden oats are built and sailed solely for that purpose, eclipsing cricket in popular-y. On holidays and in Carnival Week in August, the whole island comes to vatch and place bets on the boats which race from Sandy Ground, Meads Bay, lowing Point and Rendezvous Bay to a marker out at sea and back. ❑

Half-built houses dot Anguilla's landscape, because after a young islander leaves school, his main aim is to build a house. As soon as he's earned enough money, he lays down foundations, adding to it bit by bit as he can afford it. This can often take as long as 15 years.

BELOW: fishing boats at rest in Island Harbour.

ONLY JESUS SAVES
HAVE A GODLY DAY
MR
HOT
DOG.
Coffe
IS
HoT

YOU ARE A BORN
SINNER & YOU ARE
GOING TO HELL
THE POPE, PASTOR
CAN'T SAVE 'U' BUT
LORD JESUS

NO LIFE GUARD
SWIM AT YOUR OWN RISK
comitours

ST MARTIN

A busy island shared between the Netherlands and France, it is a aven for shoppers and sunseekers. While the French side excels in gourmet restaurants, the Dutch part is a gambler's delight

According to legend, St Martin's border was defined when a Dutchman and a Frenchman stood back to back, then walked around the island until they met face to face. The Dutch side is smaller supposedly because the utchman was fat, or slow, drinking gin as he walked, or all three. Crossing the order today is an affair of total informality, quite in keeping with the charac- r of this tiny "freeport" island, with nothing but a few solitary signposts mon- oring the tourists and locals crossing back and forth all day. Despite such formality, the border holds great symbolic value to the islanders, marking 00 years of peaceful co-existence and distinguishing two communities which e the same and yet different. Above all, it celebrates the unique character of n island which is many things in one.

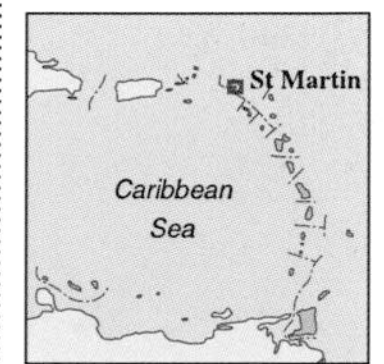

Whatever its origins, St Martin's border bisects the smallest land mass – 37 q. miles (96 sq. km) – in the world shared by two countries. The smaller south- rn half – St Maarten – is part of the Netherlands Antilles, while the northern de belongs to France. As of 1946, French St Martin is technically an *arondisse- ent* of Guadeloupe, which is a *département* of France (in the same way that awaii is a state of the US). And the difference between the two nations is nmense: St Martin is quintessentially French in style, developed on a small cale but including Parisian shopping, whereas St laarten has large resorts, casinos and fast food chains.

PRECEDING PAGES: hot dog and religion.
LEFT: Mullet Bay.
BELOW: duty-free shopping in Marigot.

ontrasting landscapes

ittingly, the island is also composed of two con- asting landscapes: the west end is an atoll of low nd surrounding a lagoon, while the east end con- sts of a range of conical hills, like a plate of candy isses. Actually, St Martin is folded into two parallel nges. One stretches north-northeast from Cole Bay ill and includes the highest peak, Pic du Paradis ,391 ft/420 m); the other runs from Point Blanche to yster Pond, creating the steep rocky cliffs along the eathered southeast coast. Between them lie Great ay and Salt Pond, the valley of Belle Plaine and the naller salt ponds at Le Galion.

There is no drama here. The hills are low and easy climb, the beautiful white beaches are sheltered, e feral boars of Terres Basses (western lowlands) e long gone. It's a fertile landscape of soft hills and asture, cattle and horses. Green and hawksbill turtles est on the shores and the fishing is good.

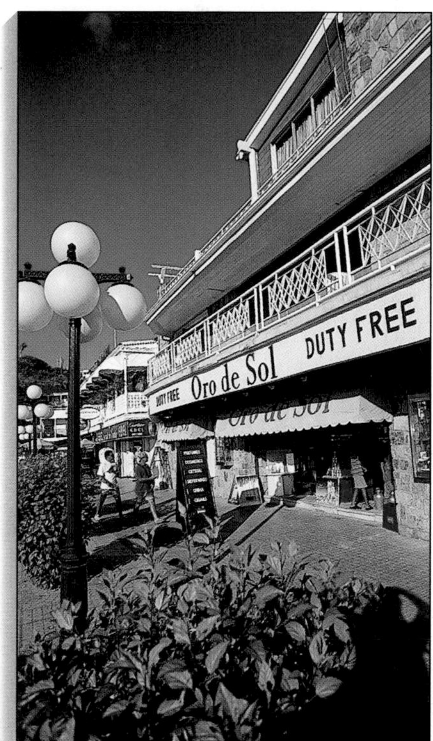

cosmopolitan stew

here is a sly elusiveness about identities on this land. For instance, it's unclear whether residents are be called St Martinois or St Maarteners. Even the opulation figures are mysterious, various sources estimate that there are at least 62,000 legal residents – 32,000 on the Dutc side and 30,000 on the French – along with thousands of illegal aliens from a corners of the world. While the French side is decidedly French, the Dutch sic is anything but Dutch. Although a significant Dutch influence remains, most c the population represents a cosmopolitan stew in which American, West India and Asian segments play equally important roles.

One result of this cosmopolitan nature is an extraordinary linguistic situa tion. The principal languages are Dutch, French, English, Spanish, patois an papiamento (which was not spoken on the island until after 1960 when it arrive as the language of an imported labor force, *see page 53*). As a rule Englis (like French) is viewed as the conqueror's language, and some form of creol as the mother tongue, the "national language". In French St Martin, everyon speaks French whereas in St Maarten, although Dutch is the official languag and taught in schools, everyone speaks English and signposts and notices are al in English too. As the early commercial language of the region, gaining impor tance when America became a major trading partner, English has always func tioned as a neutral *lingua franca* amid the raging hostilities of the colonizers

A sharing mentality

Remains of a half dozen or so Amerindian camps have been unearthed to date especially around the beaches of Terres Basses, on the southeastern shore o Simpson Bay Lagoon, revealing that St Martin was used by the Caribs as a resort or hunting ground. They referred to the island as Sualougia, "a place t get salt" and Oualichi, "a place to get women." There were probably a few Caribs on the beach just after hurricane season in 1493, when Columbus passe

BELOW: school-children in Philipsburg.

y somewhere to the south. He is supposed to have missed St Martin com-
letely, mistaking it for Nevis, or possibly St Kitts.

It was the salt, finally, that led the Dutch to lay claim to the island in 1631. Iolland was at war with Spain, and Spain had a monopoly on European salt, an ssential commodity for the preservation of food in the days before refrigeration. Iowever, the Spanish soon snatched it away and it was while the Dutch were rying to recapture the island in 1644 that the young Peter Stuyvesant, then overnor of Curaçao, lost his leg to a Spanish cannonball at Cay Bay (three ears later he became governor of the Dutch colony on Manhattan). The Span-sh abandoned the island four years later, and the Dutch moved back with the rench dividing the territory between them. The border has survived unchanged o this day, despite several armed incursions in both directions and persistent ttempts by the Dutch in the 18th century to buy the French side outright.

At the height of colonialism, sugar and salt became the island's most impor-ant exports until slavery was abolished and the plantations went into decline. alt was shipped to the US and to Holland where it was used in the herring ndustry until that too ground to a halt in 1949.

Modern-day pirates' den

While St Martin is not entirely averse to its present or past colonial connections, he rhetoric of independence has been increasingly in vogue, particularly on he Dutch side, due to unhappiness over controls exerted by the Curaçao-based Antillean government and the influence of The Hague. Tax-free status and lax controls had brought rapid tourism development on both sides of the island which spiraled to a peak in the early 1990s with undesirable side effects. To

Map on page 120

Tourism in St Martin took off after World War II as the island had been left with a ready-made airport. Juliana Airport was built as a military airfield by the US in 1943 while St Martin was occupied by the Allies, during the Occupation by Germany of France and the Netherlands.

Below: Marina Port La Royale in Marigot buzzes with life.

Seashells found only in the deepest waters were discovered on beaches after Hurricane Luis struck St Martin in 1995. The storm closed the island to tourists for three months and wrecked many livelihoods. Now, after widescale rebuilding, it is back to "business as usual."

counteract these, new regimes such as customs controls and new taxes we imposed by Curaçao, which did not go down well with the islanders, who ha survived decades of benign neglect from Europe earlier in the century by rely ing on traditional activities such as subsistence farming and smuggling.

This rapid growth in tourism had brought instant wealth to many, makin the island the envy of several of its Caribbean neighbors, and St Maartener today still take a certain pride in their island's image as a sort of modern-da pirates' den. Opinion in the bars and cafés on both sides of the island lean toward a preference for more direct self-governance, while maintaining all th benefits of ties with Europe – a happy solution indeed which would permit S Martin to enjoy the best of both worlds. Some islanders are particularly eloquen in their irritation at being ruled via another small island. After all, 600 miles (97 km) separate St Maarten from Curaçao, while five English islands and tw Dutch intervene in the 150 miles (240 km) between Marigot and Guadeloupe Marigot seems actually to have lost some autonomy, and there is a general, i rather nostalgic, sentiment that under direct rule St Martin would be less encum bered by bureaucracy and at the same time would have better access to rea executive authority and resources.

Philipsburg – the Dutch capital

In 1733 a town was founded on the sand bar that separates the Great Salt Pon from Great Bay. It was named **Philipsburg** ❽, in honor of John Philips, th Scotsman who did so much for the early development of St Maarten. The san is still very much in evidence; all over town there are unobtrusive welcom mats to keep as much of it outdoors as possible. But what's left of the pond i easy to ignore – a stretch of stagnant water with som long-term plans to clean it up and make it a bird sanctuary – so who would realize that when Back Stree takes a strange course behind the Sea Palace Hotel, it's avoiding the ghost of a huge storage pile of salt?

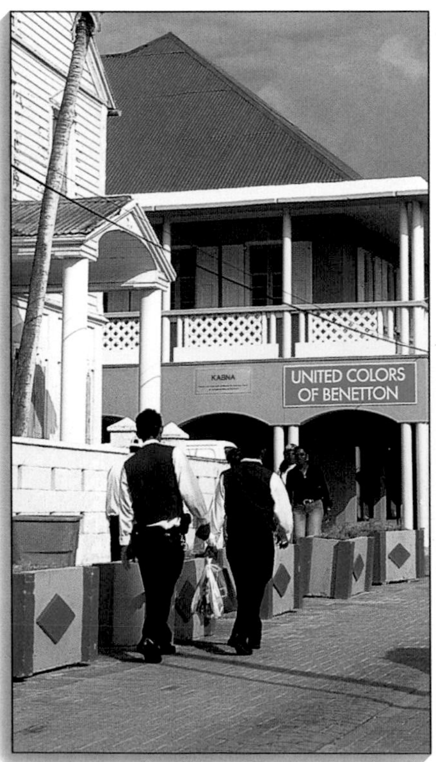

BELOW: busy Front Street in Philipsburg.

By day, Philipsburg is a lively, commercial town – its two main roads, Front Street and Back Street, are linked by a series of narrow alleys supporting a cruise ship port, several hotels, and "the shopping center of the Leewards". In the middle of everything is the **Courthouse**, built on **Wathey Square** in 1793, and still in use. A whole book has been written about its history, but now this is the place to pose for photos and pay parking tickets. The square is lined with former merchant residences that became shops as the population moved back out of the developing town. Directly in front of it, the town's characteristic excitement begins as ships' tenders, sometimes four at a time, unload crowds of passengers on to the pier, all bent on the task of spending money for pleasure.

Moving along **Front Street** the eye at first meets nothing but shop windows – Gucci, Kohinoor, Little Switzerland – selling duty-free goods, but soon the ornamental fretwork known as West Indian "gingerbread" (*see pages 76–77*) comes into focus, and next, the buildings themselves. The characteristic architecture that developed in the 18th and 19th centuries is still evident in a few two-storey structures around

Vathey Square with a warehouse or shop below, living quarters above, and teps from the street up to a front gallery or verandah. But since Hurricane Luis wept through in 1995 there are not many left.

A fascinating video showing the devasting effects of the hurricane can be een at the small **St Maarten Museum** (open Mon–Sat; entrance fee) at the astern end of Front Street and you can stop off for a drink at the **Pasanggra-an**, originally a government guest house, and now the oldest inn on the island, which has an atmosphere of disheveled charm. Queen Wilhelmina and her aughter Juliana stayed here during World War II and their bedroom is now ie Sydney Greenstreet Bar. While relaxing with a drink, perhaps the island's amous Guavaberry liqueur – a rum-based cocktail mixed with the wild red erries that grow on the hills – you can watch the boats going in and out of the iarinas on trips around the island and to St Barths, St Eustatius, and Saba.

Because Philipsburg is linear and crowded it is not really possible to "wan-er" here. There are few places to pause without stepping out of the flow alto-ether into a hotel or restaurant. Even the Great Bay beach seems somehow ut of bounds. Philipsburg keeps its back turned to the sea. While the tiny Vathey Square can in no way match Marigot's wide-open waterfront, efforts to iake it more "people friendly" and new fixtures such as the lively Reggae Café how that it could give Philipsburg a much-needed focal point.

Around the popular west coast

Getting in and out of Philipsburg and Marigot, the capital of the French side, at ush hour, or traveling the main routes between Philipsburg, Simpson Bay and Marigot can be nothing short of a bother and the historical sites around

Out of the 10 casinos in St Maarten, the Casino Royale in Maho Beach Hotel has the highest table limit at US$2,000. The slot machines at the Golden Casino in Great Bay Beach Hotel can cough up as much as US$2,500 in one win.

BELOW: planes swoop low over Maho Beach.

Spiny lobster is caught on the Saba Bank, a shallow part of the sea between Saba, about 25 miles (40 km) south of St Martin, which is also a good breeding ground for fish like grouper.

Philipsburg are only worth visiting for their views: from Fort Hill, the site o **Fort Willem** to the west, you can look over the capital below; **Fort Amsterdan** commands Great Bay from the west, looking across to the **Old Spanish Fort** o Point Blanche, and over Little Bay on the other side.

As the locations of the forts suggest, the earliest Dutch settlements were o the sand bar and around **Little Bay** ❾, now, sprawling along the peninsula i direct contrast to the ruins of Fort Amsterdam above is the modern 220-roon Divi Little Bay Resort and Casino which was given a revamp after the hammering it took from Hurricane Luis.

The road continues round to the brow of Cole Bay Hill from where there i a justly famous vista of **Simpson Bay Lagoon** and neighboring islands. Beyond the road drops to **Simpson Bay** and to the hotels and white beaches that circl the west end: the built-up resorts of **Maho** – over which the planes swoop dow into Juliana Airport – and **Mullet**, the most popular; limestone and marl sediment laid in nearly horizontal beds has created low, richly colored cliffs alon the shore of the quieter **Cupecoy Beach**, where clothes are optional. Acros the border, beaches are unspoilt and secluded with **Baie Longue** stretching fo 1 sandy mile (nearly 2 km), graced by one small, upmarket hotel, **La Samanna**

Marigot – a touch of southern France

After the sometimes crass commercialism of Philipsburg, **Marigot** ❿ seems more European and more Caribbean at the same time; more appealing, more colourful, and equally lively. There's more than a touch of southern France here, especially in the morning fruit and vegetable market (best on Wednesdays and especially Saturdays) on the quay. Wide open to the sea, the quay is a

BELOW: market day in Marigot.

Map on page 120

welcoming recess where, unlike its Dutch counterpart, it invites you to stop and watch in the cafés, bars and excellent restaurants that spill out on to the streets. It seems entirely right to sit and watch the ferries loading for Anguilla while eating chicken barbecued over a halved oil drum, or salt cod (once the food of slaves) served with rice and peas, or fresh fish with lime and garlic and spices – delicious Caribbean fare. Or, if you prefer, to survey the market square over espresso and *pâtisserie* in a cafe like **La Vie en Rose**, opposite the harbor, where French will be spoken all around you. It is then just a 15-minute walk (or a car ride) up to the ruins of **Fort St Louis** for some magnificent views of the town and Anguilla 5 miles (8 km) away.

There is fine shopping to be done along **Rue de la République** and in the chic boutiques around the **Marina Port La Royale**, which embraces the boat-filled northernmost finger of Simpson Bay Lagoon with elegant shops and cafés. On Thursday nights a carnival atmosphere pervades as shops stay open late, bands play and the restaurants fill up with onlookers and satisfied shoppers. Those too busy to sit down and eat can grab a barbecued snack at one of the many *lolos* (food stalls) scattered around the town. Significantly, much of the town still takes a siesta from noon until 2 or 3pm, as does the small **archeological museum** (open Mon–Sat; entrance fee) behind the marina – unthinkable among the driven merchants of Philipsburg, where midday belongs to the cruise ships.

Into the hills

Stretching to the west of Marigot along the northern shores of the lagoon is a strip of hotels and shopping centers. The beaches along **Baie Nettlé** are not much to write home about, but the area makes a good base. Leaving Marigot to

BELOW: cacti grows in the craggier parts.

Map on page 120

the north, the road skirts past the central hills where there is a network of hik ing trails punctuated by viewing points. Several lead to the **Pic du Paradi** which is densely wooded and alive with colorful forest birds. The countrysid to the north, around Grand Case, supported many of the sugar plantations in th 18th century and it is apparent that cane was planted virtually on the hilltops. I ushered in a long period of prosperity, which lasted until slavery was abolishe in 1848 on the French side and 15 years later in the south, causing a lot of grief especially where several plantations straddled the border.

The most popular dive site in St Martin is the 200-year-old British frigate HMS Proselyte, *just south of Philipsburg which provides excellent viewing for all levels.*

Right: a cockfight in Marigot. **Below:** restaurants in Grand Case.

Grand Case – the gastronomic capital

It has been said of the little town of **Grand Case** ⓫ that its only industry is eat ing, but there are also art galleries here and, of course, a beach. The most toute creole creativity in St Martin is culinary, and this village alone offers dozens o choices, lined up along the beachfront road.

The sand at Grand Case and **Friar's Bay**, just to the south, is golden no white, and the light seems different in this part of the island, with tones of ochre and gold. The road leads round to the east, south of the salt pond which attracts an abundance of bird life, through the rolling countryside and mangrove swamps of **Cul de Sac**, where there are boats over to **Ilet Pinel** ⓬, an offshore island that offers excellent snorkeling and a choice of places for lunch. Sheltered **Anse Marcel** to the northwest is a favorite spot with yachties who take advantage of the large Meridien resort there, the shopping mall and yacht charterers.

Acquiring an all-over tan

Along the rough Atlantic shores of the east coast, there are several isolated beaches off the road to Orléans and windsurfing is popular here – as is the odd cockfight in specially designated pits around St Martin, which, incidentally is not encouraged. At **Baie Orientale** the Club Orient is a naturist resort claiming a section of beach for those who wish to acquire an all-over tan. On the bandstand next to the club, calypso and reggae bands play in the afternoons, creating a party mood.

On the western bank of the Etang aux Poissons is the **Ferme aux Papillons** (butterfly farm) ⓭ (open daily; entrance fee) which has a fascinating collection of the beautiful creatures. The best time to come is in the morning when they are most active. **Orléans** ⓮, further south, was the capital of French St Martin until 1768, but only graves and a dueling ground recall those days. Local artist Roland Richardson lives here and opens his home every Thursday for visitors to see his work. He also has a gallery in the former *mairie* (town hall), a restored West Indian building in Marigot.

Beyond are the beaches of **Oyster Pond**, and reefs that lure scuba divers to their caves and cliffs. The coast itself is wild, with windswept scrub and cacti, including the striking Pope's Head, around **Guana Bay** (named for the iguanas once found here). An island tour used to end at a sort of salt water geyser at **Devil's Cupper**, but changes in the rock formation due to construction have eliminated that. Now it ends with a sundowner in Philipsburg. ❑

ST BARTHÉLEMY

Known affectionately as St Barths, this ultra French chic haunt of the rich and famous is a Caribbean St Tropez with magnificent yachts in the harbor and Parisian chefs in the restaurants

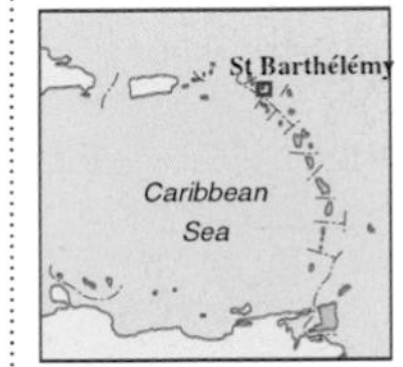

With an international renown that far outstrips its 10 sq. miles (25 sq. km) of white beaches and craggy hills, this tiny French island at the top of the Leeward Islands, less than half the size of Manhattan, is a magnet o the rich and famous. As a result St Barthélemy harbors some of the world's nost sought-after real estate. Like St Tropez in southern France, sky-high prices nly serve to enhance the allure of St Barths, as it is popularly known, among lite and average mortals alike. During primetime week at Christmas, the likes f Madonna, Sylvester Stallone, Steven Seagal and Sharon Stone are all to be ound hiding out here, along with assorted billionaires, supermodels, royalty and he scores of daytrippers who come over from St Martin every day to try and pot them.

The essence of France in a tropical haven, St Barths' convoluted coastline is ewn full of blue pockets trimmed with exceptional hideaway beaches; steep-ided mountains – the Pyrenees in miniature – are brindled with torch cactus and tunted wild frangipani; kaleidoscopic panoramas create a feeling of endless opography. In the same way an undersized athlete may overcome his limitations vith superior speed, so has nature compensated St Barths with a rugged and rregular beauty.

PRECEDING PAGES: a windswept hillside.
LEFT: only the locals are allowed to spear fish in St Barths.
BELOW: preparing the fishing boats.

It smells of France, too – *baguettes* baking in the *oulangeries*, coffee wafting from the street cafés and vhiffs of Gauloises and Gitanes from determined mokers. The absence of the aromas of the charcoal urners' woodsmoke, the incense of freshly harvested pices and the heavy sweetness of freshly cut sugar ane, which typify the West Indies, makes you won-ler if this really is the Caribbean? Yes, for still the un is relentless, the sea magnificent, the trade winds omforting, the mosquitoes annoying.

rench settlers and pirates

Christopher Columbus sighted the island in 1496, aming it for his younger brother, Bartholomew and t first appeared as a mere flyspeck on a Spanish map n 1523, identified as San Bartolemé.

In a sea of fecund, resource-laden islands, St Barths vas inimitably undiscoverable, bypassed even by the Caribs except as an overnight rest stop on their raids o other islands. However, a party of French settlers rom St Kitts set up home here in 1648 only to be nassacred by a passing band of Carib warriors several ears later.

Undeterred, a group of Huguenots from Brittany nd Normandy arrived, establishing the first perma-ent settlement, which thrived, not on farming and ishing, but on piracy. St Barths became a clandes-ine rendezvous for pirates, plundering the passing

There are many islanders whose family lines go back to the early Breton and Normandy settlers. The Norman dialect is still spoken and a few of the elderly women wear tall white hats called quichenottes.

Spanish galleons heavy with treasure. The island's rocky, arid hills, with r fresh water supply, and lack of savannah made a sugar and syrup industr unthinkable, although some cotton and tobacco were cultivated, so few slave were imported and the people continued to live the peasant life they had France. The French government reported them to be "good people, very poo honest, rather ignorant, and quite quarrelsome," this latter contentiousness su viving to this day in what seems to be an intramural sport.

Sold out to the Swedes

Nevertheless in a most unexpected and bizarre trade, in 1784, the neglectf government of Louis XVI gave St Barths to King Gustaf III of Sweden i exchange for trading rights in the port of Gothenburg. The Swedes immed ately got down to turning the island into a model possession. The capital wa given its decidedly non-French name of Gustavia while the port was declare duty free.

Spared the terror and dissolution about to overtake her French sister island Martinique (*see pages 218–27*), Guadeloupe (*see pages 194–203*), and St Ma tin (*see pages 126–35*), in the French Revolution (1789–95), the island flou ished. The local administration worked to organize the indigenous populatio not as Swedes, but as people of St Barths with their own traditions and he itage. A rational pattern of streets was laid out around the harbor, warehouse were built, the roadways cobbled. By 1806 the island wallowed in relative pros perity, with a population bloated to about 6,000. However, the following decade saw a series of disasters – natural and economic – and in 1878 Sweden sold th island with the 1,000 remaining French descendants back to France.

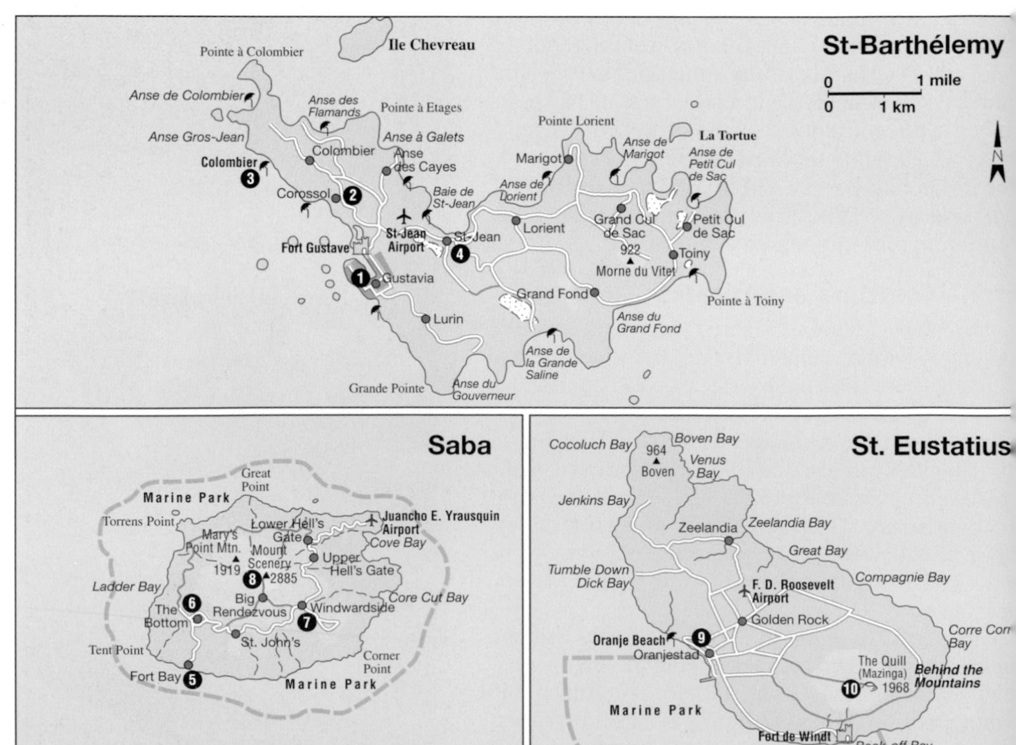

ontent to be French

day St Barths, together with St Martin 15 miles (24 km) away, both come der the administrative umbrella of Guadeloupe, an overseas department of ance (*see page 42*), each with their own mayor. Candidates for the local ministration are perennially right wing, but the islanders are not banking the es of autonomy. "It's good to have a nation like France looking out for you," ys a shop clerk in Gustavia. "Independence? Don't speak about that. Crazy ople want it."

Here there is no underclass to be placated, suppressed or promised, for unem-oyment is virtually non-existent. Fishermen, businessmen, builders, and labor-s all have plenty to do, and they know how to enjoy life, too. Long lunches and enty of breaks for surfing, fishing and hanging out in Le Select in Gustavia is e order of things – so there is little crime to speak of. As once happened when veden took control, people are trying to get on the island, not off.

hair-raising arrival

round 160,000 visitors a year come to St Barths, half of them by catamaran uttle on daytrips from St Martin 15 miles (24 km) away. Those that fly in on e tiny eight- or 12-seater planes have an experience akin to a theme park ride. he hills loom up in front at the approach to the 875-yd (800 m) runway like an npenetrable wall and suddenly the plane dives steeply and lands, with brakes uealing, stopping just short of the sea. It wasn't long ago that two approaches ıd to be made – to clear the then grass airstrip of sheep before actually landing.

St Barths is also a stop-over for yachts sailing the Caribbean between Antigua the south and the Virgin Islands. Gustavia and the scattered islets around

On St Barths, a two-storey, three-bed-room villa with a few acres of land is likely to set you back around $7 million (£4½ million). A square meter of space in St Jean is more expensive than its equivalent on the Champs-Elysees in Paris.

BELOW: landing on the runway is like a theme park ride.

Rudolf Nureyev (above) built a house on the Pointe à Toiny right on the rocks where the waves often sprayed him as he lay on his sun-deck. The house is signposted "Maison Nuryev".

provide beautiful natural harbors, attracting the serious yachtsmen and leisu palaces alike. Around the islets, such as **Isle Fourche**, the sea is rich in mari life and coral, and the marinas in Gustavia offer packages in small groups of to 10 dives. Deep-sea fishing for marlin, wahoo and tuna on boats providi lunch and an open bar can also be arranged there, although visitors are n allowed to spear the fish.

Gustavia – a Gallic town with a Swedish heritage

Set around a yacht-filled harbor and careenage too small for cruise ships (sm ships can anchor in the outer harbor), the picturesque buildings of the capit climb up the steep hillside behind. **Gustavia** ❶ is still a free port and the la est Paris fashions from Versace to Gaultier are all available right here in t exclusive boutiques, along with Gucci leathers, Vuitton suitcases and Charl Jourdan footwear. Boat-loads of shoppers arrive from St Martin, and cafés sp out on to the streets Parisian style, buzzing with a young, chic French crow There are no beggars or hucksters here; no ramshackle shops or rums, and n colorful, aromatic market clogs the waterfront – only four makeshift vegetab stalls on a side *rue*, operated by a half dozen women who sail the 125 miles (2 km) from Guadeloupe weekly.

The Swedes bequeathed three forts – Oscar, Karl and Gustav – at strateg points around the town and beneath Fort Oscar is the **Musée de St-Barth** (open Mon–Fri, and Sat am; closed for lunch; entrance fee) with exhibitions local history, traditions and island crafts. A five-minute walk past Fort Ka brings you to the popular **Shell Beach** which is just what its name implies – beach covered with shells.

LEFT: flying high. **RIGHT:** some secluded coasts.

lentiful beaches

oing west out of Gustavia, you soon reach the tradition-bound, fishing village f **Corossol** ❷, on a brown sand beach lined with colorful fishing boats and lob-er traps. The women sit outside their houses weaving hats, mats and baskets ut of latania palms to sell.

St Barths has at least 14 beautiful white sand beaches, and one of the best of e secluded ones is **Colombier** ❸ at the tip of the northwest peninsula, where a turtles come back year after year to lay their eggs. The beach cannot be ached by car, but the 30-minute walk from the village is well worth it for the agnificent island views en route. Another way in is by boat from Gustavia. round the point to the east, the wide stretch of sand edged with latania palms nd seagrapes at **Flamands** is uncrowded despite the few small hotels with all eir watersports facilities.

St Jean ❹, on the northern shore, has the most popular beach, divided in two y a spit of rock on which stands the old **Eden Rock** hotel where Greta Garbo nce stayed. Now you can lunch on freshly caught lobster, surrounded on three ides by a turquoise sea. Behind the beach are shops, hotels and snack bars giv-g an atmosphere of the French Riviera.

Further east, **Lorient**, where the first French settlers lived, offers good surf-g or snorkelling depending on the mood of the sea. Windsurfers head for **rand Cul de Sac** at the eastern end, which has a sandy bay protected by a oral reef and is backed by a large salt pond. Sand fleas can be a problem here s they sometimes are on **Anse de la Grande Saline**, in the south, a long white each also next to a salt pond. Surfers gather here for the waves while waterfowl njoy the pond. They know a good place to stay when they see one. ❑

Map on page 140

BELOW: a pelican fly-past.

SABA

A tiny volcanic peak jutting out of the crystal clear waters of the aribbean and Atlantic, Saba's dramatic mountain scenery matches the magnificent underwater world around it

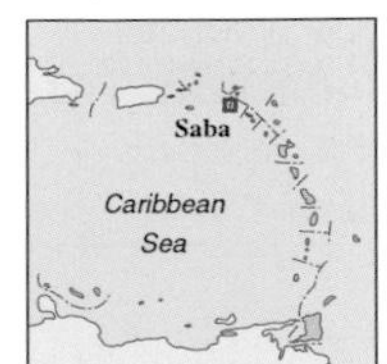

There are no white sandy beaches on the Dutch island of Saba (pronounced *Say*-bah). This miniature volcanic island's rocky slopes climb steeply out of the tropical sea rising to the highest point in the Netherlands at the top cloud-covered Mount Scenery (2,855 ft/870 m). Rugged cliffs, refuge to a riety of seabirds, support 5 sq. miles (13 sq. km) of green, mountainous ter-in dotted with small villages of pretty, pristinely kept, white houses with red ofs, and once linked only by hundreds of steps. Around 1,200 people live re, half of them light-skinned and the other half dark-skinned and they all eak English, although Dutch is the official language. As no plantation econ-ny ever existed slaves were only brought over to help on the small farms and rry goods up and down its paths.

Like St Barths 30 miles (50 km) to the northeast, landing on Saba is a nerve-racking experience. The Winair pilot heads straight for a vertical rock face, ly to fly a sharp, cool curve to the left just as you feel that your time has me and then lands seconds later on a runway the length of an aircraft carrier 1,300 ft (398 m) to be precise – so that his 10 or so passengers can disembark fely. Saba's airport, completed in 1963, is only open when the trade winds are ntle enough. In earlier days, arriving by sea was not much easier as there ere no natural harbors for protection against the rong currents and fierce gusts of wind.

PRECEDING PAGES: monstrous moss on Mount Scenery.
LEFT: a Saban family
BELOW: shoals of colorful fish to see.

hipwrecked

ristopher Columbus discovered Saba in 1493, but was only in 1632 that the first Europeans – a couple shipwrecked Englishmen – first set foot on the land. Later, eager Dutch settlers from St Eustatius, miles (27 km) to the southeast, managed to brave e waves that crash regularly against the steep coast-e. Ruled a dozen different times by the Spanish, ench and English, Saba was finally taken over for od by the Dutch in 1812, and the islanders have no ans to break away (*see page 293*).

The only inlet in the towering cliffs where boats n dock is at **Fort Bay** ❺, a relatively flat bay by ban standards but with none of the luxuries of a oper harbor. Before 1972 when the pier was built, yone who disembarked here – or at Ladder Bay on e west coast – always got their feet wet after being wed ashore in wooden jolly-boats. The first vehicle the island, a jeep, was landed in 1947 on two oops lashed together to form a makeshift raft. These ys, daytrippers from St Maarten, 28 miles (45 km) the north, arrive on high-speed ferries almost daily d the dive shop in Fort Bay gets very busy.

The first part of the road that staggers across the aggy terrain to the airport was built in 1943, under

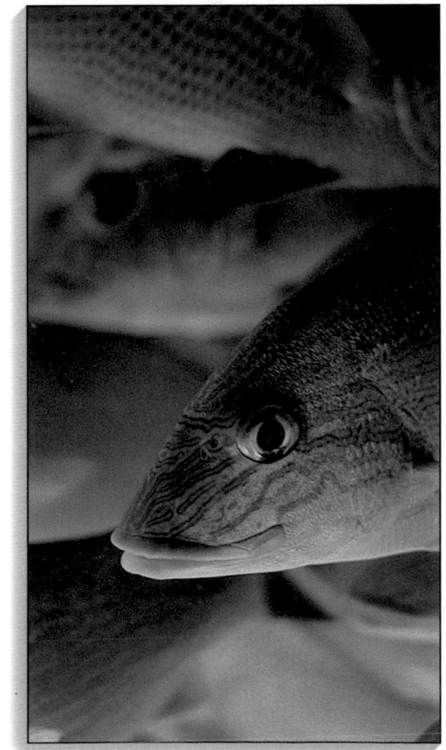

How much further to the top?

the auspices of Josephus Lambert Hassell. After Dutch engineers had declar any road construction to be impossible, Hassell took a correspondence cour in civil engineering and proved them wrong. Before that, on landing at Fc Bay people had to walk up hundreds of stone steps to the main village of Tl Bottom, and cargo had to be carried, including once a piano that took 12 mc to get it to its destination.

From The Bottom to the top

At 820 ft (250 m) above the sea, **The Bottom** ❻ does not live up to its nam In fact it is derived from *de botte*, the Dutch word for a bowl, as it stands on small piece of flat land surrounded by mountains. With around 500 inhabitant the village functions as the island's capital and the government building is su rounded by the hospital, school, **Cranstons Antique Inn**, the first guesthous established in the 1830s, and a few bars. American students from the sma medical school there give it a youthful ambience.

The road only reached the picturesque village of **Windwardside** ❼, 90 steps further up, in 1951 and, despite the souvenir shops selling Saba lace, an a few small hotels and restaurants, it is still very much a Dutch Caribbean idy in its peaceful setting against a green mountain ridge between the haze-cov ered Mount Scenery and Booby Hill. Pretty white wooden houses on grani foundations, and gardens full of flowers in bloom decorate the village. The re roofs are all very clean – they have to be as they are used for collecting rainwat for there are no rivers on the island. What at first appears to be a family cry in the vegetable gardens or orchards turns out to be the house's own cistern, cru cial to survival, and you may see a grave beside it – there is little room fc cemeteries here.

BELOW: these hikers are determined to get there.

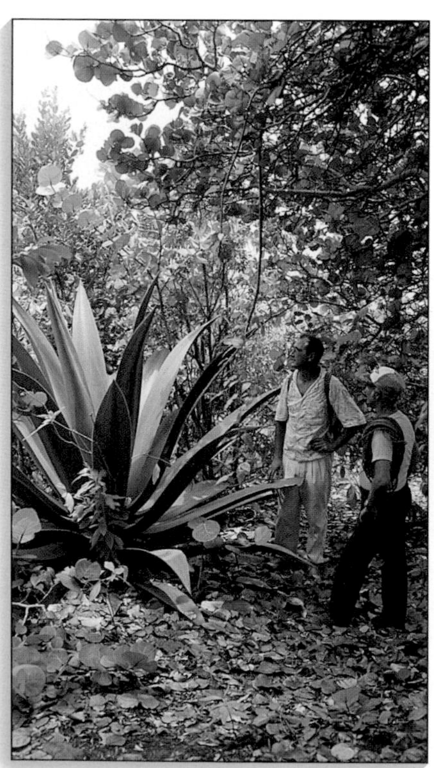

The **Saba Museum** (open Mon–Fri; close noon–1pm; entrance fee) was once a sea captain house built in 1840 and still has the original kitche A wall covered with the masters' certificates show how closely the Saban men are associated with th sea. For centuries they were fishermen and mariner plying the Caribbean trading routes. One sailor i reputed to have been paid in gold for smugglin escaped French prisoners from Guyana to Trinida

Nearby are the **Captain's Quarters** that have bee converted into a comfortable and attractive hotel. Th bright rays of sunlight are pleasantly filtered by caro and mango trees in front of the peaceful terrace, an there's a wonderful view of the island's dramatic land scape down to the sea 1,800 ft (550 m) below from th room verandahs and pool bar.

Foggy forest hikes

Waiting for a completely clear day before climbin **Mount Scenery** ❽ is not a good idea as the summi rarely peeks out of its thick cloud veil. The ascer begins on the outskirts of Windwardside (on the roa to The Bottom) and you don't need to be an expe climber, although good shoes will make the 3-hou tour easier because the 1,064 steps along the way ar steep and often wet.

Lizards scurry across the path at the start of the tra

Map on page 140

nd the bright red and yellow artificial-looking heliconia that grace the lobbies f smart hotels all over the world grow wild among the trees. The higher you limb, the more luxuriant the vegetation becomes: the trees are covered in lianas ropical vines), massive leaves darken the path, and the fog closes in. Then, just eneath the summit, a 210 ft (64 m) high radio tower (brought up in just one day y a helicopter) comes into view. The stormy wind whips through the trees and histles through the steel structure and behind it Mount Scenery drops away.

Other hiking trails around Saba may not be so dramatic but are just as satisfying and the new **National Park** opening above Ladder Bay in 1999 offers an ven wider choice.

'olcanic underwater landscapes

:old hands after a 50-ft (15 m) dive? No problem at the **Hot Springs** site where ivers can plunge their hands into the warm sand there. From 1987 the waters round Saba have been protected as part of the **Saba Marine Park**, concealing vast, spectacular volcanic landscape rich in sea life and open to divers. A mall entrance fee to this colorful experience is charged by the diving schools, r by the organizers of boat excursions from St Maarten. The 26 diving grounds only accessible by boat – provide divers at all levels with unbelievably beautiful spots such as **Tent Reef Wall**, encrusted with corals and sponges, or the ently sloping reefs where elegant stingrays cruise and nurse sharks sleep in the and. At **Third Encounter** what must once have been an underwater volcano ears up to just 100 ft (30 m) below the surface. A pillar of coral, called Needle's ye, has grown up on its western flank over the millennia – a unique collection f tube and barrel sponges, star coral, elephant ears and brain coral. ❑

TIP

Everyone has a secret recipe for the aromatic dessert drink, Saba Spice. The main ingredient is always rum, while the mix of brown sugar, cloves, fennel and other flavorings tends to vary. Try it and see.

BELOW: on a clear day – the view from Mount Scenery.

EXPLORING THE SPLENDORS OF THE DEEP

The dramatic seascape of the Caribbean is still a widely unexplored realm of beauty even though generations of settlers have changed the landscape.

Tourism has set off the spirits of invention: more and more tiny submarines seating about 20 or so passengers are being launched throughout the region to give the ordinary visitor a chance of sharing the kind of underwater experience previously only available to the rapidly growing crowd of scuba divers.

THE POOL IS OPEN

With its warm and shallow waters, 75°F (24°C) being the average temperature, the Caribbean Sea is an ideal spot to learn to scuba dive. Hundreds of dive shops certify beginners within five days of theory and practise in shallow grounds (PADI, NAUI courses). More advanced divers and budding marine biologists will also meet instructors to help them find the best sites and produce exquisite underwater photography.

Some of the most beautiful dive sites are located in protected marine areas. The boom in tourism – more fish to be caught, more sewage water to be dispensed with, more beach pollution and reef damage from ships anchors – has severely endangered the fragile and highly complex reef ecosystem. The tiny island of Bonaire was the first to protect the coastal waters around the island as a marine park, others such as Saba and the British Virgin Islands followed suit. Jacques Yves Cousteau initiated a marine park on the western shore of Guadeloupe, St Eustatius now protects its historic treasures below the water line, and Anguilla is about to start a reef care program.

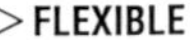

▷ **HIDE AND SEEK**
Dimly lit caverns in the reef are favorite shelters for night hunters like snapper, found in rocky notches between corals and sponges.

△ **REEF CREST**
Where the waves are broken by the elkhorn corals in the shallower part of the reef, many fish search for prey.

▽ **NEW FRIENDS**
Dolphins are very friendly and communicative and occasionally swim alongside divers.

▽ **BRAINY**
Over centuries spherically growing brain corals can reach diameters of more than 6 ft (2 m).

▷ **FLEXIBLE**
Soft corals are perfect indicators of submarine currents, look for trumpetfish in the big Gorgonians.

WATCH OUT!
ny and big fish have veloped clever tactics to de from enemies and rprise their prey.

▷ DON'T TEASE
Crabs are very quick using their pincers, when searching the ground for organic food like worms.

▽ UNDERWATER TRAIL
Some marine parks, like this one at Buck Island, introduce snorkelers and divers to specific forms of local aquatic life by marked underwater trails.

RECAPTURED BY THE SEA

Off the western shores of Aruba, around 33 ft (10 m) below land is the *Pedernales*, the remnants of a tanker, torpedoed during World War II, it is only one of almost a dozen wrecks attracting divers close to the island. Aruba is the westernmost island of the Netherlands Antilles offering an assortment of underwater wrecks including planes. At 460 ft (140 m) long the *Antilla*, off the coast of Aruba, is the biggest wreck in the Caribbean and it is living proof of nature's rapid move to integrate: corals, sponges, anemones and other invertebrates have attached themselves on to the huge hull and transformed it into a multi-colored patchwork, where Spotlight Parrotfish and Queen Angelfish enhance the dazzling scene. Its storage room in the bow is as big as a church. There are plenty of books on each island documenting their shipwrecks and other man-made sites. Old anchors can be found around St Eustatius, explore the shipwreck *Proselyte* in Great Bay (St Maarten) or the *RMS Rhone* in the Rhone Marine Park, off Tortola or a load of old cars which tumbled from a barge off Vaersenbaai, Curaçao.

P 52

ST EUSTATIUS

Peace and quiet is what you will find on this small Caribbean hideaway, along with a network of hiking trails and a vast underwater landscape just waiting to be explored

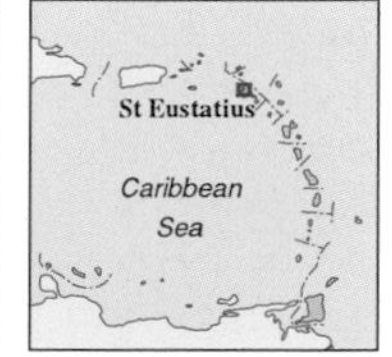

Dominated by the dormant volcano called The Quill (1,968 ft/600 m) with a lush rainforest center, this tiny Dutch island lazing in the Caribbean sunshine has so far avoided being on the beaten tourist track, making it a eaceful place to escape to. However what it lacks in beaches and shopping nis 11-sq. mile (28 sq. km) haven, with Oranjestad its only town, makes up for n dramatic scenery above and below the water. Colloquially called Statia, the sland also has a fount of fascinating tales to tell of a more prosperous era.

In 1775, minuscule Statia was a thriving trading center, known as the Golden Rock, and had as many as 10 ships a day calling at Oranjestad, then a busy own. Janet Schaw, a touring Scottish gentlewoman strolled along this seafront nd recorded her impressions in her *Journal of a Lady of Quality*: "From one end f the town of Eustatia to the other is a continued mart, where goods of the nost different uses and qualities are displayed before the shop-doors. Here ang rich embroideries, painted silks, flowered Muslins, with all the Manufac-ures of the Indies. Next stall contains most exquisite silver plate, the most eautiful indeed I ever saw, and close by these iron-pots, kettles and shovels. Perhaps the next presents you with French and English Millinary-wares. But it vere endless to enumerate the variety of merchandize in such a place, for in very store you find everything…"

PRECEDING PAGES: tidying up the backyard.
LEFT: Oranjestad architecture.
BELOW: island style in the sun.

This "Lady of Quality" would have difficulty rec-gnizing Statia today. A few crumbling ruins, some nder water, are all that is left of the warehouses and nerchants' offices along the sea front. Things are a ot quieter now.

Il-gotten gains

t Eustatius was discovered by Columbus in 1493 and aken by the Dutch for the West India Company dur-ng the 1630s – 22 changes of flag later, the island nally succumbed to the Dutch.

Plantations on the central plain – where the airport ow lies – gave the islanders a good living, but the eir jewel was the safe harbor. Well positioned on najor trade routes, in the 18th century Statia was nade a duty-free port and reaped the rewards. Valu-ble goods bought and sold filled the coffers at the umerous local trading offices and the island became center for the slave trade, too. During the American evolution (1775–83) arms and gunpowder were nuggled through the island in barrels of rum and nolasses via the merchant ships bound for New Eng-nd – and the population is reported to have swelled 20,000 – 10 times what it is today.

Such was the island's support of the rebellious ritish colonies in North America that in 1776 sol-iers fired a salute when they sighted one of their

In 1781, after invading St Eustatius, Admiral Rodney, is supposed to have found most of his booty buried in the graveyard of the Dutch Reformed Church. He ordered the coffins to be opened after an abnormal spate of funerals had taken place.

warships, the *Andrea Dorea*. This was the first salute ever fired by another la in honour of the recently formed United States of America and moved Statia the front of the world stage. The Americans were delighted, but the British we absolutely furious.

However, historians now doubt whether love of freedom was actually t motive behind the ominous salute, because signals of that kind were normal only employed to greet trading vessels (and the Dutch government also assur the seething British that they had had no intention of recognizing the sove eignty of the USA). Whether or not the guards up in Fort Oranje in Oranjest did recognize the importance of the American flag, the ship was probably ve welcome anyway because the American rebels were lucrative customers.

Rodney's revenge

Britain finally settled the score when Admiral George Rodney attacked St Eust tius in 1781 and ransacked the warehouses, banishing the merchants and ca turing their ships. He sent back to England £5 million worth of booty. Th started a steady decline in the fortunes of the island, precipitated by the end slavery in 1863 which finished off the small plantation economy. The popul tion dwindled to the less than 2,000 it is today and the island's main source income is now an oil depot on the northwest coast where supertankers load an unload. Otherwise, the Statians live by subsistence farming, money sent hon from relations abroad, and Dutch support.

However, poverty has not prevented the Statians,who mostly speak Englis from generating their warmth and friendliness to visitors and there is very li tle crime to speak of. They are still proud of their historical gesture and on

BELOW: taking a break over a game of dominoes.

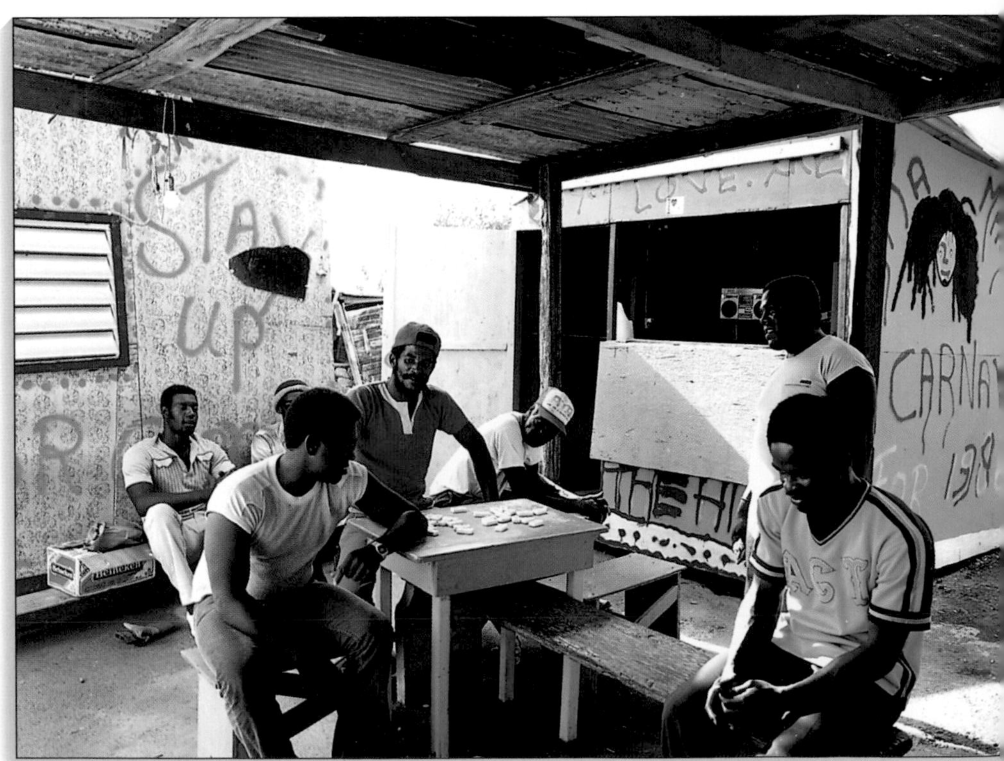

ovember each year, they celebrate Statia-America Day, when cannons are red from Fort Oranje and the islanders get together and sing a hymn which cludes the lines: "Statia's past you are admired/Though Rodney filled his ag/The first salute fired/To the American flag." The flags of the 13 American lonies are then hoisted above the fort to mark the occasion.

ranjestad – a fallen town

ot long after Admiral Rodney's sojourn in **Oranjestad** ❾ a mighty undersea rthquake caused much of the lower part of the town, where all the warehouses were, to crumble into the sea. Now some of the submerged ruins and nken ships provide great snorkeling and there are plans to restore the parts of e Lower Town left on dry land. The Old Slave Road winds up to the top of the 30-ft (40 m) high cliff where **Fort Oranje** (open daily; free) dating from 1636 id restored in 1976 for the US Bicentennial Independence celebrations, guards ver the bay, the cannons point through the embrasures at imaginary enemies. here's a fine view down to the mile-long dark sand of **Oranje Beach**, Statia's st swimming spot. Memorial plaques on the fort from Franklin D. Roosevelt id the "St Eustatius Commission of the American Revolution" commemorate e island's fateful salute.

The shore on the wild northeastern Atlantic coast has dark sand and a heavy surf only suitable for splashing about in. It is overlooked by La Maison Sur La Plage which offers fine French cooking and simple guest cottages.

Close by in the 18th-century Doncker-De Graff House, once inhabited by an xtremely wealthy Dutch merchant during Statia's heyday, is **St Eustatius Iuseum** (open Mon–Fri; entrance fee). This is where Admiral Rodney made s headquarters for 10 months in 1781 before the French pushed him out. eputedly one of the best historical museums in the region, the house gives a enuine feel of what prosperous colonial life must have been like and has some xcellently arranged archaeological and historical colctions of Arawak pottery, tools used by the early ttlers and detailed documentation of the ignoble ave trade.

The plaques along the "Historical Walk" that connues on to the main sights in Oranjestad are rather orn-looking these days. **Honen Dalim**, the second dest synagogue in the Western hemisphere, (the oldt is in Willemstad, Curaçao), has been left to decay nce the large Jewish population left with the arrival Rodney. Built in 1739, its walls of yellow brick, ought over as ships' ballast and unusual at that time, iclose a broad, two-storey room, but the outside eps lead to nowhere.

The congregation of the **Dutch Reformed Church**, e island's largest church, a few minutes further on, so departed with the drop in prosperity. The masve tower made of dark volcanic stone in 1775 is still anding after renovation in 1981, but the broad nave now roofed over by the blue of the sky.

On the other hand, the Seventh Day Adventist hurch, just past Wilhelmina Park, bulges at the ams every Saturday morning and the narrow streets ied by houses with corrugated steel roofs are empty. ie older houses have arcaded porches and balconies ith peeling gingerbread trim, whereas on the outirts of town some of the newer concrete houses are t so pretty.

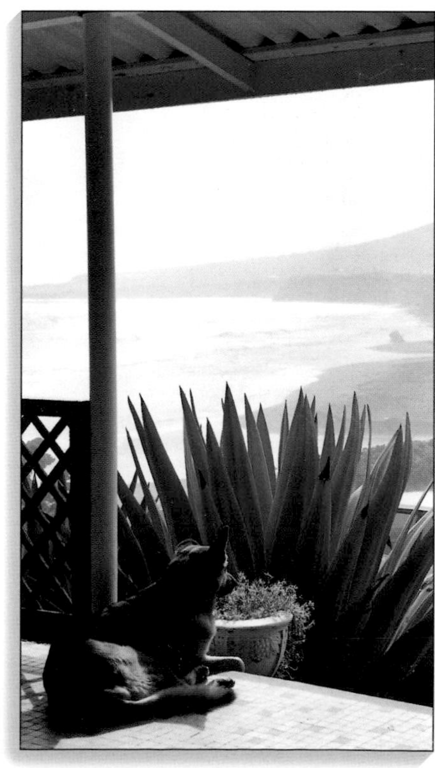

BELOW: looking out over Zeelandia Bay.

Green giants in the crater

The Statians started shooting several worried glances at **The Quill** ⓾ whe Montserrat (*see pages 188–91*) started blowing up in 1995. Old paintings of th island show massive plumes of smoke above Mazinga, the old Amerindia name for the volcano. Geologists have soothed local anxieties, however, an both slopes and the crater are accessible to hikers. A sometimes steep, but largel pleasant path, starts in the outskirts of Oranjestad on the road leading west ou of town, and continues up to the edge of the crater. When you reach the to there are three possibilities: following the crater rim either to the right or the lef or actually descending into it and the untouched rainforest growing there. Smal geckos race across the ground, and tiny hummingbirds dip into the orchid growing wild on the trees. Most startling are the hermit crabs that look lik rolling stones as they tumble towards the sea inside their shells to reproduce before making the arduous return journey back up to the crater.

In the early morning – the best time for the three–five-hour tour with guide provided by the tourist office in Oranjestad – swathes of fog hang above th gigantic trees inside the crater. Some of these ancient trees along the route hav been given biblical names by the locals. Moses, for instance, is a mighty old tre covered with aerial roots.

Further hikes, all marked on the tourist office map, are located in the are called **Behind the Mountain** on the southeastern slope of The Quill where th St Eustatius National Parks Foundation (STENAPA) is developing a botanica garden, complete with an information center, to protect the secret habitat of the rare, pink-flowered morning glory. In the lonely bush and meadow landscape i the north more trails extend across the island as far as the **Boven** (964 ft/294 m)

Below: passion-flowers grow in the wild.

Treasures in the deep

Statia has at least a dozen interesting dive sites wit a historical slant, and is a very rewarding destinatio for underwater fans, however experienced or inexpe-rienced they may be. Sometimes an ancient clay pip may be seen on the ocean bed, but leave it there, it's against the law to remove historical artefacts. STE-NAPA is in the process of establishing a Marine Par on the leeward side of the island on the same scale a Saba's (*see page 149*). By the Old Pier in Lowe Town, **Dive Statia**, the island's top dive base, offers among other things, beginners' courses and snorkel-ing around the **Old City Wall** in the bay. Betwee the ruined walls of Lower Town's submerged build-ings swim brightly colored parrotfish and angelfish

The boat trip out to the other diving grounds onl takes a few minutes. The finest ones are illuminate by the morning sun such as **Barracuda City**, wher dozens of these silvery glinting fish glide aroun 65–80 ft (20–25 m) down, beside a miniature preci-pice. An anchor has been lying here since the 18t century, and there are more at **Anchor Point** and **Los Anchor**. Two wrecked ships at **Double Wreck** hav undergone a sea change over the past 200 years an now stingrays, flying gurnards and spotted moray live inside their hulls and cabins alongside vast com-munities of sponges and sea anemones. □

ST KITTS AND NEVIS

'wo sleepy tropical islands in a sea of blue, St Kitts and Nevis have 'oken up to what they have to offer the discerning visitor – deserted eaches, a relaxed way of life and hotels in magnificent Great Houses

All seems at peace in these two Lilliputian "fragments of Eden." Long before dawn come the first chirrups, a cock crow, the asthmatic braying of some irritable donkey, and the yap of dogs lying in dust hollows under apboard cottages. A chorus of cooings and warblings begins, a sound of entice- ent, an invitation to rise or to sleep on. Then a breeze starts up, bringing the ightest murmur of leaves rubbing together, the sudden staccato showers of ew drops on tin roofs, the dry rattle of tamarind pods hanging like rusty achetes among the mango and breadfruit trees, and the sensual scents of reamy white frangipani.

The sun yolks up over curls of pink-golden sand washed by the surf; shadowy lossoms of bougainvillea, hibiscus and African tulips erupt in sparks of reds, urple and white. Over by the well, a plump pawpaw drops and rolls down a ath to rest near the nose of a fat black pig tethered like a pampered pet on the eps of a lopsided one-room cottage. The heat comes quickly. Spiral wisps of iorning mist over the banana trees vanish and floorboards creak in the clustered omes of the village. A girl picks two mangoes and a bunch of plantains from ees near the path. "You gotta be awful lazy to starve on our island," say the lder Kittitians smugly.

PRECEDING PAGES: Great Salt Pond on St Kitts' southeast peninsula.
LEFT: St Kitts farmland in Dieppe Bay.
BELOW: passing the time of day.

Couched in the gentle northern arc of the Leeward lands, these two green volcanic blips of St Kitts and evis offer a cocooned Caribbean of yesteryear with uiet beaches, remnants of the old British plantoc- acy, and dreamy days under the silk-cotton trees. /hile the native Arawak and Carib Indians called St itts, the larger of the two islands, Liamuiga (the fer- le isle), today's static combined population of around 6,000 on a land area of 100 sq. miles (250 sq. km), ttle more than the size of Rhode Island's Providence, nd an economy dependent on tourism and sugar, night suggest a chronic case of backwater blues. But, 1 fact, this nation-in-miniature, separated by a 2-mile 3 km) stretch of choppy sea, is dealing enthusiasti- ally with the challenges of a go-it-alone economy, vhile at the same time, celebrating a varied and ibrant history.

irst British settlement

'olumbus, who occasionally waxed poetic in his amings, bestowed the elegant title of *Nuesta Señora e las Nieves* (Our Lady of the Snows – in reality, louds) upon Nevis in 1493, but then resorted to a ttle self-glorification by calling St Kitts St Chris- opher. As was often the case in those hectic colony- ollecting days, claims of sovereignty were largely rgotten and the resident Carib population continued smoke the "cohiba" tobacco, and delight in their diet of turtles, iguanas and other delicacies for at least another 30 years.

The arrival on St Kitts in 1623 of Sir Thomas Warner and the Caribbean's first bunch of hardy British settlers was followed closely by a group of French colonists and the peaceful island became a microcosm of traditional Britain vs France antagonisms, in which they joined forces only to eliminate the Caribs at Bloody Point in 1626. Over a century and a half of conquests and counter-conquests ensued until the 1783 Treaty of Versailles formally acknowledged British sovereignty.

Queen of the Caribbees

By that time the islands were thriving sugar and cotton producers supported by a vast army of African slaves, which continued – with infrequent recessions – way beyond Emancipation in 1834. In the 1780s, tiny Nevis had become a more significant commercial center than New York, a veritable Caribbean social nexus ("The Queen of the Caribbees"), complete with palatial planter's mansions and a fashionable hotel-spa. Horatio Nelson (*see page 172*), sent to enforce the Treaty of Versailles, was an attractive and eligible addition to the social whirl, despite annoying the planters by chasing away the "foreign" American traders vital to their economy.

At Nevis…a spa was established; and here, to this Tunbridge Wells of the Caribbees, came all the fashionable of the West Indies…
– SIR FREDERICK TREVES
The Cradle of the Deep

The road to independence was a rather messy process. In 1967 the three islands of St Kitts, Nevis and Anguilla, long jointly administered, became an Associated State of the United Kingdom. Almost immediately Anguilla ceded, eventually regaining its Crown Colony status (*see page 119*) and the islands of St Kitts and Nevis – never very compatible bedfellows – were left to sort out a joint constitution prior to their formal independence on September 19, 1983

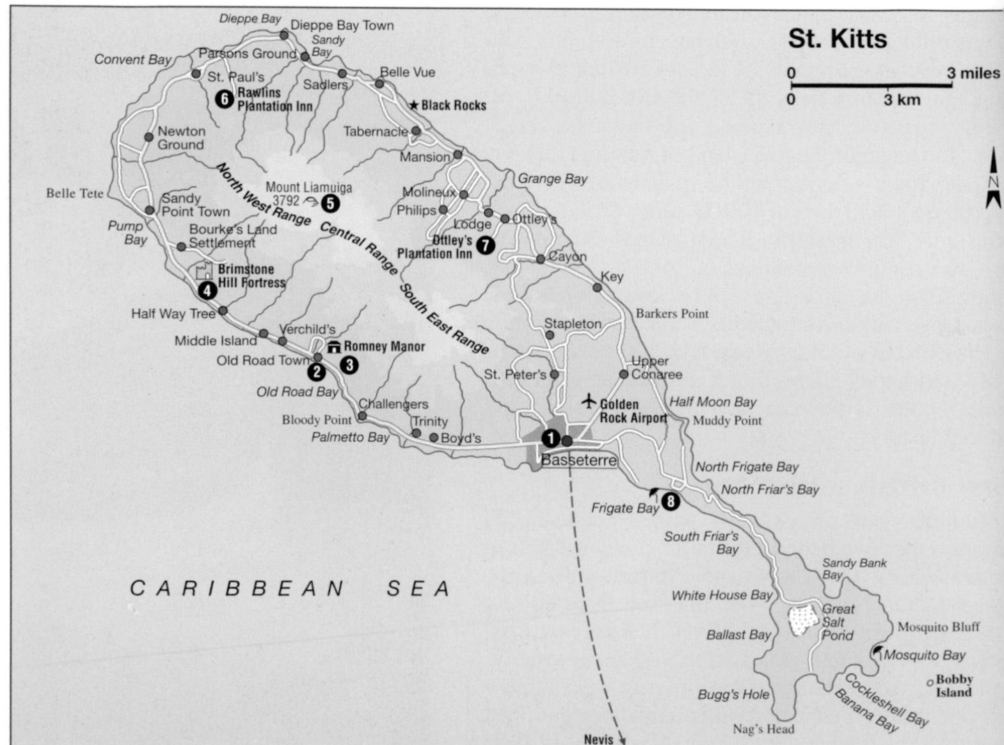

Nevis feared the economic dominance of St Kitts and made sure it had guarantees of partial self-government and even an "escape clause" if the union proved unworkable. According to many Nevisians today, that union has indeed proved unworkable and the spectre of its secession has dominated political debate in the twin-island federation since 1996. Despite arguments that secession would be a "backwards step" in an era of globalization and emerging trade blocs, those who wanted to break away remain undeterred. However, they narrowly missed their goal in August 1998 when 62 percent of Nevisians voted for secession, instead of the two thirds necessary.

The St Kitts Music Festival features top names from every type of music the Caribbean has to offer. The spectacular four-night event is held at the end of every June at the Fort Thomas Hotel.

Progress and pitfalls

While independence hasn't solved political or inter-island rivalries, it also has not cured the island of many of its social and economic inequities. The evidence that tourism is growing – along with the new wealth it promises – can be seen almost everywhere on the two islands these days, especially with the construction of Port Xante, the new cruise ship port. Many are grateful that the industry's slow start is giving St Kitts and Nevis a chance to do things right, but there are also some who feel that it is not coming quickly enough. That was evident in a recent and particularly lurid drug trafficking case involving money, drugs and the assassinations of a minister's son and the island's police chief. The case rocked the small local community and prompted the government to call in Scotland Yard for help.

The considerable influence which traffickers can wield in such small Caribbean nations is not hard to understand, given the continuing levels of poverty that prevail. It remains true that no one can really starve on these islands,

Below: the day's catch waiting for a buyer.

Political Mud-Slingers

Whatever energy is conserved in day-to-day life is devoted to exuberantly heated political discourse – always colorful, often vitriolic, but mostly confined to written diatribes in St Kitts' two rival political newspapers, *The Labour Spokesman* (for the Labour Party) and *The Democrat* (for the People's Action Movement – PAM). While the two parties sport nearly identical political philosophies, and devote equal energy to accusing the other of incompetence and corruption, most of the population is devoted to one or the other in large roughly equal sections.

Political affiliation is a major factor in everyday life – at work, at play and, of course, in the choice of which of the latest crop of scandalous political rumors to believe or to reject as "blatant lies and propaganda." The rare apolitical slanders describe this phenomenon as "Political tribalism", but while local-style politics is both highly polarized and passionate, the politicians and their supporters do abide by the rules of democracy and free speech for the most part: the bitter verbal brawling rarely becomes physical or crosses the line. If it does, their victims are quick to retaliate in court.

The critics argue that if more effort were spent on social and economic development than political mudslinging, the island would be a lot better off.

with a breadfruit tree at every corner, and there are indeed many Kittitians who like things pretty much the way they are. They enjoy the "liming" lifestyles, the laidback stop-for-a-beer-anytime spirit, the "pocket a mumps" attitude that suggests a pocketful of wages is cause for abandoning work for a while and enjoying the fruits of labor. But in these islands, like everywhere else in the world today, there are also many who want more than this. They want cars and cable TV, and they want to live in new "wall" (concrete) houses instead of in flimsy wooden cottages. And if tourism cannot bring these things quickly enough, there are other ways, for those who want them badly enough.

However, supported by the American DEA and Scotland Yard, the regional justice authorities have shown that the upkeep of law and order will prevail in the end. As a people still fired by the pride of new nationhood, there is an element of the national character which demands a better solution, even if it means a wait.

Basseterre – a gracefully revived town

This knack for patiently waiting to pick only the choicest fruits of progress, while preserving the best of the old ways, is nowhere more evident than in the bustle of a newly invigorated **Basseterre** ❶. After decades of sleepy existence and a long descent into downright shabbiness, this elegant old West Indian lady, which became the official British capital in 1727, is enjoying a second debut.

A five-year campaign to restore the town's graceful but dilapidated commercial buildings and dwellings, some of them centuries old, has resulted in one of the greatest success stories in Caribbean architectural preservation. Careful and sensitive restorations have revealed all the original charm of the traditional buildings, with their lower floors of rough-cut volcanic stone and upper stories

BELOW: a typical building in Independence Square.

f fanciful wooden gingerbread. Now what began as a successful exercise in ivic pride is rapidly turning out to be an economic success story as well. More nd more cruise ship passengers are enjoying the town's charm and beauty, and usiness is growing, with attractive shops offering duty-free products and souenirs opening up everywhere.

Yet Basseterre still booms with an irrepressible West Indian vigor. Crisply ressed traffic police sort out the snarls at the intersections around the **Circus** here an ornate cast iron clock tower, the **Berkeley Memorial**, regards the wirling scene with the pompous aloofness of a colonial plantocrat; bemused isitors and locals peer down from the balcony of the **Ballahoo,** a meeting lace and restaurant, at the frenetic salesmanship of the cab drivers ("Man, you otta want a taxi – s'way too hot to walk, man"). **Independence Square** nearby s now a pretty park, overlooked by 18th-century houses. Where once there vas a slave market is now a network of paths in a Union Jack design with a ountain in the middle.

On the Bayfront brand new **Port Zante** offers docking for cruise ships. Like verything else in St Kitts, the ambitious project took longer to materialize than xpected, and it didn't help when most of the construction barges and dredges vere shipwrecked by Hurricane Hugo in 1989. Completed at last, and described s "blended to the historic heart of Basseterre," there are now "30 beautifully andscaped acres" of prime waterfront property for which dozens of new shops nd restaurants, a hotel and a casino are on the cards.

In stark contrast, in the narrow alleys off **Bay Road**, chickens and goats nible at scraps, and opposite the almost empty official market, an impromptu fish narket draws a crowd of choosy buyers who nudge, poke and sniff the bonito,

When cruise ships dock at the brand new Port Zante in Basseterre on a Sunday, most shops open up especially for them.

BELOW: fortified view of Basseterre.

Large butterflies – orange sulfurs, malachites, mimics and Caribbean buckeyes – skim on fresh breezes after the familiar afternoon tropical downpour.

snapper, grouper, king fish and fantasy-colored parrotfish alongside a rag-taggle jumble of colorful fishing boats on the narrow beach.

The St Kitts circular

If Basseterre is basking in a vibrant new life, then the rest of St Kitts, as enjoyed on the 32-mile (51-km) loop drive, still remains mostly in a sleepy haze although there is evidence of an island in transition. The only real road wriggles through villages of pastel-shaded wood and breeze-block cottages with tin roofs overlooking black sand beaches, and backed by fields of sugar cane climbing up to the fringes of the rainforest around Mount Liamuiga (once Mount Misery).

Remnants of old sugar mills abound, as on Nevis, a handful have found a more productive use as elite inns and private homes. But in spite of the busy little sugar-cane railroad, the slow demise of the sugar industry is evident everywhere. More and more of the cane fields are being converted into residential areas, with modern "wall houses" being built.

The last of the Caribs

History interjects itself, sometimes subtly, in the form of Carib rock drawings at the side of the road in **Old Road Town** ❷, 5 miles (8 km) west of Basseterre, where the first British settlers landed. On the way, you pass the sad little ravine at **Bloody Point** where over 2,000 Carib Indians were massacred on a hot afternoon in 1626, as they were about to launch an attack on island settlers. Sir Thomas Warner, who led the first party of settlers, is buried further along the coast in St Thomas' Churchyard at **Middle Island**, in an ornate tomb topped with his rather self-serving epitaph. Above Old Road Town, are the ruins of

BELOW: Romney Manor, where batik is created.

'ingfield Sugar Estate and the lush rainforest gardens of **Romney Manor** ❸, e old estate house destroyed by fire in 1995. Here are the workshops of **Cari-ᴈlle Batik** (open Mon–Fri) where you can buy batik clothes and material and atch their creation.

Further north, **Brimstone Hill** ❹ (open daily; entrance fee) is history pre-rved atop a huge volcanic plug of andesite edged by limestone protrusions. A eat graystone fortress peers out over a panorama of ocean punctuated by the /o Fuji-shaped cones of St Eustatius and Saba to the northwest. Begun in 590, the fortress was confidently known as Britain's "Gibraltar of the West idies," until its humiliating capture by the French in 1782, just prior to their nal ejection a year later. Today a series of small museum rooms gives a use-l overview of island culture and history and café provides a welcome rest.

. walk into Mount Liamuiga

igh above the fort, the rainforest begins abruptly. Guided walking tours to the 792-ft (1,156-m) picture-postcard volcanic crater of **Mount Liamuiga** ❺, 'e available from tour operators in Basseterre. Follow sinuous paths up through ie cane and enter the gloom where the trade wind breezes suddenly cease. uzzings and rustlings in the undergrowth and treetops suggest a lively retinue f residents and possible sightings of green vervet monkeys.

On the northern slope of the volcano, off the circular road, is **Rawlins Plan-ıtion Inn** ❻, a 17th-century plantation house and ruined mill which has been ıade into a lovely hotel surrounded by beautiful gardens. Further along the tlantic coast, **Ottley's Plantation Inn** ❼, another converted sugar estate, ffers a spring-fed pool and short and easy rainforest walks.

Half Way Tree, on the Caribbean coast of St Kitts, is reputed to have got its name from the villagers cutting all of their trees halfway to ward off any jumbies (evil spirits) coming from Brimstone Hill.

BELOW: a siesta on Brimstone Hill.

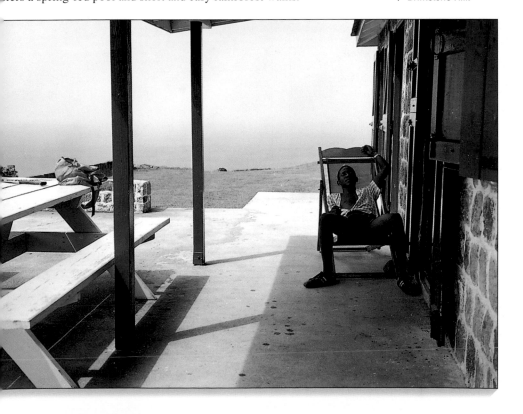

Alexander Hamilton (1757–1804), illegitimate son of a Scottish merchant, who grew up to be the first Secretary of the American Treasury alongside George Washington, kept his lowly start on Nevis quiet.

The wild beauty of the southeast peninsula

At the entrance to the 14-mile (22-km) southeast peninsula, **Frigate Bay** embraces both the Atlantic and the Caribbean with pale sandy beaches offerin watersports for all. The main island resort area, this is where hotel develo ment starts and ends – for the time being. At the end of the peninsula, the wi beauty of the scrub covered hills, desolate salt ponds and unswept seawee covered beaches is home to dozens of species of migratory birds and verv monkeys. The only sign of human life is at the very end of the road, whe Ricky Perreira will welcome you to enjoy a cold drink and sample the barbecu at his ecologically sensitive **Turtle Beach Club**.

The slow boat to Nevis

While regular short-hop flights are available between St Kitts and Nevis ever day, the ferry boat linking Basseterre to Charlestown provides an unforgettab 45-minute, 12-mile (19-km), nautical experience – a slice of island life in i most chaotic and charismatic form.

The *Caribe Queen* wallows alongside Basseterre ferry dock by the side c the massive landfill development of Port Zante as the loading takes place – mini-mountain of boxes, baskets, sacks of vegetables, a crate of startle-eye chickens, two trussed pigs (alive and squealing), three old bicycles and fiv enormous axes with brightly honed blades. The ride is choppy as the ferry rol past the velvety hills of the southeast peninsula, skirting Ballast Bay, Bugg' Hole and Nag's Head, catching the bigger waves in The Narrows between th two islands.

Outside the spray-splattered windows, the classic volcanic profile of Nevi

BELOW: schoolgirls go home shadowed by Nevis Peak.

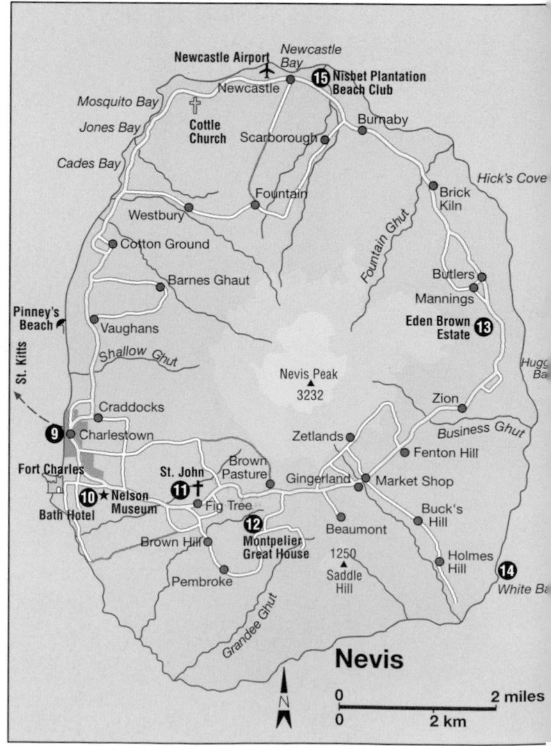

'eak rises 3,232 ft (985 m) into its perpetual cloud cap. Dense rainforest shrouds ıe higher slopes; lower down are tree-bounded fields and the remnants of old ugar mills and below that the long line of **Pinney's Beach** – 4 miles (6 km) of olden sand shaded by palms – backed by the luxury Four Seasons Resort with golf course designed by Robert Trent Jones, and several beach bars and restau- ants, this is the island's busiest beach and it still looks deserted.

Map on page 170

gingerbread capital

Emerging from its palmy setting, **Charlestown** ❾ (pop. 1,800) is a colorful prawl of pastel walls, tin roofs, and shady gardens. At the pier a hand-painted ign reads "Welcome to Nevis. Birthplace of Alexander Hamilton."

After Nevis's heyday in the 18th century, the town's fortunes fluctuated, hit y hurricanes and other disasters and the slackening demand for its sea island otton and sugar cane. However, Charlestown has retained a quaint dignity and rchitectural unity in its high-roofed, verandah-shaded, gingerbread-trimmed uildings on Main Street and around **D.R. Walwyn's Plaza**. At the top end of Main Street is the **Museum of Nevis History** (open Mon–Fri, and Sat am; ntrance fee) on the site where the 18th-century American statesman Alexander Hamilton was born in (it is believed) 1757. Set in a beautiful garden by the ea, growing typical Nevisian plants and trees, the museum charts the life of Hamilton and the island's history with all the proceeds going towards its upkeep.

Back at the Plaza, huckster ladies sell vegetables and trinkets near the **Nevis Handicraft Co-op**, where homemade fruit wines – pawpaw, sorrel, genip and gooseberry – are for sale in old soda bottles along with some fiery pepper sauce. Around the corner at the **Nevis Philatelic Bureau**, visitors flock to buy first-day

BELOW: a ramshackle house in Charlestown.

editions of colorful Nevis stamps (a useful source of revenue). And on Saturday by 7.30am, the town is bursting with life as Nevisians crowd into the fish, me and vegetable market down by the docks.

The Nelson era

By comparison, the remainder of this 36 sq. mile (93 sq. km) volcanic islan seems a sleepy, pastoral place. The 18-mile (30-km) road around the islan meanders southwards out of Charlestown to the shell of the once-fashionabl **Bath Hotel** ⑩ (open Mon–Fri; entrance fee). Built in 1778 to accommodate th cream of society visiting the natural sulphur spring (closed for renovatio nearby, the hotel spa is believed to be one of the first in the Caribbean. Th British sea captain Horatio Nelson was a central attraction here in the mid-178 when he married Fanny Nisbet, a Nevisian society widow, and the **Nelso Museum** (open Mon–Fri, and Sat am; entrance fee) has a marvellous collection memorabilia of his time in the West Indies. Their marriage certificate is on dis play in the 300-year-old **St John's Fig Tree Church** ⑪, 2 miles (3 km) furthe on, which over the centuries has been rebuilt twice and where there is a fasci nating array of tombstones.

The road continues eastward, circling **Nevis Peak** whose forested slopes hid a web of hiking trails, and wriggles past bursting bushes of bauhinias and untid bark-dripping gum trees. The spine-laden trunk of a sandbox rises out of a tan gle of Mexican creepers and lantana. A turning to the right leads to **Montpelie Great House** ⑫, the sugar estate where Horatio and Fanny actually tied th knot. In the 1960s, a plantation house-style hotel was built on the site, which i now surrounded by lovely gardens, and past guests have included Diana, th

Dick's Bar Disco, in Butlers on the east coast, shifts into gear at around midnight on Saturdays with dancing till dawn to live "steel-reggae".

BELOW: a poolside view.

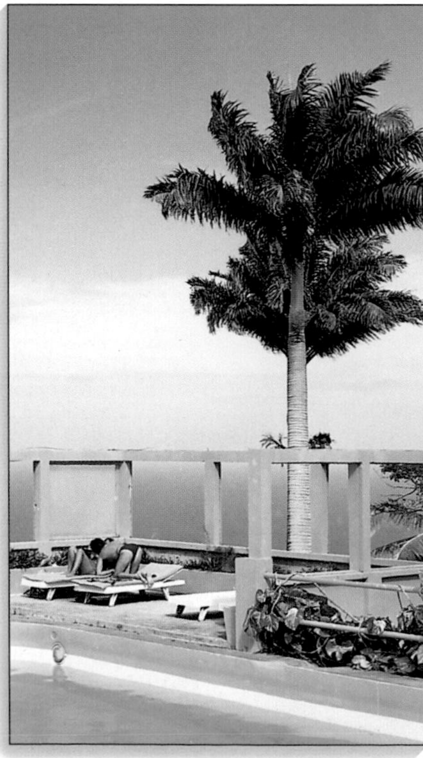

HORATIO AND FANNY

Horatio Nelson came to the Caribbean as Captain of th *Boreas* in 1784, to keep an eye out for any illegal tradin going on. After American independence, the new nation's ship were no longer allowed to trade with the British colonies, bu when Nelson impounded the goods of four disguised America merchant ships lying off Nevis, the island's merchants, wh were going to do business with them and whose livelihoo depended on them, sued him for £40,000. Their anger wa such that Nelson had to hide on his ship for eight weeks unt John Herbert, the president of Nevis and Fanny Nisbet's uncle bailed him out.

Based in Antigua in English Harbour (see page 182), Nelso hated the "infernal heat" of the West Indies and sough diversion on Nevis which was the height of fashion at the time His personal charm and his friendship with the future William I who was also based in Antigua for a time, eventually mad him a welcome guest in Nevis's Great Houses and he was soo seen with the attractive young widow, Fanny Nisbet on his arm

He married her in March 1787 and Prince William wrote "*Poor Nelson is head over ears in love. I frequently laugh a him about it...he married Mrs Nisbet on the twelfth of Marc (it was the 11th) and I had, my Lord, the honour of givin her away....*"

rincess of Wales. It is one of several tastefully converted estates on the island, here charming hosts help guests recapture the atmosphere of the old plantoc- cy days and is a perfect place to stop for lunch or a drink.

If you believe in ghosts, the abandoned **Eden Brown Estate** ⓭ (open daily; ee), halfway up the east coast, is supposed to be haunted by a bereft bride hose husband-to-be was killed in a drunken duel on the eve of their wedding. he remained a recluse in the house until her death and islanders say that she has ften been heard crying there still.

idden beaches

narrow track winds down from the road at Gingerland past typical cameos of land life to the hidden beaches of **White Bay** ⓮ on the southeastern Atlantic oast. The sea can be dangerous here, but on quieter days the surf is good and ou may have a chance to go out fishing on the reef with one of the fishermen ho keep their boats there.

On the north and west coasts, beautiful white beaches, fringed by palms and angoes, are quiet and deserted – ideal places to relax, Robinson Crusoe fash- n, and watch hummingbirds dip into wild orchids. The azure blue Caribbean a is calm and perfect for snorkeling and watersports. Popular opinion has it that e **Nisbet Plantation Beach Club** ⓯, near Newcastle, has the best beach in evis. The long, curved white strand, in front of the sensitively restored 18th- ntury Great House, is tailor-made for lovers. After dark, the sand shimmers silver moonshadows, night breezes keep the palm fronds clicking (and the oconuts falling), and the skittering surf sparkles with luminous phosphores- nce. It's hard to imagine a more idyllic setting for a romantic tryst. ❑

Below: the garden of Montpelier Great House.

US-49

ANTIGUA AND BARBUDA

With a white, sandy beach for every day of the year and waters cked by the steady northeasterlies these islands, set in the heart of the Caribbean, are a haven for beach lovers and sailors

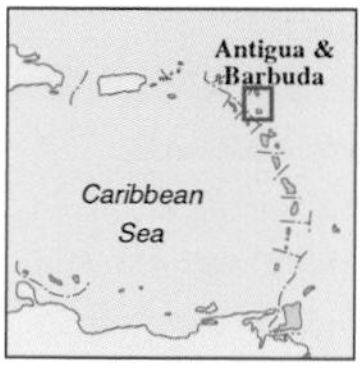

Shaped like a heart, the Leeward island of Antigua (pronounced An-*tee*-ga) shimmers in the heat of the Caribbean sun as the plane comes in to land. For many, landing on this 108-sq. mile (270 sq. km) flat island of vol-nic rock, coral and limestone is the first taste of the West Indies they have as ey wend their way to other islands. At the heart of the Caribbean archipelago ntigua, with islands Barbuda and the uninhabited Redonda, is edged by a autiful coastline abundant with bays, coves and natural harbours: 365 white ndy beaches in all so the tourist brochures say, and water sparkling in every ade of blue and turquoise between the Caribbean and the open Atlantic.

The vegetation on Antigua is limited to low scrub and dry grassland – the rests that once covered the island had to make way for the fields of Euro-an colonists, and the only real scenic variety is provided by a few green hills d scraps of forest in the southwest. But watersports enthusiasts love Antigua. vers flock to the barrier reefs surrounding the island, while windsurfers and ilors enjoy the steady trade winds. Every April, the international yachting set owd in for Antigua Sailing Week, when partying vies with sailing. The gentle aribbean Sea on the leeward side is perfect for swimming and once, during a ate visit, even enticed the Queen into its warm, soothing waters.

PRECEDING PAGES: colorful sails during Antigua Sailing Week.
LEFT: peddlers hawk their wares along the beach.
BELOW: a simple photographer's studio.

n experienced nation

ne pale pink sands of Barbuda 25 miles (40 km) to e northeast offer a desert island remoteness for those ho want to get away from it all and relax as Diana, incess of Wales did in the February before she died. is tiny 60-sq. mile (160 sq. km) island has a popu-tion of only 1,300 contributing to the nation's ,000, most of whom are dependent on tourism.

However, the self-confident islanders can look back a lot more experience than most of their neighbors nere tourism is concerned. During World War II, the SA used Antigua as a base for reinforcements and power, building a modern airport which created a itable infrastructure for tourism after the war. By 65, there were over 50,000 visitors to the island, d today the annual figure is around 270,000 counting for 75 percent of the country's revenue. an attempt to redress the balance, various agricul-al projects have been introduced and offshore bank-g and industries have been shored up with subsidies.

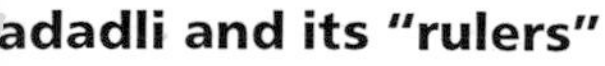

adadli and its "rulers"

1493, on his second journey to the New World, ristopher Columbus sighted the island and named after a church in his home town of Seville: Santa ara de la Antigua. It was first named Yarumaqui, eaning the island of canoe-making, by the Arawaks

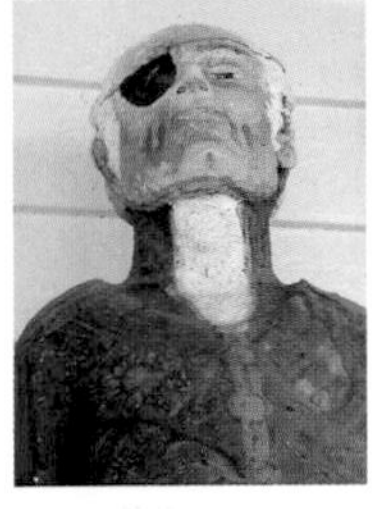

When Horatio Nelson (depicted above) was based in Antigua for three years in the 1780s, he was not enamoured with the island or the heat, calling it "a vile spot" and "this infernal hell".

and then the Caribs called it Wadadli, or Oil Island, and the name can still seen today on the bottle caps of a local beer.

During the Anglo-French colonial wars in the 17th and 18th centuries, Antig served as the Caribbean base for the British fleet. In 1666 the French briefly ca tured the island, after which it remained British when a white "plantocrac was established feeding off sugar production. When the sugar prices dropp dramatically in the late 1960s, the manor houses of the plantation owners f into disrepair; these days, only the ruined windmills are left.

The big Birds

Part of the crown colony of the Leeward Islands until 1956, Antigua was giv the status of an independent colony within the British Commonwealth in 196 and in 1981 it finally became independent with Vere Cornwall "Papa" Bird Prime Minister. From 1945, Bird and his Antigua Labour Party (ALP) had steer the fortunes of the island, and in 1994, at the ripe old age of 84, he was "su ceeded" by his son Lester.

The Bird clan's private fortune has been estimated at more than US$100 mi lion, and critics have accused the Antigua and Barbuda "family business" of level of corruption that is unique even by Caribbean standards, involving frau arms smuggling, drug running, money laundering and so on, interlaced wi the fierce rivalry between two of Papa Bird's sons, Vere Jr and Lester. In h story *A Small Place* (1988) the Antiguan writer Jamaica Kincaid provides particularly vivid account of this corruption. As long as the sun shines, howeve and the sea remains pleasantly blue, the islanders really don't seem to care a that much and Lester Bird is confidently looking forward to re-election in 199

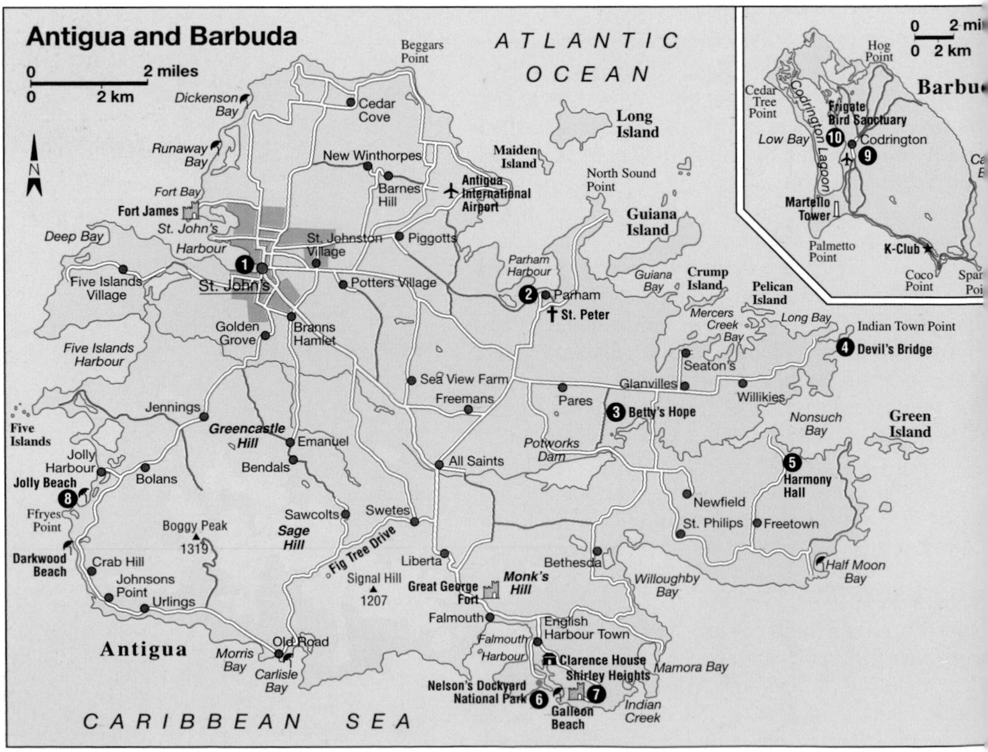

Antigua and Barbuda

John's – a thriving town and harbor

John's ❶ (pop. 40,000) in the northwest is Antigua's capital and is set ɔund its largest and most important natural harbor. The streets in the center are ɩed with typically Caribbean wooden houses; most of the historic buildings te from the late 19th and early 20th centuries, because a large part of the wn was destroyed by a seaquake in 1843.

Old warehouses by the Deep Water Harbour have been converted into shopng centers within practical reach of the cruise ships: **Heritage Quay** offers a ıs Vegas-style casino and duty-free shopping, and **Redcliffe Quay**, which ed to accommodate the newly arrived slaves before they were auctioned off the market, has been beautifully restored, retaining many of its historical feares, and is now full of restaurants and souvenir shops. Both are very pleasant aces in which to relax with a cocktail in air-conditioned elegant surroundings.

At the southern end of Market Street a block or two up the hill, the going gets tter in the colorful **Public Market** where fruit, vegetables and other produce ɔm the island are sold right on the street. The busiest days are Fridays and Satdays. No stroll through St John's would be complete without a visit to the **useum of Antigua and Barbuda** (open Mon–Fri, and Sat am; free but donaɔns welcome) on Long Street, at the other end of Market Street. Located in the ld Court House (1844), this collection of oddities provides an insight into cal cultural history. It ranges from Siboney and Arawak excavation finds to eel drums that you can try out for yourself. The most attractive items are in the ological section and include large coral skeletons.

The finest view of the busy capital is from **St John's Cathedral**, two blocks stward on Church Street. Its distinctive twin towers can clearly be seen from

TIP

Food City, Antigua's largest and most modern supermarket, is on Dickenson Bay Street on the way to the Deep Water Harbour in St John's. It is open daily from 7am to 11pm.

BELOW: shopping on Antigua.

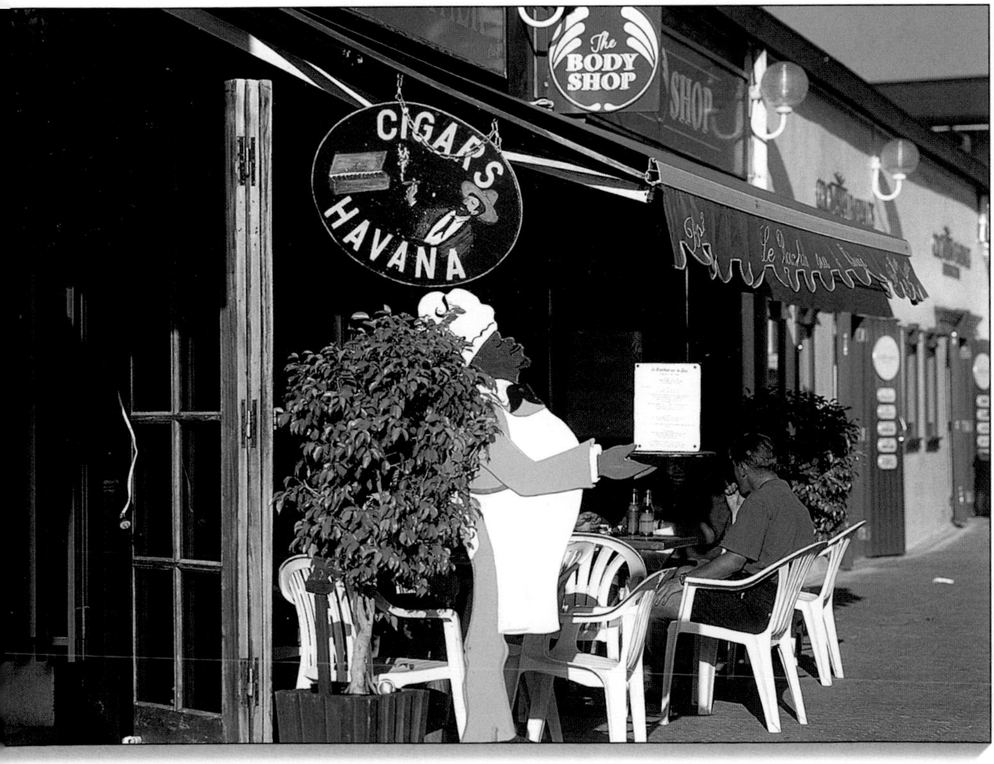

Wherever you see a huddle of men, you can be sure there will be a game of Warri (above) going on. Brought over from Africa by the slaves, it is played on a wooden board with 12 holes and 48 seeds. The aim is to capture your opponent's seeds.

BELOW: statues of St John on the cathedral gates.

all over the old town. This Anglican episcopal church is actually the third stru ture to be built on the site. The first church, built in 1682, was completely ma of wood, while the second (built in 1789) fell victim to the quake of 1843. Tl present structure dates from 1845–48 and, despite its exposed location, it turn out to be sturdy enough to withstand Hurricane Hugo in 1989 and Hurrican Luis and Marilyn in 1995, which devastated the rest of the island. The two sta ues of St John on the south gate were actually planned for a church in Guad loupe, but an English warship stole them during shipment.

The harbor entrance is protected by two 18th-century bastions: **Fort Ba rington** to the south, and on the northern promontory **Fort James**, which st has cannon dating from the colonial era and has wonderful views. The beach the bay below is St John's local beach and popular for beach parties at weekend Otherwise the impoverished-looking huts along the northern suburbs make clear that not everyone on Antigua has profited from tourism; and ironically, t streamlined luxury cruise liners still remain within full view, creating two worl that could scarcely be more different from one another.

The white beaches of the north

While driving through Antigua you need to get used to two phenomena: ama ingly fast minibuses, whose drivers prefer to hoot rather than brake, and almo no signposts. Make sure you are provided with a map by the car rental compar and ask the locals for directions – bumpy tracks included, Antigua has no mo than 60 miles (100 km) of road altogether.

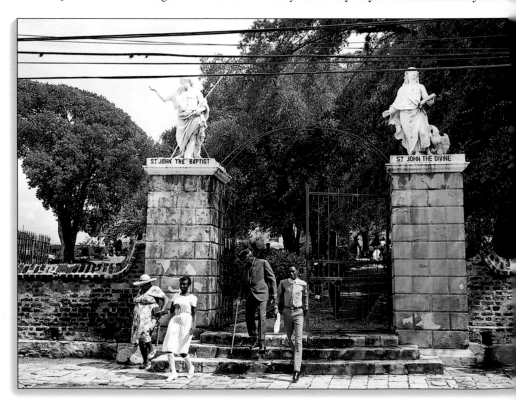

The stretch of coast to the northwest of St John's provides perfect conditior for Antigua's number one industry. **Runaway Bay** and **Dickenson Bay** are th mes of the idyllic white beaches here, whose assets the hotel industry has t been slow to catch on to. The prices bear a direct relation to how far the hotel from the water, with luxury establishments nearest the beach and medium-cat-ory ones further back in the hills. Dickenson Bay is well equipped with glass-ttomed boats, various diving schools, jet-ski rental and bars. The further north u go, the quieter beach life becomes.

uiet coasts and Betty's Hope

road, sandy bays nestle between weathered limestone crags along Antigua's stern coastline which is pounded by the Atlantic. It's advisable not to under-timate the power of the surf here, especially since no *Baywatch*-style assis-nce is at hand on these largely deserted beaches. The roads heading east out St John's lead to **Parham** ❷ where, in 1632, the first British colonists from Kitts arrived and started clearing the land of trees to plant sugar cane. The vil-ge church of **St Peter's**, built in 1840, is an unusual octagonal shape. Nearby e shoreline is bordered by several mangrove swamps which are now, owing development, a rarity on Antigua. From Crabs Peninsula to the east, you can ok over to the controversial development on Guiana Island.

About 4 miles (6 km) away to the south and east, in the middle of dry bush-nd, on the other side of the small village of Pares, stands the remains of **Betty's ope** ❸ (open Tue–Sat; free), the first sugar plantation to be established on a and scale in Antigua in 1674. In the midst of such a barren landscape, it's rd to believe that there were vast fields of sugar cane here once. The planta-n was developed by the British officer Christopher Codrington, who came to ntigua as governor of the Leeward Islands. His family lived in the Great

Christopher Codrington Jr (1668–1710) was renowned as a Renaissance man, theologian and soldier – not a contradiction in terms in those colonial days. In 1702, he founded a theological seminary in Barbados (see page 270) *and a year later he tried (and failed) to recapture Guadeloupe from the French.*

BELOW: Nelson's Dockyard, English Harbour.

An egret graces an Antiguan phone card.

House, named for his daughter, for many generations until 1921 when th abandoned sugar and moved to the USA. Today, Betty's Hope is a small ope air museum that includes the old twin windmill towers – you can see one them working – and also the foundation walls of the former boiling house.

Devil's Bridge ❹, nearly 5 miles (8 km) away at the most eastern tip of t island near Long Bay, is a natural rock bridge with several blowholes formed the incessant pounding of the Atlantic surf. Thought to have once been Arawak settlement, it is a popular weekend destination with the locals becau the offshore reef acts as a breakwater, and the sea is calm.

Another good beach at which to spend some time is **Half Moon Bay** in t south; because of its perfect almost circular shape, many consider it to be t finest on the island. Just before you get there, take a left turn to **Nonsuch B** 2 miles (3 km) away, to **Harmony Hall ❺** (open daily). A former plantati house and now known for its crafts and art gallery, it has recently been refu bished. The bar is tucked away in the old stone mill tower and moorings a available in the bay. The Antiguan Artists' Exhibition is held here in Novemb

Nelson's Dockyard and English Harbour

The quickest way to reach the southwest coast and **Nelson's Dockya National Park ❻** (open daily; entrance fee), 12 miles (18 km) from St John is to take the much-used All Saints Road. The first small town you pass is **Li erta**, which commemorates the first slaves who settled here after they we freed by the British in 1834.

A 30-minute walk takes you up Monk's Hill to the ruins of **Great Geor Fort** and panoramic views across **Falmouth Harbour,** splattered with whi

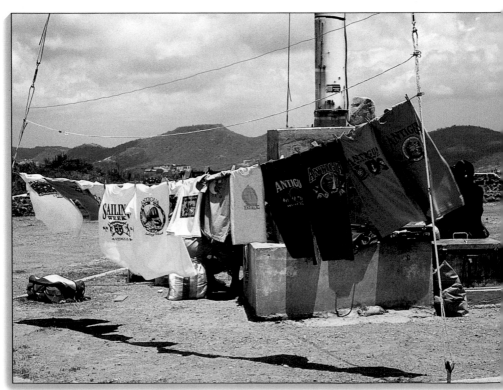

BELOW: roadside display on Shirley Heights.

ils. **English Harbour** is tucked away inside the bay, and was made a National ırk in 1985. The potential of this magnificent, protected, natural harbor was alized as early as 1671, and while tropical storms damaged numerous Royal aval vessels in most other parts of the West Indies, here in English Harbour and ılmouth Bay they were protected from the worst. Completely hidden away om the enemy out at sea, the dockyard was a safe place in which to repair the ips. Admirals Hood and Rodney have stayed at **Admiral's House** on several casions during their battles against France towards the end of the 18th century, d from 1784 to 1787, the young Horatio Nelson, commander of *HMS Boreas*, as based here (*see page 172*).

Today the former naval base is a picturesque yachting harbor. Warehouses and wder magazines have been restored with an affectionate eye for detail and ansformed into a museum, romantic restaurants and nostalgic hotels. The **dmiral's Inn** and the **Copper and Lumber Store** are two sensitively restored d atmospheric hostelries, with walls of brick brought over from England as ips' ballast. A lively place at the best of times, Nelson's Dockyard really mes into its own during the big regattas, such as **Antigua Sailing Week**, hen the bars and dignified restaurants – Colombo's, The Deck and the Galley ır – stay open all night and there's dancing till dawn.

hirley Heights – a perfect lookout

cross the harbor high up on the hilltop stand the ruins of the once protective rtress of Shirley Heights. At the foot of the hill is **Clarence House** which ıs built especially for Prince William, the Duke of Clarence, when he was ansferred to Antigua in 1787 as commander of *HMS Pegasus*. This typically

Learn more about English Harbour on an historical boat trip (departs noon, daily from outside the Copper and Lumber Store), or during the multimedia show at the Dow Hill Interpretation Centre (open daily, entrance fee) on the way to Shirley Heights.

BELOW: a "bishop" gives his blessing on Lay Day.

NTIGUA SAILING WEEK

rriving in Antigua towards the end of April you won't see suitcases rotating on the luggage bands, just bulky or's bags by the hundred. Antigua Sailing Week, 30 ırs on, is one of the biggest yachting events in the world, acting more than 250 yachts and sailors – from the rld-class cup-winners to the amateur sailing enthusiast. d you don't have to be a sailor either, for alongside the days of racing off the shores of Antigua are seven days ntensive partying.

Two days are wholly set aside for organized fun and ic in Falmouth's shallow harbor waters: Lay Day falls r three days of racing, when climbing a greasy pole, of war and a wet T-shirt competition judged by a shop" and other honorary majesties become the niest thing you've ever done; Dockyard Day celebrates finish in an even more raucous style.

lthough to some sailing is just a sideline of the week, re is serious racing all around the island for a range of sses. All sorts of boats join in from the small (with a dicap) to the high-tech 58-footer (18 m) with fiberglass s and a crew of 20 plus. And at lookout points, it's a nderful sight to see the boats turn into a westerly course release their colorful spinnakers.

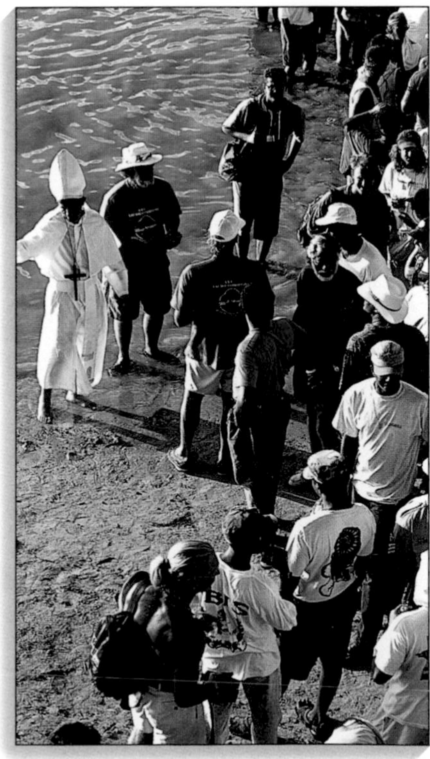

You may recognize a pinkish hue to the sand on some of the beaches in Antigua; that is because it has come from Barbuda where sand-mining is a large employer.

Georgian colonial building, with a pretty verandah and shuttered windows, nc serves as the British governor's guesthouse and country residence. But offic visitors don't get exclusive access, as the rooms full of period antiques are op to the public when the governor is away (tours are free, but a tip is appropriat

There's a perfect, 360-degree panoramic view from **Shirley Heights ❼**. 1781 Governor Thomas Shirley instigated the construction of the fortificatio to protect the harbor, and on clear days the excellent view extends as far Montserrat, 28 miles (45 km) to the southwest, and Guadeloupe, 40 miles (km) to the south. The observation point and the restaurant at the top are bc called **The Lookout** and every Saturday there is a barbecue and live mus here – steel bands from 3–6pm and then reggae until 10pm.

The feared attack by the French, which the bastion was supposed to preve never actually materialized. Most of the soldiers who died at English Harbo did so from tropical diseases rather than in battle. A marked path leads from T Lookout to the cemetery in which they lie buried; the ruins of several barrac stables and cisterns can also be seen, giving some idea of the harshness of ga rison life. **Galleon Beach**, right beneath Shirley Heights, is an ideal place fo subsequent swim, although it is only accessible by car or water-taxi from En lish Harbour.

Green hills and soft sand

Just north of Liberta, **Fig Tree Drive**, the most scenic road on Antigua, win its way down towards the southwest coast. The figs in question are not figs all but the wild banana plants which, together with a few giant trees and lian provide a vague idea of what the rainforest here was once like. At Old Road, t

BELOW: exclusivity is the name of the game on Barbuda.

Map on page 178

·ip continues northwards, hugging the coast all the way, and soon **Boggy Peak** 1,319ft/402m), the highest point on the island, comes into view.

Two of Antigua's finest beaches provide good rest-stops with a bar and restau-ınt along the way: **Carlisle Bay**, at Old Road, and **Darkwood Beach**, 5 miles 3 km) further on, both have astonishingly few visitors. In contrast, just around ıe next point, **Jolly Beach** ❽ (plus the yacht-filled Jolly Harbour) is full of ommotion and perfect service; it's part of the Club Antigua, the island's largest oliday village, and the outskirts of St John's are only 5 miles (8 km) away.

›eautiful remote beaches of Barbuda

arbuda is the ideal holiday island for those who love solitude, its sole attrac-on being the seemingly endless, shimmering and slightly pink-colored coral each on the Caribbean side. The landscape is flat as a pancake and scrubby part from the eastern "Highlands", which rise to a maximum height of just 28 ft (40 m).

LIAT, the island-hopping airline based in Antigua and co-owned by 11 'aribbean countries, provides at least two daily 10-minute flights from Antigua › Barbuda and offers an all-in day trip with a visit to the frigate bird sanctuary, ınch and some time on the beach included. Otherwise with no public transport ıere is little to see and do on this 68-sq. mile (170-sq. km) island.

Situated on the eastern edge of the 8-mile (13-km) long lagoon, **Codrington** ❾, ıe main town (or village really), where most of the 1,300 inhabitants of Bar-ıda live, is named for Sir Christopher (*see page 183*). The sugar baron was ·ased Barbuda by King Charles II in 1680 and the family kept it for 200 years. 'e resettled several particularly powerfully built slaves and their families here, ıd even today people still say that the Barbudans are lot taller than the Antiguans.

Barbuda has just three "sights" worth mentioning: ıe **Martello Tower**, a 50-ft (17-m) high former atchtower; **Highland House**, Codrington's histori-ıl manor on the highest point of the island, and the ·**igate bird sanctuary** ❿ to the north. Nesting sites f the unusually tame frigate birds are mainly located the mangrove swamps, and can be reached by boat.

On the southern tip of the island are two exclusive ·sorts, the luxurious Italianate **K-Club**, where the rincess of Wales stayed in 1997, and the relaxed **oco Point Lodge**. Both pick up their guests from ntigua in private planes.

edonda – a fantasy "monarchy"

ıe third island in this small nation, **Redonda**, 24 iles (38km) southwest of Antigua, is uninhabited – :cept for birds. This half square mile (1 sq. km) cky island, where guano was collected until the mid-e of the 20th century, has a history of its own: in 365 an eccentric Irishman named Matthew Shiell ıd the unusual idea of crowning his son Philip "King ' Redonda". He became a novelist and the title was ıssed on to members of the literati. Today's "monarch" ves in Sussex, England, and is very generous with s knighthoods: the Redondan nobility includes riter Henry Miller and pop star Sting. ❑

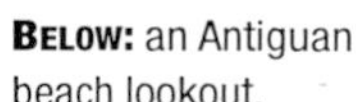

BELOW: an Antiguan beach lookout.

MONTSERRAT

Life under the shadow of the mighty volcano is not easy for the people of Montserrat, but those that remain in the "safe zone" are getting back on their feet and showing visitors around

Mountain Man used to live in a large stone house that he had built himself far up the green slopes that flanked the eastern reaches of the Soufrière Hills in southern Montserrat. After decades working as a builder in ngland, he had returned to his "Emerald Isle" home. Life was good. His house lso had a bar and restaurant where Montserratians and tourists went to relax. hen, on July 18, 1995, the mountain above Long Ground suddenly began to rrow up a dense plume of ash and steam. The "crisis" had begun, and two ears later, two thirds of the island was out of bounds. Not even the scientists an predict when it will end.

For Mountain Man, like every other Montserratian, nothing would ever be the me again. Indeed, when the mountain first spewed pyroclastic flows of rocks, sh and gases over the crater rim at 80 mph (130 kph), it was Mountain Man's ouse that was the first to be destroyed. Other flows followed, killing people (19 ed in June 1997), and devastating villages and towns, including the capital Plyouth. Nowadays, Mountain Man lives in what he calls a "shed" in the "safe" orth zone, but he is determined not to leave the island. He will build again, he ys, and restore his life to some sort of normality.

PRECEDING PAGES: a view of the volcano in August 1997, just before it destroyed Plymouth.
LEFT: buried in ash.
BELOW: examining a mud slick.

ow Montserrat used to be

or life "before the volcano" had been normal. This ay, pear-shaped island of 11 by 7 miles (18 by 11 km) rmed a gentle society. Its 11,000 or so people were ainly farmers cultivating the rich volcanic soil, civil rvants, construction workers or in the tourist industry. isitors included retired North Americans ("snow birds" ey were called) who bought or rented pleasant villas r the winter months, short-stay tourists who loved ld-fashioned" Montserrat ("how the Caribbean used be" was the marketing phrase) and, at one time, rock ars such as Paul McCartney and David Bowie who me to record and chill out at George Martin's famous r Studios, a victim of Hurricane Hugo in 1989.

Plymouth had once been pastel pretty, with gingeread houses in the Caribbean vernacular style. Everyhere had been green, except for the beaches which ere volcanic black. Like every other Caribbean and, Montserrat – which remains a British depenncy – had suffered migration, but by 1995 (despite e ravages of Hurricane Hugo), life seemed tranquil.

Montserratians are used to destruction by hurricanes but not by fire from the mountain. There were no lk memories of danger from the Soufrière Hills, spite the sulphurous fumaroles and boiling vents at attracted tourists up the trail to Chance's Peak, e highest point on the island. In historical times, ere had been some seismic activity. Nothing more.

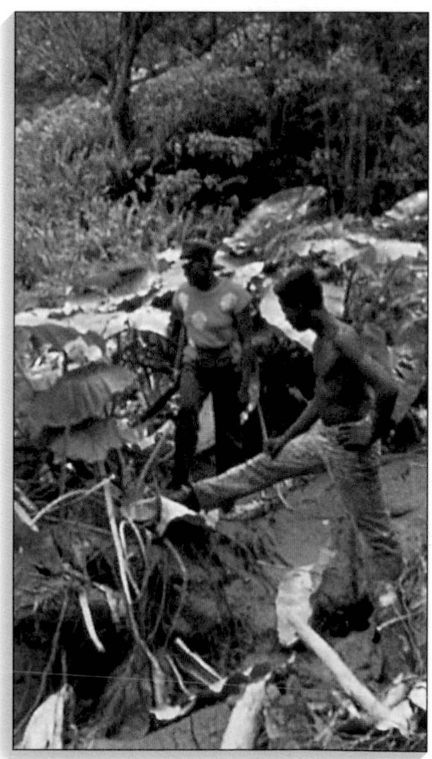

In 1907 Mrs Goodwin won a competition with her design for Montserrat's emblem (above). It portrays Ireland, as Erin, embracing Christianity with the Irish harp and reflects the island's early Irish connections.

An Irish-Catholic sanctuary

By the time Columbus saw and named Montserrat – after the mountainou ridges near the abbey of Montserrat near Barcelona – the original Amerindia inhabitants were no more. The first settlers in post-Columbian times were Iris and English Catholics finding sanctuary from Protestant persecution on St Kitts

By the middle of the 17th century, a typical Caribbean colonial structure wit an economy based on sugar had been established: a small Anglo-Irish plante class developing a social, economic and political power base over a growin number of African slaves. When sugar collapsed, and a post-Emancipatio society developed, limes and cotton became the backbone of the economy.

Gradually, a greater degree of autonomy was won from the British. And by th early 1990s most power lay with a locally elected government with a Britis governor responsible for security and external relations. Political tension between "dependent territory" and the "mother country" erupted in the "vol cano crisis" when the inadequacy of the relationship was exposed. Suspicion c Britain's commitment to Montserrat characterized the management of the crisi

In the "safe zone"

Those islanders who remain – some 7,000 had left by 1998 either for Britain c other islands – have had to relocate to the north, which remains untouched b the volcano (except for an occasional fall of ash). Its wilder landscape ends i steep cliffs, and beyond the dark sea are the purple outlines of St Kitts and Nevi (*see pages 162–73*) on one side and Antigua (*see pages 176–85*), on the othe

The "safe zone" begins at **Lawyer's Mountain**: a steadfast green ridge of tre fern and cabbage palms that would protect the north from all but the mo

BELOW: safe – an untouched estate house in the north.

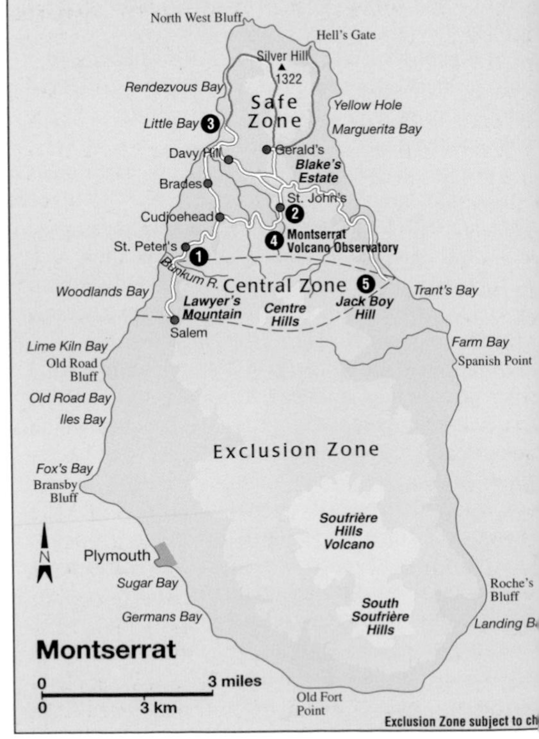

ataclysmic explosions. Close by is the hillside village of **St Peter's ❶**, whose our-square church – a shelter during the crisis – dominates the clutch of houses preading up the steep, main street. There are red poinsettias here, thorny aca-ia and, in the dry *ghauts* (gorges), breadfruit, banana, mango and soursop.

The roads in northern Montserrat wiggle, climb and plunge – designed for an thlete. What was once the least populated part has now become the hub of a ew Montserrat, with the sprawling village of **St John's ❷**, the new "center" bout 3 miles (5 km) inland. Everywhere there is evidence of dislocation and eprivation, but also change and development: people making the best of things. nd despite everything, Montserrat's reputation as one of the most crime-free ocieties in the world (so said the island's former British Police Commissioner) emains. The reasons, he said, were education and a sense of community.

While much of Montserrat's major attractions (Plymouth, for example, was rgely destroyed in September 1997) from the old days are now out of bounds, e Government is determined to reclaim its tourist industry. Where else in the aribbean can you watch a mountain grow? Accommodation, however, is lim-ed – although there are some bed and breakfast facilities. Day trips from ntigua are available (*see Travel Tips*) by the ferry (the airport has been partly estroyed) which docks in the northwest of the island at **Little Bay ❸**. What as once a deserted cove, enjoyed by divers (an activity still on offer), is now little port, and the possible site of a new capital, goats and all.

Map on page 190

On Boxing Day 1997, a pyroclastic flow of ash, gases and rock increased the width of the delta of the White River in the southwest of the island to about 1 mile (1.5 km). The water level in the area increased by 40 in (1 m).

iews of the volcano

isitors can now go to the **Montserrat Volcano Observatory ❹**, where the ehaviour of the volcano is monitored. And, of course, you can see the volcano. he best spot is at **Jack Boy Hill ❺**, on the east coast, here you can look down on to the old airport (there no longer air access to Montserrat except by heli-opter) and see the pyroclastic flow, like a grey-brown i slope, which had wiped out the people and villages its path, before almost hitting the sea.

When the clouds lift – and you may not be lucky – ou can see the new contours of the volcano. It's an ve-inspiring sight; and for those who knew the ndscape from "before", it's unbelievable. For the pography of the now gray Soufrière Hills has dra-atically changed. From inside the old crater, with its cient protective rim, a new mountain has grown. This stless dome kept growing until March 1998, say the ientists, at the rate of eight fridges per second. After at, it seemed to stop, but Montserratians were still able to tell whether it was just a brief interlude or hether the mountain had fallen back to sleep again.

But turn away from the smoking mountain, the ins of Plymouth and head to the green north. Hike the wild edges of the **Look Out cliffs**, to the moor-nd of **Blakes**, to the treefern gullies of **Bunkum ver**, a habitat of the mountain chicken (an edible og), to **Woodlands Beach** for a scuba dive, or to e coral strand of **Rendezvous Bay**. More rewarding, rhaps, is to keep company with the stoical people of ontserrat, whose lives have been refashioned since e "fire came from the mountain". ❑

BELOW: impromptu protection from the ash fall-out.

GUADELOUPE

French, but proudly Guadeloupean, this is an island of contrasts from the arid lowlands and white beaches of Grande-Terre to the mountain forests and diving grounds of Basse-Terre

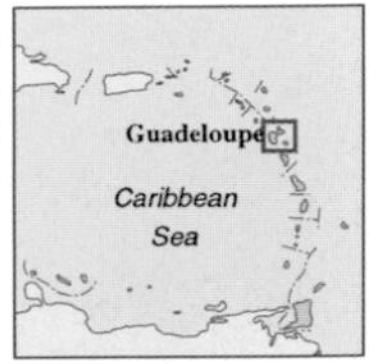

Butterflies have a short life span, but the two unequal wings of Guadeloupe – one dry and rocky, edged with its white ring of beaches, the other mountainous, luxuriant and crisscrossed with crystal-cold rivers – have een spread for centuries. This butterfly settled on the Caribbean Sea a very long me ago, many leagues from the coast of South America, and belying the gen-ral reputation of the species, it has survived tribulations that would have estroyed the more fragile of its kind. It is said that when Christopher Colum-us first set eyes on Guadeloupe in 1493, he immediately encased it in a casket nd presented the jewel to the very Catholic King of Spain.

At 555 sq. miles (1,438 sq. km) Guadeloupe is one of the larger islands of the esser Antilles and is not only diverse, but also complex. Beaches wash the ides of volcanoes wrapped in banana plantations, flat expanses of sugar cane row alongside winding mangrove swamps, international hotels contrast with vooden huts perched on four stones and major highways cross paths leading ver the mountains amidst giant ferns and dense forests.

One section of the population defends its ties with France, the other, its African heritage, although a growing minority refuses these divisions harking ack to slavery and proclaims a "Caribbean identity." Some want to keep the olitical status of French overseas possession decreed n 1946. Others brandish a red and black flag, stamped vith a crab, and demand independence. Some drive to vork in a BMW. Others trundle along in an ox cart.

PRECEDING PAGES: the magnificent cemetery at Morne à l'Eau.
LEFT: an Atlantic seascape,
BELOW: a fine place to relax.

A piece of France

Guadeloupe along with surrounding islands – Marie-Galante, Les Saintes and La Désirade – St Martin (*see pages 128–37*) and St Barthélemy (*see pages 140–45*) s a *département* of France; an integral part of the motherland – as opposed to a colony or dependency – nd of the EU. These islanders, like Martinicans, have French citizenship and French passports and have the ame rights as those living in France, around 4,500 niles (7,000 km) away. Flying or sailing into Guade-oupe from another Caribbean island may make you vonder if you have taken a wrong turning some-vhere: the four-lane highway from the airport is ammed with French cars, the large supermarkets and urniture stores are the same as those in France and the uburbs of the commercial capital Pointe-à-Pitre could e of any main town in the motherland. People hurry ome with their *baguettes* or sit in cafés reading *Le Monde* or *France-Soir* and the smell of coffee mingles vith that of Gauloises.

Financially supported by Paris, providing a higher tandard of living than most of the other Caribbean ountries, Guadeloupe's main export is bananas –

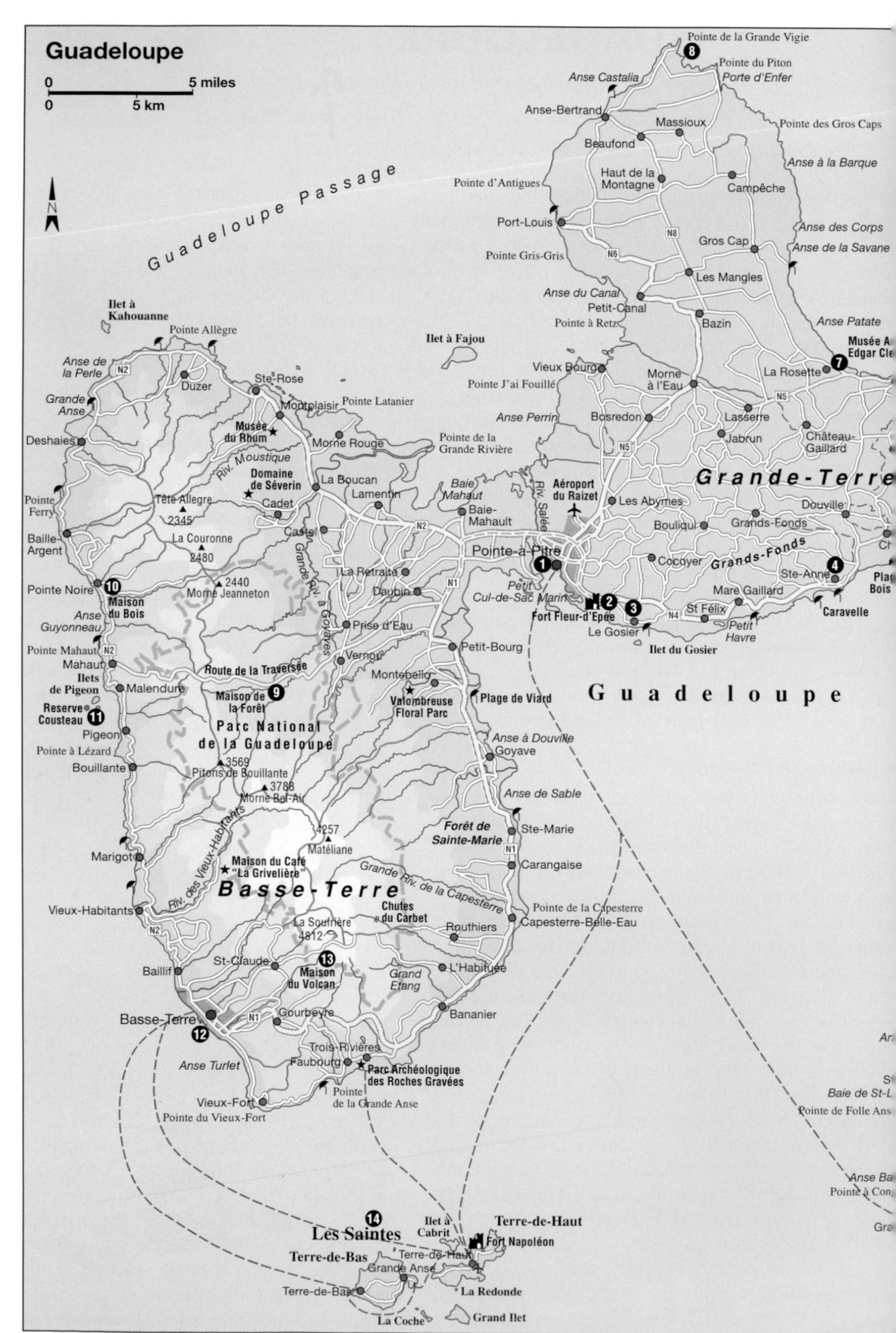
Guadeloupe
0 5 miles
0 5 km
Guadeloupe Passage
Grande-Terre
Basse-Terre
Guadeloupe
Parc National de la Guadeloupe
Les Saintes
Terre-de-Haut
Terre-de-Bas
Pointe-a-Pitre
Aéroport du Raizet
Fort Fleur-d'Epée
Le Gosier
Ilet du Gosier
Ste-Anne
Caravelle
Anse-Bertrand
Port-Louis
Petit-Canal
Morne à l'Eau
Les Abymes
Basse-Terre
Vieux-Habitants
Bouillante
Pointe Noire
Deshaies
Ste-Rose
Lamentin
Baie-Mahault
Petit-Bourg
Goyave
Ste-Marie
Capesterre-Belle-Eau
Trois-Rivières
Vieux-Fort
Gourbeyre
St-Claude
Baillif
La Soufrière 4812
Maison du Volcan
Chutes du Carbet
Maison du Café "La Grivelière"
Maison de la Forêt
Maison du Bois
Musée du Rhum
Domaine de Séverin
Valombreuse Floral Parc
Parc Archéologique des Roches Gravées
Fort Napoléon
Route de la Traversée
Reserve Cousteau
Ilets de Pigeon
Ilet à Kahouanne
Ilet à Fajou
Pointe de la Grande Vigie
Porte d'Enfer
Musée Edgar Clerc
Plage de Viard
La Redonde
Grand Ilet
La Coche
Ilet à Cabrit

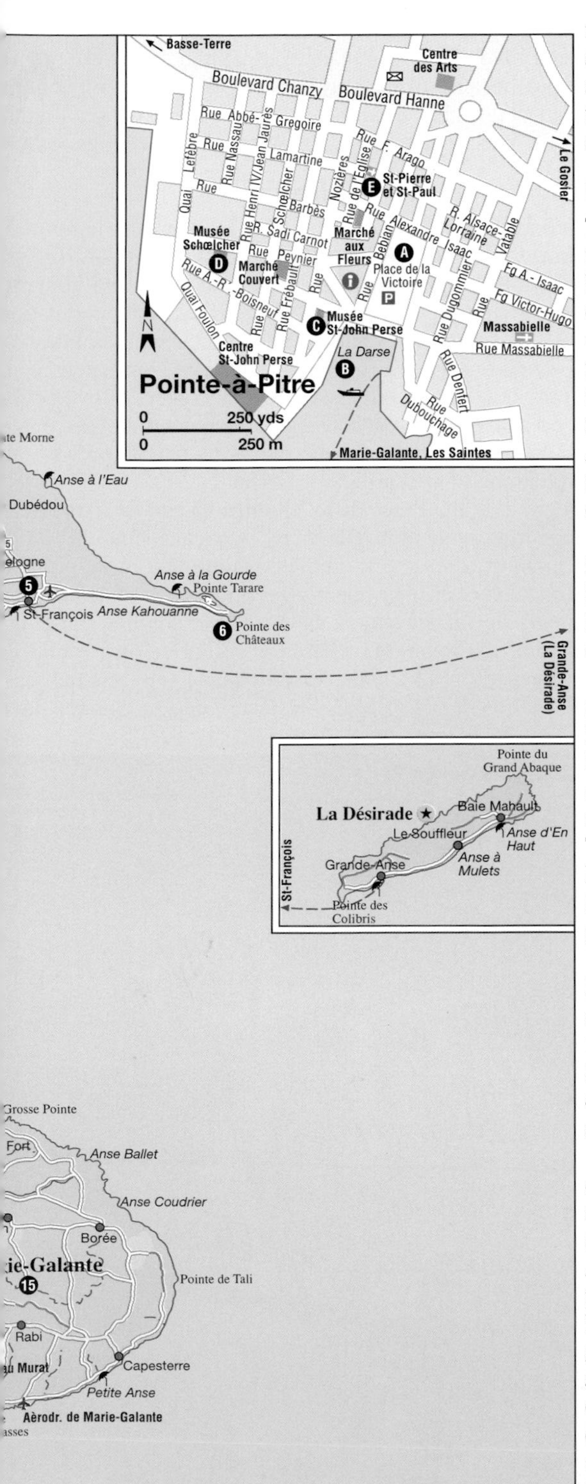

most of which are eaten in France – and sugar cane, mainly used for making rum, still accounts for 40 percent of agricultural land; tourism is rapidly taking over as the biggest earner.

Land of beautiful waters

The Spanish made several attempts to settle the island after Columbus had dropped by long enough to name it for the Virgin of Guadelupe in Spain. However, they were foiled by the resident Caribs who tenaciously guarded their Land of Beautiful Waters (Karukera) until the arrival of the French in 1635. Within five years, the Amerindians had been suppressed and soon a thriving sugar economy was in operation, underpinned by African slaves.

The British cast a greedy eye on the island, invading twice and taking control in 1759. They agreed in the 1763 Treaty of Paris to return the island to Louis XV – in exchange for keeping Canada.

Life took a downward turn for the *béké* (rich, white planters), when during the French Revolution slavery was abolished in the French colonies and a revolutionary commissioner, Victor Hugues, was sent to Guadeloupe in 1794 to enforce it. This he did with gusto, defeating the British, who had been invited in by the *béké* to maintain the status quo, and then guillotining 850 royalist planters.

When Napoleon came to power, Hugues was replaced and slavery reinstated until abolition was decreed in the 1848 Revolution that established the Second Republic in France. After that, 40,000 East Indians came to work on the sugar plantations.

Guadeloupe and Martinique went into decline during the two world wars, thousands of islanders went to fight for France and in World War II they suffered an Allied blockade during the German Occupation of France, cutting off the import of basic essentials. Afterwards, in 1946, integration into the Third Republic as *départements d'outre-mer* (overseas departments) of France seemed the only way towards economic recovery for the French islands and it would also whisk the rug from under the feet of the local colonial élite.

The two "wings" of mainland Guadeloupe are divided by the Rivière Salée. Paradoxically, the smaller flatter eastern "wing" is called Grande-Terre, which means large or high land, and the large, mountainous western "wing" is Basse-Terre meaning low land. It is believed they were named by sailors for the winds that blow greater in the east and lower in the west.

Since then, unlike Martinique, however, there have been several groups advo cating independence and many Guadeloupians who, although not wanting t break away, resent France because of the way top jobs are given to incomin French when unemployment is high; they also feel that their creole culture – a mi of African, East Indian and West Indian – is being swamped by all things French

Pointe-à-Pitre – the unofficial capital

In the high season, three daily 747s from France arrive in the modern airport o Le Raizet 2 miles (3 km) from Pointe-à-Pitre, on the southern end of the Riv ière Salée.They unleash a flow of tourists and emigrants returning home t savor a few weeks of sun and family affection (3 to 4 percent of the populatio leave each year to work in the factories and offices of metropolitan France)

Pointe-à-Pitre ❶ (*see map inset on page 197*) is the main commercial cen ter of Guadeloupe, whose population is inflated daily by a workers from the sub urbs. If you close your eyes to the low-cost housing developments and delve int the old town, you discover its appeal. In some places its balconied wooder houses rival those of the French Quarter in New Orleans.

Its many admirers regret that the **Place de la Victoire** Ⓐ and its flame tree (the century-old sandbox trees were blown down by Hurricane Hugo in 1989) where the children's nannies, dressed in creole costume and three-pointe madras headtie, used to watch over their upper-class protégés at play, has now been converted into a parking lot. Pavement cafés and old colonial building edge the square, the hub of the town and where the guillotine once stood. I opens out on to **La Darse** (harbor) Ⓑ and the boats that take you from the east ern side of the harbor to the islands of Marie-Galante and Les Saintes hav

BELOW: fresh country produce in the market.

ept the magic of yesteryear's sailboats. La Darse continues along the wharf here for three centuries the import-export houses sold red herring, lard and odfish and have now been transformed into the modern US$20 million **Centre t-John Perse,** housing 80 shops, restaurants and a hotel. Gone are the ocean iners which sailed for France, instead, a cruise ship throws anchor several imes a week and its silhouette blots out the horizon, raising the old magic.

Behind, on the Rue Nozières, the small **Musée St John Perse** ⓒ (open Mon–Sat; entrance fee) celebrates the life and work of the Guadeloupian poet who was born into a *béké* family as Alexis Saint-Léger in 1887. Although he left he island when he was 12 never to return again, he idealized the Caribbean in is poetry and won the Nobel Prize for Literature in 1960.

Mingle with the crowd thronging the **Rue Frébault**, Pointe-à-Pitre's busiest treet, another block away from the harbor, but avoid entering the shops to haggle over the price of fabrics since the sales staff are often impolite. Make a stop nstead at the **Marché Couvert** (covered market) close by, where the women sell ugar apples, sweetsops, soursops, mangoes, passion fruit and tubers such as ams, sweet potatoes, cassava and madera, as well as home-grown vegetables.

A few minutes to the west on Rue Peynier is the **Musée Schoelcher** ⓓ (open Mon–Sat; closed for lunch and Sat pm; entrance fee), dedicated to the French olitician, Victor Schoelcher, who persistently campaigned for the abolition of lavery in the French colonies and signed the decree in 1848. On the way back o Place de la Victoire turn left up Rue Nozières and, nearby, tucked away to the ight, is the **Marché aux Fleurs** (flower market) fronting the sand-colored açade of the basilica of **St Pierre et St Paul** ⓔ. Built in the 1830s with metal upports, it successfully withstood the huge earthquake in 1845.

To discover the islands' writers and artists, visit the Librairie Générale, 46 Rue Schoelcher, Pointe-à-Pitre. Here you will find books on every subject from fishing in Guadeloupe to local magic and architecture, and on the walls are paintings by local artists.

BELOW: jagged rocks at Pointe des Châteaux.

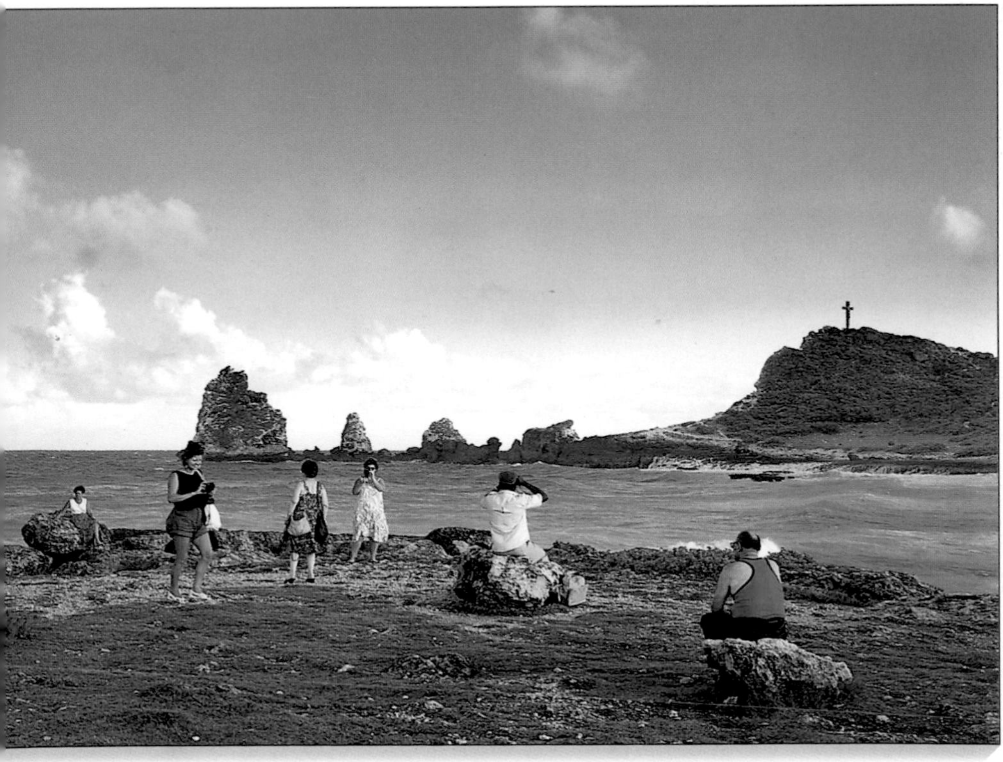

The island's only golf course is at St François, 25 miles (40 km) from Pointe-à-Pitre on the south coast of Grande-Terre. Designed by Robert Trent Jones, the 18-hole course is beautifully positioned.

LEFT: the waterfront at Basse-Terre.
RIGHT: sunset in Grande-Terre.

Exploring Grande-Terre

On Grande-Terre the flat landscape of sugar cane fields is dotted here and ther with the massive stone silhouette of a sugar mill, the dark green foliage of mango tree or the scarlet splash of a flame tree. But on leaving Pointe-à-Pitre o the N4, the south coast road, you come to Guadeloupe's main resort area startin with one of the biggest marinas in the Caribbean at **Bas du Fort**, about 2 mile (3 km) from the center. On the hilltop above, looking across to Marie-Galante an the mountains of Basse-Terre, is the coral-built, 18th-century **Fort Fleur-d'Epé** ❷ (open daily; free) which holds art exhibitions and has lovely gardens.

Le Gosier ❸, 2 miles (3 km) further on, is the hub of the holiday scen where there are countless little restaurants owned by the locals. The service i slow, but a Ti-punch (rum with sugar cane syrup) helps to pass the time. Try th humbler dishes not to be found on every menu such as breadfruit *migan* (bread-fruit slices cooked slowly with lemon juice and salt pork) and *bébélé* (plaintains green bananas, congo peas, tripe with salt pork) from Marie-Galante. This is th real Guadeloupe. The town comes alive at night to the sound of zouk (*see page 62*) emanating from the nightclubs.

There are several sandy beaches along the south Atlantic coast but the typica French West Indian village of **Ste Anne** ❹, 9 miles (14 km) away, sits on one o the best, while the Club Med resort enjoys another fine beach at Caravelle. Th road slopes down a further 9 miles (14 km) to **St François** ❺, once a quiet little fishing village and now an upmarket resort with its own airport for light aircraft and private jets, and a golf course. Ferries depart regularly from the opulen marina for the island of La Désirade 6 miles (10 km) away. The road out of th town ends 7 miles (11 km) on at the craggy **Pointe des Châteaux** ❻ where, a

final gesture, the rocks have been lashed by the Atlantic at its juncture with the 'aribbean into spectacular castle-like formations. You can walk up to the cross lanted at the Pointe des Colibris in 1951 for some fine views.

Map on pages 196–97

re-Columbian treasures

ack on the N5 heading north, after about 8 miles (13 km) you reach Le Moule, nce the capital of the island, where there is a series of beaches and restaurants erfect for lingering in over a rum punch and a plate of seafood. Just outside at a Rosette is the **Musée Archéologique Edgar Clerc** ❼ (open Mon–Sat; losed for lunch; entrance fee) which houses one of the Caribbean's largest collection of pre-Columbian items, among other treasures. This one is the work of ack Berthelot, an architect known throughout the region and a figure in the ndependence movement, who died in 1984 in a car bomb explosion.

Instead of following the coast road and taking a swim in one of the many heltered, hidden coves, push on further north, on the N8, which cuts across ountry of thornbushes and acacias for about 15 miles (24 km) to the **Pointe de ı Grande Vigie** ❽. Here the land ends in the dazzling realm of azure and the ea meets the sky. Only a few years back this area was a wild and desolate lace. Still undiscovered by the Club Med, it has become the haunt of scuba ivers and the strong swimmer who is not duped by the apparent calm of the lue, blue water.

On your way back to Pointe-à-Pitre, stop off at **Morne-à-l'Eau** faithful companion to the island's most magnificent cemetery, that is a true city of the dead vith funeral palaces of black and white chequered tiles. On All Saints Day in Iovember the cemetery at night is aglow with the flickering of tiny candles.

The racoon is a rare sight in Guadeloupe and is the emblem of Basse-Terre's massive Parc Naturel.

.OUSTEAU'S SILENT WORLD

When Jacques-Yves Cousteau (1910–97) was filming his award-winning film Le Monde du Silence (1955) : Ilets Pigeon, he discovered what he considered to be ıe of the best dive sites in the world. As a result of the ıthusiasm of this French underwater explorer and ımeraman *extraordinaire*, the Reserve Cousteau, a large 50-acre (300-ha) submarine park was set up around the ıy islands off Malendure on the western coast of Basse-ırre. Why this site should be so much more beautiful than ost others is because the hot volcanic springs around e islands have created a wonderful warm environment r a much wider variety of sea life than other Caribbean ɔasts. Forests of hard and soft corals and large ımmunities of magnificent tube and barrel sea sponges violets, yellows, flaming red and greens give shelter to a ıiverse of fish in all shapes, sizes and color schemes. orgonias gently sway in the silvery gentle sea in mperatures of around 82°F (28°C), and the visibility is ill perfect at depths of 65–130 ft (20–40 m).

To experience such a spectacular site, well-equipped ve shops with licensed instructors at Malendure organize dividual dives or courses. You can also rent tanks for each dives, as the underwater scenery starts close by.

BELOW: the *Nautilus* in Basse-Terre waters.

To the mountains of Basse-Terre

Now for the western wing, the mountainous **Basse-Terre**. Taking the N1 out Pointe-à-Pitre cut across the 60,000 acres (30,000 ha) of the **Parc National d la Guadeloupe** (also known as the Parc Naturel) on the dramatic **Route de Traversée**, 5 miles (8 km) down the road. About halfway along the 15-mi (24 km) route, edged with giant ferns, bright red flamboyants and rainforest, the **Maison de la Forêt** ❾ (open daily; free), a good information center whic provides maps for well sign-posted walks, some lasting 20 minutes – such as th one to the beautiful **Cascade de l'Ecrevisse** (Crayfish Waterfall) – or thre hours such as the Pigeon Trail. The route reaches the west coast at **Mahau** where you can turn right on the N2 and visit the **Maison du Bois** ❿ (ope daily; entrance fee) at **Pointe Noire**, 4 miles (6 km) away, a woodworking cen ter which has an exhibition of wooden household implements. Turn left an you quickly come to the dark sands of **Malendure**, the launching pad for th **Reserve Cousteau** ⓫, a marine park around the Ilets Pigeon (*see page 201*

The Parc Naturel has very few wild animals at all, and definitely no poisonous snakes, just plenty of birds, butterflies – and some beautiful flowers.

The N2 twists and turns along the coast for about 16 miles (26 km) to **Basse Terre** ⓬, the administrative capital of the *département* of Guadeloupe. Unde the shadow of the smoking **La Soufrière**, which last yawned and fell back t sleep in 1976, the old, colonial port, founded in 1634, has neatly planne squares, narrow streets and, on the south side, the ruins of an old fort.

Several roads lead up through lush countryside to the smart resort of **S Claude**, 4 miles (6 km) into the foothills of La Soufrière, where there is a informative **Maison du Volcan** ⓭ (open Tues–Sun; closed for lunch; free) an the start of some scenic trails. You can drive further up the mountain to a park ing area by steaming fumaroles and the fit can tackle the arduous 90-minut climb to the often cloud-covered crater.

BELOW: lunch outdoors.
RIGHT: heliconia dangle artificially in the forest.

Trips to the islands

At **Trois Rivières** on the coast south of the volcano two ferries a day make the 25-minute trip to **Le Saintes** ⓮ where, in 1872, Britain's Admiral Rodne foiled the French fleet's planned attack on Jamaica i the Battle of the Saints. A huddle of eight islands, onl two – **Terre-de-Haut** and **Terre-de-Bas** – are inhab ited. Without sugar cane, their tiny population is sai to be of Breton origin, descended from the pirate who used to stake out the seas. Today, they are skille sailors or fishermen, identifiable by their wide hat called *salakos*. It is worth staying the night in one o the several small hotels and inns on Terre-de-Haut t experience the tranquility of a beautiful island and th delicious seafood after the daytrippers have left.

From Pointe-à-Pitre two boats go daily to Le Saintes and three to the circular 60-sq. mile (155 sq km) island of **Marie-Galante** ⓯, which Columbu named for his own ship. Bordered by white sandy beaches, one of the most secluded being the hidde coves of **Anse Canot** on the northwest coast, the island still grows sugar for rum.

The islands of Guadeloupe abound in natura beauty. If you rush through your visit this beauty may blind you to other cultural essentials; you won't see the people for the trees. ☐

DOMINICA

The magnificent volcanic landscape of this "scrunched up" ·land provides bird-filled rainforests, spectacular waterfalls, a lake of boiling water and lovingly tended gardens everywhere

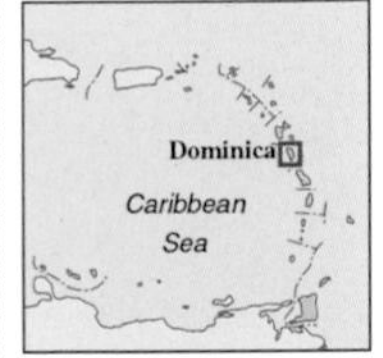

As Mr Rochester, the hero of Jean Rhys's novel, *Wide Sargasso Sea*, toiled up the path towards his honeymoon home halfway up a Dominican mountainside, he lamented: "Too much blue, too much purple, too much green. he flowers too red, the mountains too high, the hills too near.". Perhaps he ıight have said in more prosaic words: "Too beautiful for its own good". Not nly fictional characters have been overwhelmed by Dominica's physical presıce. From Columbus, who allegedly told the Queen of Spain that Dominica ›ronounced Dom-in-*ee*ka) looked like a scrunched up piece of paper, to the 9th-century British imperialist J.A. Froude and the 20th-century travel writer, atrick Leigh Fermor: all have been somewhat in awe of Dominica.

The largest of the Windward Islands (15 by 29 miles/25 by 46 km), Dominica es between Guadeloupe and Martinique. From the air, it has a dark presence, ›lcanic mountains disappearing into its dense, cloud-covered spine, forested bs of ridge and valley, carved out by the numerous rivers rushing down to the ·a, while the odd road threads a parallel to the coastline. With much of its sur-.ce still covered in some of the finest rainforest in the region, its 70,000 people ve in scattered communities beside the sea, mainly on the sheltered leeward side, · along the ridges.

PRECEDING PAGES: well cared for church in Portsmouth.
LEFT: craggy cliffs of the north.
BELOW: dramatic Trafalgar Falls.

protecting environment

he magnificent environment of this "Island of dventure" has been both a protection and a conraint. In the past, it protected the island from total ‹ploitation by even the most grasping of European lventurers and settlers as there were no great riches · be made with only small patches of flat land.

Although the colonizers managed to drive the resent Caribs from the leeward coast into the mountain ıstnesses and to the remote northeast, they were not ıtirely wiped out. The environment protected them. gain, in the 18th century, the forests provided a ınctuary for the maroons (escaped slaves) and it also ıabled a strong-minded independent peasantry to ›velop, cultivating "gardens", as they still do, in ›rest clearings.

The early settlers, at the end of the 17th century, ere small-timers, Frenchmen from Martinique, who aded with the Amerindians, cultivated tobacco, and ter coffee and cocoa on estates whose names alone *Temps Perdu* or *Malgré Tout* – evoke a sense of loss ıd resignation.

When the British finally took control in 1783, restling the island from the French (who continued · skirmish with the British through the Napoleonic 'ars) sugar, then limes and eventually bananas in the ›30s became the main crops. The banana industry

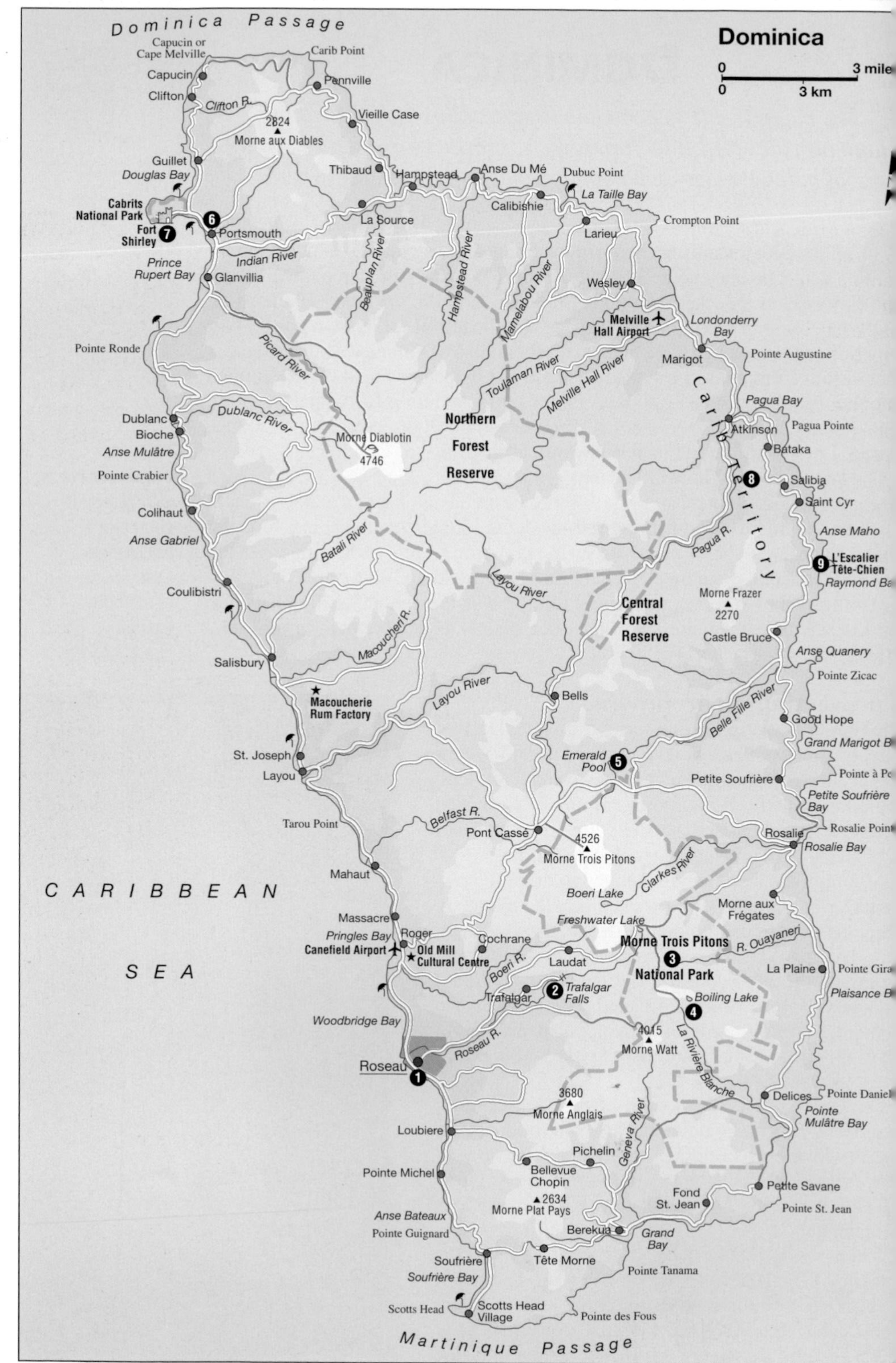
Dominica
0
3 miles
0
3 km
Dominica Passage
Capucin or Cape Melville
Carib Point
Capucin
Pennville
Clifton
Clifton R.
2824
Morne aux Diables
Vieille Case
Guillet
Douglas Bay
Thibaud
Hampstead
Anse Du Mé
Dubuc Point
La Taille Bay
Cabrits National Park
Calibishie
La Source
Crompton Point
Fort Shirley
Portsmouth
Larieu
Indian River
Prince Rupert Bay
Glanvillia
Beauplan River
Hampstead River
Wesley
Mamelabou River
Melville Hall Airport
Londonderry Bay
Pointe Ronde
Picard River
Toulaman River
Melville Hall River
Marigot
Pointe Augustine
Carib Territory
Pagua Bay
Dublanc
Dublanc River
Northern Forest Reserve
Atkinson
Pagua Pointe
Bioche
Morne Diablotin
4746
Bataka
Anse Mulâtre
Pointe Crabier
Salibia
Saint Cyr
Colihaut
Anse Maho
Anse Gabriel
Batali River
Pagua R.
L'Escalier Tête-Chien
Raymond Bay
Coulibistri
Layou River
Morne Frazer
2270
Central Forest Reserve
Castle Bruce
Macoucheri R.
Anse Quanery
Salisbury
Pointe Zicac
Macoucherie Rum Factory
Layou River
Bells
Belle Fille River
Good Hope
Grand Marigot Bay
St. Joseph
Emerald Pool
Layou
Petite Soufrière
Pointe à Peine
Petite Soufrière Bay
Tarou Point
Belfast R.
Pont Cassé
4526
Morne Trois Pitons
Rosalie
Rosalie Point
Rosalie Bay
Mahaut
Clarkes River
CARIBBEAN
Boeri Lake
Morne aux Frégates
Massacre
Freshwater Lake
Pringles Bay
Roger
Cochrane
Morne Trois Pitons National Park
R. Ouayaneri
Canefield Airport
Old Mill Cultural Centre
Laudat
SEA
Boeri R.
La Plaine
Pointe Giraudel
Trafalgar
Trafalgar Falls
Boiling Lake
Plaisance Bay
Woodbridge Bay
4015
Morne Watt
Roseau R.
La Rivière Blanche
Roseau
3680
Morne Anglais
Geneva River
Delices
Pointe Daniel
Pointe Mulâtre Bay
Loubiere
Pichelin
Bellevue Chopin
Pointe Michel
Petite Savane
2634
Morne Plat Pays
Fond St. Jean
Pointe St. Jean
Anse Bateaux
Pointe Guignard
Berekua
Grand Bay
Soufrière
Tête Morne
Soufrière Bay
Pointe Tanama
Scotts Head
Scotts Head Village
Pointe des Fous
Martinique Passage

ew spectacularly in the 1960s becoming known as "green gold" (*see page 44*). ut now challenged by the large Latin American competitors, modern ominica, independent from Britain since 1978, is looking to tourism as a main ovider of income and employment.

But unlike its neighbors, this island has no casinos; no multi-national chains, l-inclusive resorts with white marble pillars, golf buggies,"limbo nights" and cuzzis. At least, not yet. For visitors to Dominica glory in its otherness. Instead lounging on sunbeds on white sand beaches, they dive into pools at the base rainforest waterfalls or bathe in rivers whose cliffs are smothered in vines, ant ferns and the yellow-red claws of the dramatic heliconia plant. They hike to the forests, up trails that are still used by Dominicans to reach their forest ;ardens", past the buttressed trunks of great trees, such as the chatanier, or the ant of the forest, the gommier, from which the Caribs still make their canoes.

n the banks of the Roseau River

ot even **Roseau** ❶ (pronounced Ro-zo) – with a new shopping mall and ipermarkets – can escape the impact of the island's hinterland, the essentially ;ricultural base of Dominican society. For every Saturday – from before first ght until mid-morning – the capital (pop. 8,000) hosts market day. There, side the mouth of the Roseau River with its backdrop of mountain and forest, laid out the bounty of the land. From armfuls of ginger lilies, to sacks of m, from coffee beans to avocados, watercress to coconuts, all are gathered into is place of plenty, an endlessly festive endorsement of Dominica's national otto: *Apres Bondie Cest La Ter* (After God it is the land).

Roseau is a bustling little town with a small, 18th-century French quarter,

For a scuba site with a difference head for Champagne by Scotts Head in the southeast where you can swim through underwater hot spring bubbles and watch myriad sea life – it's even better at night.

BELOW: a typical shop in Roseau.

The blending of Carib, French and British cultures are celebrated on Creole Day in November, when Roseau comes alive with the swirl of 18th-century petticoats and the jangle of gold jewelry.

surrounded by 19th-century streets, their wood and stone houses support ove hanging verandahs and gingerbread fretwork. A newly built Bay Front, wi an imaginative **museum** (open Mon–Sat; entrance fee) housed in the old Pc Office, has extended the once narrow waterfront. But now that middle-cla Dominicans (known in the old days as the *gros bourg*) prefer to live in th cooler suburbs, many of the old town houses and their gardens have been pull down and replaced by somewhat charmless concrete buildings.

There are, though, the still splendid **Botanical Gardens** (open daily; free despite the destruction wrought by Hurricane David, in 1979, which reduced tl 40-acre (16-ha) site to a "junkyard of tree limbs" – the remains of a school b can still be seen beneath the large baobab tree that crushed it. Successful restored, the gardens, on the northeastern edge of the town, make the perfect se ting for a cricket ground and there is an aviary for Dominica's endangered Si serou and Jaco parrots.

Volcanic wonders

Heading inland for 5 miles (8 km) past the Botanical Gardens, you reach **Trafa gar Falls ❷** (open daily; entrance fee – tickets to attractions are also availab from travel agents, car-hire and tour operators), two spectacular waterfall They are a 10-minute walk from the tropical gardens and inn at **Papillo Wilderness Retreat** (see below). You may be besieged by guides here but yc will only need one if you want to go further than the viewing platform.

Trafalgar Falls is on the southeastern edge of the magnificent **Morne Tro Pitons National Park ❸** which covers 17,000 acres (6,800 ha) of the southe central part of the island. Those with more than an average dose of energy ca

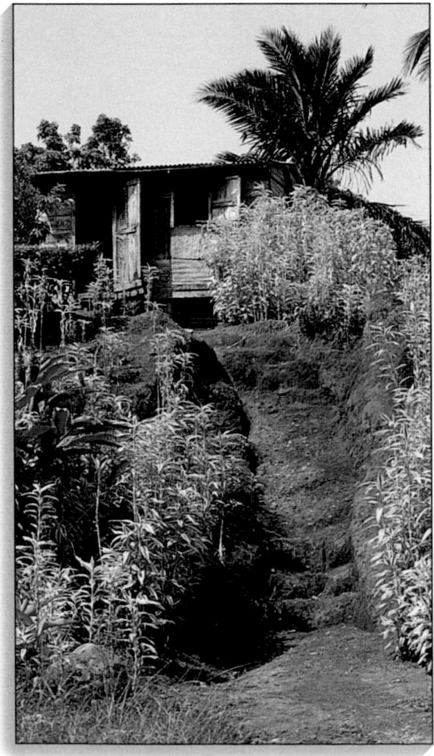

BELOW: a carefully tended Carib garden.

ISLAND GARDENS

All Dominicans are wedded to the land, from the fir Amerindians, who brought with them many of th fruit and vegetables now native to the island, the maroon who survived by farming in the forests, and the slave with their provision grounds, to the colonizers, who sa that plants from other parts of the world could flourish the Caribbean. This was particularly true of Dominic whose dramatic landscape provides a different mi climate in every corner – it seems that every flower, fru and vegetable from the garden of Eden can prosper her

Dominicans welcome visitors to their lovingly tende patches whether they be the market gardens of **Giraud** or a beautifully laid out Roseau back yard. But it's importa to call first. This you can do through the **Papillo Wilderness Retreat**, near Trafalgar Falls (tel: 448-228 open daily; garden tour fee), where an array of tropic flowers complement the natural contours and vegetation the rainforest. "They blend from nurtured collections in wilderness," says creator Anne Jno Baptiste.

Close by is **D'Auchamps Estate** (tel: 448-3346; ope daily; entrance fee) where the Honychurch family ha made delightful walkways through natural dry forest shov ing off Dominica's abundance to its best advantage.

ke to the **Boiling Lake** ❹, the second largest cauldron of bubbling hot water 20 ft/66 m wide) in the world, which lies in the heart of the park. This geo-gical phenomenon is, in fact, a flooded fumarole, from where hot gases escape rough vents in the earth's molten crust. It's a tough but extraordinary journey n 8-hour round trip), which starts at **Titou Gorge**, close to the village of **Lau-t**, 6 miles (10 km) northeast of Roseau. The track plunges and rises, crosses reams and climbs up to narrow ridges opening up into a lunar landscape of eaming vents and geysers, hot pools of boiling mud and mineral streams reaked with blue, orange, black and yellow. This is the **Valley of Desolation** and beyond that the Boiling Lake itself, stirring restlessly within its crater. nose who make the pilgrimage feel they belong to a special club…

ainforest birdlife

n the northeastern edge of the park, off the Castle Bruce road, lies the pretty **merald Pool** ❺ in the heart of lush green rainforest where you can have a pic-c, stand behind the 40-ft (12-m) waterfall and cool off with a dip.

Along the lower reaches of the **Central Forest Reserve**, travelers are some-nes accompanied by the sound of a squeaking gate. This, in fact, is the melan-nolic call of the rufous-throated solitaire (known locally as Sifflé Moutayn) hoing across the forest canopy. Local lore has it that this perky-looking thrush a magical spirit whose call tempts travellers further and further into the forest.

While Dominica cannot compete with Trinidad, for example, in its extrava-nt range of bird life (*see pages 276–81*), there are 166 species to keep bird-atchers happy. Such an assortment within the confines of a small island is a flection of the remarkable diversity of vegetation.

Map on page 208

TIP

If you are lucky you may see female whales and their young swim close to your boat on a whale-watching trip off the west coast, as well as schools of dolphin. Contact local dive shops for information.

BELOW: Indian River, once traveled by Columbus.

Fortifications in spectacular surroundings

In dramatic contrast to the gnarled and battered elfin woodland – high, win and watered by 300 in (760 cm) of rain annually – there is, for example, the d tropical forest of the Caribbean coast. The spectacular headland of the **Cabri National Park**, 25 miles (40 km) north of Roseau and close to the second tov of **Portsmouth** ❻, is covered with bay, mahogany, sandbox, white cedar a logwood. And there in the heat among the silent trees are the ruins of the 18t century British fortifications, **Fort Shirley** ❼ (open daily; entrance fee), on one of the most important military sites in the West Indies, complete with g batteries, storehouses and officers' quarters. During the colonial wars, it hous up to 600 men, protecting both the north of the island and Prince Rupert Bay the south. The Cabrits Peninsula has the added attraction of being surround by a **marine park**, rich in underwater life and excellent for snorkeling and divi

Dominica's two endangered parrots, the Sisserou and red-necked jaco, live on the slopes of Morne Diablotin in the north. You may spot one with the help of the Forestry Division (tel: 448-2401) who can provide a guide.

Another habitat, close by the Cabrits and with yet another story to tell, is t wetlands around the **Indian River**, just south of **Prince Rupert Bay**. It was in this bay that Columbus sailed on November 3, 1493, the day he first sight Dominica, and it was the Caribs of the Indian River area who provided subs quent European sailors with water and shelter, pineapples and cassava. T boat trip from the coastal road at the river mouth (avoid boats with outboa motors which disturb the vegetation) up this haunting gray-green waterway fo lows the route European sea captains took to greet the Carib chief.

A remaining Carib settlement

Today, the surviving Caribs, live along the northeastern seaboard (take the ro east from Portsmouth to Pagua Bay) in coconut and banana country– althou they still grow cassava – edging the wild Atlantic. T **Carib Territory** ❽ was set aside for them in 1903 b a well-meaning British administrator called Heske Bell, who thought they would die out unless they we guaranteed a "reservation" of their own. Today, t area is not in itself distinctive but you will see hous built on stilts, and stalls on the roadside display t unique basketwork of the Caribs (finely woven i three colors from a forest reed), the lingering legacy an ancient culture.

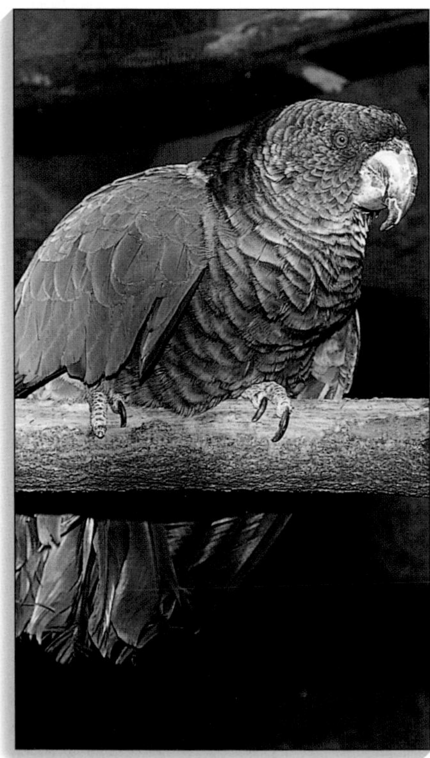

BELOW: Dominica's endangered Sisserou parrot.

L'Escalier Tête-Chien ❾ (the snake's staircase a rock formation that looks like a stone serpent slit ering up out of the ocean, further southward alon this dramatic coastline, features extensively in Cari folklore.

But while modernity has been embraced by wealth ier Dominicans – the Internet, holidays abroad an American TV soaps (electricity only reached the eas coast in the mid-1980s) – there is a characteristic gen tleness about Dominican villages, from a southeaster community such as **Petit Savanne**, set among sweet smelling bay trees, to the breezy hillside of remot **Capucin** in the north. Church, school, shop are th public face of village life, while the yard remains th center of the family's economic and social activity: place to make brooms from the vines, to store provi sions, such as yam and dasheen, to hang green bananas or to gossip in the cooler hours of the day. ☐

Carib Indians

When the first European settlers came face to face with the Caribs already living on the islands of the Eastern Caribbean at the beginning of the 17th century, it was not a time for exchanging pleasantries. These Amerindians had made their way up from South America a few centuries earlier in 75-ft (23-m) boats, hewn from massive gommier trees, which held 50 people apiece, and had fought with the resident Arawaks for their land.

They were not going to give in to the new invaders easily. After all, as one Carib chief remarked ironically to French soldiers, "We have not gone over to your country to take it, so why have you come over to take ours?"

When Christopher Columbus had arrived in the Bahamas in 1493, the Indians (as he called them because he thought he was in India) for the most part had been friendly and provided sailors with food and water. His first impressions of them, recorded in his journal were that they were timid and unwarlike: "They should be good servants and intelligent, for I observed that they quickly took in what was said to them." And he set about enslaving them to help in the Spanish quest for gold.

Word also spread at that time that these "pagan savages", with their almond eyes, high cheekbones, copper-colored skin and straight black hair, ate their captives, roasted on a spit. Historians now say that this was a scurrilous tale put about by the Spanish who wanted to justify their un-Christian methods of slavery and cruelty. However, it is understood they may have practised some form of ritual cannibalism in that they would eat a piece of heart of a courageous enemy or beloved chieftain, believing they would receive a portion of their courage or goodness.

Rebelling against Spanish cruelty, the Caribs fled to the impenetrable mountain forests of Dominica, from where they were able to launch attacks on other islands such as Antigua and Barbuda. In the 17th century they were also living on St Lucia and Grenada, keeping the colonists at bay with showers of arrows tipped with poison from the manchineel tree. Eventually, European weaponry and disease won the day and any that were left were beaten back to the protective arm of Dominica where a small enclave still remains.

Caribs painted their bodies red and wore feathers and beads of stone, bone and teeth for decoration; the chiefs wore crowns and gold ornaments. They participated in a trade network that stretched for thousands of miles between the islands and South America. They grew cassava (manioc), maize, beans, squash and peppers for food, along with tobacco, cotton (for hammocks) and annatto (for body paint). They fished, hunted and gathered shells, crabs and turtle eggs and the women planted, weeded, harvested and prepared meals which included turtles, iguanas and "pepperpot" stews (*see pages 71–72*).

Early European travelers wrote about a Utopian life of ease, in which the Caribs saw each other as equal, none richer nor poorer than another. "Each man does what pleases him," wrote one 16th-century traveler, "and permits no one to give him orders." ❑

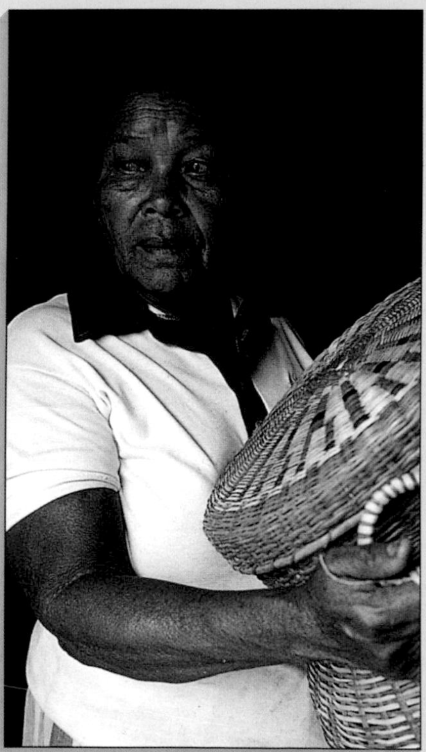

RIGHT: making basketware in the Carib Territory on Dominica.

TROPICAL BOUNTY OF THE ISLANDS

Flowers of the forest, fruit of the trees, vegetables from the ground – under the blazing sun there's a treasure trove of color, dazzling greenery and food

Like the people of the Eastern Caribbean, the flora of the region is a great melting pot. There were plants that were here before man, plants brought by the Caribs in their canoes when they paddled from South America, those which came from Africa during slavery and those brought from all over the world by the adventuresome Europeans.

For visitors to the region from North America or northern Europe, familiar only with expensive houseplants nurtured in a centrally heated room or the exotic fruit and vegetable section in the supermarket, the sudden sight of these magnificent plants growing naturally in a tropical landscape is intoxicating.

MARKET DAY

Venture into a local market in the rainier, more mountainous islands and explore the unfamiliar: the knobbly soursop (it makes an excellent juice); the pale green christophene or cho-cho of the squash family; tiny green and red peppers, some fiendishly hot. Drier islands will not have such a range, but there will be "ground provisions" – the root vegetables such as yams, which are part of the staple diet. And there are the cut flowers: the amazing red or pink gingers, artificial-looking anthurium and dramatic torch gingers. Everyone grows something somewhere.

And while there are the formal botanical gardens, or gardens of former estate houses to visit, don't forget to admire the ordinary backyard garden growing an amazing range of vegetables, fruit and exotic flowers often in just a tiny space.

△ **PINEAPPLE PUNCH**
"None pleases my tastes as does the pine," wrote George Washington in his diary during a visit to Barbados in 1751.

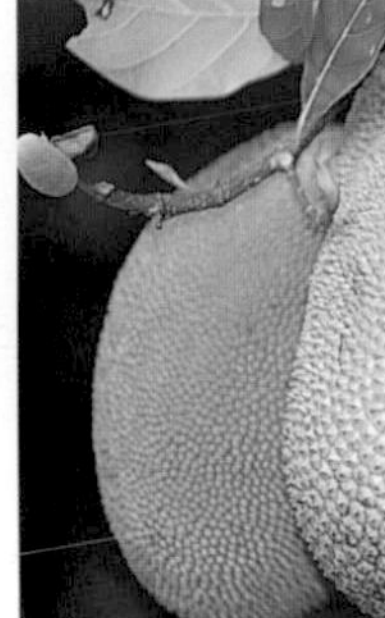

◁ **REALLY REAL**
The anthurium, part of the aroid family, looks more plastic than alive. It comes in many colors.

◁ **SPOT COLOR**
The winter-flowering immortelle is an exquisite tree of the forests, splashing the surrounding greenery with its color.

△ **RICH IN ORCHIDS**
Native orchids are found on all the islands, growing on trees in rainforests. Trinidad has some 200 species.

▽ **FLOWERING FUN**
A handsome shrub, known colloquially as Christmas candle or, less seasonally, as "ringworm bush".

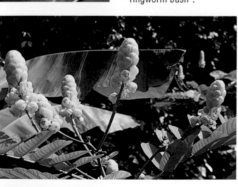

HOCOLATE DROPS
large orange pod of the ao tree grows on the k and turns dark brown. beans inside are dried nake cocoa.

READ OF LIFE
distinctive breadfruit t arrived in the Caribbean t Vincent, thanks to tain Bligh. It is best en roasted.

◁ **ALOE, ALOE**
Aloe vera, a large spiny succulent, grows in dry, thin soils. Break a leaf, and use the oozing "gel" for treating sunburn and skin problems.

▷ **ONE-OFF GLORY**
The delicate hibiscus flower comes in myriad colors, but lasts only a day. Hummingbirds love the blossoms, too.

SPICE AND ALL THINGS NICE

There is a sweetness in the Caribbean air which romantics might attribute to spice and, in particular to the vanilla plant (above), a straggly plant from the orchid family, with an exquisite-smelling flower that opens only for a few hours in the mornings. Pollinating is done by hand and it's the pods that give the much sought after vanilla flavor.

Although spices such as vanilla and nutmeg were once an important export crop, most arrived in the Caribbean in the 18th century from the Far East "spice islands". Once, Grenada grew some 25 percent of the world's nutmeg. You can still see the warehouses at Gouyave on the west coast where the spice is sorted. The outer lacy red covering is ground down into a powder and becomes mace. Visit local markets throughout the region for supplies of nutmeg and cinnamon (dried strips of bark), pale gold rhizomes of ginger, black pepper (grown on a vine) and cloves (dried flower buds).

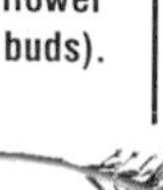

MARTINIQUE

A piece of France transported to the tropics, this beautiful, mountainous island famous for its exotic flowers exudes a kind of sophistication from the black and white beaches to the rainforest

A sign at the small beach at the base of Fort St Louis reads: *No Taking Away Sand Under Penalty of Prosecution.* In North America and in Europe people are warned about littering the ground. In Martinique they warn eople about stealing it. When Christopher Columbus landed on the island in 502, he commented, "It is the best, the most fertile, the softest, the most even, ie most charming spot in the world. It is the most beautiful thing I have ever een. My eyes never tire of contemplating such greenery." But he continued n his travels and another century went by before the first French settlers arrived 1635, led by the corsair Pierre Belain d'Esnambuc, to found St Pierre and bein the colonization of the island.

Apart from a few short-lived occupations by the British, Martinique has mained steadfastedly French, so much so that it is actually a part of France, *département* – a nail-polished fingertip on the end of an invisible arm stretchg across the Atlantic. And the first impression visitors have of the island is of tropical France: amid the palm-fringed beaches, hillside banana plantations, alleys of pineapples and volcanic mountains, the essence of the motherland can found in the *boulangeries*, the pavement cafés, the noisy mopeds, the hyperarkets and the *pissoirs*, and Parisian shops in the capital Fort-de-France. rinidadian writer V.S. Naipaul wrote in *The Middle assage* (1962): "Unlike the other islands, which have ie main town to which everything gravitates, Marnique is full of little French villages each with its iurch, *mairie* and war memorial…"

PRECEDING PAGES: an isolated farmhouse in the foothills of Pelée. **LEFT:** hanging out on the beach. **BELOW:** a splash of local art.

ropical France

t 417 sq. miles (1,085 sq. km) – 40 miles (65 km) at longest, 19 miles (31 km) at its widest – Martinique almost one-third the size of Long Island, New York. the west lies the Caribbean Sea, placid, even lakee; to the east, the Atlantic Ocean, choppier, more amatic, "like the coast of Brittany, *en France*," a artiniquan tour guide has remarked with pride.

A mountainous island, it feeds the eye with its conurs that ascend gradually from the irregular coastline d culminate dramatically, in the north in Montagne lée (4,583 ft/1,397 m), the now dormant volcano at erupted with a shattering violence in 1902. Pelée linked to other mountains – Les Pitons du Carbet ,960 ft/1,205 m) in the center, and La Montagne du uclin (1,653 ft/504 m) in the south – by a series of ntler hills, or *mornes*. The temperature, with a arly mean of 79°F (26°C), fulfils all expectations, hile the winds blowing in off the sea make for comrtable evenings. Add a thick coating of vegetation d one can understand Columbus's enthusiasm.

Today, Martinique is a largely agricultural island

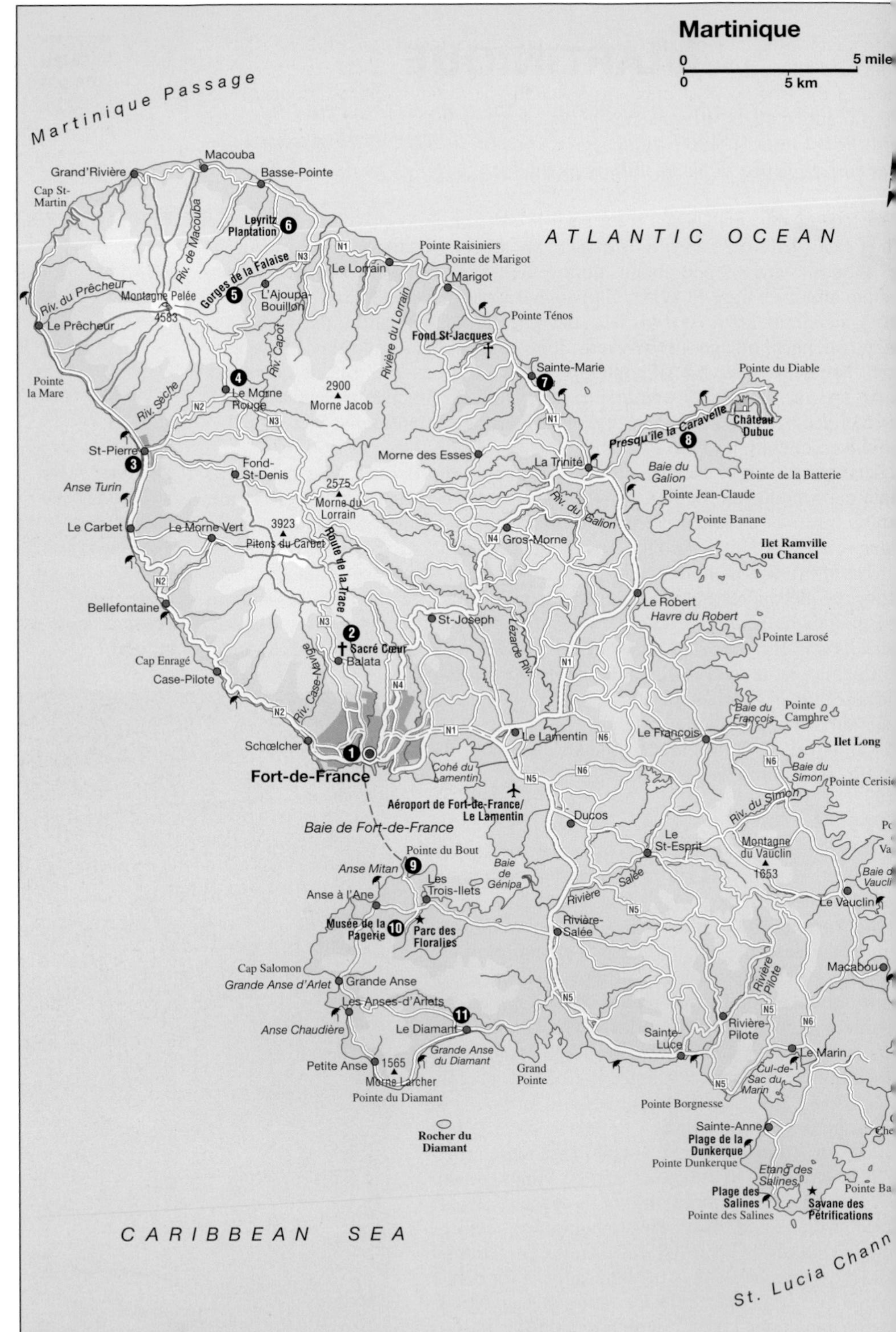
Martinique
0
5 miles
0
5 km
Martinique Passage
ATLANTIC OCEAN
CARIBBEAN SEA
St. Lucia Chann
Grand'Rivière
Macouba
Basse-Pointe
Cap St-Martin
Leyritz Plantation
Riv. de Macouba
Gorges de la Falaise
Riv. du Prêcheur
Montagne Pelée
4583
Le Prêcheur
L'Ajoupa-Bouillon
Le Lorrain
Pointe Raisiniers
Pointe de Marigot
Marigot
Pointe Ténos
Fond St-Jacques
Rivière du Lorrain
Riv. Capot
Sainte-Marie
Pointe du Diable
Pointe la Mare
Le Morne Rouge
2900
Morne Jacob
Riv. Sèche
Presqu'île la Caravelle
Château Dubuc
St-Pierre
Anse Turin
Fond-St-Denis
Morne des Esses
La Trinité
Baie du Galion
Pointe de la Batterie
Pointe Jean-Claude
2575
Morne du Lorrain
Riv. du Galion
Pointe Banane
Le Carbet
Le Morne Vert
3923
Pitons du Carbet
Route de la Trace
Gros-Morne
Ilet Ramville ou Chancel
Bellefontaine
Le Robert
Havre du Robert
St-Joseph
Lézarde Riv.
Pointe Larosé
Sacré Cœur
Balata
Cap Enragé
Case-Pilote
Riv. Case-Navire
Baie du François
Pointe Camphre
Schœlcher
Le Lamentin
Le François
Ilet Long
Fort-de-France
Cohé du Lamentin
Baie du Simon
Pointe Cerisi
Aéroport de Fort-de-France/ Le Lamentin
Riv. du Simon
Baie de Fort-de-France
Ducos
Le St-Esprit
Montagne du Vauclin
1653
Pointe du Bout
Anse Mitan
Baie de Génipa
Les Trois-Ilets
Rivière Salée
Anse à l'Ane
Musée de la Pagerie
Parc des Floralies
Rivière-Salée
Le Vauclin
Cap Salomon
Grande Anse d'Arlet
Grande Anse
Macabou
Les Anses-d'Arlets
Rivière Pilote
Anse Chaudière
Le Diamant
Grande Anse du Diamant
Sainte-Luce
Rivière-Pilote
Le Marin
Petite Anse
1565
Morne Larcher
Pointe du Diamant
Grand Pointe
Cul-de-Sac du Marin
Pointe Borgnesse
Rocher du Diamant
Sainte-Anne
Plage de la Dunkerque
Pointe Dunkerque
Etang des Salines
Plage des Salines
Pointe des Salines
Savane des Pétrifications
Pointe Ba
N1
N2
N3
N4
N5
N6
1
2
3
4
5
6
7
8
9
10
11

ith a racially mixed population of 380,000. Like the other Caribbean islands, has been through the historical horrors of colonialism and slavery; but while ıost of the British West Indies have sought their own paths in independence, Iartinique, with its sister island of Guadeloupe (*see pages 194–203*), has been bsorbed politically and economically into France as a full *département d'outre-ıer* (overseas department) of the Republic.

scape from the French Revolution

he first French settlers wasted no time in establishing sugar plantations, despite :sistance from the Carib population who moved to the Atlantic coast until they ere eventually wiped out by more sophisticated French weaponry and unfa-iliar diseases. Slaves were imported and the economy thrived, driven by the *ékés*, the traditional white élite. In 1789 at the onset of the French Revolu-on, their security was threatened by slave unrest and they invited the British) occupy the island to preserve the status quo. As a result, between 1794 and 802, unlike Guadeloupe, Martinique's *békés* avoided the guillotine.

After Emancipation in 1848, fought for by French abolitionist Victor choelcher, the sugar industry went into decline, although remaining the island's ıain export with its liquid gold by-product, rum. Nevertheless, St Pierre, the ıpital, grew into a cultural town with a "saucy" reputation, until it was oblit-:ated on May 8, 1902, killing the entire population of 30,000.

Supporters of the Vichy government in World War II, the Martinicans were eprived of their essential imports by the Allied Naval blockade and learnt to ve off their natural resources. Afterwards, the black radical Martinican poet, imé Cesaire, who had been educated in Paris and was a member of the French

Aimé Cesaire, born in dire poverty in Martinique in 1913, became part of the intellectual café society in Paris between the wars. There, he published his anti-colonial views and started a new black pride movement, called négritude. He was mayor of Fort-de-France for more than 50 years.

BELOW: Fort St Louis stands guard over the capital.

Parc Floral, on Place José Marti by the fish market, is beautifully laid out and shady with geological and botanical galleries (open Tues–Sat; closed for lunch; entrance fee) and an aquarium (open Mon–Fri; closed weekends and public hols; entrance fee).

BELOW: tying up in Fort-de-France.

Communist Party, was elected both mayor of the new capital Fort-de-France an *député* to the French Assembly on a tide of anti-*béké* feeling. He and many oth ers (not all communists) were keen to divert power from the local aristocracy t the Republic, and in 1946 Martinique and her sister islands joined the club.

Today, the islanders are happy to be part of France, appreciating the financia support of their mother country, but many rue the loss of their Martinican iden tity which has more of its roots in African rather than French history.

Fort-de-France – the island's "new" capital

Martinique's capital, **Fort-de-France** ❶, is not a large town but, with a popu lation of over 150,000, it bustles with people, traffic and noise until the closin of stores and restaurants in the mid-afternoon heat imposes a somnolence on it narrow, crowded streets. There is a seedy, tropical feel to the town; building quickly lose their newness and cloak themselves in a black mildew born of hea and the humidity wafting in across the **Baie des Flamands** (Flamingo Bay). Th strong sense of Frenchness is emphasized by the *baguettes*, mopeds and képie policemen walking in pairs, revolvers dangling, creating a setting closely re sembling those found in Graham Greene's novels – the old and the new blend ing together to create a slightly askew colonial vision of a graying town meltin in the bubbling humidity and burgeoning vegetation.

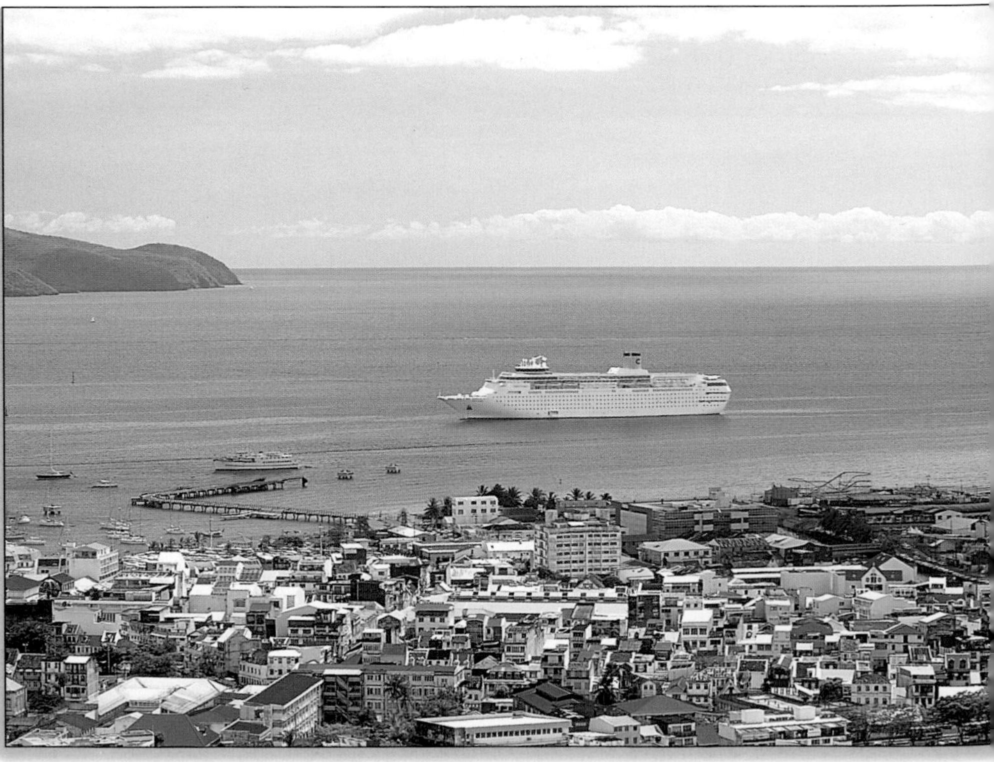

The centerpiece of the town is **La Savane,** a 12-acre (5-ha) park of lawn shady palms, footpaths and benches. Young parents, stylishly dressed, relax a their children play. In the shade of clustered ferns and bamboo, groups of me play fervent games of dominoes, the quiet broken only by the swift, click-clac of the tiles and little yelps of triumph. In a corner of the park, close to the land ıg where the ferry disgorges visitors from Pointe du Bout across the bay, stands **craft market** with paraphernalia priced in French francs and US dollars.

At the northern end stands the headless statue of Napoleon's Josephine, who 'as born at Les Trois-Ilets on Pointe du Bout. Her pedestal shows a relief of apoleon about to crown her; her date of birth (June 23, 1763); and the date of ɜr marriage (May 9, 1796). Birth, marriage, coronation: they are her most otable achievements; however, many believe that she was behind her husand's decision to reintroduce slavery in 1802 after the Revolutionary Conɜntion banned it in 1794, hence the monument's execution. And it remains ɜfaced, a potent symbol of Martinique's tortured past.

ı library and cathedral in metal

ıst across Rue de la Liberté to the right is the magnificent **Bibliothèque choelcher** (library: open all day Mon–Thurs and Fri and Sat am; free), a colɾful Baroque building crazy with Roman, Egyptian and majolican tiles, and amed for the man most responsible for the final abolition of slavery in the rench West Indies. Designed by Henri Pick, a contemporary of Gustav Eiffel, was built in metal in Paris in 1887 and then shipped out to Martinique piece y piece. **St Louis Cathedral**, on Rue Schoelcher a few minutes away, is nother of his metal constructions, built to withstand the fiercest hurricanes nd earthquakes.

On the way back down Rue de la Liberté towards the bay is the **Musée 'Archéologie** (open Mon–Fri and Sat am; closed for lunch; entrance fee), ıree floors of remnants of the Arawaks and Caribs who survive only in hisɔrical writings and glass cases. To the east of the bay looms **Fort St Louis**, orig-

French is the official language, but many Martinicans speak creole consisting of a West African grammatical structure with a basic Africanized French vocabulary .

BELOW: easy riding on the ferry from Fort-de-France.

The Compagnie de la Baie de St Pierre organizes underwater tours of the St Pierre bay, where normally clear waters allow you to see ships wrecked by the volcano as well as colorful marine fauna. The price is steep – up to 500F for an hour in the Mobilis submarine.

inally built in 1640 and added to over the years. The fort is still used as a mil tary base and is therefore closed to visitors. Opposite at **Pointe Simon**, th cruise ships dock within easy walking distance of the center.

Downtown can be a hot, humid, traffic-dominated place, but it is dotted wi colorful markets that take place in its streets. The **Marché aux Poissons** (fis market), by Place Clemenceau and next to the river, is the scene of consta activity, as fishermen unload their catch from small boats. In surrounding stree there are several other less pungent markets specializing in flowers, fruit an vegetables; the **Grand Marché** on Rue Blénac is the most tourist-oriented an is full of attractively packaged spices and sauces. Open every day, all day, bu busiest on Friday afternoon and Saturday.

To higher ground in the north

Heading north out of town for the hills, you pass through the prosperous sub urb of Didier and, a mile (2 km) or so further on, join the spectacular **Route d la Trace**, which zigzags across the the mountainous spine of the island to Morn Rouge. You may do a double take at the sight of the **Sacré Coeur de Balata** peering out of the hillside as the church is a shrunken copy of the Sacré Coeu in Paris, but not so white. The stone walls and the statue of Christ are as licked by fire, blackened in the greater humidity of the tropical rainforest.

Nearby, the **Jardin de Balata** (open daily; entrance fee) is a tropical botani cal garden with a difference. Isolated in the hills, with distant views of bot mountain and water, the calm and quiet of a monastery follow in your foot steps as you wander the meandering paths among the flowerbeds thick wit plants of unfamiliar shape and color. There are things growing here that migh

BELOW: the Pitons du Carbet behind the Sacré Coeur.

ave walked off the set of *Star Trek*, a vegetation wondrous and mesmerizing.

Originally carved out by Jesuits, the Route de la Trace is as slight as a small ıtestine; it winds upwards into the mountains, through vegetation thick and aried, creating a green background for the explosions of pink and orange ougainvillea, pink bells, and pink and yellow hibiscus dramatizing why the 'aribs called the island Madinina, Island of Flowers. Cars slice past in vehiclar displays of rapid microscopic surgery. Climbing higher, the land falls away n the left to misty valleys and, in the distance, faded folds of mountains. The egetation grows thicker and dense stands of bamboo and leafy, liana-draped ees block the view. Signposted trails disappear into the scenery on either side f the road. (Tel: 05 96 63 31 61 for information on hiking.)

Map on page 220

A relic of the volcano

Caribbean Pompeii

ı the wet twilight of the rainforest, high above **St Pierre ❸**, the Caribbean preads out dramatically and the road forks left at Le Morne Rouge descending ı sunlight to the little ghost town hugging the coast. St Pierre: the former culıral and economic center of Martinique that was once known as the "little aris of the West Indies." Behind looms **Montagne Pelée**, the sleeping volano (now constantly monitored) that, after grumbling for a few days, finally woke on May 8, 1902, at 7.50am, in a fireball of seething lava and supereated gases. Fires erupted in the town and the sea boiled. Within seconds, 0,000 people were dead. It is somehow appropriate that, on entering the town, ıe road passes the cemetery with its large white mausoleum containing the reıains of the victims.

St Pierre never recovered. Today it is a quiet little town, clean, pretty with esurgent foliage, but distinguished only by its forıer self and violent end. Ruins offer their mute testiıony: the burnt, broken stone walls of seaside varehouses; the foundations and stairways that lead owhere, the vanished theater (a replica of Boreaux's) and, on the hill that rises behind it, is the cell f the sole survivor, Antoine Ciparis, a drunkard ɔcked away the day before and protected by the trength of his dungeon. After such a reprieve, Ciparis nded up traveling America in a replica of his cell vith the Barnum & Bailey circus.

The **Musée Vulcanologique** (open daily; entrance ee), in Rue Victor-Hugo, presents personal evidence f the disaster: large clumps of nails and screws fused y heat, melted bottles, a large church bell deformed y fire, containers of scorched food. In the silence nd the sunlight outside, with the knowledge that deep own Pelée still seethes, it is a chilling display.

BELOW: An Antillean crested hummingbird at home.

hrough the Gorges de la Falaise

3acktracking 5 miles (8 km), **Le Morne Rouge ❹** its at the foot of Mont Pelée from where a rough road eads up to within 1,600 ft (488 m) of the volcano ummit and the mountain air is cool. Only experinced climbers with guides may want to attempt the eak where it rains a lot and is full of hidden dangers. Iowever, there are many trails leading from the village around the mountain suitable for different levels

Islanders are proud of their fine rum.

of fitness and experience. A hike along the River Falaise leads to the **Gorges de la Falaise** ❺, a series of impressive canyons and dramatic waterfalls, In par the trail leads you right into the river and over the smaller waterfalls creating sense of adventure.

Continuing along the road to the northeast coast, pineapple fields give way sugar cane fields which, in turn, become banana plantations, then sugar ca fields again. It is mostly women who work the pineapple fields spreading acros the Atlantic slopes of the volcano. The sugar cane, in flower, waves fluffy whi spears above its mass of tall, green stalks. The young bananas, sproutin upwards are draped for protection from parasites in blue plastic bags.

A tropical plantation house

A mile (2 km) before you reach Basse-Pointe, a tiny road veers left throug the sugar cane to the **Leyritz Plantation** ❻, now a hotel. A sign on a restore slave building reads: *SPA and HEALTH CLUB*. The former slave quarters hav been converted to tourist bungalows, the sugar mill to a restaurant. The Gre House, set in 16 acres (6.5 ha) of tropical gardens open to the public, was built i 1700. It sits on a rise dominating the plantation, its ground floor of thick ston walls and heavy wooden furniture giving a European sense of solidity, strangel unsettling in the tropical context. Unsettling, too, to think that here, in this ob ject of curiosity, lived people on whose conscience slavery sat lightly, secure i the knowledge that the Church considered blacks, like animals, soulless.

Taking the dramatic Atlantic coast road, peppered with beautiful beaches ba tered by an angry sea (swimming is dangerous), it is worth stopping off in **Ste Marie** ❼ to the **Musée du Rhum** (open Mon–Fri and Sat, Sun am; free) in th

BELOW: a ram-shackle house.

i James rum distillery. Here, exhibits tell the story of sugar and rum from 1765 nd there is plenty to sample and buy. The road meanders on down past **La rinité** to the 8-mile (13 km) long **Presqu'île de la Caravelle** ❽ which, pro-cted by the Parc Naturel de la Martinique, is criss-crossed by nature trails. here are plenty of good beaches here offering an assortment of watersports. At s tip are the ruins of the **Château Dubuc**, perfectly positioned for the pirate and nuggler who once lived there.

Cockfighting and mongoose and snake fights in specially allocated pits are popular spectator sports throughout the French islands, accompanied by heavy betting.

osephine and the south

takes 15 minutes for the *Somatour* (ferries depart regularly from the quay in ont of La Savane) to cross the Baie de Fort-de-France to **Pointe du Bout** ❾ here it ties up in another Martinique. The beaches in the north are grey with olcanic ash; here in the south they are pristine. Fort-de-France offers glimpses everyday reality, Pointe du Bout of a less troubling one with smart yachts oored in the marina, restaurants, shops and a cluster of luxury hotels.

Taxis eagerly await the ferry to drive you to the **Musée de la Pagerie** ❿ pen Tues–Sun but closed 1–2.30pm at weekends; entrance fee) just outside es Trois-Ilets. A rusted metal sign points the way to the birthplace of Empress osephine. Marie Joseph Rose Tascher de la Pagerie, later rechristened Josephine y her famous husband, left Martinique for Paris at the age of 16 in 1779, to arry the Viscount of Beauharnais. There, flighty and fun-loving, she was a ocial success; but 15 years later, in the midst of revolutionary turmoil in France, er husband was guillotined. Two years after his death, at the age of 33, she mar-ed Napoleon Bonaparte. The house in which she was born is now a ruin, estroyed by fire, and her letters and other knick-knacks from her life and noto-ous marriage are beautifully put together in the little one cottage museum.

A 15-minute walk past open fields brings you to e unspoilt, rural village of **Les Trois-Ilets** and the sh greenery of the **Parc des Floralies** (open daily; osed public hols; entrance fee), a botanical garden here picnic tables sprout up among the profusion of owers and trees with a good view of the Robert Trent ones 18-hole championship golf course alongside.

Following the winding road around the southern eninsula, you come to the pretty village of **Anse 'Arlets**, where a small wooden quay juts out into e bay's clear water. A few miles and many bends ter is **Le Diamant** ⓫, a larger village with a good oice of hotels and restaurants. Its long beach has een badly damaged by recent hurricanes, but is still onderfully white and soft to the touch. Several tracks ad to it through palm groves, and on weekends it is owded with local swimmers and surfers.

About a mile out to sea is the unmistakable hump of e **Rocher du Diamant** (Diamond Rock), an out-op of volcanic stone which was curiously once a nall part of the British Empire. In 1805, a party of 00 British soldiers, complete with cannons, took pos-ssion of the rock to control the channel between artinique and St Lucia to the south. The French ected them from their uncomfortable position, which ey named *HMS Diamond*, after 18 months. ❑

BELOW: Empress Josephine – a local who made a good marriage.

St Lucia

A luxuriant, tropical island indented with sandy coves exploding out of the surrounding crystalline waters in a volcanic heap, beautiful St Lucia is a destination for nature lovers

Fought over for more than 200 years, St Lucia (*Loo*-sha), lying between Martinique to the north and St Vincent in the south, has earned the grand-sounding title "Helen of the West Indies". A veritable treasure during colonial times for its strategic position, and caught in a power struggle between the British and French, this Caribbean classic is an incredibly beautiful and enchanting island, whose mixture of luxuriant tropical vegetation on a mountainous landscape, stunning beaches and a typically creole culture now attracts a different kind of invader, all keen to share in its natural splendors.

The most spectacular of these are the Pitons. The two majestic, cone-shaped peaks on the southwest coast, coated with lush forest, appear on the covers of so many holiday brochures and postcards all over the world that they have almost become the symbol of the West Indies. Rising straight out of the Caribbean Sea to a height of 2,600 ft (795 m), these twin peaks are proof that St Lucia actually is a pile of lava that reached the earth's surface millions of years ago after a series of mighty eruptions. So is the sand which shimmers in all kinds of shades: snow-white, cream, anthracite gray and even black.

But it is the color green that predominates as you go inland. At least one tenth of the 238-sq. mile (617 sq. km) island is covered by a thick carpet of luxuriant tropical rainforest, home to a colorful assortment of wildlife such as the St Lucia parrot (*Amazona versicolor*) and pygmy gecko, and with orchids, anthurium and the heavily scented frangipani just growing wild. The highest peak, Mount Gimie (3,116 ft/950 m), is almost permanently hung with cloud, which provides the fertile interior, rivers and streams with enough water and moisture the whole year round. Banana plantations sweep down to the craggy east coast, dramatically buffeted by the wild Atlantic.

PRECEDING PAGES: a misty, moist morning.
LEFT: a water-taxi outside Soufriére.
BELOW: colorful rastaman.

Dollars and bananas

Until the 1980s, agriculture was the island's most important source of revenue. Bananas were export article number one, despite a great many problems with pricing and marketing. Since then, tourism has outstripped all other income sources, and now more than 250,000 visitors holiday on St Lucia each year, accounting for more than half the island's foreign currency earnings.

Even though the idyll has not been destroyed by ugly high-rise hotels, tourism has still caused problems: the all-inclusive resorts on the island own one third of its beds, and even though they provide sports, entertainment and even shopping and are creating new jobs, they are simultaneously making life very difficult for small restaurants, souvenir shops and local tour offices. After all, all-inclusive holidaymakers tend

At the Marquis Estate, northeast of Castries, you can watch copra being produced.

to open their wallets just once – back home at their travel agency. The Ministr of Tourism is now trying to counter this trend by creating a marketing associa tion of smaller hotels called "The Inns of St Lucia".

One example, which in fact caused divisions among the islanders, was th development of the exclusive Jalousie Plantation Resort and Spa, as an all inclusive complex, on a spot believed to be an Arawak burial ground righ between the emblematic Pitons, which was welcomed by many in need of work it was immediately branded "a blot on the island's character" and an act of des ecration by the critics, which included the St Lucian poet Derek Walcott (*se page 67*) who likened it to opening "a casino in the Vatican or a take-away con cession inside Stonehenge." The 114-suite complex remained under-booke after it opened in 1992 and was finally forced to close down in 1995; a com promise was finally reached and it re-opened for the 1997–98 winter season a a Hilton resort with the government as a part shareholder, and no longer on a all-inclusive basis.

olorful changes of flag

. Lucia's landscapes aren't its only classically Caribbean feature: even the his-ry of the island is typical of the region. Columbus and the Spanish probably)ticed the Pitons from a distance, but were too busy heading for South Amer-a to bother with the island. After that the Caribs used guerrilla warfare to :fend their "Hewanorra" (land of iguanas) very successfully against half-:arted attempts at invasion by the British and Dutch. It was only in 1650 that me French settlers finally managed to establish a long-term base on the sec-id largest of the Windward Islands. In the years that followed the French flag id the Union Jack alternated with each other at least 14 times, until the island nally became British for good in 1814. In 1979, the island was granted inde-:ndence while remaining within the British Commonwealth.

However, French cultural influences have remained a strong factor in St ucia. English is the official language but the mother tongue is a melodic cre-e patois – a mix of African and French (*see page 72*) – and a good 80 percent f the 150,000 or so islanders are Roman Catholic rather than Anglican. Cricket played here, as elsewhere in the British Caribbean, but the people also love ancing the *beguine* from Martinique (*see page 62*) or the *merengue* from the ominican Republic. On public holidays the women wear highly colorful cloth-g, and Easter Sunday is celebrated with almost as much abandon as the Car-val in February – far more reminiscent of the French Antilles.

Walcott, who won the Nobel Prize for Literature in 1992, is very ironical)out his creole background and multiple identity: "*I'm just a red nigger who ve the sea / I had a sound colonial education / I have Dutch, nigger and Eng-sh in me / and either I'm nobody, or I'm a nation.*"

Map on page 232

The St Lucia Jazz Festival every May is claimed to be the most successful in the Caribbean, drawing around 18,000 people. Started in 1992 to fill hotel rooms, the action-packed four-day event attracts international big names.

Below: working and gossiping on the beach.

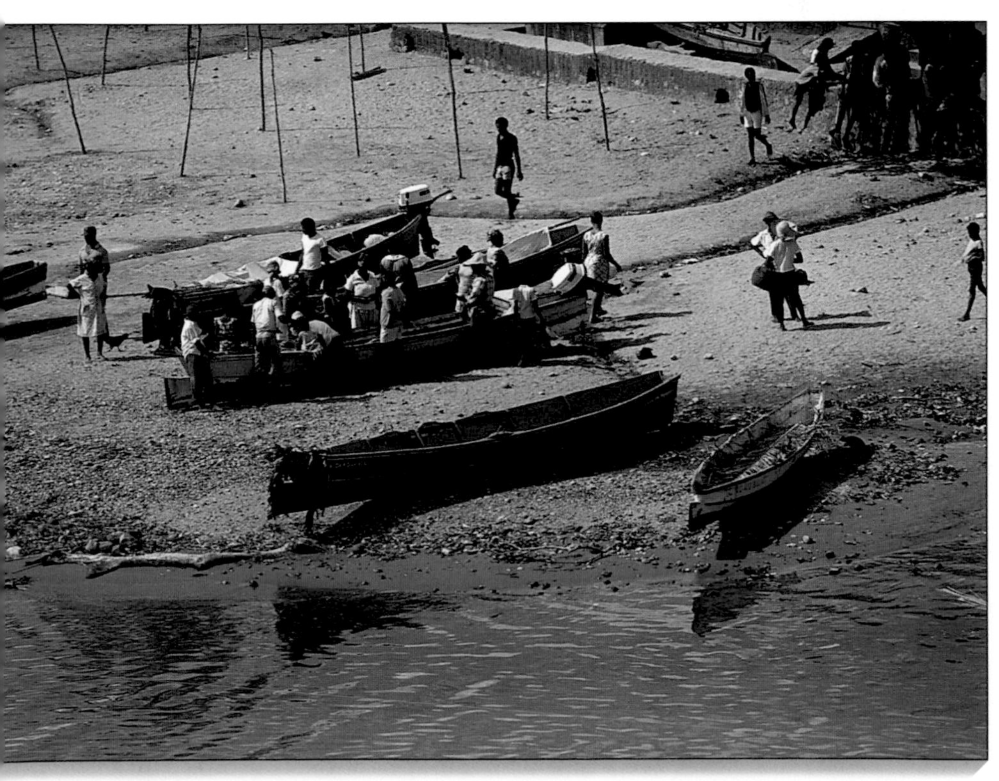

As well as in Castries cathedral, the murals of artist Dunstan St Omer and his four sons can be seen in churches at Jacmel, near Marigot Bay, Fond St Jacques and Monchy in the north, and on Manoel Street, Castries, and the sea wall at Anse la Raye.

Castries – risen from the ashes

Apart from its attractive position in the natural harbor bay, **Castries** ❶ (po 50,000), St Lucia's modern capital, has little in the way of interesting sights offer. The town was named after the French naval minister Marechal de Castrie who did a great deal to help the colony's economic development at the end the 18th century. In 1927 and 1948 two major fires reduced the entire old pa of the town to ashes and most of the rebuilding was done in concrete. A stro through the center is very rewarding in other ways, however, and provides a exciting glimpse of everyday Caribbean life.

On Fridays and Saturdays the large **Castries Market** spills out on to Jeremi Street and Peynier Street, heaving with a noisy seething mass of country fol townies and visitors. The local farmers pile up the fruits of their labors – rose colored sweet potatoes, papayas, bananas, heavy breadfruit, and all the aro matic spices that flourish in the fertile volcanic soil. Craftsmen lay out the work alongside the fishermen's catch or stalls selling old chairs and furnitur gnarled old men play Warri (*see page 180*) as bystanders egg them on.

At the southern end of Peynier Street stands the somber-looking **Cathedr of the Immaculate Conception** whose interior walls are lined with colorfu murals by the acclaimed St Lucian artist Dunstan St Omer. The main square i front, still bordered by the only 19th-century buildings that escaped the fires, wa renamed by the proud city fathers in 1993 in honor of their son Derek Walcot after he put St Lucia on the literary map, and is pleasantly shaded by a 400-yea old Saman tree. The very best view of the town and island is from Fort Charlott on **Morne Fortune**, or the "Hill of Luck", 3 miles (5 km) south of Castries. Ren ovated and used as a college, the fort was built by the French and English in th

Derek Walcott Square
This Square was re-named 'Derek Walcott Square' on 23rd January 1993 to commemorate the award of Nobel Prize for Literature to Mr. Walcott in 1992.
Derek Walcott, Poet, Painter, and Playwright, was born in St. Lucia on 23rd January 1930. He was educated at St. Mary's College, Castries and at The University of The West Indies.
Derek Walcott – Nobel Laureate Literature 1992.
CABLE & WIRELESS

BELOW: honored – the square named for the island's favorite poet.

8th century and has witnessed many a battle between the two colonial powers. oday you can watch the larger-than-life cruise ships battle it out for the prime oot in the port next to **Pointe Seraphine**, a new air-conditioned duty-free, opping complex.

Map on page 232

eaches and nightlife in the north

he island's best white beaches stretch northwards from where the island-hoping planes take off at Vigie Airport, just outside Castries. Lined with hotels and ll-inclusive resorts reminiscent of pearls on a necklace, the calm blues and reens of the Caribbean Sea are splattered with the white sails of yachts as if icked from a paintbrush. Sleek catamarans and luxurious windjammers lie at nchor in the new 1,000-berth marina tucked away behind **Rodney Bay**, once US naval base built to protect the Panama Canal, while close by on **Reduit each**, young people dressed rasta-style hawk their wares between the sunbeds. t sunset the sound of reggae and steel bands begins, inviting everyone back for e Manager's Cocktail at the hotel pool.

There's a very special kind of party every Friday night from 10pm when the therwise rather sleepy fishing village of **Gros Islet** ❷, on the north side of the arina, wakes up for a "jump-up" lasting well into the early hours. Anyone an come and the smell of grilled chicken fills the streets together with the eady thump from mobile discos. Everyone loves a party on St Lucia!

Connected to the "mainland" by a causeway near Gros Islet is the **Pigeon sland National Park** ❸ with inviting beaches and a well-tended network of ootpaths. The ruins of **Fort Rodney** overlooking the bay and a small museum open daily; closed Sun; entrance fee) commemorate Admiral George Rodney's

TIP

Several boat tours sail down the west coast to Soufrière for lunch and a visit to the volcano, Diamond Falls and Botanical Gardens. *The Unicorn*, a replica of a 19th-century brig, leaves from Vigie Marina several times a week (tel: 452 6811).

BELOW: Soufrière – where the forest meets the sea.

A mural in Choiseul, on the southwest coast between Soufrière and Vieux Fort, brightens up the quaint West Indian village where visitors can watch mahogany furniture being made at the Arts and Development Center.

BELOW: leaving church in Soufrière.

departure from here in 1782 just before he inflicted his crushing defeat on tl French at the Battle of the Saints, off the coast of Guadeloupe (*see page 202* You can also see the northernmost **Pointe du Cap** where the gentle waters the Caribbean meet the wild currents of the Atlantic. Before that **Club St Luc** comes into view, complete with golf course, stables and rather solitary grande

The scenic route to Soufrière

Beyond Morne Fortune south of Castries, the road twists and turns and goes u and down through spectacular scenery to **Marigot Bay** ❹, 8 miles (13 kn away, through jungle vegetation, up mountains and down past the broad banar plantations dominating the valley. "Yachties" flock to the natural harbor an large marina, where once Admiral Rodney bamboozled the French by disgui ing his fleet with palm fronds, and you can enjoy a drink in Doolittle's, a bo ride across the bay, named for the 1966 movie *Dr Doolittle* shot here.

The main road now winds its way south across the mountains in a series c hair-raising hairpins; several rivers have formed natural harbor bays along th coast, and the villages of **Anse La Raye** (from where it's just a 15-minute wal to a wonderful waterfall) and **Canaries** are filled with colorful fishermen houses. At **Anse La Liberté**, just outside Canaries, a new campground an Environmental Educational Center is opening up complete with hiking trail tent huts and an outdoor cooking center, reachable by water-taxi.

At **Soufrière** ❺, about 5 miles (8 km) further south, old wooden building line the streets, slender coconut palms border the dark volcanic sand, fishin boats and yachts bob in the emerald-green bay, and the dark-green woode peaks of **Petit Piton** (2,414 ft/736 m) and **Gros Piton** (2,600 ft/795 m) creat nagnificent backdrop. This is Caribbean landscape that seems too good to be ie. Not even the rain, frequent on the west coast, can spoil the joy of being in place like this. Indeed, the locals refer to the brief showers as liquid sunshine.

The dramatic scenery continues underwater at the **Anse Chastanet Marine ark** ❻, a few minutes north of Soufrière, where the diving and snorkeling is putedly the best on the island, with more than 25 different types of coral in the efs and impressive sponges at the foot of Petit Piton across the bay.

ulfurous smells and restorative springs

ot far from the Pitons you may notice a sudden aroma of "bad eggs" in the air. ie crater region of **Sulfur Springs** ❼ (open daily; entrance fee) just outside oufrière is praised by the (partly self-appointed) guides from the town as "the ily drive-in volcano in the world", because car parking was possible between e two bubbling springs for quite some time. Now the last few yards have to covered on foot, because, of course, it got out of hand.

The restorative powers of the steamy springs are harnessed in the water at the storic **Diamond Botanical Gardens** (open daily, Sun 10am–2pm; entrance e) close by, which Louis XVI presented to the three plantation-owning Devaux others just before the French Revolution for their services to the colony. In the iddle of a splendid garden, where orchids, flame trees and hibiscus bushes oom, the hot water streams out of the ground into tiled basins at a temperature around 100°C (212°F). A commemorative plaque announces that a creole rl from Martinique named Marie-Josèphe Rose Tascher de la Pagerie (*see ige 227*), Napoleon Bonaparte's wife-to-be, used to spend her holidays here the 18th century because her father owned a plantation near Soufrière.

Experienced climbers can try their hand at scaling Gros Piton, but the difficult ascent may only be made in the company of local guides familiar with the terrain. Call the Forest and Land Department on 450-2231.

BELOW: playing on the beach.

The St Lucia Naturalist Society organizes turtle-watching camps on Grande Anse Beach on the east coast on Saturday nights between mid-March to the end of July, where the leatherback sea turtles come ashore at night to lay their eggs. Call 452-8100 before Friday evenings.

Charming plantation houses

The region around Soufrière is just the right place to get a feel for what life mu have been like on plantations during colonial times. Ever since agriculture we into gradual decline, an increasing number of the traditional old manors a opening their doors to the public. The old **Soufrière Estate**, for instance, still owned by the Devaux family and has a restored water mill (1765), whic used to crush sugar cane and provide Soufrière with electricity. You can also pa take in a candlelit "Planter's Dinner". (Call 459-7565 to book in advance.)

Halfway between the quiet, picturesque fishing villages of Choiseul ar Laborie, and hidden away inside an enchanted 100-acre (40-ha) park, lies 20(year-old **Balembouche Estate House** ❽ (tel: 459-3244). If you stay here yc may see the ghosts of slave drivers walking among the trees at night!

The green heart of the island

The only way to penetrate the green heart of the island is to join an organize rainforest hike through one of the main tour agencies – hiking alone is not pe mitted, both for safety reasons and to safeguard the forest's sensitive ecolog cal balance. The **Barre de l'Isle Trail**, named after the spinal mountain rang dividing the island, is a pleasant 2–3 hour tour providing unforgettable views c sea and forest. In contrast, you have to be very fit to enjoy the **Central Rair forest Walk**, which is 6 miles (10 km) long and goes straight through the cer tral highlands, beneath Mount Gimie. With a bit of luck, especially if you ar with a small, quiet group, you may spot a rare St Lucian Parrot. It nearly becam extinct in the 1970s, but today after strict protective measures, several hundre of the parrots are thriving on the island again. A lot easier is a walk along th **Union Trail**, which begins inland from Rodney Ba This looping, hour-long trail, financed by the state owned Forestry and Land Department, also include a medicinal herb garden.

Below: typical West Indian cottage. **Right:** Red roof.

Frigate birds and whales

The east coast, which has plenty of rainfall, fev inhabitants and a raw Atlantic atmosphere, is the mos rewarding part of the island for nature lovers to visi At the **Fregate Islands Nature Reserve** ❾ (guide tours only) near Dennery, vast colonies of frigat birds have made their home. With a wingspan o nearly 7 ft (2m), they are true acrobats to watch a they chase the seagulls and pelicans, forcing them t drop their prey.

The **Maria Islands Nature Reserve** ❿ (open o request; guided tours only), just off the southern cap near **Vieux Fort** – the banana port – is a bird-watch ers' dream, home to, among others, the sooty tern, th red-billed tropic bird and the brown noddy, whicl tucks its nests under the prickly pear cactus. Also liv ing there are two endemic reptiles: the large, colorfu ground lizard and a non-venomous snake.

A new local attraction is whale-watching. Hump backed whales, sperm whales and dolphins can b spotted, if you are lucky, swimming off the Atlanti coast at various times of the year from boats orga nized by Toucan Travel (tel: 452-0896). ❑

ST VINCENT AND THE GRENADINES

Map on page 244

An area of time-warped quaintness, numerous islands, some of the world's finest beaches, and a sea of such incredible blues remains a prized discovery for the more adventurous traveler

A savored retreat for West Indians themselves, St Vincent and its 32 sister islands and cays, scattered like shells dropped from a child's overflowing bucket as she walks along the beach, are still untouched by the overt hand tourism. There are no neon lights, no high-rise buildings, no traffic jams, no and name fast-food joints, no crowds, no noise.

Completing the lower arc of the Lesser Antilles and the Windward Islands, tween St Lucia in the north and Grenada to the south, only eight of the islands e inhabited, accounting for a population of 113,000, most of whom live on St ncent. The largest, at 18 miles (30 km) long and 11 miles (18 km) wide, the sh, craggy island of St Vincent looms out of crystalline waters presided over the somnolent volcano La Soufrière (4,048 ft/1,234 m). The "untouched" ands of the Grenadines, encompassing only 17 sq. miles (44 sq. km) all gether, are havens of natural beauty whose charms extend across some of the ost beautiful beaches in the world into seas of many hues rich in marine life – rfect for sailors and divers, and beachcombers in search of privacy.

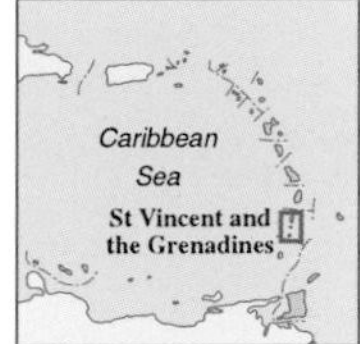

PRECEDING PAGES: Palm Island – loved by West Indians. **LEFT:** leatherback turtle on a mission. **BELOW:** view from the hills.

Among the populated islands, the manicured Mustique and Petit St Vincent e the hideaways of the rich and famous while the eming coral reefs of Bequia, Canouan and Mayreau fer spectacular diving and snorkeling. Union Island, e most southerly, is the sailing gateway to the region.

In searching for new and interesting destinations hich have yet to be spoiled by the inevitable flood of ckaged holidaymakers, travelers often discover that e benefits of visiting "untouched" islands can be mpered by the accompanying disadvantages of moteness. St Vincent and the Grenadines does not l into this category and offers a delightful compromise for those who feel more at home with the beauty nature but also enjoy creature comforts such as sy accessibility, a comfortable place to sleep and e occasional pleasure of a good meal in a restaurant.

rceful Caribs

was not until the early 18th century that St Vincent s finally settled by the French after many wrangles th the resident Caribs. Having already eliminated e Arawaks, keeping their women, the Caribs were t going to let go of their domain without a fight. owever, in 1675 they took in some African slaves und shipwrecked between Bequia and St Vincent. ermarriage produced the "Black Caribs", distinct om the indigenous "Yellow Caribs", and eyewitness ports of the time describe many a battle between em. But united in their fight against the European

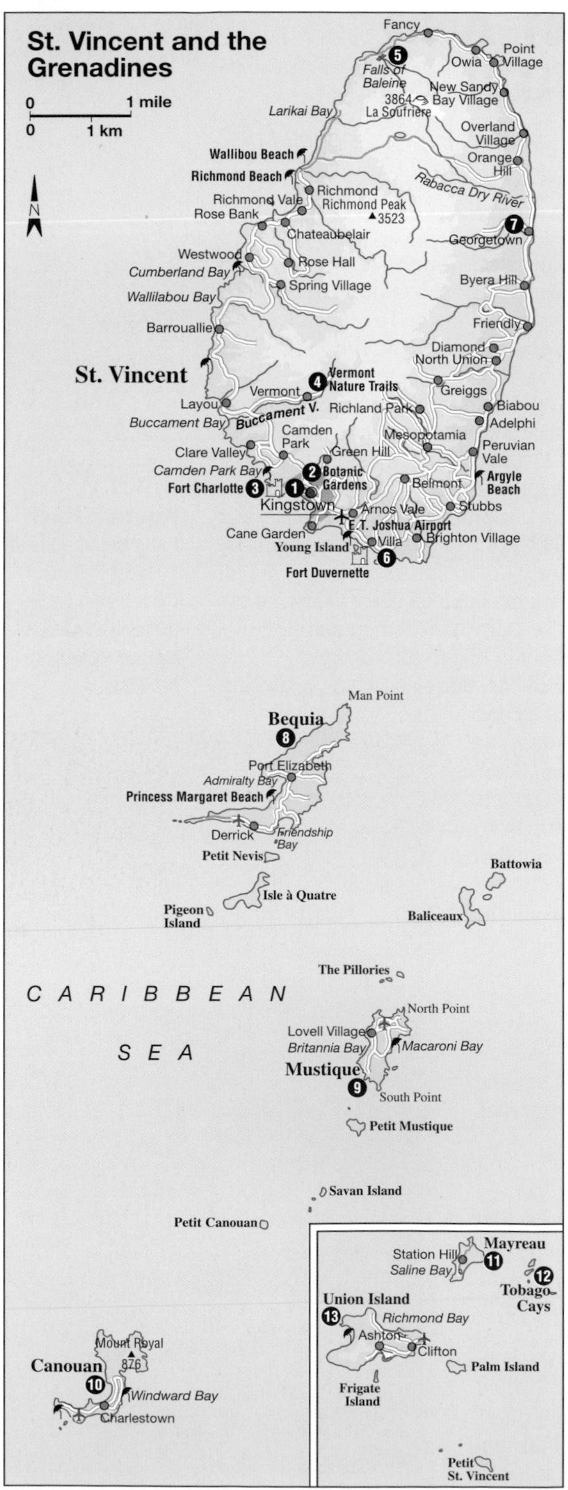

intruders, they lived alongside t French in an uneasy truce.

In 1722, the British moved in a throughout the rest of the century t two countries were involved in a tug war over the island, already plant with indigo, cotton, tobacco and sug Alongside this conflict the Bla Caribs waged war against the Briti colonists in what is known as the Car Wars, followed by the Brigand Wa that were finally ended in 1795 wh 5,000 Caribs were deported to an isla off the Honduras. There is still, ho ever, a small settlement of the Bla Carib descendants in Sandy Bay in t north of St Vincent.

British landlords

With the British at the helm, by 1829 Vincent contained 98 sugar estat manned by slaves. Most of these we run by landowners who lived in En land. By the end of the century, mo of the arable lands in St Vincent were the possession of just five owne using a labor force largely of Po tuguese and East Indian immigran

However, natural disasters took the toll in the form of a hurricane in 18 and an eruption of La Soufrière in 19 – two days before the catastroph eruption of Mont Pelée on Martiniq (*see page 225*) – which killed arou 2,000 people and finished off the pla tation economy.

Run down and poor, St Vince along with the Grenadines, was grant independence in 1979, just a fe months after another volcanic erupti had wrecked the island's agricultur already suffering from a series of hu ricanes. As a result, modern civilizati has taken a little longer to arrive her

Island cultures tend to blur on ration loosely based on the length the airport runway. The small one at Vincent's E.T. Joshua Airport allow only small planes to land here, meani fewer tourists and a culture, island an people spared from the forces that ha homogenized many other parts of t Lesser Antilles.

ingstown – the heart of a nation

ı the mornings, the cobblestone streets of **Kingstown** ❶ are full of uniformed :hool children, government workers, dollar taxi cab drivers, Rastafarians peding sandals and old women selling from upside-down cardboard boxes the ldest collection of goods – packs of chewing gum, peanuts wrapped in cellonane and pieces of ginger. Hustlers appear out of alleyways to coax tourists on des to the volcano or to the Falls of Baleine, or to sell recordings of local ılypsonians and bands such as Blaksand and New Direction. As the afternoon eat grips the town, government officers, bankers and lawyers take their lunch : the **Bounty**, a café on Halifax Street, or perhaps at the more cosmopolitan oftop restaurant in the **Cobblestone Inn**, a converted sugar and arrowroot arehouse in Upper Bay Street.

Nonetheless, this town, little more than several dusty blocks carved in a ıgged shoreline, is the heart of St Vincent and the Grenadines. There are no uildings of colonial grandeur here, but the Roman Catholic **St Mary's Cathe-ral,** beside Victoria Park to the west, makes up for this by providing a fascinating selection of architectural styles and features in one – Romanesque, Ioorish, Byzantine and Flemish spires, turrets, towers, belfries, crenellations ıd castellations are all here – built throughout the 19th century and renovated 1940. Opposite, the plain old Anglican **St George's Cathedral** has some teresting stories inside to tell.

Although Kingstown may be the most visible source of activity in this tiny ation, the real power comes from the rich volcanic soil. This is an island of ırmers, a world where practically everyone knows how to furrow a hillside to ant sweet potatoes. Agriculture is part of the school day and the more fortunate

Hairoun was the Carib name for St Vincent.

BELOW: St Mary's – an architectural mish mash.

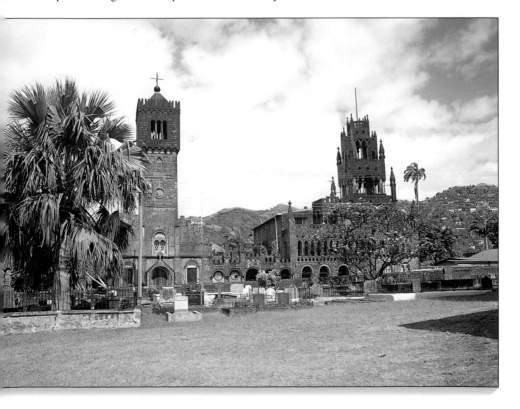

St Vincent is the world's largest producer of arrowroot. Once mainly used as a sauce thickener, the starch from the rhizome now coats computer paper. The creamy-white flowered plant, which grows up to 6 ft (2 m) tall, was named by the Arawaks who used it as an antidote for poisoned arrow wounds.

students go away to study it further in one of the West Indian universities.

On Fridays and Saturdays you can get an idea of just how productive that s is when the farmers ride dollar taxis into town loaded down with their produ of fruit and vegetables such as ginger, breadfruit, cashews, dates and cassava A large, new **Central Market** under construction on Upper Bay Street is cau ing a great deal of controversy and has been described as "a four-storey eyeso with no aesthetic appeal." Kingstown is not growing any prettier. On t reclaimed land on the harbour in front stands the new concrete **Little Tok Fish Market**, built with Japanese aid, to nurture support for continued whali in the region. Minibuses bound for the rest of the island depart from here.

In the port, the dockside hubbub reaches a crescendo every Tuesday when t large white Geest Industries freighter arrives to ship the week's crop of banan to the rest of the world. The banana industry is estimated to account for 40 pe cent of St Vincent's exports and 30 percent of the island's economy.

The oldest botanic gardens in the West

Leaving Kingstown via the Leeward Highway to the west, on the edge of tow you come to the **Botanic Gardens** ❷ (open daily; free), founded in 1765 propagate spices and medicinal plants, and the oldest in the western hemispher Chances are young men will come up to you at the gate entrance and offer yo a tour of the 20-acre (9 ha) gardens that contain teak and mahogany trees, an nearly every flower and tree that can grow in the Caribbean, including a 50- (15 m) breadfruit tree, one of the original seedlings brought to the West Indi in 1793 by Captain Bligh on his famous ship *The Bounty.*

Perched some 600 ft (180 m) on a promontory above the town, 15 minute

BELOW: bringing in the catch to sell at Little Tokyo Fish Market.

ive to the west, the ruins of **Fort Charlotte** ❸, built in 1805, command speccular views across the Caribbean to the Grenadines and, on a clear day, as far
Grenada 60 miles (95 km) away. In the barracks a series of paintings (1972)
ortrays the early history of St Vincent.

search of the St Vincent parrot

ne Leeward Highway provides a dramatic two-hour drive along the west coast ith beaches of gold or black sand. What would take 10 minutes to drive in a atter world can take hours here, as you circumvent mountains and jungles. In e **Buccament Valley** about 2 miles (3 km) from Kingstown you can wander rough rainforests along the **Vermont Nature Trails** ❹. Maps of hikes are pro- ded at the information center and you may see the endangered St Vincent rrot or the whistling warbler, both unique to the island. **Richmond Beach** der the dark gaze of La Soufrière marks the end of this beautiful winding ad and a boat is necessary to go on any further. Many boat operators offer trips which can include snorkeling and a lunch stop – to the **Falls of Baleine** ❺, miles (11 km) to the northern tip of the island. There you can swim in the pools led by these freshwater falls on a river that flows from the volcano.

The St Vincent parrot hides in the rainforest.

long the Windward coast

ne Vigie Highway leaves Kingstown from the east to the airport about 15 inutes away. Close by is the **Arnos Vale cricket ground**, the home (or shrine) Vincentian cricket which hosts international Test matches between the West dies and England, Australia, New Zealand, India and Pakistan. Vincentians ve their cricket and come out in droves to support their team, making it a

BELOW: on the front deck of a cat in Tobago Cays in the Grenadines.

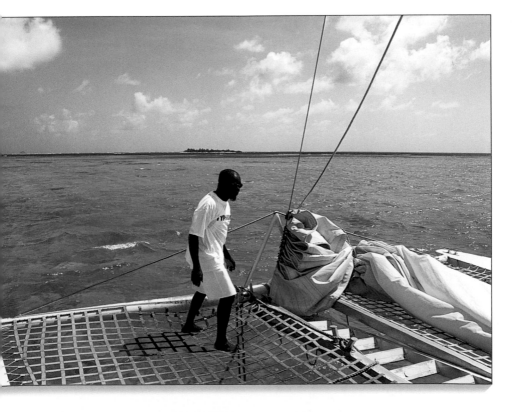

festive social occasion with loud music and dancing whether they win or los

A little further east, on the south coast road, **Villa ❻**, colloquially known "The Strip", is the island's main resort area with several hotels, guest hous restaurants, bars and watersports facilities. Just 200 yds (180 m) off shore, t tiny, privately owned resort on **Young Island**, linked to the mainland by a sm water-taxi, becomes officially child free between January 15 and March 1 Beside it on a rock is the 19th-century **Fort Duvernette**.

At least three times a day banana farmers will inspect each stalk to see if there are leaves pressing against the fruit. Bruised fruit will not be accepted by the buyers.

The Vigie Highway winds through what the Vincentians call the "breadba ket" of their island. On the Atlantic side the soil is more fertile and from t unbarricaded road you have views, somewhat frightening, of deep valleys do ted with small farms and banana plantations. You may experience the odd tra fic jam on the narrow coastal road that leads north to Georgetown, but they a usually only caused by drivers stopping for a chat, or someone going over inspect a fish for sale on the roadside. Such impromptu markets are commo

Georgetown ❼, the second largest town on St Vincent, was once the pro perous sugar capital of the island: when the price of sugar fell, the sugar pla employing most of the laborers in this valley, was closed down. Now there's sense of driving through a ghost town, although rum is still produced nearby the **Mount Bentick Rum Refinery** (open Mon–Fri; entrance fee).

A little further on is the **Rabacca Dry River**, once a hot river of lava. You c drive or walk along here to well-marked trails that lead to the crater of I Soufrière. A six-hour round trip, it is an arduous hike best started as early in t morning as possible only by the fit and healthy, but it is worth the effort wh you finally crest the rim and look down into that awesome volcano. It is oft cloudy, cold and wet at the top so be well equipped and take a guide.

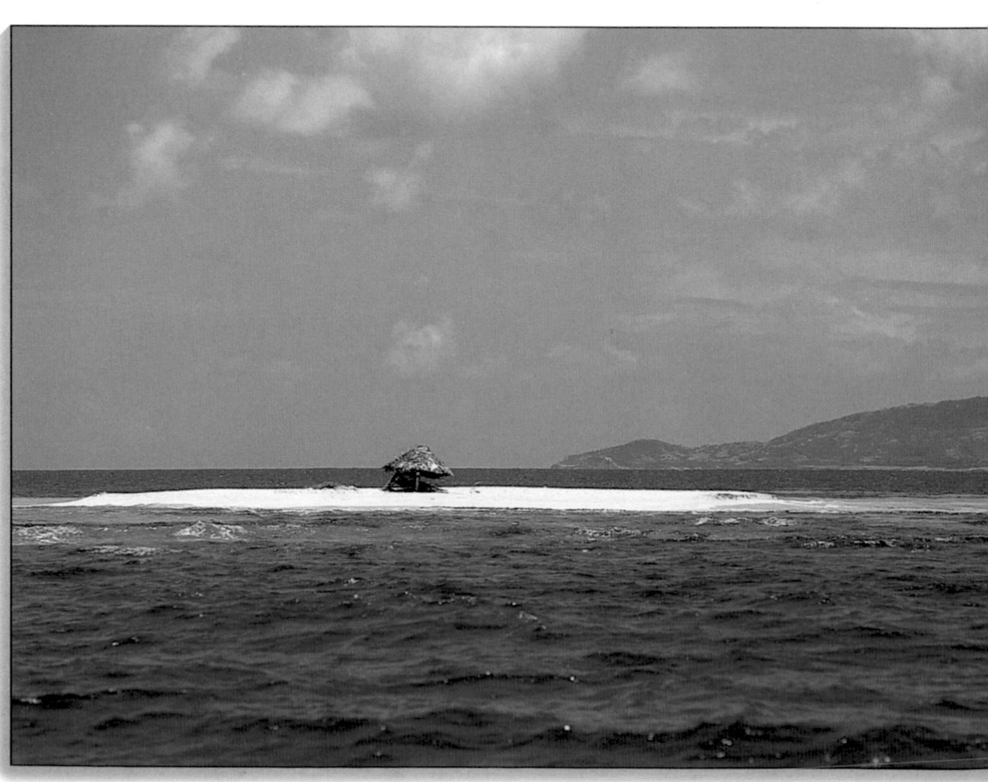

BELOW: a whole island to yourself.

sland-hopping in the Grenadines

Иost people arriving on an island in the Grenadines do so by sea, and many are nder sail either on their own private yacht, or they have chartered a yacht or are are boating (*see pages 116–17*). More and more anchorages are being proided to protect the coral reefs surrounding the islands from damage. Waterixis zip around the bays waiting to take yachtsmen on shore and boys often ome out to the boats with goods for sale. Ferries regularly leave Kingstown for ie islands, and Bequia, Mustique, Canouan and Union Island all have small airorts for light aircraft.

The focal point of **Bequia** ❽ (*Bek*-way), 9 miles (14 km) from St Vincent, is ie stunningly beautiful **Admiralty Bay**, an enormous, clear harbor bordered by teep green cliffs, holding several yacht anchorages. Around the island is a Иarine Protected Area looking after 30 superb dive sites, many of which are uitable for snorkeling too. **Port Elizabeth**, is little more than a road, a small tore and a few tiny restaurants, and along the shore unfinished sloops are being uilt by the skilful local boatbuilders.

During the 19th century, the New Bedford whalers used Bequia as a whaling tation and now the island's last whale harpoonist, Aytheneal Oliverre, lives in small house in the south which he has turned into a **whaling museum** (open aily; entrance fee). His front door is framed by a whale jawbone and inside is vertebra of the first one he killed in 1958. When and if a whale is caught Dliverre caught his last one in 1992 – the International Whaling Foundation ermits the islanders to harpoon two a year) the whole island comes to watch.

Visitors to **Mustique** ❾, 15 miles (24 km) south of St Vincent, are often reeted by the island's only policeman checking that everyone has a proper estination. Not that there are many places to go. 'here are approximately 80 houses on the 3-sq. mile 3 sq. km) island. About 50 of those belong to people ke Mick Jagger, Princess Margaret and other roylty, and a contingent of wealthy businessmen. However, on the western shore, fishermen have set up amp on the beach near **Basil's Bar**, the only public estaurant, and they eat the conch they fish for, leavng a mountain of shells.

The small, crescent-shaped island of **Canouan** ❿, as some of the Caribbean's best and most private eaches, and recently a new luxury resort, complete 'ith the Grenadines' only golf course has been pened. Tiny **Mayreau** ⓫ is less than 2 sq. miles (5 ı. km) and is inhabited by about 100 people. There e no roads, a small salt pond and one very subdued esort. Nearby a tiny clutch of five uninhabited lands, known as the **Tobago Cays** ⓬, offers speccular snorkeling and diving – although popular.

Mountainous **Union Island** ⓭, the most developed f the smaller Grenadines, is the sailing center of the egion, and is an ideal starting point for trips to the urrounding islands. Across the bay is beautiful **Palm Island**, once known as Prune Island and now a popılar resort with West Indians after some peace.

Furthest south is **Petit St Vincent**, an island resort onsidered to be one of the best in the region, where xclusive privacy is the order of the day. ❑

Map on page 244

Conch shells on the beach on Mustique.

Below: island-hopping offered on Bequia.

BENSON

FARM & GARDEN
CENTRE
FAO
FIAT PANIS

GRENADA

To the south of the Grenadines, this aromatic island is known as the Spice Island of the Caribbean, most famous for nutmeg. A relatively new holiday destination, Grenada has an alluring air

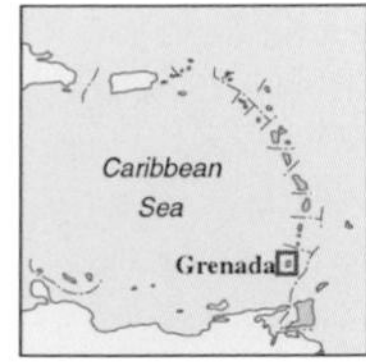

A colorful gem of an island, Grenada (Gre-*nay*-dah) is, by any definition, small. Only 21 by 12 miles (35 by 20 km) in size, it seems bigger than it really is, partly because its mountainous interior looms large and is slow) cross and partly because its landscape is so varied. Its fertility is largely ıanks to the 160 in (4,060 mm) of rain deposited on the island's interior each ear by the trade winds. This creates lush and often impenetrable rainforest, reams that cascade down to the sea and ideal conditions for the generations of nall farmers who have worked their smallholdings since the British freed the aves in 1834. The island is astonishingly fertile; bananas, cocoa, citrus, mangoes nd coconut grow in dense groves or by the roadside. Further up in the interior, ast ferns and ancient mahogany trees drip in the humidity.

Known as the Spice Island of the Caribbean, it is nutmeg (*see page 215*) 'hich gives Grenada its most delicious and distinctive aroma. Nutmeg has been rown here since the 1780s when the British brought it over from East India and, ›gether with cinnamon, ginger and cloves, replaced sugar as the island's main xport. The crop still accounts for about a fifth of Grenada's export earnings and rovides a living for many small farmers. Known affectionately as the "retire-ıent tree" as it is thought to guarantee a comfortable old age, the nutmeg tree rops an apricot-like fruit which splits when ripe to :veal its seed and the surrounding red membrane hich makes the separate spice, mace.

PRECEDING PAGES: market day.
LEFT: nutmeg and mace in the raw.
BELOW: a safe perch for a traffic policeman.

he prettiest capital

›me might dispute Grenada's claim to be the pretti-›t island in the Lesser Antilles, but few would dis-›gree that its capital, **St George's ❶**, is the finest ›wn. In a region regularly ravaged by natural disas-r or crass development, it has retained its picturesque ıarm and small-town warmth against all the odds.

The geography of St George's is unusually attrac-ve, as the town is built around the rim of a volcanic 'ater which forms its almost landlocked harbor. From 'ound the waterfront Carenage, edged with solid one warehouses, the town rises steeply, houses, ıurches and forts ringing the inner horseshoe bay. ver the promontory, where the French-built **Fort eorge** (open daily; free) commands panoramic ews of the town and harbor, is another, newer part of ›wn, joined to the Carenage by the 100-year-old ›ndall Tunnel. Here, **Market Square** is the scene ' hectic and colorful activity every Saturday morning ; farmers bring their vanloads of yams, mangoes and ınanas to town.

Delicate French provincial architecture rubs shoul-›rs with robust Georgian stonework, a happy con-›quence of Grenada changing colonial hands several

A perfect spot to watch the sun set is from the scruffy St George's Cemetery perched above the capital on Cemetery Hill. Here you can see a bust of Maurice Bishop, a poignant memorial to a charismatic leader.

times in the 18th century. Pink fish-scale roof tiles date from the time when the crossed the Atlantic as ballast in French ships. Pastel-colored wooden house clinging to the hillsides contrast with the dour stone of **St Andrew's** Presbyteria Kirk's belfry and the imposing walls of **Fort George**. From almost every var tage point you can see the coastline stretching hazily away to the next headlan

There is little in the way of conventional tourist attractions in St Georg apart from the **Grenada National Museum** (open Mon–Fri and Sat an entrance fee), near the Sendall Tunnel, which is housed in the former prison cel of 18th-century French barracks. One of the best ways to pass the time is sin ply to sit and admire the view, towards sea or mountains, preferably from th shady terrace of the waterside **Nutmeg**, famous for its rum punches.

The "intervention"

The town exudes history, but most Grenadians prefer not to discuss the even of October 1983 which brought their island brief notoriety. In 1979, a group c

Grenada

oung radicals turfed out the eccentric and dictatorial Prime Minister Eric Gairy n a bloodless coup. Four and a half years of People's Revolutionary Govern- ıent, led by the charismatic Maurice Bishop, ensued in which long overdue eforms were introduced. But Grenada's "revo" disintegrated as a hardline fac- ion tried to snatch power. Bishop was arrested, freed by a crowd and then, in cenes of appalling brutality, was executed with several supporters in the court- ard of Fort George. The US, long suspicious of Grenada's links with Castro's Cuba, seized the opportunity to invade. More than 6,000 US Marines landed in vhat is euphemistically known as "the intervention". As much of the world truggled to locate Grenada in atlases, Soviet television announced that the US ad invaded Granada and a map of southern Spain appeared behind the newsreader.

It seems long ago, but the scars remain. Those convicted of the murders are till in jail in **Fort Frederick** on Richmond Hill. Others still mourn their dead. 'he promised post-intervention bonanza of foreign investment never material- zed. Grenada returned to obscurity, traumatized and still unable to forget...

In October 1961, a fire ripped through the Italian liner, Bianca C, *in St George's Harbour. Boats of all types rushed to the rescue, saving the 400 passengers, and the ship's owners erected a bronze statue,* Christ of the Deep, *in their honor. The ship is now the largest wreck dive in the Caribbean.*

pice of Grenadian life

'he center of Grenada's nutmeg industry is the west coast town of **Gouyave** ❷ pronounced Warve), about 6 miles (10 km) north of St George's. A ramshackle ne-street fishing community, populated by as many goats as people, it has a ungent **Nutmeg Processing Station** (open Mon–Fri and Sat am; entrance fee lus tip), where visitors can see the grading, drying and packing process. Just efore Gouyave, down a dirt track, is the crumbling **Dougaldston Spice Estate**, nce a prosperous nutmeg plantation but now fallen on hard times. Small bags f nutmeg, cinnamon or cloves are on sale here for a few dollars.

From Gouyave the road follows the coast north- vards, providing spectacular sea views, before turning nland through several poor villages to the small orth-coast town of **Sauteurs** ❸. The French name literally "leapers") recalls a grisly moment in irenada's colonial past when French forces sur- ounded the last community of indigenous Caribs in 651. Rather than surrender, the 40 Caribs jumped rom the 100-ft (30-m) cliff into the sea below. On the romontory by **St Patrick's** church there you can peer own on to the rocks and spray.

A rough road leads eastwards out of Sauteurs to the **evera National Park** ❹, a wild and varied area of crubland, mangrove and palm-lined beach. From the illtop, there are spectacular views of the offshore and ninhabited **Sugar Loaf**, **Green** and **Sandy Islands**. **athway Beach**, looking out to Sandy Island, is a ormally deserted expanse of white sand, where eagrapes provide welcome shade. Currents are eportedly strong, despite a protective reef, but there a natural 33-ft (10-m) long natural rock pool perfect or swimming.

peppertpot lunch

'he main road south of Sauteurs takes you to the **Iorne Fendue Plantation House** ❺ (tel: 442-9330), gray stone house that looks like a Derbyshire vic- rage. Here for a reasonable price, the veteran owner,

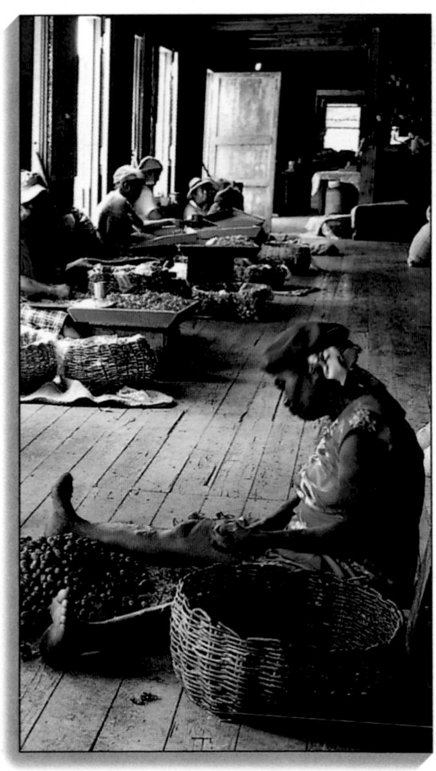

BELOW: taking the mace off the nutmegs.

TIP

Serious hikers can take a five-hour walk in the Grand Etang National Park to Concord Falls, where it's possible to swim, and on to Fedon's Camp, where a rebel planter held out against the British in 1795. The good news is there is a bus back to St George's from nearby Concord.

BELOW: there is dense rainforest in Grand Etang Park.

Betty Mascoll MBE, will provide a traditional Grenadian lunch of pepperp (*see page 72*), complete with rum punches (*see page 75*). It is essential to phor in advance. Heading south through **Mount Rose** village there is a turn-off to th **River Antoine Rum Distillery** ❻ (open Mon–Fri and Sat am; entrance fe where guided tours demonstrate 18th-century rum distilling techniques based c a water-powered cane crusher. From the distillery it is a short drive to **Lak Antoine**, a lonely crater lake teeming with birdlife.

Nature in the raw

At **Grenville**, a sprawling, rather unattractive town with a dirty beach on the ea coast, the picturesque coastal road leads to **La Sagesse Nature Centre** ❼ about 10 miles (16 km) south. Here, you drive through a banana plantatio before arriving at a shaded beach, overlooked by a small guesthouse and restau rant terrace. Within walking distance is a microcosm of Caribbean coastal eco ogy: a mangrove estuary, salt pond, coral reefs and cactus woodlands.

But Grenada's natural *tour de force* is the **Grand Etang National Park** ❽ an area which covers the mountainous backbone of the island, from Mount S Catherine (2,755 ft/840 m) to Mount Sinai (2,306 ft/703 m). The Grenville–S George's road winds tortuously up into rainforest and occasional warm mis About halfway is Grand Etang itself, a water-filled volcanic crater at 1,900 f (580 m). Legend has it that the lake is bottomless, and certainly few feel the urg to swim in the strangely still water.

A **Visitors' Center** offers a wealth of information on the surrounding flora an fauna, and there are well-marked hiking trails which take from 15 minutes t three hours to complete. It is wet, sweaty and sometimes slippery high in th nountains, but walkers will be rewarded with panoramic views and sightings of rchids, hawks and even opossums (considered a delicacy locally).

On the way back to St George's it is worth making a half-mile detour to **nnandale Falls ❾**, where a cold stream drops 50 ft (15 m) into a pool used y locals and tourists alike for swimming. The site has attracted fair numbers of elf-appointed "guides" as well as those eager to sell spices.

The southern tail of the island is comprised of a series of inlets, promontories nd beaches. The most celebrated of these is **Grand Anse ❿**, several miles of erfect white sand fringed with palm trees and hibiscus hedges. This is the ourist strip, with hotels bordering the beach and a road of restaurants and shops unning parallel. Smaller and more secluded is **Morne Rouge**, lying in a pro-ected cove further round, east of **Point Salines** airport (claimed by the US, in ne heady Cold War days of 1983, that it was being built by Cuba as part of its xpansionist designs in the Caribbean) is **Prickly Bay**. Here is the popular **pice Island Marina** alongside smart hotels such as **The Calabash**, whose wns sweep down to the beach.

'achting hideaways

irenada's two even smaller island dependencies, **Carriacou ⓫** and **Petit Mar-inique**, a three to four-hour boat ride off the northeastern coast are a haven for nose who want to get away from it all. Boats leave twice weekly from the 'arenage or you can fly, but sailing into Carriacou's natural harbor is an expe-ience to be savored. Carriacou is famous for wooden boat-building, the African-nfluenced Big Drum Dance and (some say) smuggling; the tiny, volcanic Petit Iartinique also has a reputation for illicit supplies of whisky. ❑

Carriacou Regatta, held every August, was started in 1965 to show off the hand-crafted schooners built by the descen-dants of Scottish set-tlers. It is now a huge festival with street parties and Big Drum Dances.

BELOW: hauling in the nets at Gouyave.

H

BARBADOS

A coral island set apart from the rest of the Eastern Caribbean chain, this "singular" island has a character and landscape of its own with an emphasis on beauty, fun and friendliness

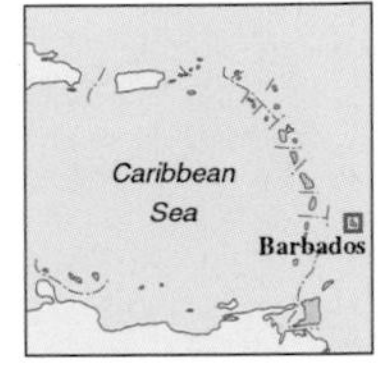

The breakers of the Atlantic – "white horses" as the Bajans call them – slam against the jagged cliffs of River Bay, a vast, barren plateau and dry river bed at the isolated northern tip of Barbados.

Ordinarily it is deserted here. But today is Boxing Day. A lengthening line of public buses curves along the road that leads to this rugged area, intruding on the landscape like a monstrous blue and yellow snake. Clusters of people swarm toward a hillside shaded by a grove of long-needled casuarina trees. Women wearing their Sunday best – brilliant turquoise skirts or scarlet dresses that look even brighter next to the muted browns and greens of the landscape – step gingerly across a narrow stream and stake out the best picnic spots on the hillside. The few trees, gnarled and stunted by the ever-present trade winds, provide a canopy under which the women unveil their elaborate holiday fare.

With a total area of only 166 sq. miles (431 sq. km), Barbados has some of the most varied terrain in the Caribbean. Divided into 11 parishes, each has its own character and landscape. The north is the least populated section; its shores punctuated by dramatic cliffs and crashing waves. Equally unspoiled is the scenic east with miles of windswept beaches along the Atlantic coast fringing the hilly "Scotland District." As the Atlantic Ocean rushes wildly along the south coast westward towards the Caribbean Sea, the sand becomes whiter, hidden away in rocky coves edged by palm trees, washed by the breakers that are finally lulled into submission on the heavenly beaches of the west coast. The center of the island is covered with gently rolling cane fields, rural villages, and lush tropical vegetation.

Although some of the hills are very steep, Barbados is considered a flat island. Coral rather than volcanic, its highest point, Mount Hillaby, is just 1,115 ft (340 m) above sea level. Off the beaten track, 100 miles (160 km) to the east of the rest of the Lesser Antilles, Barbados is often referred to as "the singular island." During the days of sailing conquerors and Caribbean settlement, this isolation provided Barbados with an unwitting defense: it is difficult to sail here from the other islands because of the prevailing easterly winds.

The first Bajans

Once a British colony and nicknamed "Little England," Barbados can appear very British with afternoon teas and starched school uniforms. One 19th-century visitor declared it "more English than England itself." There is a Hastings, a Brighton and a Worthing – all names of English towns – and a Trafalgar Square in Bridgetown, the island's capital, in which stands a statue of Admiral Nelson. The game of cricket is practically the national religion.

PRECEDING PAGES: repairing the fishing boats on the beach.
LEFT: fun and games at Carlisle Bay.
BELOW: a happy face in the sun.

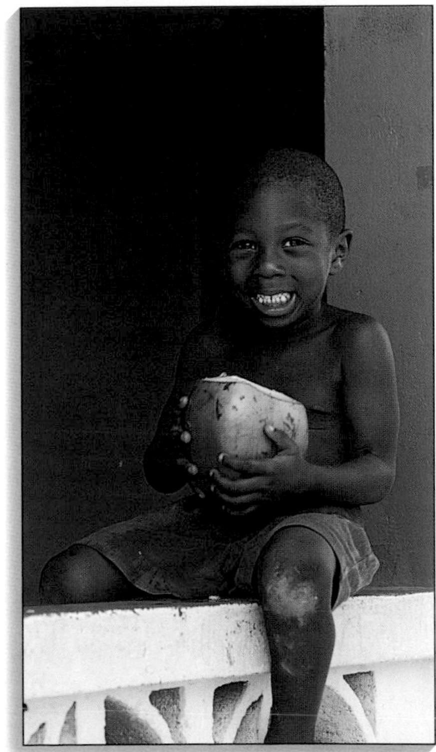

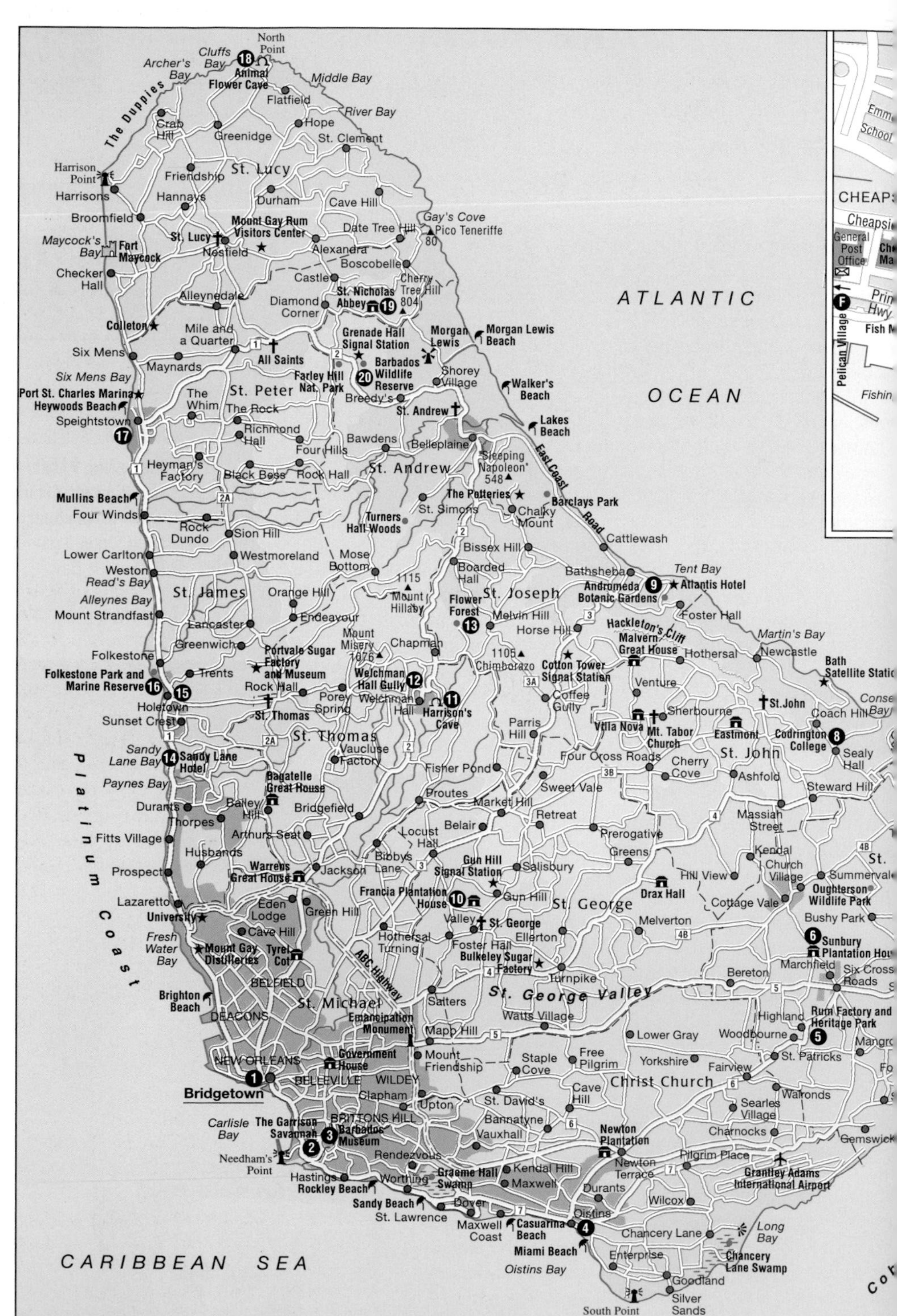
ATLANTIC
OCEAN
CARIBBEAN SEA
Platinum Coast
Bridgetown
St. Lucy
St. Peter
St. Andrew
St. James
St. Joseph
St. Thomas
St. John
St. George
St. Michael
Christ Church
St. George Valley
East Coast Road
ABC Highway
North Point
Animal Flower Cave
Harrison Point
Speightstown
Holetown
Oistins
South Point
Needham's Point
Grantley Adams International Airport
Barbados Wildlife Reserve
Farley Hill Nat. Park
St. Nicholas Abbey
Andromeda Botanic Gardens
Flower Forest
Harrison's Cave
Welchman Hall Gully
Sunbury Plantation House
Codrington College
Gun Hill Signal Station
Francia Plantation House
The Garrison Savannah
Barbados Museum
Mount Gay Distilleries
Mount Gay Rum Visitors Center
Folkestone Park and Marine Reserve
Sandy Lane Hotel
Port St. Charles Marina
Rum Factory and Heritage Park
Emancipation Monument
Government House
Chancery Lane Swamp
Graeme Hall Swamp

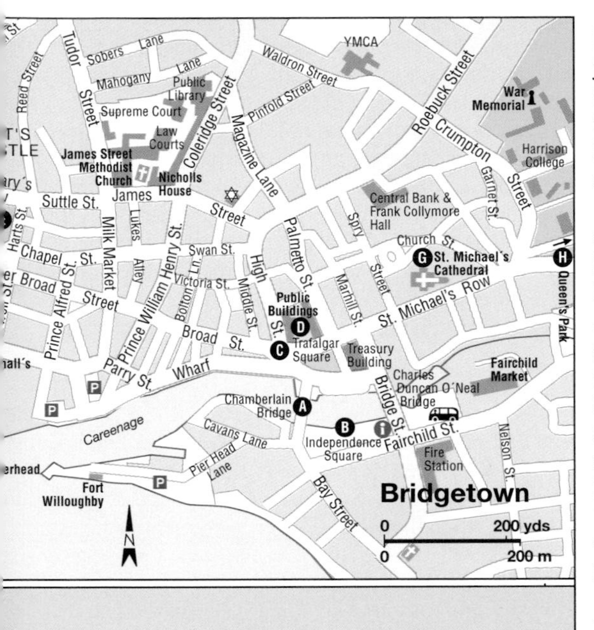

This tiny coral island is densely populated – about 265,000 people live in a space just 14 miles (22 km) wide and 21 miles (33 km) long, yet Barbadians, or Bajans, as they are generally known, have one of the highest incomes per head in the West Indies and a literacy rate of over 98 percent.

The first Bajans were Amerindians, who came in canoes from Venezuela in around – it has recently been discovered – 1600 BC. Different tribes came and went, with the Arawaks remaining most evident, but these gentle fishermen and farmers are believed to have been captured by the Spanish at the beginning of the 16th century and taken as slaves to Hispaniola – no archaeological evidence has been found that Caribs ever lived here. When the English arrived in 1625, all they found was a population of wild hogs left by Portuguese explorers who had anchored briefly in 1536.

The brightest jewel

On February 17, 1627, 80 English settlers and 10 African slaves, captured from trading vessels en route, landed on the calm west coast of the island, which became the first British possession to cultivate sugar on a large scale. By the 1650s, Barbados had a booming economy based solely on sugar cane and became known as "the Brightest Jewel in the English Crowne." As the sugar cane plantation system evolved, the institution of slavery (*see pages 33–35*) became firmly entrenched, but not without some notable uprisings – in 1675, 1696 and 1702 – cruelly quashed by the planters. The final 5,000-strong rebellion came in 1816 after the abolition of the slave trade had not given the slaves the freedom they, mistakenly, thought they were due. That didn't come until 1834.

New challenges

Between 1850 and 1914, around 20,000 adventurous laborers left for Panama to help build the canal, and many returned wearing flashy clothes, their pockets stuffed with US currency, with which they bought land, educated their children and increased their standard of living. However, afterwards there were few opportunities for black Bajans and most returned

Many believe that the island was named in 1536 by Portuguese explorers calling it Los Barbudos ("the bearded ones") after the bearded fig trees (above) which grew there. But this name has appeared in a Spanish document dated 1511.

BELOW: engrossed in a game of Warri.

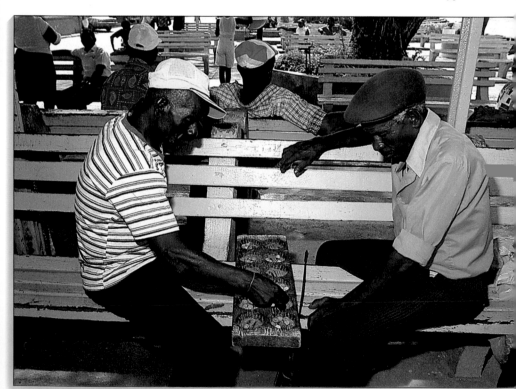

to the plantations as laborers. The poor conditions there and a lack of political power sparked a half century of intense political and social change.

Perhaps the most noteworthy figure to challenge the ruling white planter class was Grantley Adams, the acknowledged leader of the Barbados Progressive League, the island's first mass movement political party formed in 1938, which over the course of 30 years and eventually under the title of the Barbados Labour Party (BLP) helped attain fair labor laws and universal voting rights.

Political independence from Britain finally came in 1966, with Errol Barrow of the Democratic Labour Party (DLP) at the helm. Remaining in the British Commonwealth, the island has continued with a Westminster-style parliament consisting of a Senate and a democratically elected House of Assembly and now the government swings between the BLP and DLP.

Creation of a new culture

While Barbados has managed to forge a political identity, it has taken much longer to escape a cultural limbo and develop its own indigenous culture. Alongside its African heritage, brought over by the slaves, and long known for its "Britishness" and the old-fashioned lifestyle of its people, Barbados's reputation began to change in the 1970s, when the Black Power movement and Rastafarianism had a profound impact on island identity. At the same time, the tourist industry was rapidly growing, widening its appeal across the board, attracting visitors who were not rich and famous and who congregated around an increasingly lively south coast.

Another powerful influence on Bajan culture in the past two decades has been American television and music. As the island's most famous calypsonian, the

Map on pages 262–63

lighty Gabby, sings, "*All dem shows on TV, you must agree, are not for we/ Show*
ıe some Castle of My Skin by George Lamming/ Instead of that trash like Sanford
nd M.A.S.H./ Then we could stare in the face/ And show dem we cultural base."
Now, after more than 30 years as an independent nation, Barbados is finally oming into its own culturally. There is a growing appreciation of things Bajan, nd a movement to preserve aspects of the folk culture that have been dying out. he enthusiasm the revived annual Crop Over Festival in July and August genrates is one sign of the new cultural pride and the wildly popular calypsonians re a major force in Bajan society. The festival, a three-week long traditional celbration of the end of the sugar cane harvest, is the highlight of a virtual 12ıonth calendar of events, which reflects a boom period in Barbados enhancing s reputation that there is always something exciting going on.

Bussa, the monument to freedom outside Julie'n supermarket.

ridgetown – colorful contrasts

is in **Bridgetown** ❶, the bustling capital of Barbados, that the contrasts charcterizing the island are most evident. While duty-free shops sell luxury items like ameras, crystal and cashmere, a Rastaman peddles coconuts from a wooden art outside and country women, or hucksters, sit by their stalls of fresh fruit nd vegetables picked from their gardens. Old ramshackle colonial buildings and next to multi-million dollar office blocks and the strains of calypso emanate om juke boxes in back-alley cafés.

Early British colonists established a settlement here in what was no more than swamp, where they found a bridge left by the Arawak Indians – hence the name. he first harbor was built in the outer basin, called the Careenage where the boats ere "careened" or keeled over so that their hulls could be repaired and cleaned.

BELOW: colonial grandeur.

Baxter's Road, in Bridgetown, is called The Street That Never Sleeps. It comes alive at night with meals grilled by the roadside and rum shops selling beer and rum, resounding to the steady throb of calypso and reggae.

Now there are two bridges across the river, which in fact is just an inlet of se the wider Charles Duncan O'Neal Bridge and **Chamberlain Bridge** Ⓐ, t gateway to Bridgetown, which used to swing back to allow boats to pa through. Down on the south bank, as part of a major renovation program, the c warehouses are being converted into shops and cafés, such as the **Waterfro Café** where you can relax and watch the water world and city life unfold front of you. At night the tempo rises with a jazz band to dance to. In t Careenage, where the island's trading center once was, smart yachts bob alon side catamarans offering sightseeing trips along the coast, and sportfishing boa all set to hunt down the big wahoo and marlin.

Nelson – a controversial monument

Between the two bridges sprawls **Independence Square** Ⓑ, a car park day and a meeting place by night. It is also a popular spot for political rallie Over Chamberlain Bridge past the stalls of colorful fruit and vegetables, yo come face to face with a bronze statue of Nelson located suitably in **Trafalg Square** Ⓒ. A remaining symbol of colonialism, the monument was erected 1813 (17 years before Nelson's Column in London's Trafalgar Square) in a wa of patriotism after his death a few months after he'd docked in Barbados. Ho ever, since 1833, the statue has been a controversial figure with many wanti a Barbadian hero commemorated in its place.

Behind the square stand the **Public Buildings** Ⓓ, built in the 1870s to accor modate the Houses of Parliament. Founded in 1639, this parliamentary body the third oldest in the Commonwealth after Bermuda and Britain.

At the top of Broad Street, northwest of the square, is the **Verandah A**

BELOW: cricket commentators at the Oval.

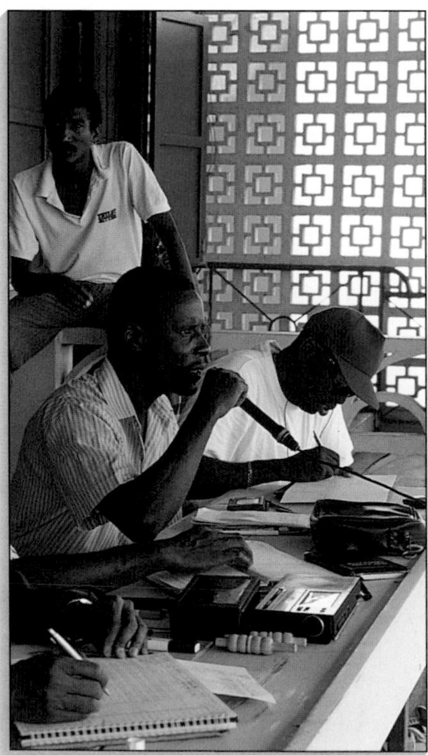

CRICKET, LOVELY CRICKET

Cricket is much more than a game in Barbados; it is national religion, inspiring the islanders with a fier passion, particularly when the West Indies meets Englan their old colonial masters, in a Test Match.

For five days, the **Kensington Oval**, the island's cricketi headquarters and national shrine, takes on a carniv atmosphere as supporters of both teams (Barbados almo sinks under the weight of the English fans who fly out for t event) pack the stands. With a "We must win but if we don then we must still have a good time" attitude, the We Indians welcome their visitors, encouraging them to join the fun and share their picnics and "liquid sunshine".

The game of cricket has been described as "like abstra art – you only understand it when you have watched it fo long time". Introduced to the island almost 200 years ago the British as a character builder, cricket now has no cla boundaries and Barbados has produced many heroes. T "Three Ws" – Clyde Walcott, Frank Worrell and Evert Weekes – were knighted in the 1960s; Gordon Greenid and Desmond Haynes, one of the world's best opening pai several fast bowlers and the greatest cricketer of all tim Garfield "Gary" Sobers, who was knighted in 1975, havi scored 8,032 runs, taken 235 wickets and held 110 catche

Gallery (open Mon–Fri and Sat am, free) which holds regular exhibitions of local artists' work on sale at reasonable prices. Downstairs in the Women's Self Help shop women sell their own special recipes of guava jelly and hot pepper sauce.

Broad Street is the main shopping area with several large duty-free stores; many of the buildings, such as Barclays Bank and Da Costa's, retain their old colonial grandeur. At the far end is the Georgian **St Mary's Church** Ⓔ (open daily; donations welcome), which also serves as a hurricane shelter surrounded by beautiful gardens. Opposite, the concrete facade of **Cheapside Market** fronts a typically colourful Caribbean scene on Saturday mornings.

Westwards along the seafront is **Pelican Village** Ⓕ, a network of passages containing craft, clothes and souvenir shops, art galleries and cafés – handy for the passengers of the cruise ships which dock in the **Deep Water Harbour** – is being redeveloped. Before the docks were built in 1961, passengers and freight had to be rowed ashore. Around 500,000 visitors arrive on cruise ships each year, usually for a one-night stopover, and the terminal is well stocked with banking facilities and duty-free shopping.

Back in Trafalgar Square, take the road east to **St Michael's Cathedral** Ⓖ (open daily; donations welcome). Dating from 1665, the original building was destroyed by a hurricane in 1780. However it was rebuilt in solid limestone coral nine years later, with the help of lottery money, ironically lending a Church blessing to gambling! Inside is a single-hand clock. A few blocks further to the east lies the tranquil oasis of **Queen's Park** Ⓗ with the magnificent **Queen's Park House** (1780) as its centerpiece. This fine Georgian building, with an impressive wooden balcony, houses a small theatre that puts on plays with a West Indian flavor, and an art gallery exhibiting the work of local artists.

Map on pages 262–63

The Synagogue, built in 1834, off James Street, has a beautiful interior.

BELOW: horseplay at the racetrack.

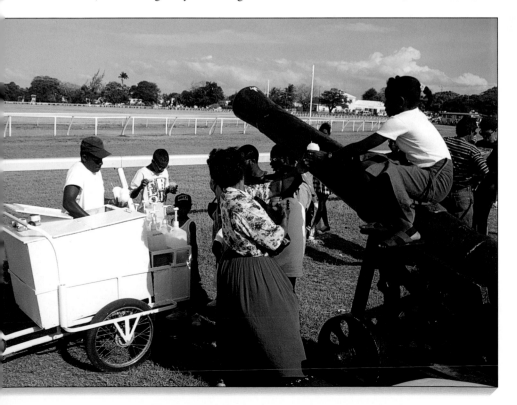

The Garrison Historical Area

Leaving Bridgetown via the Charles Duncan O'Neal Bridge, you pass the bu terminal for the south and **Fairchild Market** and continue along Bay Street t the **Garrison Historical Area**, where the **Garrison Savannah** ❷ was once parade ground for the British West Indian forces. Now a racecourse and spor venue, the Savannah is where the Independence Day Celebrations are held o November 30 with parades of spectacular pomp and splendor.

Tyrol Cot, the former home of the first Premier of Barbados, Sir Grantley Adams, and his son Tom, the second Prime Minister, is part of a Heritage Village (open Mon–Fri; entrance fee) north-west of Bridgetown.

East of the Garrison is the **Barbados Museum** ❸ (open Mon–Sat and Su pm, closed public hols; entrance fee; tel: 427-0201) housed in an early 19t century British military prison. Beautifully presented in the old preserved priso cells, this portrayal of island history with an art gallery and children's hands-o gallery is one of the best in the Caribbean. There is also a café in the shad courtyard and a twice-weekly historical show, *1627 and All That*, with a buffe

Southern hot spots

The road hugging the south coast leads through a built up area of hotels, shop and restaurants punctuated with glorious white beaches which offer plenty o fun and watersports but no seclusion. This part of Barbados is literally "jumping after dark with islanders and visitors all after some nocturnal action. From **Harbour Lights** on Bay Street, an open air nightclub on the beach outside Bridgetow brimming with Caribbean atmosphere, to the cluster of bars and restaurants at **S Lawrence Gap**, 3 miles (5 km) away off Highway 7. Each nightspot is uniqu with its own ambience and following, but they all rock with the sounds of liv soca, calypso, reggae, soul, or jazz.

Oistins ❹, further on, the fishing "capital" of Barbados, is another hot spo

BELOW: a portrait of a flying fish.

try out on Friday nights, but of a different kind. Here, a Fish Fry – fish and ips cooked outside in enormous pans over burning coals – is held in an area small, wooden imitation chattel houses, serving as bars and shops, adjacent the famous fish market. Rum and beer is sold by the bottle and the music is rned up loud. At around 4pm on weekdays you can watch the fishermen lay eir catch of dolphin (dorado), snapper, king fish, tuna and the national delicacy, ying fish, on the cool, wet slabs of the covered terminal, and see the women ftly gut and fillet them for sale.

Oistins also has an historical tale to tell: in 1652 the Royalist islanders had en besieged for weeks by Cromwell's Roundheads. The *contretemps* was ally settled in the Charter of Barbados which pledged the islanders to obeence to the hated Cromwell and his Commonwealth Parliament in exchange r the right to religious freedom and consultation over taxation.

Map on page 262–63

TIP

The Barbados National Trust (tel: 426-2421) offers a Heritage Passport allowing entry into their sites at a discount. It also runs an Open House scheme in which private houses – old and new – are open to the public for an afternoon.

lantation house and a pirate's castle

eading inland from Oistins into the parish of St Philip, you reach **The Rum actory** and **Heritage Park** ❺ (open daily, entrance fee) at Foursquare off ighway 6, for a tour of the most modern rum distillery in the world. In the joining heritage park is an amphitheatre, an art gallery and several craft shops lling locally made products. Further north off Highway 5 is **Sunbury Plantion House** ❻ (open daily, entrance fee), a beautifully restored 300-year-old antation house, full of colonial antiques, which gives a real feel of what it ust have been like to be a wealthy plantation owner. You can stop for lunch re in the café at the back and return for a typical lavish evening banquet.

Back across Six Cross Roads to the southeast coast are two hotels each worth ending a day at for their history and beautiful spoilt beaches. This is where the Atlantic meets the aribbean and the waves build up some force making e sea ideal for body surfing, especially at **The rane Beach** (open daily, entrance fee redeemable bar or restaurant). Opened in 1887, it was once Barados's most exclusive hotel and was patronized by e island's wealthy.

Before that the bay contained a small working port here boats arrived with goods from Bridgetown. A ane at the top of the cliff unloaded the boats, hence e name. Now you will recognize the beautiful cliffp view and colonnaded swimming pool from the ges of glossy magazines worldwide, as it is a fashn photographer's dream location.

Sam Lord's Castle ❼ (open daily, entrance fee), rther along this craggy coastline, reached via Highay 5, was extravagantly created in the late 18th cenry by Sam Lord, a notorious planter who is one of the st-known characters in Bajan folklore. He is reputed have made his money by luring ships on to the reef hanging lanterns in the palm trees on the beach so at the sea captains thought they were heading into rt. They were inevitably shipwrecked and Sammy le their cargo. Much of his original furniture and cor can still be seen in the house, the main part of the tel, and you can enjoy the still palm-fringed beach, d choice of pools and restaurants.

BELOW: new view points from a horse.

The wild and rugged east

To explore Barbados's magnificent, windswept east coast, it is a good idea make a day of it, and you could stay overnight in one of the old Barbadi hotels traditionally used by the islanders for their holidays. From west to ea across the island may not be very far in miles but along the hilly network roads it can take time, especially if you get lost.

Discover deepest Barbados on horse-back, mountain bike or Shank's pony. Highland Outdoor Tours (tel: 438-8069) offers hikes over Mount Hillaby, through the original forest cover of Turners Hall Woods.

The scenery changes dramatically along the East Coast Road compared to t flat pastureland of the south and as it cuts through tropical woodland, the impre sive entrance of **Codrington College** ❽ (open daily, entrance fee), with a lo drive lined with majestic royal palms, hoves into view. Founded in 1702 Christopher Codrington, the Barbados-born governor general of the Leewa Islands and *de facto* owner of Barbuda, (*see page 181*), the limestone coral th ological college has a fascinating nature trail in the grounds, leading throug primeval forest. The adventurer and travel writer Patrick Leigh Fermor describe it in the late 1940s as "in a hollow beyond a spinney of tall mahogany, south the township of Bathsheba, a beautiful Palladian building, reclining dreamily the shores of a lake among lawns and balustrades and great shady trees, sudden appeared, its columns and pediments conjuring up, in the afternoon sunligh some enormous country seat in the Dukeries." And it has barely changed.

Continuing north on the East Coast Road, the undulating sugar cane fiel change to steep hillsides of banana plantations that drop to the sea. A right tur ing plunges down to **Bathsheba** and the **Andromeda Botanic Gardens** (open daily; closed public hols; entrance fee) which has one of the finest displa of tropical flowers and shrubs in the Caribbean. Created in 1954 on a rock hillside by amateur horticulturist Iris Bannochie, who died in 1988, the garde

BELOW: waiting for the bus to town.

intelligently designed and harbors exotic tropical plants that she collected n her travels around the world. There is a splendid example of a bearded fig tree ongside collections of orchids and bromeliads. A stream cuts through the 6-cre (2 ha) profusion of tropical flora, now run by the Barbados National Trust.

At Bathsheba is the rundown **Atlantis Hotel**, where Barbados's most famous uthor, George Lamming, always stays when he returns. One of the oldest hotels n the island, it may not look much from the outside but the food is delicious. urfers flock to Bathsheba for the Soup Bowl, where the waves are a challenge.

You have to go back up the hill and down again at the next turn to Cattlewash here the road runs beside a long golden beach washed by Atlantic rollers. sually deserted during the week, the sea is dangerous for swimmers. Nearby re two more traditional Barbadian hotels – the **Edgwater Inn** and **Kingsley lub** – offering excellent local food, especially at the Sunday lunch buffets, pop-lar on the island.

he hills of the Scotland District

omesick British colonists likened the lush landscapes of Barbados to Eng-nd and the rolling hills and bizarre rock formations to the Scottish Highlands, arning the nicknames Little England and the Scotland District. An excursion to the island's interior will take you through open countryside, past acres of ane fields and small hamlets of chattel houses (*see page 77*) each with a rum op-cum-store. Leaving the ABC Highway in Bridgetown on Highway 3 and ollowing the signposts to **Gun Hill** – a former military signal station where ere is a small museum (open daily; entrance fee) and a white, stone lion – you ach **Francia Plantation House** ❿ (open Mon–Fri, closed public hols;

Map on pages 262–63

World-class opera is staged al fresco at a 17th-century plantation house during Holders Season every Easter. In recent years, performers have included Luciano Pavarotti and Lesley Garrett.

BELOW: Colony Club hotel on the Platinum Coast.

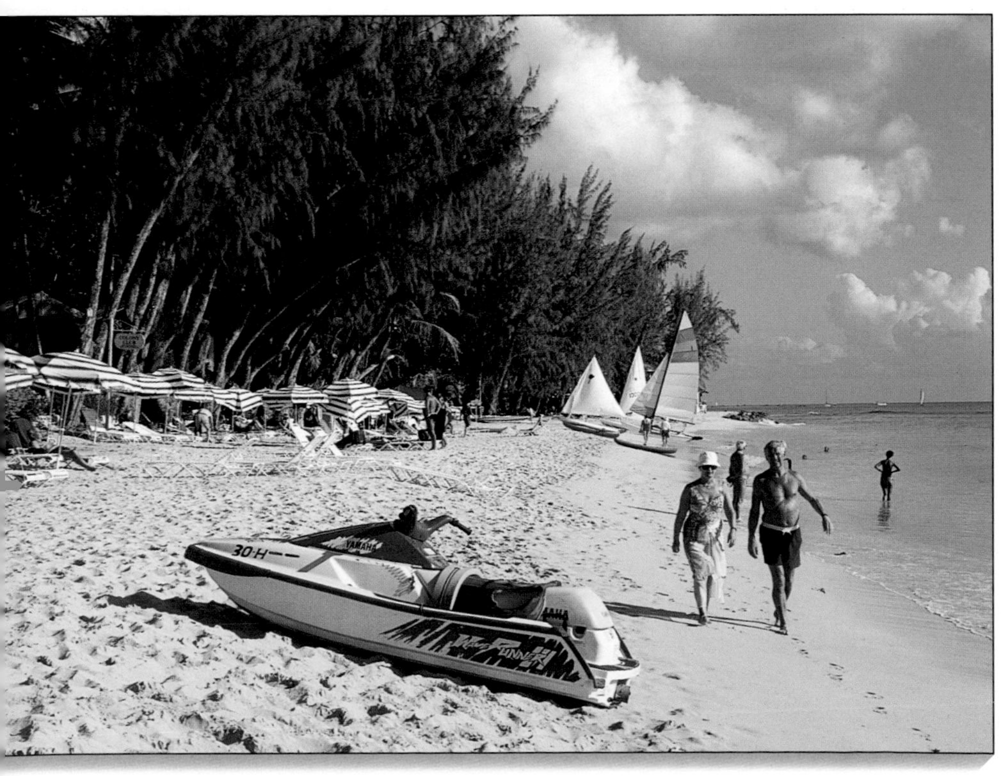

entrance fee). Still lived in by the family of the original owner who built and fu nished it in 1913, many of the rooms are open to the public and contain som fine antique pieces. The house, built in a mahogany wood is surrounded b Mediterranean-style terraced gardens.

Further north, **Harrison's Cave** ⓫ (open daily; entrance fee; tel: 438-664 is a geological feast for the eyes, a crystallized limestone underworld of gorge grottoes, streams and waterfalls encrusted with spectacular stalactites and st lagmites which you can marvel at from an electric tram.

For tranquil, natural beauty above ground, walk through the luxuriant jung greenery of **Welchman Hall Gully** ⓬ (open daily; entrance fee) nearby. Th half-mile (1 km) long ravine was once part of a series of caves, whose roofs fe in, and connected with Harrison's Cave. Now looked after by the Barbad National Trust (*see page 269*), there are over 200 species of plants, flowers an trees, plus large families of green monkeys who snap up the fruit.

Another botanical delight is the **Flower Forest** ⓭ (open daily; entrance fe a little further north, where you can touch and smell the wonderful array of tro ical flowers and plants set against magnificent views of the east coast. In the ce ter is a young baobab tree, traditionally grown in the middle of African village

White beaches on the Platinum Coast

The west coast of Barbados is lapped by the deep azure blue of the tranqu Caribbean Sea with pinky white coral sand beaches edged with casuarina tree and palms, living up to the tropical island dream. Earning the tag Platinu Coast, this is where the smart hotels jostle for the best sea view each in their ow landscaped paradise and sporting such tantalizing names as Glitter Bay, Cor

BELOW: the Animal Flower Cave on the rugged north coast.

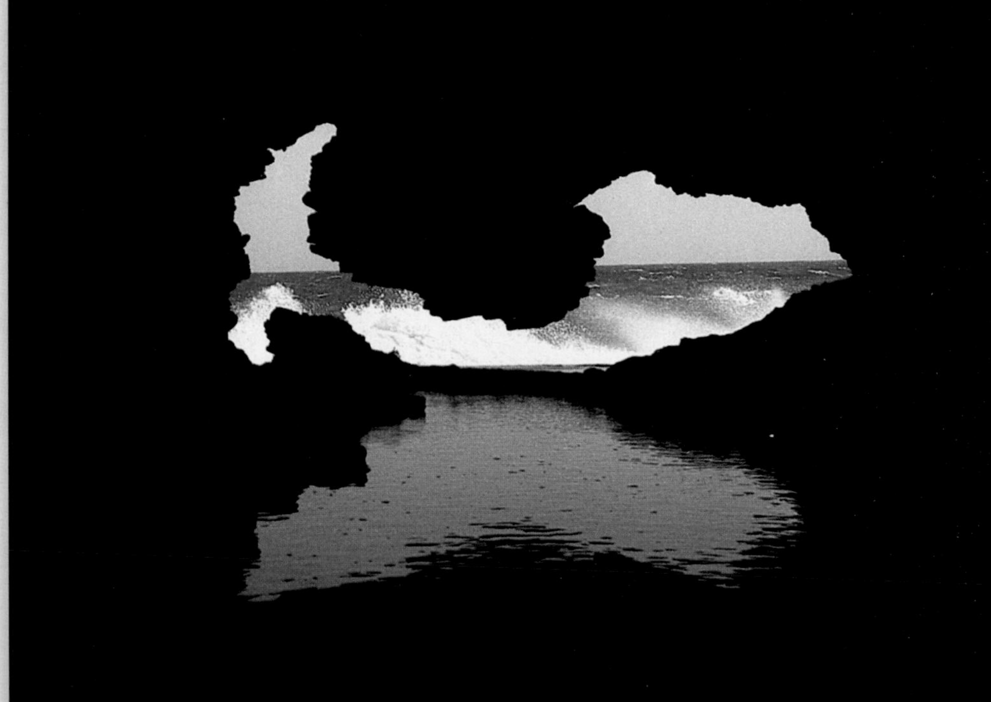

:ef and Tamarind Cove. As no one can own a beach in Barbados, it is possi- : to walk for miles along the water's edge, stopping at the beach bars for a rum nch and trying out the wide variety of watersports on offer.

The world-renowned **Sandy Lane Hotel** ⓮ and holiday refuge to the rich and mous is tucked away in Sandy Lane Bay just south of Holetown (about 3 les/5 km north of Bridgetown on Highway 1). Built in 1961, it is now closed r a controversial (according to some regular clientele) revamp and is due to open in November 1999 in time for the millennium.

Captain Henry Powell accidentally landed in **Holetown** ⓯ in May 1625 on s way to somewhere else. He took a fancy to what he saw as a nice piece of al estate and, as any true Englishman would have done in those days, he stuck Jnion Jack in the ground and claimed it on behalf of the King. He returned in bruary 1627 with an expedition to settle the island and, today, the Holetown stival celebrates the anniversary with street parties and a waterski show.

Further on you can learn how a coral reef is formed at the **Folkestone Park d Marine Reserve** ⓰ (open Mon–Fri; entrance fee) and go snorkeling along underwater trail around Dottins Reef. Further out to sea is a shipwrecked eek freighter deliberately sunk to form a coral reef.

The Story of Sugar is told at Portvale Sugar Factory and Museum (open Mon–Sat; entrance fee – factory only open Feb – May) just east of Holetown. The sequel is at Mount Gay Rum Visitors Center (open Mon–Fri; tel: 425-9066) north of Bridgetown.

ound the spectacular north

eightstown ⓱, the island's second town, was once an important port for nsporting sugar to Bristol in England. It is now returning to some of its for- r glory with the help of the Barbados National Trust, which is restoring the th-century balconied buildings. Another reason for its revival is the new **Port Charles Marina**, just to the north, an upmarket, environmentally friendly velopment, with a berth for a yacht attached to each cury residence.

Highway 1 continues through the pretty fishing vil- ;e of **Six Men's Bay** and into the rugged, sparsely pulated northernmost parish of St Lucy. Here you ll find the best picnic spots on the island, such as **cher's Bay**, a peaceful, grassy area shaded by a ove of casuarina trees, which is usually deserted, d **River Bay**. At the very northern tip of the island the **Animal Flower Cave** ⓲ (open daily; entrance :), named for the tiny sea anemones that grow in ols on its floor. The ocean's relentless pounding has :ated steep, jagged cliffs and rocky, barren land that sembles a moonscape. The small bar sells delicious memade sandwiches and lemonade and the propri- r's sheep, Pepita, drinks 7 Up out of the bottle.

From here the road cuts inland to the Jacobean plan- ion house **St Nicholas Abbey** ⓳ (open Mon–Fri; trance fee). Thought to be the oldest original build- ; on the island, it has never been a religious insti- ion, despite the name, and is full of fascinating tures and antiques set in a beautiful garden.

Further south you reach the main road back to the st coast and **Barbados Wildlife Reserve** ⓴ (open ly, entrance fee). Here the only caged creature is a ssive python – the green monkeys, otters, tortoises, anas, porcupine *et al* roam free alongside the vis- rs in a mahogany woodland. ❑

BELOW: flamingos in the Wildlife Reserve.

MATIC

TRINIDAD

;eologically part of South America and politically the stronger half of an island republic, this exhilarating, cosmopolitan, tropical island is also a land of natural beauty

Pulsating with life, Trinidad is a noisy, vibrant country, much noisier than Tobago, its calm, tranquil partner, 21 miles (33 km) away, in the two-island republic of Trinidad and Tobago. And it reaches a crescendo every :bruary at Carnival time when the capital Port of Spain, the birthplace of ılypso and steel pan, throbs to the rhythms of the bands and the dancing in the reets. Here you can see the true flamboyant nature of the islanders as they ırade in the most resplendent costumes you have ever seen and have a ball in e "greatest street party on earth" (*see pages 282–83*).

The music permeates the very heart of the countryside where more than 400 ›ecies of birds take up the tune, silently accompanied by myriad butterflies. ;inidad was not called Land of the Hummingbird by the Amerindians for noth-g. In the mountain rainforests of the north, the coastal swamps and the flat ılm-fringed beaches of the east, it is easy to escape the west coast's modern ıbbub of industrialized life, spawned by the riches of offshore oil fields.

The oil boom of the 1970s created an economic climate comfortable enough ›r Trinidad not to encourage tourism, unlike its sister islands in the rest of the ntillean chain, which means that many beaches are deserted and "untouched". owever, that is now changing as new resorts are being planned and built. Out-de the hurricane belt, the sheltered bays of the north-est are a haven for yachties who are buying ɜrmanent moorings for their boats in the top class ıarinas that have recently been developed there.

PRECEDING PAGES: early morning in Queen's Park Savannah.
LEFT: Port of Spain market.
BELOW: it's Carnival time again!

outh American influences

would be wrong to eulogize the beautiful blue 'aters that surround Trinidad, because they are rown. The southernmost and largest island in the astern Caribbean chain (1,864 sq. miles/4,660 sq. m), it is washed by the waters of the Orinoco delta ıst 12 miles (20 km away) in Venezuela, but the sea ; still mostly warm, clear and pleasant to swim in. ailing or flying across to Tobago, you can see the ɔlor dramatically change to blue halfway.

Long before Christopher Columbus sighted three ıountain peaks on the horizon on July 31, 1498 and amed the island they belonged to "La Trinidad" Γrinity), Amerindians had canoed across from the ›rinoco region and settled its shores. The Spanish ɔlonizers failed to find the gold of El Dorado here, ut they did use the island for tobacco plantations. To ultivate them they enslaved the local Indians, who ractically died out within a century as a result.

English sailors, Spanish farmers, French planters nd their families, adventurers, thousands of African laves and, from the 19th century onwards, numerous sian laborers have formed the basis of today's mul-

The acrobatic limbo you see (and attempt) in hotels comes from a symbolic dance guiding the soul to the next world.

ticultural society of 1.5 million people, who now live largely at peace with o another. During the Carnival in particular all social and ethnic barriers fall resulting in a sharp rise in the birth rate during late autumn.

Rich resources

When slavery was ended in 1834, cheap labor was suddenly very much demand on the cocoa plantations and in the sugar cane fields – and East Indi and Chinese contract laborers were lured to the Caribbean by clever promise The terms of many of their contracts were such that they often had to work the fields for up to 10 years just to pay their transport costs. Soon villages wi their own Hindu temples and their own social order began to appear in the sug belt of the south.

In the industrial centers on the west coast, a multi-racial middle class admi isters the profits from the oil wells near La Brea, manufactures products f the whole of the Caribbean, makes a good living from international tradir

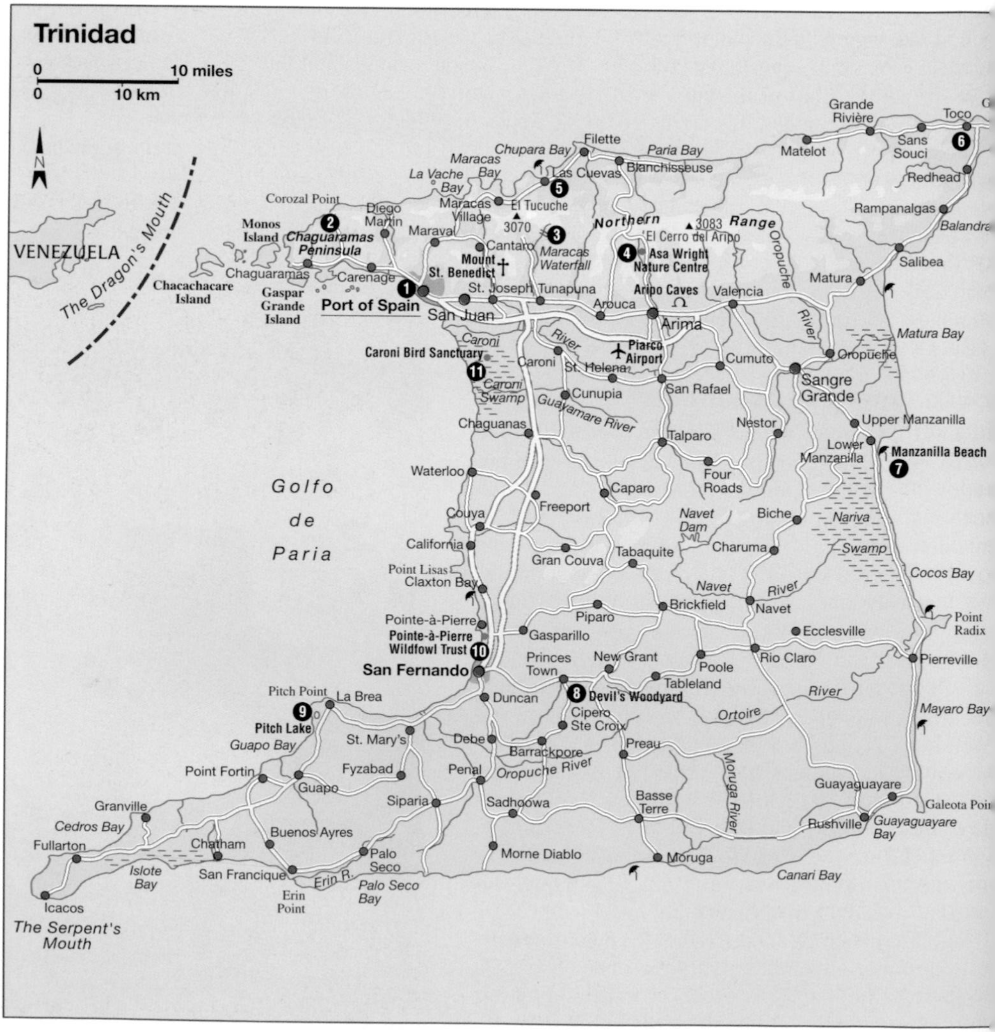

Trinidad

0 10 miles

0 10 km

ɔnnections, and praises the "American way of life". In the early 1970s, rich oil elds and gas in the coastal regions had nourished the Trinbagonians' hopes of future as free from financial worries as that of the sheikhs of Saudi Arabia. In e ensuing oil crisis, European money prevented complete economic collapse.

Politically, the two very different islands of Trinidad and Tobago have been ɔllectively run by Britain since 1889; in the 1950s political parties began to ɔurish under the clever leadership of Dr Eric Williams, and in 1962 gained dependence, creating the Republic in 1976. Now the government is domi-ɑted by Trinidadians of Indian descent, while Muslim groups are mainly in ıarge of the armed forces – a situation that is causing tension between the var-ɪus ethnic groups and also in relations between the two islands.

ort of Spain – a modern city

olorful and turbulent – that's **Port of Spain ❶**, the capital of the island repub-c, situated at the foot of the Northern Range. Established in 1754 by the Span-h, today modern skyscrapers, such as the 300-ft (92m) high Twin Towers, ıd elegant shopping centers contrast sharply with dilapidated gingerbread-yle villas, wooden huts and rusty fences. A stroll during the daytime through ıdependence Square and Queen's Park Savannah to the attractive buildings f the Magnificent Seven is not too strenuous. In the evenings, however, it is nsafe to walk in the city centre and the southeastern suburbs.

Independence Square is bordered to the east by the neo-Gothic cathedral of ıe **Immaculate Conception**. Extending away westwards towards the cruise ter-ıinal on both sides of this long square are shopping centers, banks, the color-ıl rasta market of **Tent City**, a statue of Christopher Columbus, and the Twin owers, containing government offices. The attrac-ve promenade along the center is named for Brian ara, who has done much to make Trinidad famous as cricket-playing nation.

Frederick Street, lined with street traders, leads n to the park on **Woodford Square**. This is where issatisfied citizens keep the Speaker's Corner tradi-on alive by loudly criticizing the various decisions ıade in the imposing **Red House**, the seat of parlia-ıent, at the western end of the square. The Anglican athedral of the Holy Trinity, the Supreme Court, the own Hall and police headquarters surround the park nd its magnificent old trees.

To the north, a 15-minute walk away, Frederick treet ends at the large but by no means green or ɛafy-looking **Queen's Park Savannah**. Nearby, in ıe **National Museum and Art Gallery** (open 'ues–Sun; free), you can see documents dating from ıe colonial era and also an amazing collection of litzy Carnival costumes; they provide a suitable sam-le of the annual highlight.

West of the Savannah, the **Magnificent Seven** – a ine of very fine colonial buildings dating from the urn of the century – give Maraval Road a great deal f flair and elegance. All seven buildings may only e admired from the outside, and the time to appreci-te their architectural splendor is during the early ıorning, when the sun shows them at their best.

Map on page 278

North to south the Magnificent Seven are: Stollmeyer's Castle (1904); White Hall, the prime minister's office; Archbishop's House; Mille Fleurs; Roomor; Hayes Court, the Anglican bishop's residence, and Queen's Royal College with an eye-catching clock tower.

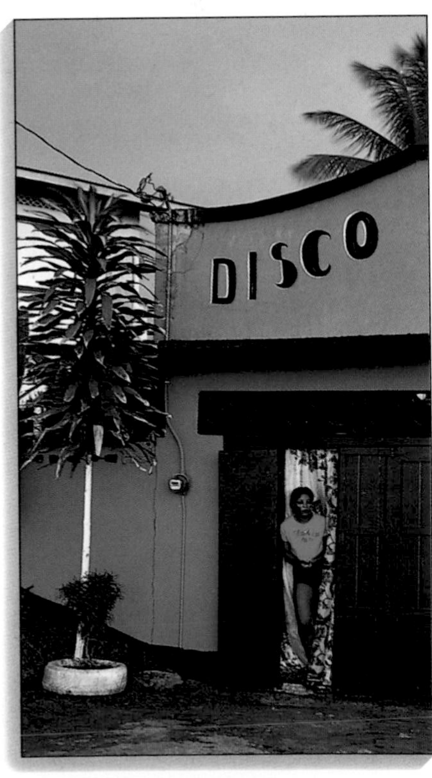

BELOW: a day in the life of a disco.

The Hindu temple of Sewdass Sadhu Mandir built right next to the sea, near the village of Waterloo, is a beautiful spot.

BELOW: a boatload of goats going to market.

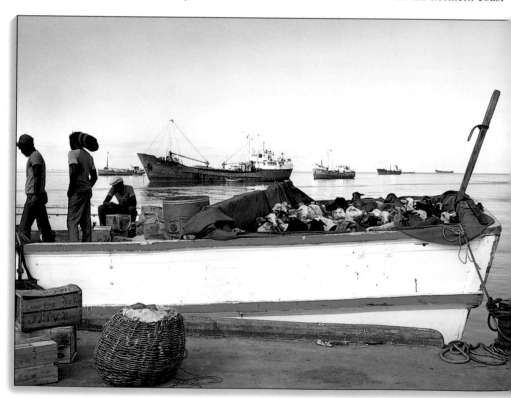

To the northern rainforest

The rugged coast of the **Chaguaramas Peninsula** ❷, a US naval ba (1945–64) to the northwest of Port of Spain, is a popular sailing region and being developed by the yachting industry – big business in Trinidad now. On t island of **Gaspar Grande**, a 20-minute boat ride away from Chaguaramas tow the young unemployed are happy to take visitors on guided tours of the **Gaspar** limestone caverns (entrance fee).

On excursions from the capital to the **Northern Range**, it takes quite a whi before the big city with all its residential suburbs, supermarkets and side stre finally gets left behind. Once that happens the mountainous hinterland arriv quite suddenly. The Eastern Main Road leads out of Port of Spain to **Tun puna**, where there are some good Chinese restaurants, and the Royal Ro plunges north through thick forest to the 320-ft (100 m) high **Maracas Wate fall** ❸, but it can be a little disappointing when it hasn't rained.

Back on the main road, you see high on the hill **Mount St Benedict**, the ol est Benedictine monastery in the region (founded 1912), and 8 miles (13 kı later, you reach **Arima**, the island's third largest town. From here the road noı twists and turns through orchards and gardens to the **Asa Wright Natu Centre** ❹ (open daily; entrance fee). This 182-acre (74 ha) site contains a va amount of fascinating tropical flora and fauna, which researchers from the Ne York Zoological Society have been studying closely for decades. Over 100 di ferent species of bird, including several rare hummingbirds, can be observe here. For a guided dawn or evening birdwatching hike, accommodation is avai able in the old plantation manor above a magnificent tropical garden.

The wildly romantic coastline near **Blanchisseuse** on the northern coast ached by 23 miles (37 km) of hairpin bends with stunning views and dangerous potholes. The half-moon-shaped sandy bay at the fishing village of **Las Cuevas** ❺ to the west is particularly attractive, while **Maracas Bay** 10 miles (16 km) from Port of Spain is the more busy beach.

Map on page 278

Never-ending palm-fringed bays

At the northeastern tip of the island are the dramatic cliffs of **Toco** ❻, a two-hour drive from the capital via the Eastern Main Road and a rather bumpy route through some mountain rainforest. Leatherback turtles lay their eggs on the secluded beaches here between April and June, when swimming is forbidden.

The East Coast Road leads back down to **Matura** from where three seemingly endless sandy bays sweep down the coast for 40 miles (64 km). Edged by dense coconut plantations, **Manzanilla Beach** ❼ in the middle has some new public amenities and **Mayaro** at the southern end has some houses to rent, otherwise these beaches are deserted and unspoiled. However, swimming in the Atlantic here is dangerous, due to a strong undertow and high waves.

Behind the palm trees is the mangrove swamp of **Nariva**, and young boys can often be seen at the roadside driving their water buffalo out into the fields – very reminiscent of India. The rural south of Trinidad is mainly inhabited by East Indian families, who earn just enough as farmers and sugar cane workers to pay for their families – most of the huts at the roadside look dilapidated.

A colorful bird from the Northern Range where the wonders of the Aripo Caves can be seen by genuine potholers with a knowledgeable guide.

Where the earth bubbles

At **Devil's Woodyard** ❽, about 8 miles (13 km) east of Trinidad's second largest town, San Fernando on the southwest coast, gas bubbles can be seen inside the mud holes of one of the island's 18 mud volcanoes. This is a holy site for Hindus, who leave sacrificial offerings here such as flowers or coconut oil. These mud volcanoes, and also the pitch lake of **La Brea** ❾, 13 miles (20 km) southwest of San Fernando, are connected with the crude oil and natural gas beneath the South American continental shelf that were discovered in 1897. The largest natural lake of asphalt in the world and up to 320 ft (100 m) deep in places, La Brea was found in 1595 by the English captain Sir Walter Raleigh, who used the sticky pitch to help keep his ship waterproof. You can walk on the surface of the lake, but since it is dangerous in places, don't explore it without an experienced guide.

Just to the north of San Fernando, some rare wildfowl have found a refuge right at the centre of a crude oil refinery. The **Pointe-à-Pierre Wildfowl Trust** ❿ has been devoting itself to breeding threatened species and preserving natural habitats in this largely industrial part of the island since 1966.

The national bird of Trinidad is the crimson ibis. Every evening flocks of these elegant creatures with long curved beaks can be seen settling on trees for the night in the bird sanctuary at **Caroni** ⓫ just south of Port of Spain. This extensive mangrove swamp is also an important breeding ground for shrimps, lungfish and species of waterfowl which can be observed on boat trips (departures daily at 4pm). ❑

BELOW: greased up for J'Ouvert.

THE GREATEST STREET PARTY ON EARTH

Carnival in the Lesser Antilles is alive and well and getting bigger every year as the islands fill up with revelers from all over the world

Neither age nor profession, nor money or skin color matter when every February, 2 million Trinidadians and visitors seem to drown in a sea of colors, feathers, rhythm and rum. From Jump Up, the wild street party from dawn on the Monday (J'ouvert) before Ash Wednesday until King Momo's fire death in the last hours of the Tuesday, Port of Spain is one big anarchic Carnival party. The heroes are witty calypso singers and ingenious costume designers highly revered by a hip-swinging crowd dizzy with the beat and pulsating rhythm of the steel pans.

NEW CARNIVALS

Trinidad hosts the biggest Caribbean Carnival, originating in the Christian tradition of having a last big feast before fasting during Lent and Celtic festivities for expelling the gloomy spirits of winter. In Guadeloupe and Martinique people dress in black and white on Ash Wednesday and bury King Vaval. On St Barths King Moui Moui is burnt and on St Kitts Christmas and the New Year are the best times to enjoy parades and street fetes. Other so-called carnivals in the summer months have developed from the harvest festivals after the sugar cane had been cut, such as Crop Over in Barbados. Some islands have only recently established carnivals for tourism's sake – any excuse for an extended street party…

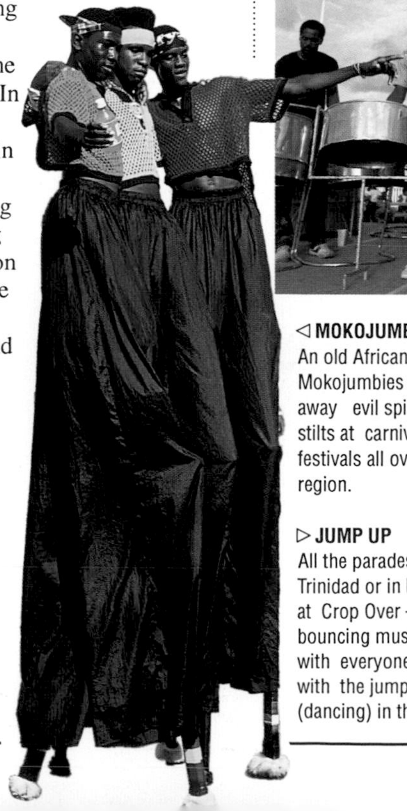

▽▷ BIRDS OF PARADISE

Feats of engineering, some of the magnificent outfits are so cumbersome that wheels have to be fixed on to facilitate movement.

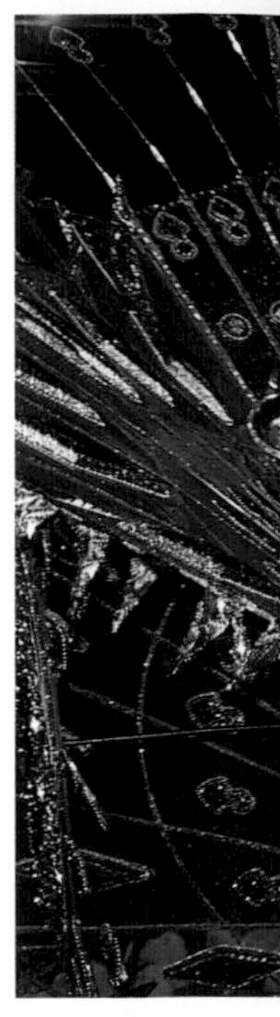

▽ STEELY COMPETITION

Months before, steel bands compete with their Carnival songs, and calypso singers prepare to fight for the title of "Calypso Monarch".

◁ MOKOJUMBIES

An old African tradition, Mokojumbies dance away evil spirits on stilts at carnivals and festivals all over the region.

▷ JUMP UP

All the parades – be it in Trinidad or in Barbados at Crop Over – are bouncing musical events with everyone joining in with the jump up (dancing) in the streets.

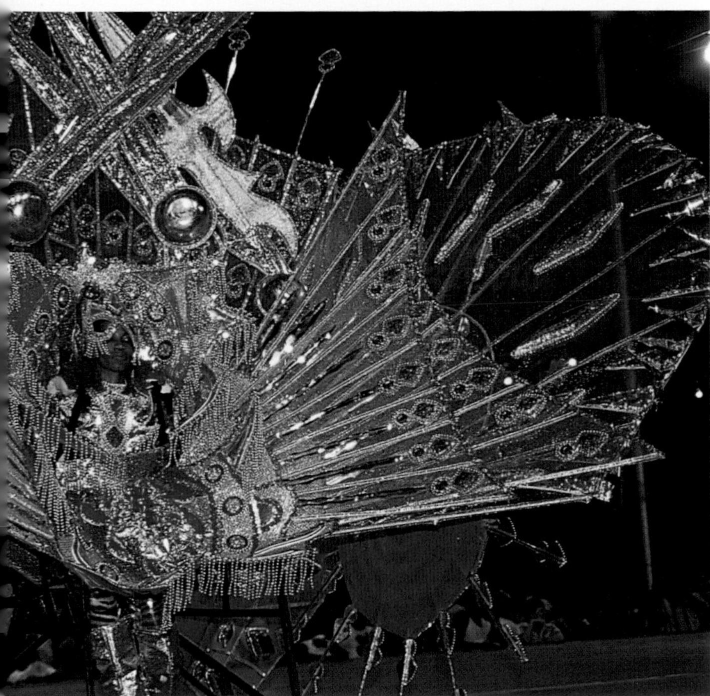

PLAYING MAS IN TRINIDAD

As soon as one Carnival ends the designers' imaginations are hard at work on the next one. Great Carnival couturiers such as Trinidadian Peter Minshall – whose renowned costumes led him to design the costumes for the opening of the Olympic Games in 1992 and 1996 – set up Mas Camps (workshops) in which vast numbers of costumes are made on a theme for their bands. Each band has a Carnival King and Queen who wear the masterpieces which are judged on Dimanche Gras, the night before Carnival officially begins.

The Mas tradition started in the late 18th century with the French plantation owners organizing masquerades (mas) and balls before they had to endure the fasting of Lent. The slaves copied and buffooned their masters, and once set free from forced labor, their frustrations found a platform in clever calypso lyrics and steel pan music.

UDDERS
Monday morning, ivert (joo-vay) begins n groups of revelers ar themselves with mud hug anyone in white.

IDDIES CARNIVAL
y of the island carnivals e a special day set aside the children just before official start. Their tumes are often made in Mas Camps of Trinidad.

▷ **BEAUTIFUL DEVIL**
When the slaves started creating their costumes the mythology of their African ancestors inspired them to figures of good and evil. Over the years even nasty devils have been clad in shiny robes and jewels.

TOBAGO

Only a 20-minute plane flight away from frenetic Port of Spain, 'obago is an oasis of calm in a bright blue sea of tranquility offering copious white beaches, sheltered coves and wild forest interior

Trinidad's other half in the Republic of Trinidad and Tobago, this small tropical island 21 miles (34 km) to the northeast lies in stark contrast to its twin's cosmopolitan bustle, industrialization and magnitude. Rural tranuility and Caribbean enjoyment of life go hand in hand in Tobago and the ıagnificent beaches and the colorful coral landscape just offshore are an effecve means of dispelling stress.

At only 26 miles (42 km) long and 3 miles (5 km) wide, Tobago is a contin-al feast for the eyes: picturesque, bumpy roads wind around the coast past nspoiled bays of white sand and bright blue sea, and climb up across the moun-ainous backbone through high stands of creaking bamboo and dense rainforest, ive with colorful birdlife, before plunging into panoramic views on the other de. No wonder Columbus named it *Bellaforma* (beautiful shape) in 1498.

Tobago does not share the cultural mix that enriches Trinidad, despite having nanged colonial hands 29 times in 160 years; the population of around 51,000 re mainly descendants of the African slaves making a living from farming or shing. The crime rate is much lower here and the people are friendly and welcoming to the steadily increasing flow of visitors to their island.

LEFT: seventh heaven at Arnos Vale.
BELOW: tropical idyll at Pigeon Point.

obago's colonial past

Iope, Courland, Shirvan, Les Coteaux – the place-ames are all reminders of Tobago's past colonial hases. At the beginning of the 17th century, the first utch and English settlers arrived only to be wiped ut or chased off by the Caribs. Eventually, 80 fami-es from Latvia succeeded in settling on Courland ay in 1654 and planted sugar cane, tobacco, pepper nd cotton. Adventurers, smallholders and pirates om all over Europe followed in their footsteps, and ıany were killed either by tropical diseases or by 'arib arrows.

Slaves were set to work on the first sugar cane and otton plantations 100 years later. In 1793, when the nglish had managed to seize control of Tobago yet gain, the island was inhabited by 14,170 blacks, 850 hites and five Amerindians.

When slavery ended in 1834 most of the planta-ons went broke as the freed slaves left and started ıbsistence farming to ensure their survival. French lanters in particular took the opportunity to buy up ınd very cheaply and started several coconut planta-ons – they then settled on Trinidad in fine manor ouses and lived very comfortably on the proceeds.

To save money the British decided from 1889 nwards to treat Trinidad and Tobago, their two south-rnmost islands in the Caribbean, as a collective dministrative unit. In 1962 the twin-island state was

Delicious soursop ice cream and many other home-made specialties can be bought from the market women in the niches at the large round market building in Scarborough. Fresh coconut milk, and ice cream coated in syrup are just two of the many delightful ways to refresh yourself around here.

given independence (*see page 279*), and since 1987 Tobago has had an intern autonomy separate from Trinidad, though it is still heavily dependent on sul sidies from Port of Spain. There are no large industrial centers on this large agrarian island, and tourism is only growing slowly because of competitic from other Caribbean destinations.

Scarborough – a village capital

The little town of **Scarborough** ❶ (pop. 16,000) on Rockly Bay is Tobago main harbor as well as the island's center of trade and administration. It wa founded by Scottish settlers in the 16th century, and has been the island's cap ital since 1769. More like a village than a town, the center consists of two roa junctions and concrete structures housing the post office, the market, the ferr and cruise ship harbor, Scarborough Mall, and the bus station. On market day half of Tobago meets up here to go shopping.

An oasis of calm behind the mall is the **Botanic Gardens**, where native tree bushes and flowers can be found in graceful and shady arrangements. Fror the harbor, Carnett Street leads up steeply past several tradesmen's stands t **James Park**; at the top end is the imposing-looking, Georgian-style **Cou House**, built between 1821 and 1825.

Follow Fort Street uphill, and a few steep curves later you reach the impres sive **Fort King George**, built in the late 18th century 490 ft (150 m) abov Rockly Bay. Severely damaged by a whirlwind in 1847, the fort was rebui according to old plans. Today, the complex contains not only the small **Nationa Museum** (open Mon–Fri; entrance fee), including exhibits of Amerindian pot tery and jewelry, but also the town's hospital and prison.

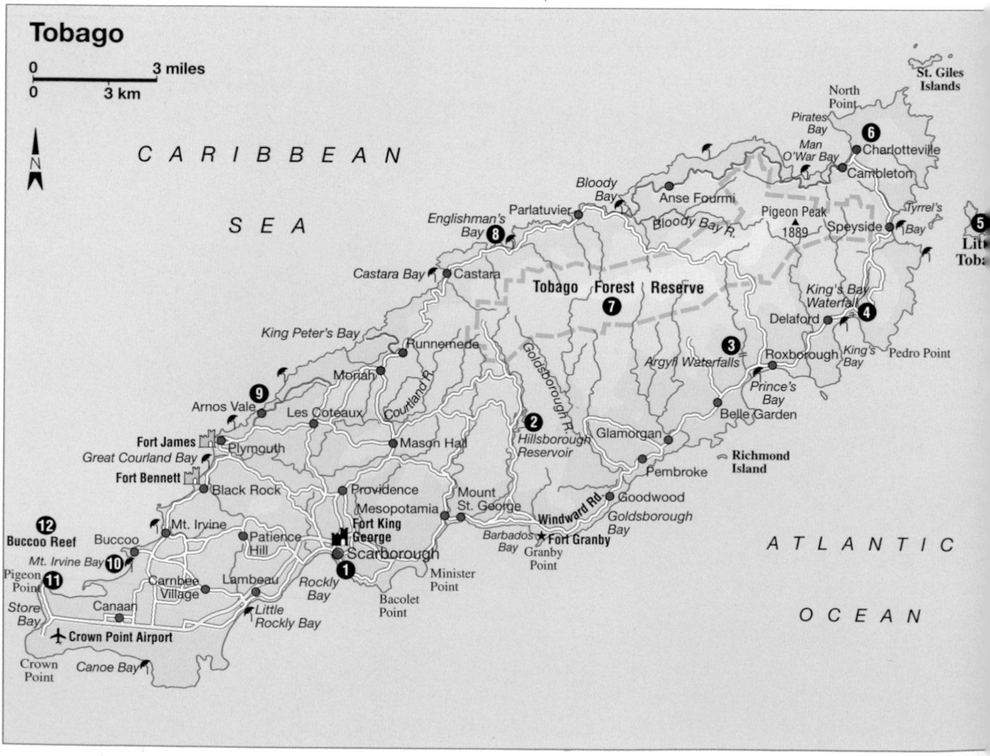

Map on page 286

ugged coasts and dense forests

een car drivers with good nerves will adore **Windward Road**, which winds ; way along the southeast coast of Tobago in steep curves. Spectacular views ' the Atlantic, pot-holes which are often knee-deep, and idyllic villages at the adside all make this route an unforgettable experience. Leave Scarborough via acolet Street and **Gun Bridge** named after the two old cannon there.

The only reminder that **Mount St George**, about 4 miles (6 km) along the ad, was once the British seat of government is the renovated court building ıting from 1788. A left turn shortly afterwards leads inland 2 miles (3 km) to e **Hillsborough Reservoir** ❷, an artificial lake providing the islanders with :inking water and also the natural habitat of many rare species of bird; the agonflies are very colorful, and you may even see a cayman (alligator).

A humming bird gathers nectar.

Back on Windward Road, all that remains of **Fort Granby** is a weathered-oking gravestone. During the 18th century this once-proud structure, looking :ross Barbados Bay, was home to the English 62nd Regiment, now it makes a :rfect picnic spot. The road winds along the coast, between the dark fringes of e rainforest and the spray of the Atlantic, passing through picturesque vil-ges like **Pembroke** and **Belle Garden**. Outside the village bars, at road junc-ɔns and in mini-markets, the Tobagonians enjoy their spare time "liming" – the cal word for "hanging out".

easonable waterfalls

tanding out amongst the tropical greenery high above the rocky coast (just :fore you reach Belle Garden) is **Richmond Great House**, a renovated manor ɔuse dating from 1766 which today is a popular guest house with New York

BELOW: King Peter's Bay from afar.

When driving in Tobago remember that the locals are familiar with every pot hole and hairpin bend and are prone to overtaking at dangerous places. To avoid stress, slow down and when it's safe to do so, cheerfully wave past any traffic behind you.

intellectuals. Just before Roxborough 3 miles (5 km) on, the road branches le to the **Argyll Waterfalls** ❸, which pours out of the mountainside in two sep arate cascades during the rainy season. Even though it's little more than a tir trickle at other times of year, there's still enough water for a refreshing "showe after the muddy 15-minute walk to reach it. Another 3 miles (5 km) past **Ro borough**, the largest town in the north – where some free but badly paid blac workers caused the Belmanna Uprising in 1876 – is **King's Bay Waterfall** the highest on the island at 100 ft (30 m) but not that copious. Nestling beneat the forest-covered hills, the beach seems cooler and wilder than most.

In the fishing village of Speyside, nearly 3 miles (5 km) away, tucked in beautiful broad blue bay, young men offer excursions to the bird sanctuary c **Little Tobago** ❺ just offshore. It's also known as Bird of Paradise Island, a those birds flourished on the island from 1909, when 48 were brought ove from New Guinea, until 1963 when the colony was destroyed by Hurrican Flora. It's more rewarding, therefore, to go diving and snorkeling along th spectacular reefs around there. Glass-bottomed boats (plenty to choose from) ar the most comfortable way on calm days to admire the marine life on show Some captains have special books with the names of the fish, corals and sponge

The picturesque northeast

Windward Road leaves the coast at Speyside and winds its way up a stee incline to a good viewpoint of the rough northeastern point of the island, wher the Atlantic and the Caribbean meet. The houses and huts of **Charlotteville** on the other side cling to the steep slope above **Man O'War Bay** rather lik bird's nests. The town's 600 or so inhabitants live mainly off fishing and touris

BELOW: top-class golf at Mount Irvine.

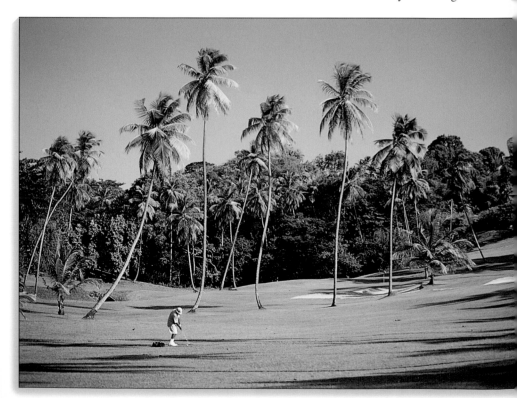

Map on page 286

visitors here appreciate the simple private quarters, and the idyllic tranquility this end of the island. A flight of 68 steps leads down to **Pirates Bay**, where cal women spread out their clothes on the rocks to dry. Just offshore is a reef eming with life and, instead of pirate ships, elegant yachts lie in the bay.

ne oldest nature reserve in the world

s the road from Charlotteville along the northern Caribbean coast is often passable, you have to return to Roxborough and cut across the island through e **Tobago Forest Reserve** ❼. This thick jungle in myriad shades of green reads along the Main Ridge between Hillsborough and Charlotteville and is e oldest section of intact rainforest, unaltered by man, in the world; the British clared it a nature reserve on April 8, 1776. The road and the several hiking utes here only allow visitors to cover a very small proportion of the entire area; e green thickets contain black-and-yellow weavers, green parrots and dazngly colorful hummingbirds, and the tropical vegetation is fascinating. Yelw poui and red flame trees stand out against the green forested hillsides. The ths are sometimes steep and muddy, which is why it's best to go with an perienced guide.

The cocrico is the national bird of Tobago and tends to descend on gardens in enormous flocks. When the pheasant-like bird starts squawking loudly it is considered a sure sign that rain is on the way.

At Bloody Bay, the road follows the coastline westwards for 2 miles (3 km) **Englishman's Bay** ❽, a magnificent beach where the forest comes down to e edge, coconut palms wave gently in the breeze, and the waves lap against the sually) deserted beach. Further along, in the steep orchards lining the road, en can be seen working with machetes among banana bushes, cassava plants d dark-green citrus trees. A track branches off at Runnemede, 4 miles (6 km) wn the coast, to stunning panoramic views over **King Peter's Bay**.

Several more small bays are tucked away at the end **Arnos Vale** ❾, down a small road further west, fering the best snorkeling and birdwatching in bago. Not far from the village, surrounded by fort, is the **Arnos Vale Waterwheel Park** which has a nall museum, shop and restaurant recently estabhed around an old waterwheel which used to prode power to the plantation estates.

uccoo – an endangered reef

ack Rock marks the beginning of the southwestern, liday side of Tobago. There are several expensive edium-category hotels on the broad beaches here, cluding **Mount Irvine Bay** ❿ where there is a ampionship golf course and good waves for surfers. anders in the villages rent out rooms privately to pplement their livelihoods. Locals and tourists all eet up in **Buccoo** every Sunday evening for the unday School" open-air disco.

At the incredibly idyllic **Pigeon Point** ⓫, one of e most-photographed beaches in the Caribbean, the ass-bottomed boats can be seen taking snorkelers the largely destroyed coral gardens at the now protected **Buccoo Reef** ⓬. Boats offer trips that include barbecue and a wallow in the shallow turquoise aters of the **Nylon Pool**. However, this is one place here it's obvious that promoting tourism isn't always the best interests of an island like Tobago. ❑

BELOW: the waterwheel at Arnos Vale.

THE ABC ISLANDS

Aruba, Bonaire and Curaçao are little pieces of the Netherlands in the Caribbean, with excellent diving in translucent seas, pink flamingos and friendly people

Off the coast of Venezuela are Aruba, Bonaire and Curaçao, otherwise known as the ABC Islands, three of the six islands which comprised the Netherlands Antilles until Aruba became self-governing in 1986. The remaining Dutch territories lie towards the northern tip of the Lesser Antilles chain, south east of Puerto Rico, they are Saba, St Eustatius and St Maarten. The ABC islands enjoy a degree of autonomy from the Netherlands government on most matters except defense and foreign policy. Bonaire and Curaçao have a Dutch Crown appointed governor to deal with their affairs, while Aruba is an autonomous member of the Kingdom of the Netherlands.

The official language is Dutch, but papiamento, an intriguing mix of European and African tongues, is widely spoken throughout this part of the Caribbean. This blend of Dutch, Spanish, Portuguese, English, French and African dialects reveals much about the nations which have shaped the islands and influenced their heritage. Spanish and English are also spoken.

Physically the ABC Islands' landscape is similar with their hilly and desert-like dry terrain which is a stark contrast to the shimmering turquoise oceans which lap at the fine sandy coastlines. The similarity ends right there though because each island provides travelers with an experience of its own. If you crave watersports action, hectic nightlife, casinos, luxurious places to stay and shopping till you drop then Curaçao and Aruba are for you. Bonaire on the other hand, offers peace and tranquility with its flocks of pink flamingos, marine parks and excellent diving.

The choice is yours. ❑

PRECEDING PAGES: a swirl of Aruban gulls.
LEFT: fading beauty, Willemstad.

CURAÇAO

The largest island in the Dutch Antilles is a cosmopolitan kaleidoscope of people and with its sheltered bays, turquoise water and coral reefs it is also a world of discovery for divers

The most important island in the Dutch Antilles, Curaçao is home to 150,000 people from over 60 nations, together with some unique "wedding-cake" colonial architecture and many attractive bays with shimmering water – nd a bizarre and wonderful world for divers to discover beside the coral reefs ffshore. Willemstad, the island's capital, is like a small tropical Amsterdam – a ascinating mixture of the Caribbean and attractive Dutch-style architecture.

Long before the arrival of Spaniard Alonso de Ojeda, the first European to set oot on this rocky island off the north coast of South America in 1499, the land 'as settled by tall Indians from the Caiquetío tribe. Which is why today's uraçao was called the "Island of Giants" by its Spanish conquerors who came n search of treasure. They failed to find the legendary gold of El Dorado here, nd limited their colonization of the island to a few cattle farms. In the 17th century the Dutch built a military base at Schottegat, a natural harbor with a deepater entrance, and it soon became an important trading center.

Since agriculture on the dry soil was both exhausting and unprofitable, the setters – who included numerous Jewish families from Amsterdam and northastern Brazil – switched to trading in indigo, cotton, tobacco...and slaves. fter suffering the rigors and inhuman conditions of their transatlantic voyage, undreds of thousands of African slaves were "freshned up" in the camps around Willemstad, and then old like cattle at the slave market – a practise which ontinued until well into the late 18th century. A loody slave uprising in 1795 did nothing to alter the tuation: the leaders of the rebellion, named Tula and arpata, were executed by Dutch soldiers in Punda ogether with 25 other slaves. It was only in 1863 that e Netherlands finally abolished slavery for good.

The island experienced an economic upswing rough the opening of a massive oil refinery on the at "isola" in the Schottegat, where crude oil from ake Maracaibo in Venezuela was refined. However, nce the oil crisis of the 1980s Curaçao has been rning a great deal less in petrodollars than it would ave hoped for. Tourism has become another imporant earner here alongside the lucrative finance busiess, international services and a flourishing harbor ith ultra-modern docks. Around 200,000 holidayakers and 160,000 cruise liner passengers visit this xotic island with its dash of Dutchness every year.

LEFT: old and new meet in Willemstad.
BELOW: sunny smile.

tropical mini-Amsterdam

illemstad ❶, the busy capital of Curaçao (pop. 25,000), impresses visitors most with its candyolored painted, renovated colonial buildings dating om the 16th to the 19th century. Magnificent merants' houses with steep, red-tiled roofs, town houses

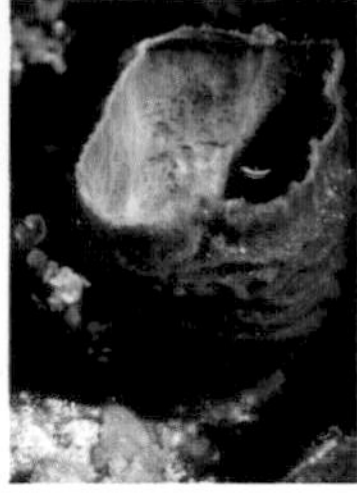

Strange sponge.

with beautiful stucco facades, three well-preserved forts, picturesque little stree and large airy churches all stand as reminders of the prosperity of the first Euro pean settlers.

The town is one large sprawling development around the **Schottegat**, a larg deep inlet of water creating a perfect hidden harbor, with **Sint Annabaai** as th narrow entrance. Take a stroll through the historic center of **Punda** ("point") an you won't find it difficult to locate its hub. The streets here and in **Otroband** ("other side") on either side of Sint Annabaai are mainly pedestrianized, an lined with attractive cafés and snack bars.

Sacred treasures

The most important sight is the **Mikveh Israel Emanuel Synagogue**, which ha been in continuous use since it first opened at the Passover Festival in 173 Sephardic settlers from Amsterdam and northern Brazil founded the communit of "Mikveh Israel" (Hope of Israel) in the 17th century. The guard at the gate i the **Hanchi di Snoa** is the only outward sign that something special is hidde behind the high yellow walls with their decorative gables. White walls, blue wir dows and dark-brown mahogany furniture contrast pleasantly with each othe in the three-aisled prayer room of the synagogue; the enormous brass chande liers come from an Amsterdam workshop, and the fine sand on the floor is reminder of the Israelites' march through the Sinai Desert.

The central courtyard is surrounded by the 200-year-old ritual bath, or mik vah, and two renovated residential buildings which today house the **Jewis History Museum** (open Mon–Fri; closed Jewish and public hols; entrance fee An interesting display here includes valuable torah rolls, seven-branche

BELOW: testing the produce in Willemstad market.

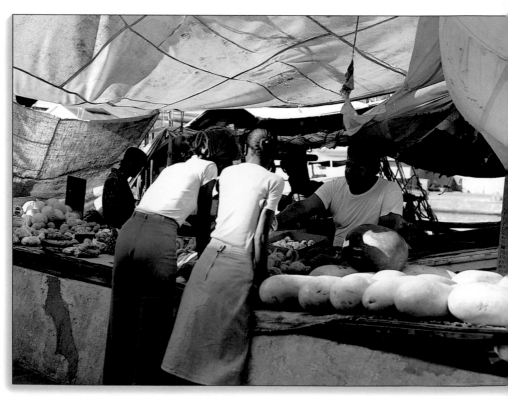

andlesticks and numerous ancestral objects belonging to the influential Luck-nann and Maduro families. Along the walls of the courtyard you can see copies of ancient gravestones from the Jewish cemetery of Beth Chaim on the out-kirts of the town, across the Schottegat, where the originals have been severely roded by sulfurous vapors from the nearby oil refinery.

Morbid charm and renovated magnificence

Next to the ugly concrete structure housing the main market on the **Waaigat**, where the female traders are almost completely concealed from view behind mountains of fresh fruit and vegetables, the **Queen Wilhelmina Drawbridge** eads across to the old Jewish quarter of **Scharloo**. Take a walk along **Schar-looweg**, where the morbid charm of crumbling walls alternates with the mag-nificent renovated villas. Stars of David on some of the garden fences here erve as reminders of the buildings' former owners. Today these attractive struc-ures are largely occupied by banks, legal practises and administrative offices. mpressive examples of the elaborate architecture typical of the 19th century nclude the yellow-and-white Kranshi, the registry office and the "Wedding Cake" or *Bolo di Bruid*, as the very decorative green-and-white building at number 77 is referred to in papiamento, the well-used patois of this island (*see page 53*). Today it is home to the **National Archive**.

On the way back along the Waaigat it's worth stopping at the **Marsh**, the old narket hall by the post office, where cooks serve enormous helpings of stew *stoba*) and other delicacies. Or buy more nutritious fare from the Venezuelan oast boats at the **Floating Market** (Sha Caprileskade).

The gently swaying **Queen Emma Bridge** with the colorful façade of the **Handelskade** in the background is the most pho-ographed scene in the whole town. This pontoon bridge has connected the business center of Punda with the picturesque old residential quarter of Otra-banda since 1888. Whenever a freighter or cruise ship needs to enter or leave the harbor through the St Annabaai, a powerful motor pulls the bridge aside; at he same time, a bell rings to warn pedestrians. Two erries transport passengers across the bay while cars oar across the spectacular 175-ft (55 m) arch of the **Queen Juliana Bridge** (1974) to the north, flying high above the massive ships below.

Enormous forts are situated on either side of the harbor entrance. Iron rings were set into their walls in order to prevent access to the harbor with a heavy chain or metal net. The **Riffort** in Otrabanda today provides an atmospheric backdrop for pleasant dining n the Bistro Le Clochard; in contrast, on the opposite bank a large and rather ugly hotel building towers above the walls of the Waterfort. Beside it is yellow **Fort Amsterdam** (open Mon–Fri; entrance fee), built n 1641 and now the seat of the regional government. The inner courtyard houses the Protestant church 1742) and a small museum containing religious arti-acts. A cannonball is still lodged in the masonry here: n 1804, during a 26-day long siege of Willemstad, he English Captain Bligh's men fired on the fort.

The stylish shop windows along **Heerenstraat** and

TIP

Architect Anko van de Woude and art historian Jenny Smit give tours of the old part of Willemstad on Thursday at 5pm and Friday at 9am, call 46 13 554. Professor Joopi Hart tours the town at 5.15pm on Wednesday. Call 76 73 798.

BELOW: all roads lead to Willemstad.

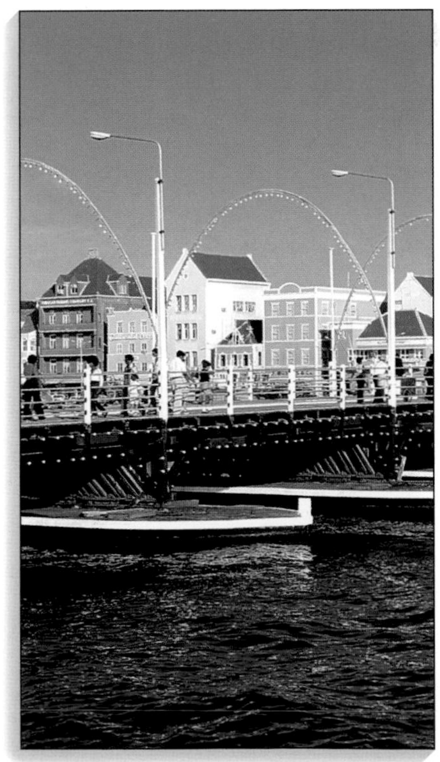

There is always time for sailing.

Breedestraat contain expensive cameras, watches and cosmetics; designer clothes, perfumes and elegant household items are sold duty-free in the local boutiques. The gables above, like many façades in this area, have been renovated. Pay special attention to the magnificent yellow-ochre Penha Building in Punda, which dates from 1708, next to the pontoon bridge. Initially the gallery on the upper storey was left open so that air could circulate freely through the house; the arcades were closed up later on to create more space inside.

The winding streets of Otrobanda also contain around 200 smartly renovated houses, the area has become increasingly popular since architects, conservationists and politicians realised how unique an ensemble the old town represents. In 1997 Willemstad joined the UNESCO global cultural heritage list.

Stroll back through the centuries

Burnt-out buildings on the **Brionplein** still survive from the riots of May 1969 when a mob of unemployed people: refinery workers and harbor workers gave vent to their frustration at social injustice. However, the bright-blue Otrobanda Hotel, the numerous bars at the Koral Agostini, the pleasant, family-run hotel and casino Porto Paseo, and several other renovated buildings on **De Rouvilleweg** all make it very clear that Otrabanda is no longer the run-down area it was. It has been transformed into a chic residential, business and entertainment district. Don't venture along these streets at night, though: despite numerous police patrols, prostitutes, drugs dealers and crack addicts have become a regular feature here.

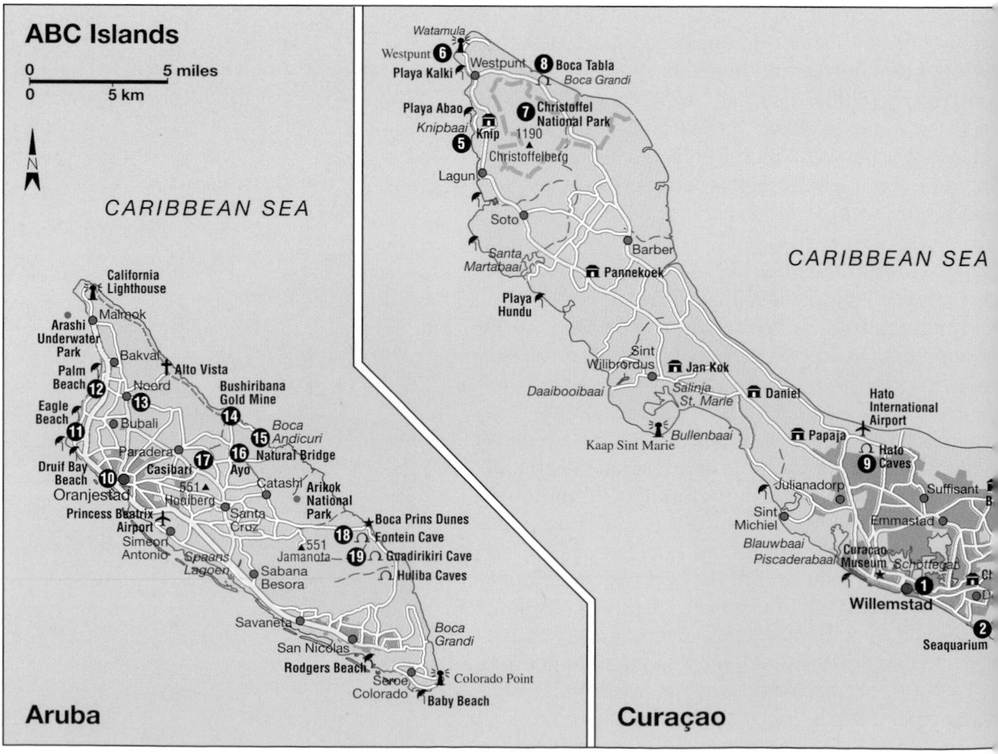

During the day a stroll along busy Breedestraat, past the attractive Haus Sebastopol and the picturesque buildings on Nanniestraat as far as the elaborately novated Haus Belvedere takes you back through two centuries of history. An eal place for a rest, with a view right across the harbor, is the Keizershof with ; bars and terraces, or you could also visit the cruise ship terminal, where the illery in the **Kas di Alma Blou** and the **Arawak Clay Products** crafts center the Mattheywerf (St Annabaai) both contain a good selection of souvenirs.

Just outside Otrobanda, inside the former Dutch military hospital, is the **uraçao Museum** (open daily; closed Sat; entrance fee) with its unusual and :lectic collection of antique furniture, old kitchen equipment and modern art.

rom Bolívar to beer

ietermaai, the district to the southwest of Punda, is undergoing a similar :velopment to Otrobanda. Expensively renovated office buildings and the tractive **Avila Beach Hotel**, once the governor's residence, are certainly worth specting. The South American freedom fighter Simón Bolívar is commemo-ted in a small museum in the **Octagon** (open daily; entrance fee): he took fuge here with his two sisters for a while in the early 19th century.

In the Landhuis Chobolobo in the Salinja quarter, the Senior family has been stilling the world-famous "**Curaçao of Curaçao**" liqueur for over 100 years, ıd in the modern Amstel Brewery on the Schottegat, the island's delicious :er is produced using desalinated sea water and imported ingredients. The xury hotels owned by international chains and also the locally run establish-ents are almost all located in the outer suburbs: on the Piscaderabaai or the Jan hielbaai.

The latter is also famous for the **Curaçao Seaquarium** ❷ (open daily; ıtrance fee) where rare and exotic tropical fish, turtles and crustaceans can be

Map on page 298–99

Genuine Curaçao is distilled in the ancient copper vats at the Landhuis Chobolobo from the dried peel of local oranges and then refined with the addition of several secret ingredients. Taste some on a tour (open Mon–Fri; free).

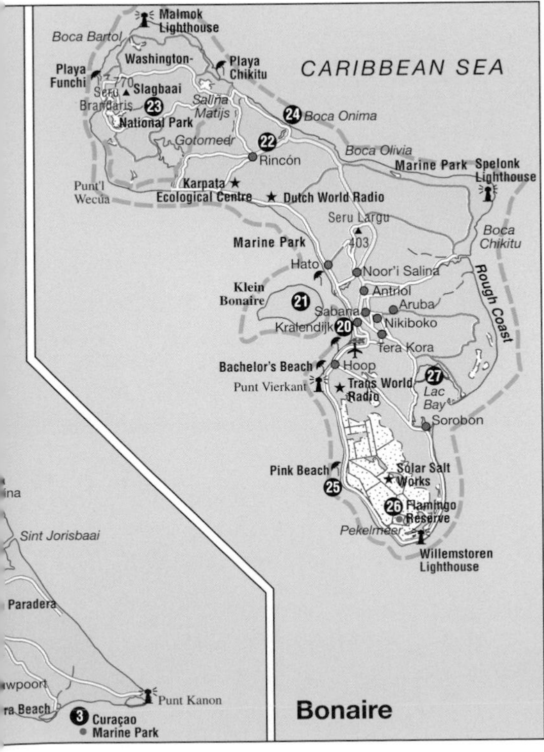

BELOW: imposing entrance of the synagogue.

admired from a boardwalk. Feeding time is especially entertaining. In the "Ar mal Encounter" section, divcrs and snorkelers can feed sharks from behind Plexiglass screen while having their photograph taken.

Although Bonaire is the most famous undersea sports center in the Caribbea Curaçao does have several spectacular diving grounds for the experienced dive The **Curaçao Marine Park** ❸, extends from the Oostpunt and along the sout west coast as far as Jan Thielbaai. Most of the diving areas can be reache directly from the shore, and the clear water is also excellent for snorkelin with colorful coral reefs, massive sponges and tropical fish to be found ve close to the coast. Anyone eager to discover the undersea world in all its ma nificence and also visit the wreck of a Dutch steamer without getting their fe wet should board the glass-bottomed, semi-submarine **Seaworld Explorer**.

TIP

Dance the night away to local bands at the *salsa* and *merengue* parties on the broad terraces of Landhuis Brievengat just north of Schottegat. An ideal way to keep fit!

Kunuku – wild and beautiful hinterland

Banda Riba, the eastern part of Curaçao, has numerous attractions includin broad, flat and sandy **Santa Barbara Beach** ❹, where children can splas about and play quite safely in the clear warm water, and also the hidden bay **Playa Kanoa**, where courageous surfers brave the waves and local bands co gregate for dancing parties at weekends. If you are interested in medicinal herb visit schoolteacher Dinah Verijs and her beautiful garden, **Den Parader** located at the foot of the Tafelberg: she'll give you all kinds of ideas from cu ing hair thinning to upset stomachs (call in advance: 76 75 608).

During any trip through the hinterland, or kunuku, to Westpunt you'll notic several magnificent, mostly yellow-ochre plantation manors – some close to th road, others nestling among hills. These residential and administrative building

BELOW: tranquil beauty of a Curaçao hidden bay.

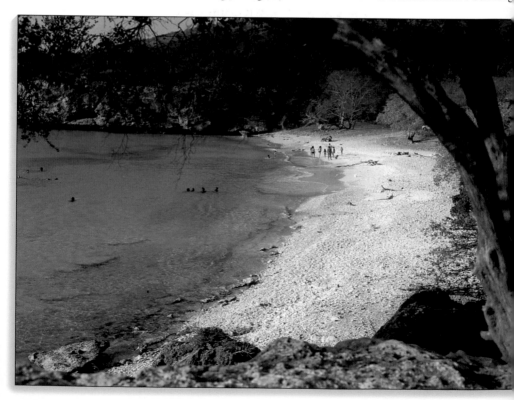

Map on page 298–99

ice belonged to influential families who kept them as country estates alongle their business premises in Willemstad. Today they have been converted to restaurants, small hotels and museums. The owner of the **Landhuis Jan ok**, for instance, serves fine Dutch pancakes every Sunday; the **Landhuis of root Sint Martha** contains workshops for the disabled; the **Landhuis Daniel** a gourmet restaurant – the other majestic buildings along the road are either ivately owned or the property of official institutions. Back on the eastern side the Schottegat, the **Landhuis Groot Davelaar** contains the renowned De veerne restaurant with its excellent local and international cuisine.

ough wilderness

ith a bit of luck, on a tour through the **Banda Abao** – the western part of the and – you may see some of the shy flamingos which live on the **Salinja St arie**, or sea turtles on the **Knipbaai** ❺. Here the sandy beaches, the best on e island, are surrounded by rocks making an attractive setting for a rest stop. e majestic Landhuis Kenepa (Knip), once at the center of the wealthiest planion on Curaçao, now hosts cultural events on a regular basis (for more inforation consult current program brochures).

Pelicans are the only creatures courageous enough to brave the waves off the **estpunt** ❻, where the sea crashes down with unbelievable force onto the cky shoreline off Watamula. Just a few miles to the east of the sleepy fishing lage of Westpunt, a fence on either side of the road marks the **Christoffel tional Park** ❼. This large nature reserve was opened in 1978 on land forerly occupied by three vast plantations; it can be explored by jeep, mounnbike or on foot. Guided tours led by expert rangers introduce visitors to the pical local flora and fauna. Keep an eye out for the een parrots native to the island: they usually fly in irs and enjoy landing on the enormous cacti. A short t exhausting climb leads to the top of the 1,230-ft 75 m) high **Christoffelberg**, where the view tends as far as Bonaire. Further attractions in the rk include Indian rock drawings, spectacular etches of coastline on the Boca Grandi, and numers rare palm trees and fragrant orchids in the wilderss of Zevenbergen.

To the northeast, the Christoffel National Park is rdered by the Die Shete Boka, a beautifully atmoseric piece of coast with its hidden grotto of **Boca bla** ❽ and breathtaking scenery whenever the werful breakers smash down on the cliffs. It was eakers similar to those which created the original ve system of **Hato** ❾ (open daily; closed Mon; trance fee) not far from the international airport. ese limestone caves contain ancient Indian drawgs rumored to date back to more than 1,000 years o. Guided tours are available.

Since the ABC Islands rose up from the sea on sevl occasions during their genesis, the landscape ceived a whole series of terraces filled with counts grottoes and caverns. The graceful walls of stamites and curtains of stalactites, combined with an derground waterfall, make these limestone caverns ascinating but crowded place to visit. ❑

Kas di Pali Maishi, near Tera Kora, on the road to Westpunt, is a reconstructed Kunuku hut thatched with straw showing how simply the country folk used to live (and some still do). Surrounded by a prickly cactus fence, the open air museum is open daily; closed Mon; entrance fee.

BELOW: perfect example of Dutch West Indian architecture.

ARUBA

:xplore an underwater shipwreck and natural reefs, laze on miles of white sandy beach, swim in gentle blue ocean and shop in modern malls, Aruba has something for everybody

Map on page 298–99

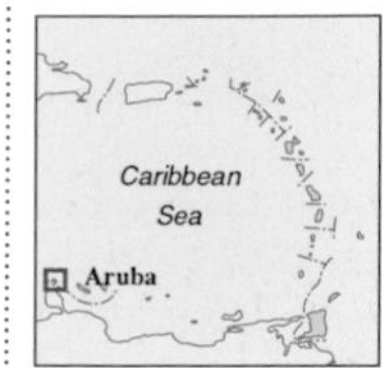

Aruba, the smallest and richest of the ABC Islands has cosmopolitan shopping centers, elegant restaurants and a refreshingly deserted hinterland which provide highly attractive alternatives to lazing away happily under ıe palms all day long on the island's 7 miles (11 km) of white sand lapped by entle turquoise and dark-blue waters.

For more than 50 years, the massive Lago oil refinery at San Nicolas was ıruba's main source of foreign revenue and not only as the biggest employer on ıe tiny island. Lago financed schools, doctors, houses, streets and even a golf ourse for its workforce. When the refinery was unexpectedly closed down in arly 1985 it came as a great shock not just to Arubans but also to the numerus workers throughout the Caribbean. On an island with a population of around 3,000 people, unemployment rose dramatically and affected thousands.

The potentially devastating economic problems struck just as Aruba offiially assumed special autonomous status. Tourism was seen as a way of attractıg much needed foreign currency and this gamble has paid off, today visitors rrive from all over the world but especially from Holland, the US and nearby outh America. High-rise hotels appeared above the palm trees on Eagle Beach nd Palm Beach, and the small town of Oranjestad soon developed a colorful ıopping center. Cunning entrepreneurs created a hollay industry that catered to every taste, whether on 'ater or land: undersea diving along the natural reef, 'ith spectacular underwater scenery around wrecked ıips and airplanes; romantic candlelit dinners on oard sailing ships; tours on party buses, and Las 'egas-style shows on the stage of the Alhambra – plus asinos where visitors can try their luck at roulette ıbles, computer games and one-armed bandits.

LEFT: all kinds of watersports in Aruba. **BELOW:** Las Vegas style at the Alhambra.

. holiday bonanza

he customer is definitely king here, as long as they ave enough dollars in their pockets and purses to pay ır it, because perfect service does have a high price. Iore than half a million holidaymakers spend a few leasant days each year at Eagle Beach and Palm each, and that figure doesn't include the 320,000 or) passengers from cruise ships who visit the bars and outiques in Oranjestad, eager to take advantage of ıe bounty of duty-free goods and impressed by the laxed and polite service. Shopping can be an expenve business especially when you're after European oods such as English and German porcelain, Belan chocolates and Swiss watches.

The horrors of the colonial era largely passed Aruba /, because the island was only inhabited by a handıl of settlers, soldiers and Caiquetío Indians. Agriılture, animal husbandry, cultivation of aloes and

Practically every type of watersport is on offer on the beaches from sailing to parasailing. And you can have a go on an assortment of "toys" such as jet skis, wave runners and banana boats.

BELOW: modern shopping malls in Oranjestad.

export of tree bark containing tannin enabled the islanders to lead a largel self-sufficient existence. Papiamento (*see page 72*), the local creole language sounds far more Spanish here than elsewhere and is also very melodious.

Spruced up: Oranjestad

A handful of shopping streets, administrative buildings, and churches, a sma harbor with a cruise-ship pier, and some magnificently restored hotels com plete with shopping malls and casinos – that just about sums up the center o **Oranjestad ❶**. If you feel like taking a break from the numerous cafés and bar around the yachting harbor where you can enjoy the view and soak up som local atmosphere and the sunshine, take a stroll past the colorful, Dutch-styl façades and visit the few sights Aruba's capital has to offer.

The most noticeable relic of colonial times here is the small **Fort Zoutma** (open Mon–Sat; entrance fee) and **Willem III Tower**, the oldest surviving struc ture on the island. The fort was built right beside the **Paardenbaai** in 1796 and since then the land reclamation at the harbor has pushed it back aroun 300 ft (100 m) inland. Its ancient walls contain the **History Museum**, where th exhibits include sea shells, sections of coral, 19th-century household items, an a mechanical barrel organ from Italy that still works. From the clock towe there's a fine view across the island, which is only 22 miles (30 km) long an 4 miles (9 km) across at its widest point. At 6.30pm every Tuesday the wel organised **Bonbini Festival** is held inside the fort, where you can sample loca culinary and liquid specialties and learn some traditional dances like the ener getic Latin American *tumba* and *merengue*.

Funeral urns, jewellery and simple artifacts in the **Archeological Museum**

Map on page 298–99

oerhaavestraat, adjoining the Protestant church of St Francis of Assisi; open on–Fri; entrance fee) document the largely unresearched culture of the Caiuetío Indians and other pre-Columbian peoples, who settled the ABC Islands ng before the Europeans arrived. Unfortunately the exhibits provide rather ant information about the Caiquetío.

The streets around the busy main street the **Caya G.F. (Betico) Croes** (forerly Nassaustraat) are where the locals tend to do most of their shopping. hey still contain a few traditional-style Aruban houses with typically steep nd flat torto-style roofs.

Cacti are a common sight in the arid countryside.

raggy coastline and stunning beaches

he terrace-shaped northeast coast of Aruba, with rough landscape, hidden sand unes, large limestone caverns and thorny scrubland is a striking contrast to e tourist regions of the west coast. **Eagle Beach** ⓫ 380 ft (120 m) wide in ome places, is lined by the so-called Low-Rise Hotels, which blend in harmoiously with the landscape despite their colorful mix of styles. Powdery-white **alm Beach** ⓬ is just as beautiful, but high-rises predominate here. Follow the gnposts to the High-Rise Hotels along the multi-lane highway that runs north om Oranjestad: they provide total luxury and the best of entertainment, and nyone who gets tired of the beach can invest any sum they like in the air-conitioned boutiques, restaurants and casinos here.

Further north the sea becomes rougher, but that is welcomed by the windrfers off **Malmok**, and doesn't affect the divers down at the wreck of the erman warship *Antilla* either (*see page 151*). It was surrounded off Aruba by e Dutch navy on May 10, 1940, during World War II, and rather than hoist the hite flag, the captain set the ship alight and sank it. he crew were interned in the Caribbean for the rest f the war, and at the end several of them were llowed to settle on the ABC Islands for good.

BELOW: another beautiful day.

ocky attractions

he 100-ft (32 m) high **California Lighthouse** towers bove the craggy Noordpunt and the sand dunes ound it. Built between 1914 and 1916, it stands ose to the bright green **Tierra del Sol** golf course, t in the midst of the reddish-brown scrubland. A usty track, which should only be attempted with a ur-wheel drive vehicle when muddy, leads along e east coast, passing the **Alto Vista Pilgrimage hapel** and a section of rocky landscape. The divivi trees here, bent by the northeasterly trade winds, e like natural signposts always pointing southwest.

Art and architecture lovers should take a detour to e unpretentious little church of **St Annakerk** in **oord** ⓭. It contains a surprisingly good neo-Gothic tar of carved oak by Hendrik van der Geld (1870) om Antwerp, as well as stained-glass windows from e Wilhelm Heinrich workshop in Kevelaer. The ins of the **Bushiribana Gold Mine** ⓮ are another opular and also very photogenic destination. They and in memory of the gold rush that took place here 1820 when a young boy found some nuggets in the y valleys on the northeast coast.

Apparently the Arubans say that if you kiss amidst the water vapour on th **Natural Bridge** ⓯ at the **Boca Andicuri** – the largest of a total of seven suc rocky bridges on Aruba – you are assured of a long and happy life. Whateve having a kiss 32-ft (10 m) above the raging surf, which has worn away th coral rock to form the 97-ft (30 m) long bridge, will certainly give you a bri rush of adrenaline.

The large iguana, indigenous to the island is protected but it has a long history of making a very tasty and nutritious soup – and today some locals are not averse to bagging the odd one or two for the pot.

Diorite boulders – a geological rarity – can be seen up close in **Ayo** ⓰ an **Casibari** ⓱: enormous, cushion-like rocks with large sections gouged out c them, some of them decorated with Indian rock drawings. The 551-ft (168 m high **Hooiberg** provides a fine view of the **Arikok National Park**, with its fas cinatingly desolate wilderness of cactus fields. Near a small renovated farm house called **Kunuku Arikok** you can see wooden troughs in which the gree juice of the aloe vera plant was collected and boiled. The juice from this plan is believed to purify the blood and regenerate the skin, and is highly treasure worldwide as an ingredient for health foods, skin creams and sunburn balms

Mysterious spirals

The cave systems of **Fontein** ⓲ and **Guadirikiri** ⓳ contain several strange an largely inexplicable Indian symbols such as spirals, circles, and lines of dots; i addition there are rare bats, bizarre rock formations, and also some rather ugl graffiti left behind by ignorant visitors. The cave walls and roof are bein cleaned by experts and guards and grilles are in position to ensure no furthe damage is done.

While surfers balance on the high waves out at Colorado Point, a good plac to relax from the tour of southern Aruba is in the shallow waters at **Baby Beach**

BELOW: Cas di Flor, a house decorated Italian style.

lternatively, visit Charlie's Bar, which is right beside the refinery at San Nico-as. This bar is a virtual institution. Over the past 50 years, guests from all over e world have lined the walls and ceiling with a scurrilous collection of personal ementoes. Such a unique setting is the hangout of local thespians, artists and usicians as well as lots of tourists who enjoy coming here for a drink, a deli-ous snack and a chat with the owner.

Aruba made its giant leap from small island to international industrial nation 1924, when the Lago Oil & Transport Company from America built a mas-ve refinery in a bay near the southwestern point of the island, not far from San icolas. The large oil companies chose Aruba and also Curaçao as safe and asily accessible locations for their enormous tankers because of the political stability in nearby Venezuela. After the oil crisis of the 1980s, parts of the efinery were shut down, but crude oil and smoking chimneys still dominate the ndscape and daily life in San Nicolas today.

talian inspiration

n the other side of the main road between Oranjestad and the island's former apital of Savaneta, a turn-off leads to the ruins of the **Balashi gold mine**, and rough the narrow defile known as **Frenchman's Pass**, where legend claims at French soldiers surrounded and shot a group of Indian warriors. The village f **Sabana Besora** still contains some typical small houses, such as the Cas di igura and Cas di Flor, with decorative patterned strips. Italian construction orkers probably scratched the attractive ornamentation into the plaster around e turn of the century. Colorfully painted flowers, stars and other decorations an also be seen in the church of St Francis of Assisi in Oranjestad. ❑

Paardenbaai (Horses' Bay) off Oranjestad got its name from the colonial merchants who used to unload horses from the boats by tying one to the beach and then shoving the rest overboard. They swam straight to their companion on the shore.

BELOW: the Natural Bridge – an ideal spot for a kiss.

BONAIRE

The waters around this island are a diver's paradise with spectacular views of a magical underwater world, a stark contrast to its cacti-strewn desert and national park

Map on page 298–99

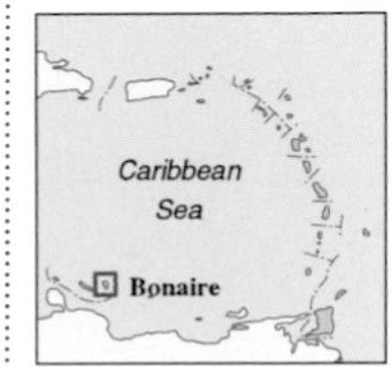

The tiny boomerang-shaped, barren-looking island of Bonaire lies just a few feet above the seemingly endless blue of the Caribbean Sea – the top of an underwater mountain. Most of its delights can be found under the sea, in the world-famous diving grounds of the Bonaire Marine Park. Despite all the marine marvels, life here is a slow-motion affair: there's picturesque Kralendijk (*Kroll*-en-dike), the barren cactus-filled wilderness of the Washington-Slagbaai National Park, and the graceful sight of more than 10,000 pink flamingos in the salt pans of the Pekelmeer.

In 1634 the Dutch established a small military base on a coral dike, the *kralendijk*, on the west coast of the island. Bonaire was only interesting to the colonizers because of its grazing land for cattle and goats; the slaughtered animals were loaded on to ships at Slagbaai ("Slaughter Bay") in the north, to be taken to market in Willemstad, Curaçao. It was during the 17th century that the Dutch West India Company first discovered the possibility of evaporating sea-water in shallow basins to produce salt cheaply, which at that time was much in demand as a preservative for fish and meat. The arduous labor involved was carried out under the scorching sun by so-called "government slaves". Today salt from the Pekelmeer remains a major export for the chemical industry, but over the past 35 years tourism has steadily grown to become the most important foreign currency earner.

LEFT: Bonaire is host to more than 10,000 flamingos. **BELOW:** coral is well-protected on the reefs.

Below as well as above the water, Bonaire takes ecotourism and environmental issues very seriously compared to other Caribbean islands: use of plastic bags is discouraged, rubbish is separated, and sewage is treated. Since the island is thinly populated (14,000 inhabitants dotted across 288 sq. km/111 sq. miles), and has no industry to speak of apart from an oil storage facility, nature is still largely intact. The only really endangered species here is the spider conch – its pink shells are sold as souvenirs, while the meat can be found on menus described as *lambi*.

A friendly and colorful capital

There's nothing hectic about **Kralendijk** ⓴, the island's peaceful capital. All of the public buildings are located along two streets on the waterfront, with most of the hotels, restaurants and a few budget boarding houses frequented by diving enthusiasts indifferent to the quality of their accommodation. On the **Kaya Grandi** a few colorfully painted façades and coral mosaics shaped like flamingos create a tropical atmosphere, and the small harbor promenade is a pleasant place for a sundowner in the evening.

You won't need a map to find Kralendijk's few sights. **Little Fort Oranje**, built in the 17th century, is beside the cruise ship pier, and there's a lighthouse

Iguanas of all sizes love the arid conditions.

built in 1932. **Plaza Reina Wilhelmina**, in the center, contains an unpretentiou Protestant church (1847) and a few attractive neoclassical municipal buildings The former residence of the governor, the **Pasangrahan**, is an elegant blend o Indonesian and Caribbean styles.

In the pseudo-Greek market pavilion on the waterfront, traders fron Venezuela sell freshly caught fish, and tropical fruit and vegetables. The bes views of Kralendijk can be had either from **Karels Beach Bar** or from the ter race restaurants at the harbor side. It is only when a cruise ship sails into tow that things get busy, and the **Museo Bonairiano** (Mon–Fri; entrance fee), wit an amazing collection of furniture, pictures, colonial household items and bric a-brac, fills up. The town's art galleries show interesting pieces of art, made b the islanders from island materials – from driftwood to car tyres, "carved" an painted in brilliant colors.

Underwater magic

The entire west coast of Bonaire is lined by coral reefs (*see page 150*) that pro vide some of the best diving anywhere in the Caribbean. The sea right round th island is part of the **Bonaire Marine Park**, and since 1978 has been strictly pro tected together with the uninhabited island of **Klein Bonaire** ㉑, situated t the west of **Kralendijk Bay**. Harpoon diving is forbidden, and it is also illega even to touch – let alone collect – any of the coral. Bonaire's west coast is ful of spectacular diving grounds, mostly situated where the reefs gradually slop down into the surrounding sea; snorkelers swimming close to the coast her will often find themselves above magnificent elkhorn coral or brain coral, an surrounded by colorful parrotfish and even Moray eels.

BELOW: conch shells lie discarded in Lac Bay.

horns, salt and pink feathers

nspoiled nature begins a few miles beyond the former slave settlement of **incón** ㉒, a collection of yellowish-brown houses among the flat hills of the *nuku* (countryside). With thorny steppe in the north and flat salt pans in the outh, Bonaire's landscape is similar to the hinterland on Aruba and Curaçao.

The **Washington-Slagbaai National Park** ㉓ was established on the site of o former plantations in 1978. It takes up the entire northern part of the island, d its freshwater swampland is an important stopover for birds migrating tween North and South America. Depending on the season you may see wild ese or scoopers here, and the budgerigars, parrots and pelicans native to the land can be observed the whole year round. There's a good view of the park om the observation point on the Gotomeer, and the idyllic beach of **Playa hikitu** is an excellent place to relax – swimming is forbidden, however, cause of the dangerous undertow. Two routes for car drivers and a lot of hiking paths lead through the varied scenery and up to the 791-ft (241-m) high **eru Brandaris**, the highest point on the island.

An only slightly bumpy road leads to the **Boca Onima** ㉔. Here, beneath a cky outcrop in the limestone terrace along the north coast, Indian drawings can ill be seen; executed in a reddish color, they include spirals, circles and styled birds. No one is certain of their precise origin, though it is believed that cenries ago, Arawak Indians prayed to the goddess Onima for calm seas here fore undertaking the voyage across to Venezuela.

In the flat, southern part of the island, the scenery is dominated by shiny hite mounds of salt and pink flamingos. A popular destination here is **Pink each** ㉕, where the pink hues of the sand are the result of the pink encrustans on the coral being powdered down by the sea. ear the salt pans of the **Pekelmeer**, where a chemil firm continues to extract salt from seawater, a imber of small slave huts still stand here and there, vealing the inhuman treatment the former masters of e island inflicted on their workers: the stone houses, ch roughly the size of a dog-kennel, had to sleep to six men during the working week. Their families ved in Rincón or Tera Kora, and the men were only lowed to go back and see them at weekends.

lamingo Reserve

part of the old salt pan area is taken up by the **lamingo Reserve** ㉖, one of only four nestingounds for pink flamingos in the Caribbean. The rds are disturbed by noisy visitors, and may only be served from afar. During the day these elegant creares fly off to Venezuela or Curaçao to filter algae, ed on shrimps and other crustaceans (which give e older flamingos their striking pink hue) and tiny eatures from the shallow coastal waters there – so if u want to see them, get up early, and bring along a od pair of binoculars. **Lac Bay** ㉗, surrounded by angrove swamps on the east coast, is a popular prace area for windsurfers – and also a breeding ground r many reef fish as well as the endangered spider nch. Many conch shells can be found lying disrded at the end of the bay. ❑

Map on page 298–99

Queen Angel fish.

BELOW: these tiny dwellings each slept six slaves.

INSIGHT GUIDES

TRAVEL TIPS

CONTENTS

Getting Acquainted

The Lesser Antilles

Area: The Lesser Antilles are a 1,500-mile (2,400-km) long archipelago of more than 20 islands, stretching from the US Virgin Islands by Puerto Rico in the north in an arc down to the ABC Islands off the north coast of Venezuela.
Language: Several languages are commonly used on the islands, including: English, French, Dutch, Spanish, and various versions of patois.
Time Zones: All of the islands except Trinidad and Tobago are in the Atlantic Time Zone, which is one hour later than Eastern Standard Time and four hours earlier than Greenwich Mean Time. When the United States goes onto Daylight Saving Time, the islands do not change, so during this time of year, time in the eastern part of the US is identical to Island time. Trinidad and Tobago are both in the Eastern Time Zone which is identical with the eastern US during Standard Time.
Currency: There are six major currencies officially used:
Barbados Dollar (BDS$): Barbados.
Eastern Caribbean Dollar (EC$): Dominica, Grenada, Montserrat, St Kitts and Nevis, St Lucia, St Vincent and the Grenadines, Anguilla, Antigua, and Barbuda.
French Franc (FF): Martinique, Guadeloupe, St Martin, St Barthélemy, Saba and St Eustatius.
Netherlands Antilles Florin or Guilder (NAf): Aruba, Bonaire, Curaçao, and St Martin.
US Dollar (US$): The US and British Virgin Islands.
Trinidad and Tobago Dollar (TT$): Trinidad and Tobago.
Electricity: Different islands run on different electrical currents:
110–120V/60 cycle (US current): US Virgin Islands, British Virgin Islands, Aruba, St Martin (Dutch side), Trinidad, and Tobago.
110–130V/50 cycle: Anguilla, Bonaire, Barbados, and Curaçao.
220–230V/60 cycle: St Kitts and Nevis, Montserrat, Antigua, and Barbuda.
220–240V/50 cycle: Bonaire, Curaçao, Dominica, Grenada, St Barthélémy, Saba, St Eustatius, St Martin (French side), Guadeloupe, Martinique, St Lucia, and St Vincent and the Grenadines.

Climate

The principal characteristic of the Caribbean's climate is the relative lack of temperature change from season to season. The islands' proximity to the equator means that seasonal temperature changes are limited to less than 10°F (6°C). An added bonus is the trade winds, which bring regular, cooling breezes to most of the islands.

Year round, temperatures average around 80°F (27°C) throughout the region. During the "winter" – which is peak season for tourists in the islands – nighttime lows can reach about 60°F (16°C), with daytime highs reaching as much as 90°F (32°C).

Rainfall varies widely, ranging from around 20 inches (50 cm) a year in Curaçao and up to 75 inches (190 cm) a year in Grenada. Rainfall is generally heaviest during October and November, though June is wettest in Trinidad and Tobago. Hurricanes can strike from July to October. The "dry" period, coinciding with the peak tourist season, is from December through April or May.

What to Do if a Hurricane Strikes

- **During the storm** Stay indoors once the hurricane begins buffeting your area. When the eye (the low-pressure area at the center of a hurricane) passes over, there will be a temporary lull in wind and rain for up to half an hour or more. This is not the end of the storm, which will in fact resume (possibly with even greater force) from the opposite direction. Wait for the all-clear from the authorities before starting to venture out of your shelter.
- **If ordered to evacuate** Stay tuned to local radio stations for up-to-date information and instructions. Follow designated routes as quickly as possible. Take with you blankets, a flashlight, extra clothing and medications. Leave behind pets (which are not permitted inside public shelters).
- **After the storm passes** Drive with caution when ordered to return home. Debris in the roads can be a hazard. Roads near the coast may collapse if soil has been washed away from beneath them. Steer clear of fallen or dangling utility wires. Stay tuned to radio stations for news of emergency medical, food, housing and other forms of assistance. If you have been staying in a rented home, re-enter the building with caution and make temporary repairs to correct hazards and minimize further damage. Open windows and doors to air and dry the house. Be particularly careful when dealing with matches or fires in case of gas leaks.

Hurricane Categories

Hurricanes are categorized from one to five according to the Saffir Simpson Scale, which measures wind speed:
Category 1: 74–95 miles (119–153 km) per hour.
Category 2: 96–110 miles (154–177 km) per hour.
Category 3: 111–130 miles (178–209 km) per hour.
Category 4: 131–155 miles (210–249 km) per hour.
Category 5: over 155 miles (249 km) per hour.

Hurricanes

Hurricanes are one of the most damaging and dangerous phenomena affecting the Lesser Antilles (*see page 18* for a description of how a hurricane forms and develops). Recent devastating hurricanes have included Hugo in 1989 which affected the Leeward Islands, Luis in September 1995 which pounded Antigua, St Martin, and nearby islands, and Marilyn a month later which caused flooding in Antigua but most damage to the US Virgin Islands.

Hurricanes usually occur between July and October, although visitations have been known in June and November, and the "hurricane season" stretches from the beginning of June to the beginning of November, when some islands celebrate with a Hurricane Deliverance Day. The average lifespan of a hurricane is eight to ten days.

In summer months, tropical disturbances are common all over the tropics. It is from these that tropical depressions and then tropical storms develop, which can bring gales of up to 73 miles (117 km) per hour and heavy rains. A hurricane warning is issued when the storm reaches winds of at least 74 miles (119 km) per hour and high water and storm surges are expected in a specific area within 24 hours. Warnings will identify specific coastal areas where these conditions may occur. Once you have heard a warning, be ready to evacuate your home or hotel. Finish getting together the things you need to take to a shelter or anything else you will need if you stay home.

Business Hours

The siesta, happily, is alive and well in the Caribbean, and throughout the region small shops close for a couple of hours in the early afternoon, when the tropical sun is at its hottest. As a result, business hours generally follow this pattern: shops open early, usually by 8am, certainly by 9am. They begin closing for siesta at noon or a little before, though in some areas, shops may stay open until 1pm. Business resumes about 2 hours later – 2pm in most places – with stores remaining open until 6pm. Again, there is some variation; on a few islands, closing time may be as early as 4pm. On Saturday, most stores are open in the morning, and many have full afternoon hours as well. Sunday is generally a day of rest.

In Barbados, Trinidad, and Tobago, shops generally do not close in the early afternoon.

Public Holidays

Christmas and New Year are public holidays, but otherwise holidays vary from island to island. See under individual island listings for specific dates.

CARNIVAL

Carnival is celebrated at different times on different islands, with the dates falling roughly into three main groups:

- On Trinidad and Tobago, Dominica, St Thomas, Aruba, Bonaire, Curaçao, St Lucia, Martinique, Guadeloupe, St Martin (French side), and St Barthélemy Carnival preserves an association with Easter, being celebrated (on all of these islands except St Thomas) in the period leading up to and sometimes including Ash Wednesday. On St Thomas, the celebration occurs after Easter.
- On St Vincent, Anguilla, St John, Barbados, Grenada, the British Virgin Islands, Antigua, Saba, and St Eustatius, Carnival takes place in June, July, or early August. On these islands, Carnival is often held in association with the "August Monday" holiday, which marks the end of the sugar cane harvest and the freeing of slaves in the British islands around that time in 1834.
- On St Kitts, Montserrat, and St Croix (in the US Virgin Islands), Carnival takes place in December and early January, in conjunction with the Christmas season.
- On St Maarten (Dutch side), Carnival takes place in late April, coinciding with the Dutch Queen's birthday celebrations on April 30.

Planning the Trip

Passports and Visas

For travel in and around the islands – except Trinidad and Tobago – it is not always necessary for US or Canadian citizens to bring their passports, although it is recommended (re-entry to the US is almost impossible without a passport.) US travelers must, however, have some proof of citizenship – a birth certificate, naturalization card, voter registration card or affidavit. Canadian citizens traveling without passports should carry a birth certificate as proof of citizenship. Citizens of both countries should also have some form of photo ID.

Citizens from outside North America need to carry a passport. All travelers going to – or even passing through – Trinidad and Tobago must have passports. Visas are usually required only of visitors from Eastern Europe and Cuba. In addition to proper documents, all travelers must have, upon entering the islands, a return or onward ticket, and adequate funds to support themselves for the duration of their stay.

Customs

Travelers arriving in the Antilles are generally allowed to bring in the following duty-free items:

- personal effects.
- a carton of cigarettes or cigars, or half a pound (225 g) of tobacco.
- one bottle of an alcoholic drink.
- a "reasonable" amount of perfume.

US TRAVELERS

For US travelers returning to the United States from the USVI, there are a number of importation options. Each individual can bring back up to US$400 worth of purchases duty-free. Travelers may also mail home an unlimited number of packages valued at US$50 or less, provided not more than one such package is mailed to any one person in a single day. If you exceed your US$400 limit upon returning to the States, the first US$600 worth of merchandise in excess is assessed at a flat duty rate of 10 percent.

JEWELRY AND ART

US law allows the importation, duty-free, of original works of art. Because of concessions made to developing countries, jewelry made in the Antilles may qualify as original art, and thus be duty-free. If you purchase jewelry, be sure to obtain a certificate from the place of purchase stating that the jewelry was made in the islands. To make sure that the articles you want to bring back fall into this category, contact the US Customs Service for further details.

PETS

If you intend to bring a pet with you on your trip, make arrangements with your destination country long before you plan to travel. Many countries do not allow foreign pets on their shores because of the danger from highly infectious diseases such as rabies; others require animals to endure substantial quarantine periods. Your local tourist office, consulate, or embassy should be able to provide details.

FIREARMS

The importation of firearms, including air pistols and rifles, is generally prohibited.

Health and Insurance

HEALTH HAZARDS

The main (though small) health risk to travelers in the Caribbean is infectious hepatitis or Hepatitis A. Although it is not a requirement, an injection of gamma globulin, administered as close as possible before departure, gives good protection against Hepatitis A. In addition, make sure you observe scrupulous personal hygiene, wash and peel fruit, and avoid contaminated water (drink bottled water if you are unsure).

SUN PROTECTION

To a traveler who is not adjusted to the tropical sun, 80–90°F (27–32°C) may sound "just like summer temperatures back home". Don't be fooled! The sun in the tropics is much more direct than in temperate regions.

Bring a high-factor sunscreen and wear it whenever you go out. For starters, expose yourself for only brief periods, preferably in the morning or late afternoon when the sun's rays are less intense. As your tan builds, you can increase your sunning time and decrease your protection factor – though you will still need some sort of protection. Bring a brimmed hat, especially if you plan to do any extended hiking, walking, or playing in the midday sun.

DRINKING WATER

In undeveloped areas away from resorts, it is best to avoid drinking tap water, especially after hurricanes, when water supplies can become contaminated. In these areas, stick to bottled water, and avoid ice in your drinks.

INSECTS

To combat mosquitos, pack a plentiful supply of insect repellent. At night, a mosquito net over the bed provides the best protection, although the

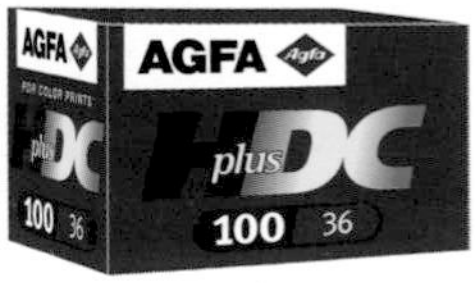

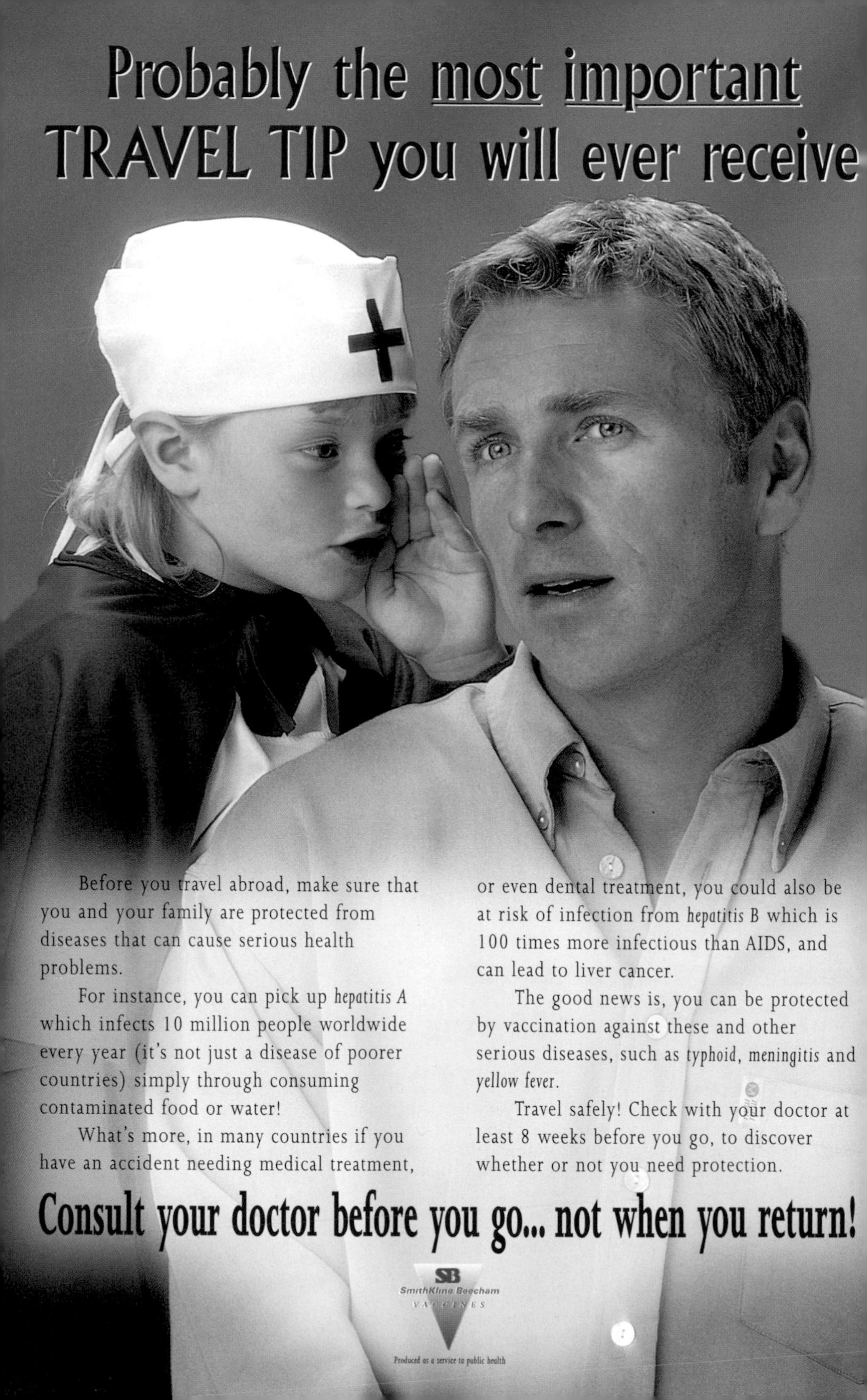

Probably the most important
TRAVEL TIP you will ever receive
Before you travel abroad, make sure that you and your family are protected from diseases that can cause serious health problems.
For instance, you can pick up hepatitis A which infects 10 million people worldwide every year (it's not just a disease of poorer countries) simply through consuming contaminated food or water!
What's more, in many countries if you have an accident needing medical treatment, or even dental treatment, you could also be at risk of infection from hepatitis B which is 100 times more infectious than AIDS, and can lead to liver cancer.
The good news is, you can be protected by vaccination against these and other serious diseases, such as typhoid, meningitis and yellow fever.
Travel safely! Check with your doctor at least 8 weeks before you go, to discover whether or not you need protection.
Consult your doctor before you go... not when you return!
SB
SmithKline Beecham
VACCINES
Produced as a service to public health

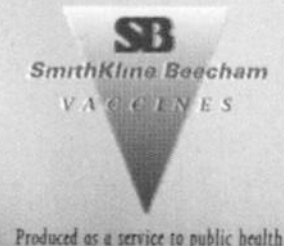

plug-in repellents are also useful (check the voltage). Mosquitos can carry malaria and dengue fever (causing fever, muscle ache, headache), although both are rare in the Lesser Antilles.

IMMUNIZATION

No immunizations are required for travelers to the Antilles, unless the traveler is coming from an infected or endemic area. However, it is a good idea to have a tetanus shot if you are not already covered, and possibly gamma globulin (*see Health Hazards, above*). Check with a Public Health Department or other source before traveling, just to make sure there are no precautionary steps to take.

INSURANCE

Though you are highly unlikely to have to claim, you should never leave home without comprehensive travel insurance to cover both yourself and your belongings. Your own insurance company or travel agent can advise you on policies, but shop around since rates vary. Make sure you are covered for accidental death, emergency medical care, trip cancellation, and baggage or document loss.

Money Matters

A range of currencies is used in the islands. Whatever the official currency, the US dollar and sometimes the British pound are readily accepted throughout the islands. In addition, major credit cards and traveler's checks are welcome at most major hotels, restaurants and shops. On French islands, the French franc is the preferred currency, although the dollar is accepted.

If you are bringing US dollars or pounds sterling, it is a good idea to check around before converting your currency, especially if you are on a limited budget. Try to get price quotes in both the local currency and the currency you are carrying. Then check the applicable exchange rate. You may find you can save some money by making purchases in whichever currency gives you greater value.

BANKING HOURS

Banks are normally open mornings, Monday through Friday – from 8am or 8.30am until noon. Many banks also have afternoon opening hours, especially on a Friday. A few banks open on Saturday mornings. As US dollars, credit cards, and travelers' checks are widely accepted in the islands, visitors need not worry about finding a money exchange facility immediately upon arrival. You can also use your credit and debit cards to withdraw cash from ATMs (Automatic Teller Machines). Before you leave home, make sure you know your PIN number and find out which ATM system will accept your card. See under Travel Tips for individual islands for variations in bank opening hours, and for locations of ATM machines.

Tax

Two taxes which you might not expect will be levied on you during your travels in the Lesser Antilles. The first is a government room tax, charged on all hotel room bills, which generally averages 5–10 percent of the total bill. The second is the departure tax. This fee, around US$10–15, but as high as US$25 in certain islands, is payable upon departure from each of the islands. Remember to keep enough cash to pay the departure tax, usually required in local currency.

What to Wear

"Casual" is the word in the Antilles. Light cotton dresses, trousers, skirts, shorts, and blouses for women, and informal trousers, shorts and comfortable open-necked shirts for men should make up the majority of your wardrobe. The breezes are cooler at night during the winter, so women are advised to bring a light jacket or cotton sweater, just in case. Men should bring a jacket and tie, especially if they plan to visit any casinos – most of them (and some of the fancier restaurants and hotels) require at least a jacket for the evening. For the feet, light sandals are appropriate and comfortable on the beach and around town. A light raincoat or an umbrella are useful in case of sudden showers. A pair of sturdy walking shoes is essential for those planning walks or hikes in the mountains and rainforests.

Swimsuits and other beach attire are definitely not appropriate around town. When you venture from beach or poolside into town, cover up – a simple T-shirt and a pair of shorts should do the trick. By following this rule, you will show respect for the standards of many island residents.

Nude or topless (for women) bathing is prohibited everywhere except for Guadeloupe, Martinique, St Martin, St Barthélemy, and Bonaire. Guadeloupe, St Martin, and Bonaire have at least one designated nudist beach.

Tourist Offices

Addresses of on-island tourist offices, and representative offices in other countries can be found in the listings for individual islands. In addition, you can turn to the following offices for any enquiry about the islands:

Caribbean Tourism Association, 20 East 46th Street, New York, NY 10164. Tel: 212-682 0435.

High Commission for Eastern Caribbean States, 10 Kensington Court, London W8 5DL, UK. Tel: 0171-937 9522.

Getting There

BY AIR

As far as accessibility goes, the islands fall fairly neatly into two groups: those that can be reached by direct flights from North America, South America, and Europe, and those that cannot. Islands which can be reached by direct flight are as follows:

- Antigua
- Aruba
- Barbados
- Curaçao
- Guadeloupe
- Martinique
- St Kitts
- St Lucia
- St Martin
- US Virgin Islands

All other destinations must be reached by inter-island airline from the nearest direct-flight island. All the islands, including those listed, can be reached from various points in the Caribbean via numerous carriers, on a tangled spider's web of routes (*see Inter-Island Travel, page 321*). If you want to know which islands can be reached from a particular island, see the listing for that island. Note that inter-island schedules and itineraries are liable to change. Once you have decided on all the places you want to visit, talk to a travel agent, tourist board or airline company to determine the most efficient way to get to your destinations.

A good travel agent will help you plan your trip and find the flights which best suit your pocket and your timetable. Fare prices can vary according to the season and special offers from airlines, so shop around. Many scheduled services are supplemented by charter flights, but even so, flights become heavily booked during high season. Cheap fares to Martinique and Guadeloupe are available if you fly with Air France or Aéromaritime from an international airport in France.

Airline Numbers

Telephone numbers of major airlines serving the Lesser Antilles:

- **American:** 800-433 7300
- **Air Canada:** 800-776 3000
- **Air France:** 800-237 2747
- **British Airways:** 800-247 9297
- **British West Indies Air International:** 800-327 7401
- **Continental:** 800-525 0280
- **KLM:** 800-374 7747
- **Lufthansa:** 800-645 3880
- **United Airlines:** 800-241 6522

Inter-Island Carriers

Inter-island airlines include the following:

- Aero Virgin Islands
- Air BVI
- Air Guadeloupe
- Air Martinique
- Air Mustique
- Air St Thomas
- ALM (Dutch Antillean Airlines)
- American Eagle Carib Express
- BWIA
- Caribair
- Crown Air
- Eastern Caribbean Airways
- LIAT
- Prinair
- Sunair Express
- Virgin Islands Seaplane Shuttle
- Winair

Cruise Lines

A large proportion of visitors to the Caribbean arrive by cruise ship, the combination of staying in a luxurious floating hotel and making short visits to different exotic locations being increasingly popular. The days on which cruise ships call see hundreds of passengers flooding into usually low-key ports, and in many places shopping complexes, such as Heritage Quay in scruffy St John's, Antigua, have sprung up to accommodate them.

The Lesser Antilles are on the itineraries of several cruise lines, though frequency of service to the different islands in the group varies widely – from hundreds of port visits each year to the US Virgin Islands, to no stops at all at certain other islands. Itineraries change constantly. The best way to plan your trip is to decide first where you would like to go, then contact a cruise operator or travel agent to see if there is a current itinerary that covers all or most of your destinations.

The following cruise ship companies have ships that call at islands in the Lesser Antilles:

Carnival Cruise Lines, 5525 NW 87th Avenue, Miami, FL 33166. Tel: 800-327 9501.

Clipper Cruise Line, 7711 Bonhomme Avenue, St. Louis, MO 63105. Tel: 800-325 0010, 314-727 2929.

Commodore Cruise Line, 1015 North America Way, Miami, FL 33132. Tel: 305-358 2622.

Costa Cruises, One Biscayne Tower, Miami, FL 33131. Tel: 800-447 6877, 305-358 7325.

Cunard Line, 555 5th Avenue, NY, NY 10017. Tel: 212-880 7500.

Epirotiki Lines, 551 5th Avenue, Suite 1900, NY, NY 10017. Tel: 800-221 2470, 212-599 1750.

Fantasy Cruise, 1052 Biscayne Boulevard, Miami, FL 33132. Tel: 305-358 1588.

Holland America Cruises, 300 Eliot Avenue West, Seattle, WA 98119. Tel: 206-281 3535.

Norwegian Cruise Line, One Biscayne Tower, Miami, FL 33131. Tel: 305-358 6670.

Ocean Cruise Line, 1510 SE 17th Street, Fort Lauderdale, FL 33316. Tel: 305-764 3500.

P & O Cruises, c/o Princess Cruises, 2029 Century Park East, LA, CA90067. Tel: 800-

252 0158 (California only); 800-421 0522; 213-553 1770.
Paquet French Cruises, 1007 North American Way, Miami, FL 33132. Tel: 800-327 5620, 305-374 6025.
Royal Viking Line, One Embarcadero Center, San Francisco, CA 94111. Tel: 415-398 8000.
Sea Goddess Cruises Limited, 5805 Blue Lagoon Drive, Miami, FL 33126. Tel: 305-266 8705.
Star Clipper, 4101 Salzedo Avenue, Coral Gables, FL 33146. Tel: 305-442 1611. Sailing cruises on four-masted clipper ships.
Windjammer Cruises, PO Box 120, Miami Beach, FL 33119. Tel: 305-534 7447. Sailing cruises on tall-masted ships.

Yachting Information

The "yachtie" community in the Caribbean is a thriving one. Apart from people employed in the charter business, it is comprised of many adventurers: those passing through, whole families sometimes, perhaps on their way round the world, and those who can't tear themselves away. For yachtsmen and women who want to stay put for a while, there are community anchorages in St Martin, Bequia (Grenadines), Grenada, and Trinidad. Throughout the islands, there are pleasant, well-equipped marinas with slips of different types and facilities for repairs and provisioning which have mushroomed over the past few years, and are continuing to be built. Several of the larger ones have dry-dock facilities for boat storage. Cruising guides to the region include those by William T. Stone and Anne M. Hays (published by Sheridan House), by Donald Street (published by W.W. Norton, New York), by Chris Doyle Publishing, and by Michael Marshal (published by Adlard Coles).

Cargo Ships

For the traveler in search of something out of the ordinary, a cargo ship offers a different type of cruise: comfortable cabins for only a handful of passengers (evening meals are generally taken with the officers) on a working cargo ship. Geest "banana boats", for example, leave Southampton on a round trip lasting 25 days, and calling at Antigua, Barbados, Dominica, Grenada, Guadeloupe, Martinique, St Kitts, St Lucia, St Vincent, and Trinidad. Enquiries can be made to the following:
Cargo Ship Voyages Ltd (agents for Geest), Hemley, Woodbridge, Suffolk, IP12 4QF. Tel: 01473-736265.
Freighter World Cruises, 180 South Lake Avenue, Pasadena, CA91101. Tel: 818-449 3106.
Strand Cruise and Travel Centre, Charing Cross Shopping Concourse, The Strand, London WC2 4HZ. Tel: 0171-836 6363.

Weddings in the Caribbean

There are those who still prefer a traditional wedding at home, followed by a honeymoon away, but others – in increasing numbers – decide to combine the two, and bring family and friends along as well. A Caribbean island makes the perfect destination. Choose a hotel which employs a full-time wedding organizer, or, through your travel agent, choose one of the tour operators who now offer all-in wedding packages. Here are some points to note:

- Rules vary from island to island (contact tourist offices for information), but in most cases it is required that couples be over 18, and for the wedding to be conducted after three working days. Hotels prefer you to be resident there for seven days.
- You will need valid passports, birth certificates and any relevant divorce or death certificates. Allow approximately half a day to complete administration prior to the ceremony (paperwork can be done only during government business hours, so check that public holidays don't intervene). On English islands, non-English documents must be translated by an officially recognized translator.
- The marriage may be carried out by a marriage officer or a clergyman. In the latter case, it may be necessary for your home minister to liaise with the island minister; this is always the case for Catholic services.
- The marriage is legally binding.
- The bride and bridegroom can usually choose their own music.
- Wedding outfits (remember the heat and the relaxed setting when planning yours) can usually be pressed before the ceremony; major airlines all have arrangements for transporting them, either boxed or hanging in garment sleeves.
- Wedding photographs and videos can be provided, but the quality may not be the same as in the US and Europe.
- Apart from the cost of staying in the hotel, couples pay an extra fee for the wedding ceremony. Prices vary considerably, depending on the standard of hotel and what extras are offered (these might include anything from a souvenir T-shirt to a sunset cruise).

Sailing

YACHT CHARTER

One of the most exciting ways to explore the Caribbean is on a private yacht, either with your own crew to sail the boat for you or bareboat – just the boat – for experienced sailors. Popular destinations are the Grenadines and the Virgin Islands as the islands are close together and easily explored in a week or two. A three-week trip might take you, for example, from Antigua to the Virgin Islands or Antigua to Grenada, making leisurely calls at the islands along the way. Short charters of just a few days can also be arranged, and for those who prefer to sleep on dry land, most islands have day-sail operators too. Whatever your itinerary, if you are at home on a boat, this is a wonderful way to see the islands.

CHARTERING A YACHT

If you want to rent a crewed yacht, make sure you are happy with your choice – that the yacht is safe, comfortable and well-equipped and the crew congenial enough to share close quarters. Don't deal direct with yachts unless they come recommended through friends. Leave it to a reputable agency to match you with the right boat and crew. Two long-established agencies are:
Nicholson Yacht Charters, 78 Bolton Street, Cambridge, MA 02140. Tel: 800-662 6066.
The Moorings, 19345 US 19 North, Clearwater, FL 34624. Tel: 800-535 7289.

An exhaustive list of companies offering bareboat Caribbean charters is published in the March issue of *Sail* magazine, while the August issue covers crewed yachts. *Sail* is available in many libraries, and back (or current) issues can also be ordered from the magazine's publisher. Contact: **Sail Publications, Inc.**, 34 Commercial Wharf, Boston, MA 02110. Tel: 617- 241 9500.

Practical Tips

Telephone and Fax

Public card phones in several denominations are available from Cable and Wireless on the islands from which the company operates. They are useful for avoiding the usually high hotel charges on phone calls. Residents of the US and Canada can use AT&T USA Direct public phones with a charge card. Some public phones allow holders of a European charge card, such as a BT Chargecard, to access the home operator. Public fax centers are also available to send and receive faxes.

Traveling with Kids

West Indians love children, and children love the sun, sea, and sand, so the islands are a perfect holiday destination for a family. Many resorts now offer children's programs including babysitting facilities.

Facilities for Disabled Travelers

Generally, there are few special facilities such as ramps in public places. However you will find them in new shopping centers, restaurants and many modern resorts. Resort hotels may well have a few specially adapted bedrooms or, failing that, ground-floor rooms and minimal steps to public rooms.

Religious Services

All the mainstream church denominations can be found on the islands, as well as little-known cults. Attending a local service, perhaps Baptist or Seventh Day Adventist, is a wonderful way to experience an important aspect of Caribbean life, and you will be assured of a warm welcome, as long as you dress smartly and act with decorum and respect. Local tourist offices and free tourist publications should be able to advise times of services.

Tipping

On most restaurant and hotel bills, you will find that a 10–15 percent service charge has been added by the management. If this is the case, tipping is unnecessary, although a small gratuity given directly to an attentive waitress or bellman is always appreciated. If you are unsure whether or not service has been included in your bill, feel free to ask. When service is not included, a tip in the 15–20 percent range is appropriate. Taxi drivers should be tipped within this range as well.

Etiquette

Common politeness is as desirable on the islands as it is anywhere else. "Please", "Thank you", and a respectful and friendly demeanor will go a long way toward returning the warm welcome you are likely to receive. "Hello","Goodbye", "Good Morning" and "Goodnight" are always used to friends, family or just to people you might pass on the road. If you need to ask directions or advice always greet the person *before* asking a question.Two more points: don't take anyone's picture without first asking permission – it is often seen as invasive; and don't drag up shades of colonialism and old B-grade Hollywood movies by referring to island residents as "natives".

Getting Around

By Car

The islands are well stocked with auto-rental agencies. Travel by car allows great freedom and flexibility to explore the nooks and crannies of the islands, but there are a few things the driver should be aware of. Many of the islands are mountainous, and on all of them, roads are narrower than most US and European drivers will be familiar with. Driving thus may be a little more harrowing than at home – not for the faint-hearted. Also, in some areas yearly rainfall is quite light and this allows a film of oil to build up on road surfaces. When it does rain on these roads, they become especially slick, requiring extra caution. All in all, drivers should prepare to drive defensively and with caution, perhaps following the advice of one of the islands' tourist agencies to "sound the horn frequently", especially when approaching bends. Regulations on driver's licenses vary from island to island – see under the listings for individual islands.

By Taxi

Perhaps the most common means of transportation for visitors to the islands is the taxi. Not only are taxis convenient and, by US standards, often quite inexpensive, but taking a taxi also gives you access to the resources of the driver. Where else could you chat with an island expert for the price of a cab ride? Most taxi drivers will gladly help you find things you are looking for, or that you aren't looking for but may be delighted to find. It is usually possible to find a taxi driver who is willing to give you a tour of his or her island and, in some places, drivers are specially trained to do this.

Another positive feature of taxi travel for island visitors is that rates are generally fixed and published. Often, printed sheets with detailed rates are available from points of entry, drivers, and tourist offices. If you plan to travel much by taxi, one of the first things to do upon arrival is to familiarize yourself with the rates to different destinations and at different times of day.

Taxi drivers are usually friendly and extremely helpful. If you receive good service, return the favor with a good tip – say, 15–20 percent.

By Bus

Most of the islands have local bus services which many residents use to get around. Though they are not as flexible as taxis and rental cars, buses are quite inexpensive and have the advantage of allowing travelers to get a small taste of how local residents live. Your hotel, a tourist office, or a police station should be able to supply information on schedules, and fellow riders and drivers are friendly and helpful in making sure that bewildered visitors get off at the right stop.

Tour buses (mini and full-sized), vans, jeeps, and "communal taxis" are available on all the islands, for taking groups sightseeing.

Inter-Island Links

As you might expect in this region of small-to-tiny islands cut off from one another by the sea, the options for getting around between islands are legion. For the traveler desiring quick transfers (and, perhaps, the novelty of a ride in a seaplane), there are at least 20 airline companies operating inter-island routes. LIAT is probably the largest and best-known of these, although ALM (Dutch Antillean Airlines) has a monopoly on flights between Aruba, Curaçao, Bonaire, and St Martin. For a list of inter-island air carriers, *see Getting There, page 317*.

On the sea, an armada of ferries operates regularly between islands, and there is even a regular run between Aruba, Curaçao, and Venezuela. Some of these ferries are the familiar steel-and-smokestack variety, while the inquisitive and adventurous traveler will find hydrofoils, schooners, and other types of sailing vessel plying the waters between islands. *El Tigre*, for example, is a 60-ft (20 meter) catamaran making a daily run between St Barthélemy and St Martin. It is often possible for travelers to bargain with fishermen and other small boat owners to arrange rides out to the many small islands which lie off the shores of the major islands.

Where to Stay and Eat

Choosing a Hotel

As there is a variety of currencies in the islands, our price guide (*see below*) is given in US dollars. See under individual islands for detailed and specific listings.

When writing to a hotel, be sure to complete all mailing addresses, unless otherwise noted, with: (name of island), WI. For full details and reservations (which are recommended), contact the hotel directly, or a travel agent. Alternatively, try the Caribbean tourist office in your preferred country.

ACCOMMODATION PRICE CATEGORIES

Price categories are based on the cost of a double room, for one night:
$ = less than $100
$$ = $100–200
$$$ = more than $200.

Choosing a Restaurant

Our price guide (*see below*) is given in US dollars. *See* individual islands for detailed listings. Reservations are recommended, especially in the winter season, and at some restaurants they are essential.

THE COST OF EATING OUT

Price categories are based on the cost of a meal for one person, excluding drinks:
$ = less than $20
$$ = $20–30
$$$ = more than $30.

Nightlife

Nightlife on the islands ranges from relaxing over a leisurely dinner in a restaurant with a verandah onto the beach to frittering your money away in a casino. In between these options are nightclubs, bars, discos, and live music. The larger hotels provide much of the evening entertainment on the islands, including music and dancing both during and after dinner, flashy floor shows usually featuring a limbo dancer, and "folkloric evenings" composed of elements of the music, dance, and drama native to the Caribbean. Travelers with an interest in the cultural lives of island residents may wish to venture beyond hotel walls in search of steel band, calypso, and reggae music, and of bars and clubs frequented by local people. Discos may be found both in and outside hotels.

The intensity of nightlife varies substantially from island to island. The more heavily touristed islands may have several special entertainments every night of the week, while the quieter islands may sometimes have little more to offer than dinner to the accompaniment of recorded music, followed by a stroll along the beach. In the latter category, things may pick up a little during the weekends; several establishments have discos that open only on Friday and Saturday nights. On all the islands, the peak tourist season – approximately December to April – is also the peak nightlife season; things are slower during the rest of the year.

Active Nightlife

The following islands are known for having a particularly lively nightlife:

- Aruba
- Barbados
- Curaçao
- Guadeloupe
- Martinique
- St Lucia
- St Martin (French and Dutch)
- Trinidad and Tobago
- US Virgin Islands

Casinos

Visitors will find plenty of opportunities to gamble in the Antilles. A number of the islands have several casinos, and even some of the region's more relaxed islands have a casino or two.

If you do plan to gamble, be sure to bring along some appropriate clothes. Dress codes in the casinos tend to be a little more formal than those prevailing elsewhere.

The legal gambling age is 18 on most islands, but on Guadeloupe and Martinique you must be 21. Photo ID will sometimes be required for admittance, and some casinos charge an admission.

Islands with Casinos

- Antigua
- Aruba
- Bonaire
- Curaçao
- Guadeloupe
- Martinique
- St Kitts
- St Martin

Outdoor Activities

Sport

The climate and geography of the Antilles make the islands perfect for sports enthusiasts, and tourism has helped spark the development of a variety of sports facilities. Following is a list of some of the more popular sporting activities; see listings under individual islands for more detailed information.

GOLF

Golf is available on Antigua, Aruba, Barbados, British Virgin Islands, Curaçao, Grenada, St Kitts and Nevis, St Lucia, St Martin, the US Virgin Islands, St Vincent and the Grenadines, Guadeloupe, and Martinique. Guadeloupe, Martinique, Nevis and the US Virgin Islands each have an 18-hole Robert Trent Jones course. The BVI has two small practice courses, and Aruba has one of the oddest courses in the world, with "greens" made out of oiled sand.

TENNIS

Tennis is played on all islands, to varying degrees. Courts are found primarily within the premises of hotels, but arrangements can be made to use these courts even if you are not a hotel guest. Some islands also have private clubs which are open to visitors, and public courts which operate on a "first come, first served" basis. The more popular islands offer instruction and equipment rental, and many hotels have resident tennis pros to help you improve your game.

WINDSURFING AND SAILING

From mini Sunfish to two-masted yachts and large motorboats, a variety of rental options is available for sailing. Equipment can be hired, and classes are conducted on almost every island.

Waterskiing is available on most islands and all the necessary equipment may be rented. If you are interested in chartering a yacht, either crewed or bareboat, for a day or a considerable period of time, *see Getting There pages 319–20.*

DEEP-SEA FISHING

Fishing is a popular watersport throughout the Caribbean. Most fishing boats can be chartered by the day or half day, and can usually accommodate several passengers. Many will quote rates which are all-inclusive of lunch, drinks, snacks, bait, equipment and any other essential items you might need on your fishing trip.

HIKING AND HORSEBACK RIDING

Rainforests, mountains, waterfalls and gorgeous views await you. Many of the islands have good sized national parks with prime hiking opportunities (Dominica, Guadeloupe, Grenada, St Kitts, and St John in the US Virgin Islands, are particularly good), and St Lucia's Pitons offer experienced mountain climbers a chance to test their skills. Guides are often available to lead excursions. For details see under individual islands listings.

BIRDWATCHING

Trinidad and Tobago are noted for their birds. In the US, bird-watching tours are organized by: **Field Guides Incorporated**, Box 60723, Austin TX; tel: 512-327 4953.

Scuba Diving and Snorkeling

The clear blue waters of the Caribbean are the setting for a marine landscape of breath-taking beauty, a hidden world – accessible only to divers and snorkelers – in which gloriously colored and patterned fish vie for attention with extraordinary coral formations and reefs teeming with life.

All the islands offer equipment and excursion packages, including training packages for those who have never dived before. Addresses of well-reputed dive operators (always check on the reliability of operators and ask to see instructors' certificates) are listed under individual islands. The following islands are particularly renowned for diving:

- Barbados
- Bonaire
- British Virgin Islands
- Curaçao
- Saba
- St Lucia
- Tobago
- US Virgin Islands

Destinations with limited facilities, but wonderful diving include:

- Anguilla
- Dominica
- St Vincent and the Grenadines.

If you are a swimmer but not a diver, most hotels rent out snorkeling equipment. The lists of best diving islands apply equally to snorkeling, but even if an island is not listed, you are still likely to be bewitched by the variety of marine life that you will find there. Ask the staff at your hotel as they should know the best spots to go. Always wear a T-shirt while snorkeling to protect your back from sunburn.

Outdoor Hazards

Manchineel trees: these are usually indicated by red stripes painted on them and a warning notice. The apple-like fruit and the resin contain a poisonous substance (the Amerindians used it on their poison arrows) and when it rains they secrete an irritant that burns the skin – so never shelter underneath one. Don't handle the leaves or rub them either.

Sea urchins: when swimming over rocks be careful where you put your feet – stepping on one of these spiny balls is a very painful experience, as a spine may get stuck in your foot.

Sea lice: however tired you may be don't hang on to a buoy or anything else covered in a fine green seaweed because the sea lice living in it can cause a very itchy, painful allergic skin reaction.

Snakes: the only poisonous snake in the Lesser Antilles is the Lance de Fer found in the dry scrubland and river valleys of St Lucia and Martinique. If it bites it is not usually fatal but hospitalization is necessary.

Language

Primary Languages

The multiplicity of languages in the Antilles reflects the region's checkered colonial past. All of the islands use their own patois language as well as a whole array of primary languages which include:

- **English:** Anguilla, Antigua and Barbuda, British Virgin Islands, Dominica, Grenada, Montserrat, St Kitts and Nevis, St Lucia, St Vincent and the Grenadines, St Maarten, Barbados, Trinidad and Tobago, and the US Virgin Islands.
- **French:** Dominica, Guadeloupe, Martinique, St Barthélemy, St Lucia, and St Martin.
- **Dutch:** Aruba, Bonaire, and Curaçao.
- **Spanish:** Aruba, Bonaire, and Curaçao.
- **Papiamento** is the local language of Aruba, Bonaire, and Curaçao. It has evolved from Spanish, Dutch, Portuguese, English, and African and Caribbean languages.

In addition to the primary languages listed above, Chinese is among the languages spoken on Aruba. English (and, to a lesser extent, other European languages) is spoken in several areas throughout the islands which have a high concentration of foreign travelers, but don't expect everyone to understand you – especially in rural areas and smaller towns. Efforts to communicate with island residents in their own languages are always appreciated.

Further Reading

History, Economics and Culture

A History of Modern Trinidad 1783–1962 by Bridget Brereton, Heinemann, London (1981).

A Short History of the Netherlands Antilles by Cornelius Ch. Goslinga, M. Hijhoff, The Hague (1979).

A Short History of the West Indies by J.H. Parry, P.M. Sherlock, and A. Maingot, Macmillan Caribbean, London (1987).

America's Virgin Islands: A History of Human Rights and Wrongs by William H. Boyer, Carolina Academic Press, Durham NC (1983).

Barbados: A History from Amerindians to Independence by F.A. Hoyos, Macmillan Caribbean, London (1978).

The Dominica Story: A History of the Island by Lennox Honychurch, Letchworth Press, Barbados (1975).

From Columbus to Castro: The History of the Caribbean 1492–1969 by Eric Williams, Harper and Row, New York (1971).

Gentlemen of Fortune: The Men who Made their Fortunes in Britain's Slave Colonies by Derrick Knight, F. Muller, London (1978).

Last Resorts, The Cost of Tourism in the Caribbean by Polly Pattullo, Cassell and Latin American Bureau (1996).

Pirates, Shipwrecks, and Historic Chronicals by Edward Rowe Snow, Dodd, Mead, New York (1981).

The Poor and the Powerless, Economic Policy and Change in the Caribbean by Clive Y. Thomas, Latin American Bureau (1988).

A Good Read

James Ferguson, author of the excellent **Traveller's History of the Caribbean** (Windrush Press, 1998) and **Traveller's Literary Companion to the Caribbean** (In Print, 1997), and contributor to this guide, recommends the following books, available in paperback:

- **In the Castle of My Skin** by George Lamming – growing up in a 1930s Barbadian village during the demise of colonialism. a novel of adolescence and political awakening.
- **A House for Mr Biswas** by V.S. Naipaul – classic, bitter-sweet account of a Trinidadian man's search for security.
- **The Lonely Londoners** by Samuel Selvon – comic masterpiece of a Trinidadian immigrant's life in 1950s London.
- **The Wide Sargasso Sea** by Jean Rhys – an atmospheric classic prequel to a Brontë classic – read it to discover which one!
- **The Orchid House** by Phyllis Shand Allfrey – acclaimed novel of family tensions and colonial decline in Dominica.
- **A State of Independence** by Caryl Phillips – a wry study of small-island politics and an exile's return to his homeland.
- **Omeros** by Derek Walcott – contemporary working of homeric epic by St Lucian Nobel Prize-winning poet.
- **The Dragon Can't Dance** by Earl Lovelace – captures all the exuberance of Trinidad's Carnival.
- **The Penguin Book of Caribbean Verse in English**, ed. Paula Burnett – the best available collection of verse from English-speaking Caribbean poets.
- **Tree of Life** by Maryse Condé – tale of several generations of a Guadeloupean family.

The Slave Trade by Hugh Thomas, Picador, London (1997).

Natural History

A Field Guide to Reefs of the Caribbean and Florida by Eugene H. Kaplan, Houghton Mifflin, Boston (1982).
Birds of the West Indies by Christopher Helm (1997).
Caribbean Reef Fishes by Dr John E. Randall, T.F.H. Publications, Inc. (1996).
Exploring Tropical Isles and Seas: An Introduction for the Traveler and Amateur Naturalist by Frederic Martini, Prentice-Hall, New Jersey (1984).
The Gardens of Dominica by Polly Pattullo and Anne Jno Baptiste, The Papillote Press, 23 Rozel Road, London SW4 0EY (1998).
Tropical Flowers and Plants by Stirling Macoby, P. Hamlyn, New York (1974).

Sport

Caribbean Afoot by M. Timothy O'Keefe, Menasha Ridge Press, US.
The Complete Diving Guide, Caribbean Volume I by Colleen Ryan and Brian Savage, Complete Dive Guide Publications, Corinth VT.
The Diver's Handbook by Alan Mountain, New Holland (1996).
Diving Guide to the Eastern Caribbean by Martha Watkins Gilkes, Macmillan Caribbean, London (1994).
Snorkeling: A complete guide to the underwater experience by John R. Clark in cooperation with the Oceanic Society, Prentice Hall, New Jersey (1985).
West Indies Cricket Annual by Tony Cozier (ed.), Barbados, Caribbean Communications (published yearly).

Getting Acquainted

US Virgin Islands

Located about 40 miles (64 km) east of Puerto Rico, the United States Virgin Islands (USVI) is composed of over 60 islands with a total land area of 136 sq. miles (352 sq. km). The inhabited islands are St Thomas, St Croix and St John.

Public Holidays

January 1 **New Year's Day/ Three King's Day**
January 6 **Martin Luther King Day**
February (3rd Monday) **President's Day**
March 31 **Transfer Day**
Easter **Good Friday, Easter Monday**
June 18 **Organic Act Day**
July 3 **Emancipation Day**
July 4 **Independence Day**
July 23 **Supplication Day**
October **Friendship Days** (Puerto Rico/ BVI)
November 1 **Liberty Day**
(last Thursday) **Thanksgiving Day**
December 25 **Christmas Day**
December 26 **Boxing Day**

Calendar of Events

December–January 6 **St Croix Christmas Festival**
March 17 **St Patrick's Day Festival, St Croix**
Easter week **Rolex Regatta**
April (third week) **St Thomas Carnival**
July (week of the 4th) **St John's Carnival**
October **St Croix Music and Arts Festival**

Planning the Trip

Customs

The USVI is a renowned shopping spot, and visitors will find a large variety of duty-free items to choose from. For regulations for US travelers returning to the United States, *see* under Customs (*page 316*).

Money Matters

The currency is the US dollar (US$). Normal banking hours are 9am–3pm Monday–Thursday, 9am–5pm Friday. There are ATMs (Automatic Teller Machines) at the airport on St Thomas and in the Banco Popular, Sunny Isles Shopping Center in St Croix, among other places. All major credit cards are accepted on the main islands.

There is no departure tax at the airport; it is included in the price of your ticket.

What to Bring

Plan to pack light clothing made from natural fibres and plenty of high factor sunscreen. In general, casual elegance is enough for the evenings, although some of the upscale places may require their guests to wear more formal attire.

Tourist Offices Abroad

IN PUERTO RICO

US Virgin Islands Tourism, 1300 Ashford Avenue, Condado, Santurce, Puerto Rico 00907. Tel: 809-724 3816.

IN THE US

Chicago: 343 South Dearborn Street, Suite 1108, Chicago, IL 60604. Tel: 312-461 0180.
Los Angeles: 3450 Wilshire Boulevard, Los Angeles, CA 90010. Tel: 213-739 0138.
Miami: 7270 NW 12th Street, Suite 620, Miami, FL 33126. Tel: 305-591 2070.
New York: 1270 Avenue of the Americas, New York, NY 10020. Tel: 212-582 4520.
Washington: 1667 K Street NW, Suite 270, Washington DC 20006. Tel: 202-293 3707.

IN CANADA

234 Eglinton Avenue East, Suite 306, Toronto, Ontario M4P 1K5. Tel: 416-488 4374.

IN THE UK

Molasses House, Plantation Wharf, Clove Hitch Quay, London, SW11 3TN. Tel: 0171-978 5262. E-mail: usvi@destination-marketing.co.uk

WEBSITE ADDRESSES

http://www.usvi.net
http://www.st-croix.com

Practical Tips

Media

As a territory of the US the USVI receives all of the TV channels available in America and the same goes for newspapers and magazines. Local newspapers include the *Virgin Islands Daily News* on St Thomas and St John and the *St Croix Avis*. Weekly tourist publications include *St Thomas This Week* available on St Thomas and St John and *St Croix This Week. The Virgin Islands Playground* is a free visitors' guide to all the islands packed with useful information.

Postal Services

Post offices can be found in the main towns of the three islands, including:

- 1 Marshall Hill, Frederiksted, St Croix.
- Sugar Estate Road, Charlotte Amalie, St Thomas. Tel: 774 1950.

Telephone, Telex & Fax

The area code is **340**. Direct-dialed and operator-assisted long-distance calls may be placed from most hotel and pay phones. Some hotels may also be able to provide telex, fax, and telegraph services.

If you have difficulties in making any sort of telephone or wire communication, the place to go is ITT. Their offices are located at:

- 51-A Kronprindsens, Charlotte Amalie, St Thomas. Tel: 774 1870.
- Caravelle Arcade, Christiansted, St Croix. Tel: 773 2525.

Local Tourist Offices

There are visitor information offices at the two airports and in Charlotte Amalie near Main Street and Emancipation Garden. Alternatively you can write to the following addresses for information:

St Thomas: PO Box 6400, Charlotte Amalie, USVI 00801. Tel: 774 8784.

St John: PO Box 200, Cruz Bay, USVI. Tel: 776 6450.

St Croix: PO Box 4538, Christiansted, USVI 00840. Tel: 772 0357.

Medical Treatment

Excellent medical and dental facilities are available on all three islands. There are two hospitals and clinics on St Thomas, a clinic on St John and three hospitals (medical centers) on St Croix. All have 24-hour emergency services. Hospital telephone numbers:

St Thomas. Tel: 776 8311.

St Croix. Tel: 778 6311.

St John. Tel: 776 6222.

Pharmacies include:

- Sunrise Pharmacy, Red Hook, St Thomas.
- The People's Drugstore, Christiansted.
- The Pharmacy, Sunny Isles Shopping Center, St Croix.
- St John Drug Center, Cruz Bay.

Emergency Number

- **Police, Fire, Ambulance:** 911

Shopping

The USVI enjoy a duty and sales tax-free status so that most things are 20–50 percent cheaper than on the mainland. Wednesday and Friday are the most crowded shopping days, due to the number of visiting cruise ships.

St Thomas has the widest choice of duty-free shopping with a large proportion in Charlotte Amalie; Havensight Mall by the cruise ship docks and Red Hook on the east coast are shopping malls packed with outlets selling jewelry, watches, cameras, liquor, and other duty-free goods. St Thomas also has a selection of handicraft outlets.

St Croix's King's Alley Walk is a new shopping area in Christiansted. In St Croix Leap in the west, there are some excellent wood-carvers.

St John features a variety of local arts and crafts. The most popular shopping areas are Mongoose Junction and Wharfside Village in Cruz Bay.

Voltage: 120 volts 60 cycles.

Religious Services

Charlotte Amalie is home to the second oldest synagogue still in use in the western hemisphere (1833), located on Crystal Gade. Two other notable places of worship are the Dutch Reformed Church, the first established church on the island (1660), and the Frederick Lutheran Church, which is popular for weddings.

Culture

Reichhold Center for the Performing Arts is an outdoor theater in St Thomas which hosts performances of every kind. Local artists are joined by visiting international performers.

Dance

The dance styles that have developed in the US Virgin Islands are particularly interesting. There are regular performances, and classes are taught on St Croix and the other islands. During Carnival, look out for the Mokojumbies, dancers dressed in colorful costume who perform their art – on stilts.

Getting Around

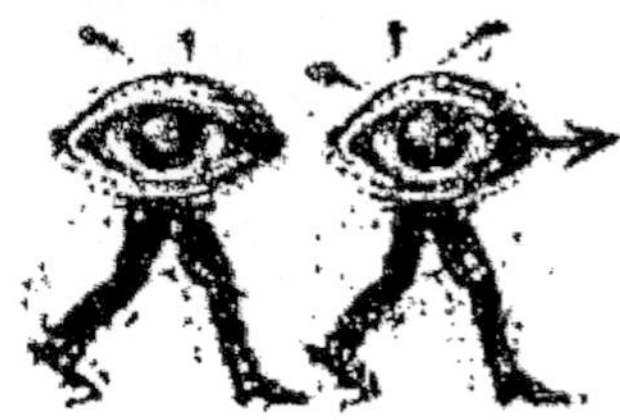

By Car

Note that cars drive on the left, British style, in the US Virgin Islands, despite the fact that most steering wheels are on the left, American style.

A US driver's license is valid in the USVI. If your license is from another country, and you wish to drive here, contact the Division of Tourism before you go to see what arrangements need to be made.

In St Thomas and St Croix, rental cars may be picked up at the airport. In St John, cars are available in Cruz Bay. Car hire companies include:
St Thomas: ABC Auto Rentals, tel: 776 1222; Budget, tel: 776 5774.
St Croix: Budget, tel: 778 9636.
St John: St John Car Rental, tel: 776 6103.

By Taxi

Whether you arrive by plane, cruise ship or ferry, you will find taxis waiting for you at your point of entry to take you to your hotel or wherever else you want to go. Taxi fares are published by the Virgin Islands Taxi Association, but you should discuss the charge before boarding.

If taking a day trip to St John, an open-air taxi tour of the island is recommended. Taxi companies include:
St Thomas: VI Taxi Association, tel: 774 4550.
St Croix: St Croix Taxi Association, tel: 778 1088.

Good Beaches

St Thomas: Magen's Bay, Morningstar Beach, Sapphire Bay, Lindberg Bay, Secret Harbour.
St Croix Buccaneer Bay, Cane Bay, Grapetree Beach, Davis Bay.
St John Trunk Bay, Caneel Bay, Hawk's Nest Bay, Salt Pond Bay, Maho Bay, Cinnamon Bay.

By Bus

There are no public buses on St John (transport is usually by foot, taxi, or jeep), but there are regular services on St Thomas and St Croix; look for the Vitran bus stop signs. On St Croix buses run every half hour between Christiansted and Frederiksted.

Inter-Island Links

There are airports on St Thomas and St Croix. You can fly between the US Virgin Islands on Virgin Island Seaplane (tel: 777 4491). There are regular ferry services from St Thomas (Charlotte Amalie) to St John, Tortola, and Virgin Gorda. There is no regular ferry service to St Croix.

Local airlines link the USVI with nearby islands including the BVI, Anguilla, and St Martin. Airlines include:
- Air Anguilla, tel: 246-497 2643.
- LIAT, tel: 246-495 1187.
- American Eagle, tel: 800-433 7300.

Where to Stay

Choosing a Hotel

Rates for hotels and guest-houses can usually be quoted inclusive or exclusive of meals. Apartments, condominiums, cottages, villas, and campsites are also available.

Hotel Listings

ST THOMAS

Bolongo Bay Beach Club
7150 Bolongo, St Thomas, VI 00802.
Tel: 775 1800.
Fax: 775 3208.
All-inclusive resort hotel with high-quality accommodation, food, and facilities. **$$$**

Elysian Beach Resort
Cowpet Bay, St Thomas, VI 00802.
Tel: 775 1000.
Fax: 779 0910.
A superb pool plus excellent watersports and fitness center. **$$$**

Island View Guesthouse
PO Box 1903, St Thomas, VI 00801.
Tel: 774 4270.
Fax: 774 6167.
Fantastic views from this guesthouse, and a beautiful location on Crown Mountain. **$$**

Mafolie
PO Box 1506, Red Hook, St Thomas, VI 00804.
Tel: 774 2970.
Fax: 774 4091.
A family-run hotel with splendid harbor view. Free shuttle to Magen's Bay beach, or stay by the pleasant hotel pool. **$**

Ritz Carlton
699 Great Bay, St Thomas, VI 00802.
Tel: 775 3333.
Fax: 775 4444.
A luxury hotel in a magnificent setting. Superb restaurant, pool, beach and diving facilities on East Point facing St John. **$$$**

Wyndham Sugar Bay Beach Club
6500 Estate Smith Bay, St Thomas, VI 00802.
Tel: 777 7100.
Fax: 777 7200.
Excellent facilities for all the family. All-inclusive prices. **$$**

Price Guide

Price categories are based on the cost of a double room, for one night:
$ = less than $100
$$ = $100–200
$$$ = more than $200.

ST CROIX

Caravelle
44a Queen Cross Street, Christiansted, St Croix, VI 00820.
Tel: 773 0687.
Fax: 778 7004.
Traditional hotel with its own jetty at the old harbor in the old town. **$$**

Chenay Bay
PO Box 24600, St Croix, VI 00824.
Tel/fax: 773 2918.
Pretty bungalows built into a slope by the sea and set within a vast wildlife park. **$$$**

Pink Fancy
27 Prince Street, Christiansted, St Croix, VI 00820.
Tel: 773 8460.
Fax: 773 6448.
Old Danish town villa with a fascinating past, originally owned by an ex-showgirl. Decorated with glitzy showbiz memorabilia and interesting antiques. **$$**

Tamarind Reef
5001 Tamarind Reef, Christiansted, St Croix, VI 00820.
Tel: 773 4455.
Fax: 773 3989.
Opened in 1994 in West Indian style, fronting the beach. Many of the rooms have kitchenettes. Watersports facilities on offer. **$$–$$$**

ST JOHN

Caneel Bay
PO Box 8310, Great Crux Bay,St John, VI 00831.
Tel: 776 6111.
Fax: 693 8280.
Resort hotel built in the 1950s by Laurence Rockerfeller, restored in mid-1996, situated on a peninsula right in the heart of the National Park. Very quiet. Seven different beaches. **$$$**

Gallows Point Suite Resort
PO Box 58, Cruz Bay, St John, VI 00831.
Tel: 776 6434.
Fax: 776 6520.
Neat wooden houses with fully-equipped apartments. **$$$**

Hyatt Regency
PO Box 8310, Great Crux Bay, St John, VI 00831.
Tel: 693 8000.
Fax: 693 8888.
Resort hotel with huge pool and extensive grounds. **$$$**

Raintree Inn
PO Box 566, Cruz Bay, St John, VI 00831.
Tel/fax: 693 8590.
Friendly guesthouse with verandah and green patio. **$**

Where to Eat

What to Eat

The multinational, multi-ethnic history of the USVI, combined with its tropical location and international reputation as a vacation spot, have contributed to a rich cuisine on the islands. Locally-produced fruits and vegetables and fresh seafood provide some of the raw materials for island cooks, who create anything from bullfoot soup (what it sounds like) and *fungi* (cornmeal pudding) to French, Italian and Chinese food.

Restaurant Listings

ST THOMAS

Banana Tree Grill
Bluebeard's Castle, Charlotte Amalie.
Tel: 776 4050.
Elegant dining combined with a beautiful view across the harbor. **$$**

Café Lulu
Blackbeard's Castle, Blackbeard's Hill.
Tel: 714 1641.
A new restaurant with a varied menu and very fair prices. **$$**

Caesar's
Frenchman's Reef Hotel, Flamboyant Point.
Tel: 776 8500.
Good Italian food at reasonable prices. **$$**

Eunice's Terrace
66–67 Smith Bay, Route 38.
Tel: 775 3975.
Generous helpings of good West Indian food are served in a wonderful setting. **$**

1829 Government Hill
1829 Government Hill, Charlotte Amalie.
Tel: 776 1829.
Excellent continental food and service in an historic house.
$$–$$$

Hervé's
Kongens Gade, Government Hill, Charlotte Amalie.
Tel: 777 9703.
New restaurant serving excellent French cuisine in a relaxed bistro-style setting.
$$–$$$

Vergilio's
18 Dronningens Gade, Charlotte Amalie.
Tel: 776 4920.
Superb Italian food in a quaint European-style setting. **$$–$$$**

Price Guide

Price categories are based on the cost of a meal for one person, excluding drinks:
$ = less than $20
$$ = $20–30
$$$ = more than $30.

ST CROIX

The Buccaneer
Gallows Bay, Christiansted.
Tel: 773 2100.
Four different restaurants, including Gina's, serving gourmet Italian dishes, under one hotel roof. **$$–$$$**

Duggans's Reef
Route 82, Teague Bay.
Tel: 773 9800.
Outdoor dining overlooking Buck Island. Pasta with a Caribbean touch. **$$$**

Frigate
Mafolie Hotel, Red Hook.
Tel: 774 2790.
Superb views and steaks and salads at reasonable prices. **$**

Tutto Bene
2 Company Street, Christiansted.
Tel: 773 5229.
Excellent pastas made with Italian flair. **$$**

ST JOHN

Fish Trap
Raintree Inn, Cruz Bay.
Tel: 693 9994.
Fresh fish, chicken and steak. **$$**

Morgan's Mango
Cruz Bay.
Tel: 693 8141.
Seafood and steak; imaginative dishes with a West Indian flavor; outdoor dining. **$$**

Paradiso
Mongoose Junction.
Tel: 693 8899.
Good food, fair prices, a casual but classy setting, and tasty Italian dishes. **$–$$**

Outdoor Activities

Diving

Some of the finest diving in the Caribbean is to be found in the USVI. There are many schools and most hotels offer diving as part of their watersports program.

On **St Thomas**, a particularly lively spot is Coki Beach which specializes in beginners. Dives start at US$25 and you can do an exciting night dive from the beach for US$40 (tel: 775 4220). Aqua Action at Secret Harbour Beach Resort (a beautiful bay) pride themselves on only dealing with small groups and will organize dives to suit you (tel: 775 6285). The Chris Sawyer Diving Center, Red Hook, is very popular, with its custom-built dive boat. There are day trips to the *Rhone* every Friday offering full gear, two dives, and lunch for US$110 (tel: 777 7804).

On **St John**, located in Wharfside Village, Cruz Bay, is Low Key Watersports, the only PADI 5-star IDC facility in St John. They offer daily diving from beginners to advanced and also kayaking, a popular sport on St John (tel: 693 8999).

Watersports

ST THOMAS

Windsurfing equipment and lessons are widely available (at Sapphire, Magen's, Morningstar beaches, and others) as well as Sunfish sailboats. Snorkeling is good off Sapphire, Hull and Coki beaches; equipment can be hired. Sailing is available every day, with most boats leaving around 9.30am, and returning by about 4pm; the cost is roughly US$90. There are many boats available at the marinas or even at your hotel. A couple to note are *Nightwind* at Sapphire Beach Marina (tel: 775 4110), and *Winifred*, a classic wooden sailing ship at Red Hook (tel: 775 7890). You can combine onland tours with sailing in the catamaran *Spirit* (tel: 775 9500). For power boats try Nauti Nymph, American Yacht Harbor, Red Hook (East End), which has a large fleet for self-drive or with a friendly captain (tel: 775 5066). If you want to explore beneath the ocean but don't dive, consider a trip on Atlantis Submarine, Building V1, Havensight Mall (tel: 776 5650).

ST CROIX

A trip to the snorkeling trail at Buck Island National Monument is highly recommended. Companies offering half-day excursions (equipment provided) include Llewellyn Charter (tel: 773 9027). For other watersports try St Croix Water Sports (tel: 773 7060).

ST JOHN

There is an underwater snorkeling trail off Trunk Bay; Cinnamon Bay and Salt Pond Bay also offer good snorkeling. Windsurfing equipment can be rented at Cinnamon and Maho. Atlantis Submarine *(see above)* leaves Cruz Bay once a week. Day sailing trips, including lunch and snorkeling, can be taken on the catamaran *Adventurer*, sailing daily from Cruz Bay to the idyllic island of Jost Van Dyke (tel: 771 6950). Try also Cruz Bay Watersports (tel: 776 6234).

Golf

St Thomas has a championship course with beautiful views – Mahogany Run (tel: 775 5000). **St Croix** has two 18-hole courses – Carambola (tel: 778 5638), and Buccaneer (tel: 773 2100).

Hiking

Two-thirds of **St John** is US National Park so there are many trails. The National Park Visitors' Center in Cruz Bay will give you all the information (open daily 8am–4pm, tel: 776 6201).

Reef Bay Trail (tel: 776 6330) is a lovely downhill hike incorporating a sugar mill, petroglyphs and a spectacular beach.

Horseback Riding

On **St John**, whether you want a horse or donkey, full or half day, sunset or full moon, contact Carolina Corral, Coral Bay (tel: 693 5778).
On **St Croix** try Sprat Hall Plantation (tel: 772 2880).

Getting Acquainted

British Virgin Islands

Located at the top of the Lesser Antilles, near the USVI and Anguilla and a short hop from Puerto Rico, the British Virgin Islands (BVI) are made up of over 50 islands, cays, and rocks. The largest is Tortola, at 12 miles (19 km) long and 4 miles (6 km) wide which has the highest elevation in the BVI, at 1,760 ft (540 meters). Though most of the islands in the group are volcanic, Anegada to the northeast was formed from coral, it is almost invisible to passengers arriving by sea.

Public Holidays

January 1 **New Year's Day**
March (2nd Monday) **Commonwealth Day**
Easter **Good Friday, Easter Monday**
Whit Monday
June (2nd Monday) **Queen's Birthday**
July 1 **Territory Day**
October 21 **St Ursula's Day**
November 14 **The Prince of Wales' Birthday**
December 25 **Christmas Day**
December 26 **Boxing Day**

Calendar of Events

Easter Festival: Virgin Gorda's Carnival.
Bacardi HIHO: International windsurfing competition end of June/beginning of July.
Festival: Tortola's week-long Carnival commemorating the slaves Emancipation. Official holiday on first Monday, Tuesday, and Wednesday in August.

Planning the Trip

Money Matters

The currency of the BVI is the US$. Banking hours are 9am–2pm, although some banks are open until 3 or 4pm. There are banks in Road Town (Tortola) and Spanish Town (Virgin Gorda). Most hotels change travelers checks and cash.

Tourist Offices Abroad

IN THE US

Toll free: 800-835 8530.
New York: 370 Lexington Avenue, Suite 1605, New York, NY 10017. Tel: 212-696 0400. Fax: 212-949 8254. E-mail: bvitouristboard@worldnet.att.net
San Francisco: 1804 Union Street, San Francisco, CA 94123. Tel: 415-775 0344. Fax: 415-775 2554. E-mail: bvitbsfo@pacbell.net
Los Angeles: 3450 Wilshire Boulevard, Suite 108–17, Los Angeles, CA 90010. Tel: 310-287 2200. Fax: 310-287 2753.
Atlanta: 3390 Peachtree Road NE, Suite 1000, Lennox Towers, Atlanta, GA 30326. Tel: 404-240 8018. Fax: 404-233 2318.

IN THE UK

FCB Travel/Marketing, 110 St Martin's Lane, London WC2N 4YD. Tel: 0171-240 4259. Fax: 0171-240 4270. E-mail: christine.oliver@fcb.co.uk

WEBSITE ADDRESS

http://www.britishvirginislands.com

Practical Tips

Media

The *Island Sun* and The *BVI Beacon* are two weekly newspapers. The weekly *Limin' Times* has entertainment information.

The best information for visitors is in *Welcome: The British Virgin Islands Tourist Guide.* This bimonthly brochure can be found in tourist offices and hotels, and has a website: http://www.bviwelcome.com

There are four local radio stations: ZBVI 780 AM; Z Gold 91.7 FM; The Heat 94.3 FM, and ZROD 103.7 FM.

Postal Services

The main post office on Tortola is on Main Street (take the lane off Waterfront Drive at the Ferry Dock). There are branches on Virgin Gorda and in the villages.

Telephone, Fax and Internet

The area code is **284**. International phone calls may be made from most phones, and some will take phone cards. Most hotels are able to send faxes or e-mails. Also available is AT&T USA Direct Service: 1-800-872 2881.

Local Tourist Office

Tortola: PO Box 134, Wickhams Cay, close to the Crafts Market, Road Town. Tel: 494 3134. Fax: 494 3866.
E-mail: bvitourb@caribsurf.com
Virgin Gorda: Virgin Gorda Yacht Harbour. Tel: 284-495 5181.

Emergency Number

- **Police, Fire, Ambulance:** 999.

Medical Treatment

Peebles Hospital on Porter Road, Road Town, is the best equipped hospital. B&F Medical Complex (open daily from 7am; tel: 494 2196) and Medicure Ltd have lab and x-ray facilities. There are also private clinics on Tortola and Virgin Gorda. Other islands have doctors or nurses on call.

Shopping

An assortment of shops, including duty-free, line Tortola's Main Street in Road Town including the famous Pusser's Company Store, which apart from its own rum sells all things nautical, clothes and antiques and has branches in Soper's Hole Wharf in the west and Leverick Bay in Virgin Gorda. On Wickhams Cay I is a Crafts Alive Market selling locally made products. BVI Apparel has factory outlets selling clothes and gifts at low prices at Soper's Hole, Baugher's Bay and Road Town. Dive BVI Ltd stocks diving equipment. On Anegada, Pat's Pottery & Art features items all made on the island.

Voltage: 110 volts AC (in some hotels also 208 volts), 60 cycles.

Good Beaches

Tortola: Smuggler's Cove, Cane Garden Bay, and Elizabeth Bay.
Virgin Gorda: The Baths, Little Dix Bay, Savannah Bay and the Beach at Bitter End Yacht Club.
Peter Island: Deadman's Bay.
Jost Van Dyke: White Bay.
Anegada: the western half of the south coast.

Getting Around

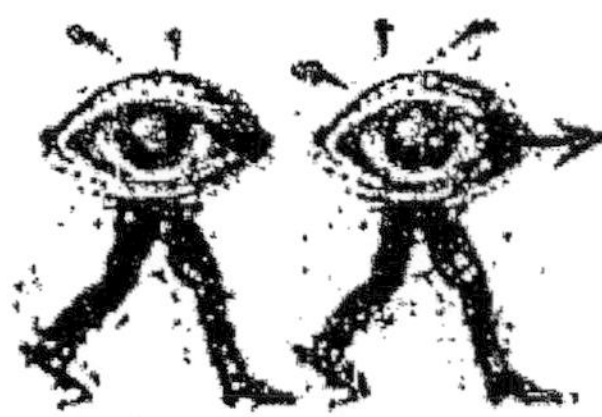

By Car

Driving is on the left, but many cars are Japanese or American and have the steering wheel on the left. To drive here, a temporary BVI driving license is required. It can be obtained through the rental agency (for about US$10) on presentation of your valid driver's license. Advance booking is recommended in peak season. Hotels are very helpful in organizing car rental, and a car can be delivered to your hotel.

There are many international and local car rental companies including:

Hertz, West End Ferry Dock, Tortola. Tel: 495 4405. Fax: 494 6060.

Budget Rent-a-Car, Wickhams Cay I, Road Town. Tel: 494 2639, 494 5150.

Mahogany Car Rentals, Spanish Town, Virgin Gorda. Tel: 495 5469.

D.W. Jeep Rentals, The Settlement, Anegada. Tel: 495 9677, 495 8018.

By Taxi

Taxis are easy to find on the BVI. They stop if hailed on the road, and can be found waiting at the airports and at ferry docks. On Virgin Gorda small converted lorries with benches run a shuttle service between the main tourist points at a reasonable price.

The taxis have fixed prices, but it is always best to ask for the fare before you start out on a journey.

Inter-Island Links

BY AIR

There are good connection flights from the international airports on St Martin and Puerto Rico; smaller airlines connect BVI with the US Virgin Islands and Tortola with Anegada:

- **Air Sunshine,** tel: 495 8900; in the USA: 800-327 8900.
- **Air St Thomas,** tel: 495 5935.
- **American Eagle,** tel: 495 2559.
- **Carib Air,** tel: 787-791 1240.
- **Gorda Aero Services,** tel: 495 2271.
- **LIAT,** tel: 495 1187, 495 2577.
- **Winair,** tel: 494 2347.

BY FERRY

Timetables are available in hotels, at the tourist board, and in the *Welcome* magazine.

There are regular services:

- from Road Town, Tortola to Spanish Town, Virgin Gorda and Peter Island.
- from West End, Tortola to Jost Van Dyke.
- from Beef Island, Tortola to North Sound and Spanish Town, Virgin Gorda (North Sound Express).
- from Road Town, Tortola and West End to St Thomas and St John (both USVI).
- from Virgin Gorda to St Thomas (USVI).

There is also a free ferry from Beef Island, Tortola to Marina Cay (Pusser's).

Where to Stay

Choosing a Hotel

It is easier to find a four or five-star deluxe hotel on the BVI than a budget guesthouse. However, there are five camp grounds, three on Anegada, one at White Bay on Jost Van Dyke, and one at Brewer's Bay on Tortola.

All the hotels are surrounded by lovely gardens, and some of them have prize-winning chefs. There are also many superb villas for rent (on a weekly or monthly basis).

Hotel Listings

TORTOLA

Cane Garden Bay (Rhymer's) Beach
PO Box 570, Cane Garden Bay, Tortola, BVI.
Tel: 495 4639.
Fax: 495 4820.
Simple, clean rooms close to the beach. Evening entertainment mainly at weekends. **$**

Fort Burt Hotel
PO Box 3380, Road Town, Tortola, BVI.
Tel: 495 2587.
Fax: 494 2002.
The historic site of a fort tower has been integrated into a romantic hotel with a pleasant restaurant overlooking Road Harbour. It is connected with Fort Burt Marina which has extensive yachting facilities. **$$–$$$**

Frenchman's Cay Hotel
PO Box 1054, West End, Tortola, BVI.
Tel: 495 4844, 800-235 4077.
Quiet resort overlooking

Tortola's south coast, small beach. **$$–$$$**

Jolly Roger Inn
PO Box 21, West End, Tortola, BVI.
Tel: 495 4559.
Fax: 495 4184.
Six colorfully decorated rooms, some with shared bathrooms. Friendly atmosphere. The restaurant is popular with locals and serves Creole cuisine. Live music at weekends. **$**

Lambert Beach Hotel
PO Box 509, Elizabeth Bay, Tortola, BVI.
Tel: 495 2877.
Fax: 495 2876.
E-mail: lambert@caribsurf.com
Pleasantly furnished rooms in small villas scattered along the quiet and magnificent white beach of Elizabeth Bay with shady spots under palms and seagrapes; pool, pretty gardens. Delicious Caribbean and international cuisine. Very friendly ambience. **$–$$**

Long Bay Beach Resort
PO Box 433, Long Bay, Tortola, BVI.
Tel: 495 4252, 800-729 9599.
Beautiful resort with elegantly furnished studios and villas, good watersports facilities on a long white sandy beach; two restaurants. **$$–$$$**

Moorings – Mariner Inn
PO Box 139, Road Town, Tortola, BVI.
Tel: 494 2333.
Simple rooms with kitchenettes. There are dockside moorings and facilities for bareboat charters. **$$**

Prospect Reef Resort
PO Box 104, Road Town, Tortola, BVI.
Tel: 494 3311.
Fax: 494 5595.
Large complex around a marina west of Road Town, good facilities for yachting and other watersports. **$$–$$$**

Sebastian's on the Beach
PO Box 441, Apple Bay, Tortola, BVI.
Tel: 495 4212, 800-335 4870.
Friendly, informal place especially popular with young people and surfers, right on the beach. West Indian dishes in the restaurant overlooking the bay. **$–$$**

VIRGIN GORDA

Biras Creek Hotel
PO Box 54, North Sound, Virgin Gorda, BVI.
Tel: 494 3555, 800-608 9661.
Fax: 494 3557.
32 luxury suites in a secluded area with breathtaking views over the Atlantic and the North Sound. Excellent sports facilities plus a pool, quiet sandy beach, and renowned restaurant. **$$$**

The Bitter End Yacht Club and Resort
PO Box 46, North Sound, Virgin Gorda, BVI
Tel: 494 2746, 800-872 2392.
VHF Channel 16.
Sailors' paradise, with a maritime atmosphere. Spacious well-furnished rooms in villas spread over a hill with beautiful flowering plants. All watersports facilities (windsurfing, sailing, and diving classes); pool and a fine sandy beach. The bar and restaurant right on the water has barbecues in the evenings. **$$$**

Guavaberry Spring Bay
PO Box 20, Virgin Gorda, BVI.
Tel: 495 5227.
Lovely cottages situated in beautiful gardens, close to The Baths. **$$**

Little Dix Bay Hotel
PO Box 70, Virgin Gorda, BVI.
Tel: 495 5555.
Fax: 495 5083.
Deluxe villa accommodation set in quiet, pretty gardens. Offers some watersports activities, body shaping and free refreshments as well as a water-taxi to nearby beaches. International specialties. **$$$**

Olde Yard Inn
PO Box 26, The Valley, Virgin Gorda, BVI.
Tel: 495 5544.
Fax: 495 5968.
E-mail: oldeyard@caribsurf.com
Small comfortable inn in four acres of tropical gardens with a pool. A short shuttle ride to Savannah beach. Romantic tropical dining with Creole and local dishes. **$$–$$$**

OUTER ISLANDS

Anegada Reef Hotel
Setting Point, Anegada, BVI.
Tel: 495 8002.
Fax: 495 9362.
A perfect place to relax, only 16 rooms; mooring facilities, dive shop. **$$**

Price Guide

Price categories are based on the cost of a double room, for one night:
$ = inexpensive, under $100
$$ = moderate, $100–200
$$$ = expensive, over $200

Peter Island Hotel and Yacht Harbour
PO Box 211, Road Town, Tortola, BVI.
Tel: 494 2561.
Fax: 494 2313.
Deluxe harbor and beach rooms, furnished in a flowery Caribbean style on a 1,000-acre (405-ha) island. Exquisite restaurants next to the pool and under the palms of beautiful Deadman's Beach; walking/jogging and mountain biking trails. Regular ferry service to and from Peter Island ferry dock, Tortola. **$$$**

White Bay Sandcastle
White Bay, Jost Van Dyke, BVI.
Tel: 494 2462.
Fax: 495 9999.
E-mail: sandcastle@caribsurf.com
Six timber cottages on one of the best beaches in the Caribbean, next to the Soggy Dollar bar with romantic candlelit dinners. **$$**

Where to Eat

What to Eat

The cuisine of the BVI includes touches of American and Continental cooking, in addition to such Caribbean creations as *fungi* (cornmeal pudding) and *roti* (curry wrapped in a thin chapati). Seafood and tropical fruits and vegetables are fresh and plentiful. Cocktails as starters are very tempting.

Restaurant Listings

Try to get a copy of the *BVI Restaurant Guide* (with map), a free annual publication available at the tourist board and in hotels. It gives details of restaurant addresses, main dishes, opening hours, prices, credit cards, reservations, dress codes, etc. Also check the listing "Dining Out" and the mouthwatering adverts in the *Welcome* magazine.

All hotel restaurants are open to guests from outside. Dinner reservations are recommended especially during peak season. All Pusser's Restaurants (Waterfront Drive, Road Town; Soper's Hole, West End; Marina Cay and Leverick Bay, Virgin Gorda) serve good salads, huge sandwiches, juicy steaks and tasty fish. Try a "Painkiller".

TORTOLA

Brandywine Bay
East of Road Town, Brandywine Estate.
Tel: 495 2301.
Italian gourmet-style cooking with Caribbean ingredients. There is a magnificent view over the Sir Francis Drake Channel. **$$$**

Callaloo
Overlooking Prospect Reef Lagoon.
Tel: 494 3311.
Serves international and Creole-style gourmet cuisine. **$$$**

C & F Restaurant
Purcell Estate, Road Town.
Tel: 494 4941.
A cosy family place in the backyard of Road Town; local cuisine, especially seafood, that is popular with local residents and visitors alike. **$$**

Chez Bamboo
The Valley.
Tel: 495 5752.
Bistro-style Caribbean and Creole cuisine with a touch of French elegance. Mouthwatering desserts. **$$**

Spaghetti Junction
Waterfront Drive, near Wickham's Cay, 1 Road Town.
Tel: 494 5309.
A small, pleasant place for an evening meal Italian style. **$**

Mrs Scattcliffe's
Carrot Bay.
Tel: 495 4556.
Homely atmosphere. The chef cooks mainly with home-grown vegetables. Specialties include soursop sherbert, coconut bread and papaya soup (see page 106). Reservations necessary. **$**

Price Guide

Price categories are based on the cost of a meal for one person, excluding drinks:
$ = less than $20
$$ = $20–30
$$$ = more than $30.

VIRGIN GORDA

The Mad Dog
The Baths.
Tel: 495 5830.
Small casual bar serving tasty sandwiches. **$**

The Lobster Pot
Spanish Town.
Tel: 495 5252.
A romantic place to enjoy West Indian seafood, but also steak and chicken. **$$**

JOST VAN DYKE

Foxy's
Great Harbour.
Tel: 495 9258.
This place buzzes with life but is especially busy on the weekend because of its famous barbecues on Friday and Saturday serving great salads, grilled fish and chicken. During the week the bar offers snack lunches and mainly seafood or *rotis* are available for dinner. Expect a warm welcome with local songs from Foxy himself playing the guitar (see page 112). **$**

Outdoor Activities

Watersports

Snorkeling is fun on the rocky edges of many beaches, such as Smuggler's Cove, Tortola or Deadman's Beach, Peter Island. Norman Island and the rocks nearby called the Indians are also a good choice.

Apple Bay, Cane Garden Bay, and Josiah's Bay are popular windsurfing beaches on Tortola; there are also good conditions in Trellis Bay. Boardsailing BVI offers lessons for beginners and sailing classes (tel: 495 2447). In November, the surfers arrive in these bays.

Diving

The wreck of the *RMS Rhone* west of Salt Island is the most popular dive site in the BVI and is also a marine park. Other dive sites are close to the Indians. The reefs around Anegada have been badly damaged due to too many divers and heavy anchoring. Diving has now been banned in that area in order to speed up recovery of the reef and establish a marine park there. Dive operators in the BVI include:

Dive BVI, tel: 495 5513; fax: 495 5347
e-mail: divebvi@caribsurf.com
website http://www.britishvirginislands.com/divebvi

Baskin in the Sun, Prospect Reef and Soper's Hole, Tortola. Tel: 494 2858, 800-650 2084.

Kilbride's Underwater Tours, Bitter End Yacht Club, Virgin Gorda. Tel/Fax: 495 9638, 800-932 4286.

Sailing

The BVI is one of the best sailing areas in the Caribbean. Some big hotels have small catamarans and Sunfish for their guests, others like Peter Island and Bitter End Yacht Club (with Nick Trotter's Sailing School, tel: 494 2745) also provide bigger yachts, some with a crew for day sails.

International yacht charterers like Moorings, Stardust or Sun Sail have branches on Tortola. Check with the tourist board or the *Welcome* magazine for the long list of smaller charter companies. In general yachts are rented on a weekly basis.

Fishing

The following operators offer sport fishing tours for bonefish and marlin:

Anegada Reef Hotel, tel: 495 8002; fax: 495 9362.

Pelican Charters, Prospect Reef Harbour. Tel: 496 7386.

Getting Acquainted

Anguilla

Anguilla is 16 miles (26 km) long and 3 miles (5 km) wide and lies at the top of the Lesser Antilles' Leeward Island chain, near the Virgin Islands and St Martin. Its terrain is dry and flat with its highest point at 215 ft (65 meters) above sea level.

In 1980, Anguilla became a British Dependent Territory, which was changed to a British Overseas Territory in 1998.

Public Holidays

January 1	**New Year's Day**
March/April	
Easter	**Good Friday**
	Easter Monday
	Whit Monday
May 30	**Anguilla Day**
June (2nd Saturday)	**Queen's Birthday**
August (1st Monday)	**August Monday**
(1st Thursday)	**August Thursday**
(1st Friday)	**Constitution Day**
December 19	**Separation Day**
December 25	**Christmas Day**
December26	**Boxing Day**

Calendar of Events

January 1	**New Year's Day boat race**
May 30	**Anguilla Day athletic contest and boat race**
August Monday	**Regatta boat race**
August Thursday	**Boat race**

Carnival: week-long celebrations beginning the Friday before the first Monday in August.

Planning the Trip

Money Matters

The currency is the East Caribbean (EC) dollar. US dollars are also accepted. Normal banking hours are 8am–1pm, Monday–Thursday, 8am–noon, 3–5pm on Friday. There are banks in The Valley and at George Hill.

There is a departure tax of US$10 at the airport and US$2 at the ferry.

Tourist Offices Abroad

IN THE US

Medhurst and Associates, 1208 Washington Drive, Centerport, New York 11721. Tel: 516-425 0900.

Anguilla Tourist Board, World Trade Center, Suite 250, San Francisco, Ca 94111. Tel: 415-398 3231.

IN THE UK

Anguilla Tourist Board, 3 Epirus Road, London SW6 7UJ. Tel: 0171-937 7725. E-mail: anguilla@btinternet.com.

Website address

http://www.candw.com.ai

Plant a Tree

Since so many of the few trees Anguilla had were blown down by Hurricane Luis in 1995, the Anguilla Beautification Club (ABC) has set up a tree-planting scheme through which you can adopt a tree. Contact them at: ABC Trees, PO Box 274, Anguilla BWI.

Practical Tips

Media

Anguilla has several newspapers and magazines including *What We Do In Anguilla*, a local tourism magazine, which is widely available in stores and hotels. Daily newspapers include the *Chronicle* and the *Daily Herald*.

While on the island you can tune in to the local radio stations Radio Anguilla, Caribbean Beacon and ZJF 105.3 FM. There is also a community TV channel.

There is a small library located in The Valley.

Postal Services

There is a post office in The Valley (tel: 497 2528, open 8am–noon and 1–3.30pm Monday–Friday; 8am–noon Saturday). Areas outside The Valley are served by mobile postal services.

Telephone, Telex & Fax

The area code for Anguilla is **264**. International telephone calls, cables, and telexes may be made from the offices of Cable and Wireless in The Valley (open weekdays, Saturday and holidays 7.30am–10.30pm, Sunday 10am–8pm). Anguilla has direct-dial telephone services and international calls may be received 24-hours a day.

Local Tourist Office

Old Factory Plaza, The Valley. Tel: 497 2759.

Useful Numbers

- **Emergencies:** 911/999.
- **Police:** 497 2333.
- **Doctor:** 497 3792; 497 6522; 497 2882; 497 2632; 497 3233.
- **Hospital:** 497 2551; 497 2552.
- **Pharmacy:** 497 2738.

Medical Treatment

There is a 24-bed hospital in The Valley plus three clinics, one each in The Valley, East End, and South Hill. Limited but qualified dental services (one dentist, two dental auxiliaries) are available. Seriously ill patients are transferred to Puerto Rico or Tortola, BVI.

Good Beaches

Highlights among Anguilla's 45 beautiful beaches include: Maunday's Bay, Shoal Bay East and West, Little Bay, Rendezvous Bay, Mead Bay, Crocus Bay and Sandy Ground.

Culture

On Thursday evenings the **Mayoumba Folkloric Theatre** perform at La Serena Hotel in Meads Bay (tel: 496 6827). The group keep Anguillan traditions alive through music, dance, and the spoken word.

Shopping

The most interesting shopping is in the studios and shops of local artists. Amongst them: **Cheddie's Carving Studio**, The Cove, West End Road. Tel: 497 6027 (carvings using driftwood). **Devonish Art Gallery**, The Valley. Tel: 497 4971.

Voltage: 110 volts AC 60 cycles.

Getting Around

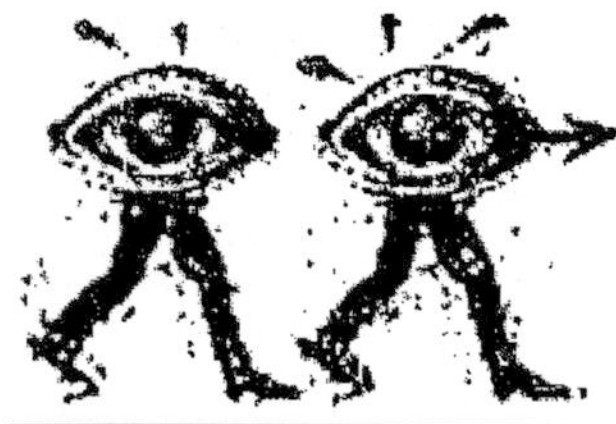

By Car

Cars drive on the left, British style. To purchase a temporary Anguillan driver's license, which is good for up to three months, present a valid driver's license from your country of origin, with a small fee, to the police station in The Valley. The ports of entry can also perform this service.

Car hire companies include:
Avis, Blowing Point. Tel: 497 6221.
Triple K Car Rental (Hertz), Airport Road. Tel: 497 2934.

By Taxi

Taxis are available at all points of entry including Wallblake Airport, which is located more or less at the center of Anguilla, a couple of miles from The Valley, the island's principal town. Passengers arriving by boat will disembark further west at Blowing Point. Taxis are not metered, but there are fixed charges for taxi rides; confirm the price before you start.

Island tours take about 3 hours and start from the airport or Blowing Point.

By Bicycle

Bikes can be rented from your hotel or from:
Multiscenic Bicycle Rentals, George Hill Road. Tel: 497 5810.

Inter-Island Links

From Wallblake Airport you can fly to St Martin, St Kitts, St Thomas, BVI, Antigua, and San Juan, Puerto Rico. Airlines include:
Air Anguilla, tel: 497 4264.
American Eagle, tel: 497 3131.
Winair, tel: 497 2748.
LIAT, tel: 497 2238.
Tyden Air, tel: 497 2719.

Marigot in St Martin is a 20-minute ferry ride away from Anguilla and makes a good day trip. Ferries leave Blowing Point every half hour 7.30am–5pm. Don't forget your passport or ID and immigration card to show in St Martin.

Where to Stay

Choosing a Hotel

Hotels are scattered throughout the island. Given Anguilla's size and population, the range of accommodation available is astonishing. Prices range from US$40 for a room at the guest-house Norman 'B' to US$1,500 for a villa at the Malliouhana. Further information, mailing addresses, and reservations are available through the Anguilla Department of Tourism.

Hotel Listings

Cinnamon Reef
Little Harbour, Anguilla, BWI.
Tel: 497 2727.
Fax: 497 3727.
The resort's 14 villas are built to withstand hurricanes and look a bit like tanks, especially with their cute, color-coded flags. Inside, however, they are lovely, spacious and very private, each with terrace and hammock. Free tennis and watersports, very relaxed atmosphere; local calypso and reggae performers. **$$$**

Easy Corner Villas
South Hill, Anguilla, BWI.
Tel: 497 6433.
Condominiums perched on South Hill with a sweeping view of Road Bay. **$$**

Malliouhana
Mead's Bay, Anguilla, BWI.
Tel: 497 6111.
Fax: 497 6011.
One of the Caribbean's most costly hotels, this is an exclusive, jet-set haunt. Security is tight and its huge rooms are hung

with a glorious collection of Haitian art. Gargantuan bathrooms have deep tubs and bidets. The wine cellar stocks 30,000 bottles and the restaurant is overseen by a prestigious French chef. **$$$**

The Mariners
Sandy Ground, Anguilla, BWI.
Tel: 497 2671.
Fax: 497 2901.
Managed and part-owned by Anguillans, this is a happily relaxed hotel with West Indian-style cottages nestled between a seagrape grove and a beautiful garden. **$$–$$$**

Price Guide

Price categories are based on the cost of a double room, for one night:
$ = less than $100
$$ = $100–200
$$$ = more than $200.

Norman 'B'
Northside, Anguilla, BWI.
Tel: 497 2242.
Simple guesthouse; basic rooms with ceiling fans. **$**

Rendezvous Bay
PO Box 31, Rendezvous Bay, Anguilla, BWI.
Tel: 497 6549.
Fax: 497 6026.
The grandaddy of the island's hotels, built before the Rebellion by Jeremiah Gumbs, a descendant of one of the founding fathers of Anguilla, this hotel is still run by his family and infused with his personality. Perched on the beautiful half-moon beach, the commodious verandah is the setting for family-style meals and an open bar. **$$**

Shoal Bay Villas
Shoal Bay West, Anguilla, BWI.
Tel: 497 2051.
Privately owned, differently decorated condominiums on the island's most gorgeous beach. **$$**

Where to Eat

What to Eat

As you might expect on a boatbuilding, sea-faring island, locally-caught seafood is Anguilla's specialty. Conch, spring lobsters, whelks, and tropical fish may be found, prepared in either Continental or the local Creole style. Barbecues – of fish, or of the islands' ever popular chicken and goat – are another distinctive aspect of local cuisine.

Barbecues often take place on the beach, and the fishing visitor who charters a boat can often make arrangements to cook the day's catch on the beach. Check with the local Tourist Office.

Restaurant Listings

Aquarium Bar and Restaurant
Round-a-Bout, South Hill.
Tel: 497 2720.
Simple place which serves tasty local cuisine, and seafood specialties. **$**

Arlo's
Lower South Hill.
Tel: 497 6810.
Popular Italian eatery with a varied menu, home-made pasta and pizza to eat in or take out. **$$**

Price Guide

Price categories are based on the cost of a meal for one person, excluding drinks:
$ = less than $20
$$ = $20–30
$$$ = more than $30.

Eclipse at Cap Fuluca
Maunday's Bay.
Tel: 497 6666.
A beautiful very expensive restaurant in an idyllic location serving Caribbean and International dishes. Its executive chef has won several prizes in culinary competitions in both the Caribbean and the US. Herbs are fresh from the hotel garden. **$$$**

Johnno's
Sandy Ground.
Tel: 497 2728.
Informal atmosphere; local seafood and barbecue restaurant and bar on the beach; popular hangout with live music some evenings and every weekend. **$**

Scilly Cay
Scilly Cay, Island Harbour.
Tel: 497-5123.
Lovely setting on its own tiny islet surrounded by coral reefs. **$$–$$$**

Outdoor Activities

Diving

Unspoilt, uncrowded diving is on offer on Anguilla, with several wrecks to explore, as well as excellent sites which include Sandy Island, Prickly Pear Cays, and Little Bay. Organize your diving through your hotel or with:
Anguillian Divers, Island Harbour. Tel: 497 4750.
The Dive Shop, Sandy Ground. Tel: 497 2020.

Watersports

Good snorkeling can be found off many of the beaches; the reefs off Shoal Bay East are very close to the shore, while Scilly Cay (ferry from Island Harbour), Crocus Bay, and Little Bay are also good. Snorkeling can be organized via:
Hoo Haa Charters, Island Harbour or Sandy Ground. Tel: 497 4040. Snorkeling charters.
Rollins Ruan, tel: 497-3394. A day sail, including lunch, on *Chocolate* is available. Glass-bottomed boats for two can be also be hired.

Fishing

Fishing from a traditional Anguillan boat can sometimes be arranged, either through a formal charter or through an informal arrangement made with a local fisherman. Ask the fishermen you see launching their boats from the beach. Another possibility is a fishing boat trip to one of Anguilla's tiny neighboring islands, such as Sombrero Island, which has a lighthouse open to the public.

Contact:
Sandy Island Enterprises, tel: 497 6359.
Neville Connor, tel: 497 5643 (for sport fishing).

Tennis

Non-residents can play tennis at several hotels, including Cinnamon Reef, Carimar Beach Club, and Rendezvous Bay.

Horseback Riding

Expeditions on horseback, and riding lessons, are offered by:
El Rancho Del Blues, tel: 497 6164.

Anguilla Boat Racing

Wooden boat racing is a major interest on Anguilla, in fact it is the national sport, with races taking place on almost every public holiday. The beautiful and distinctive boats are built on Anguilla, and used for fishing as well as racing.

Getting Acquainted

St Martin

At the top of the Lesser Antilles, between Anguilla and St Kitts, lies the island of St Martin. Shared by France in the north and the Netherlands (Sint Maarten) in the south, the 37-sq. mile (96-sq. km) island is a popular cruise, vacation, and shopping spot. For the most part, St Martin is rolling and green, and Pic du Paradis (the highest point) rises to only 1,391 ft (420 meters).

On Arrival

Most visitors arrive at Juliana Airport on the Dutch side of the island. Sea passengers are likely to land at Philipsburg, the capital of St Maarten, and a popular cruise port, or at Marigot or Grand Case on the French side. Take a taxi from the airport (*see Getting Around page 342*)

Public Holidays

DUTCH SIDE

April 30	**Coronation Day**
May 1	**Labor Day**
	Ascension Day
	Whit Monday
November 11	**St Maarten Day**
December 15	**Kingdom Day**
December 25	**Christmas Day**

FRENCH SIDE

January 1	**New Year's Day**
March/April	**Easter Monday**
May 1	**Labor Day**
May 8	**VE Day**
	Ascension Day
	Whit Monday

Late May	**Slavery Abolition Day**
July 14	**Bastille Day**
July 21	**Schoelcher Day**
August 15	**Assumption Day**
November 1	**All Saints Day**
November 11	**St Martin Day**
December 25	**Christmas Day**

Calendar of Events

DUTCH SIDE

Mid April **Carnival**, three-week celebrations at Carnival Village, Philipsburg

FRENCH SIDE

Before Lent	**Carnival**
Easter	**Easter Parade**
July 14	**Bastille Day** street celebrations and boat races
July 21	**Schoelcher Day** street celebrations in Grand Case

Good Beaches

Dawn Beach, Guana Bay, Mullet Bay, Maho Beach (under descending aircraft), Little Bay.

Planning the Trip

Money Matters

The French franc and the Dutch florin or guilder are the official currencies, but US dollars are also universally accepted. Normal banking hours are 8.30am–3pm, Monday–Friday. Several banks have ATMs. A departure tax is payable at the airport: US$12, or US$5 if you are leaving for the Netherlands Antilles islands.

Tourist Offices Abroad

IN THE US

St Maarten Tourist Bureau, 675 Third Avenue, New York, NY 10017. Tel: 212-953 2084.

French West Indies Tourist Board, 610 Fifth Avenue, New York, NY 10020. Tel: 212-757 1125.

French Government Tourist Office, 444 Madison Avenue, New York, NY 10022. Tel: 212-838 7800.

IN THE UK

French Government Tourist Office, 178 Piccadilly, London WIV OAL. Tel: 0891-244123.

IN CANADA

French Government Tourist Office, 1981 Ave McGill College (490), Montreal, Quebec H3A 2W9. Tel: 514-288 4264.

French Government Tourist Office, 1 Dundas St W, Suite 2405, Toronto, Ontario M5G 1Z3. Tel: 416-593 4717.

Website addresses

http://www.franceguide.com
http://www.st-maarten.com

Practical Tips

Media

Useful addresses, local events, and details of church services are listed in the free weekly paper *Today* (English language). While on the island, you can tune into PJD2 Radio.

Postal Services

In Marigot, the post office is on Rue de la Liberté. In Philipsburg, telegrams, calls and telexes are sent through the Landsradio central communications office in the Pondfill section of town, between Loodsteeg and Market Street. The Philipsburg post office is right behind the Landsradio building. Stamps may be bought at your hotel or, on the French side, at a *café tabac*.

Telephone, Telex & Fax

The area code for the Dutch side is **5995**; for the French side: **590**. On both sides of the island, overseas calls can be made from most phones, including pay phones; large hotels can send and receive faxes and e-mail.

Local Tourist Offices

Dutch side: St Martin Tourist Board, Imperial Building, 23 Walter Nisbeth Rd. Tel: 22337.
French side: Blvd de France 97150, Marigot. Tel: 875723.

Medical Treatment

There are hospitals in Marigot, tel: 295757; Philipsburg, tel: 31111. There are also pharmacies in Philipsburg, tel: 22321; Marigot, Rue Général de Gaulle, tel: 875409.

Emergency Numbers

- **Police:** (Dutch side) 22222; (French side) 878833.
- **Fire:** (Dutch side) 54222; (French side) 875008.
- **Ambulance:** (Dutch side) 22111; (French side) 878625/877200.

Nightlife

On the Dutch side, nightlife is concentrated around the Las Vegas-style casinos in Philipsburg and the resorts in Simpson Bay and Maho.

With no casinos on the French side, the focus is on the fine restaurants in Grand Case and Marigot, several good nightclubs can be found on both sides of the island, including:
Le Privilège, Anse Marcel.
Studio 7, Grand Casino, Mullet Bay (start the evening at **Cheri's Café**, Maho).
Casinos include:
Casino Royale, Maho Beach Hotel; **Pelican Casino**, Pelican Resort; **Mount Fortune Casino**, Sheraton Port de Plaisance; **Golden Casino**, Great Bay Beach Hotel; **Coliseum Casino**, Philipsburg.

There is plenty of live music and dancing in the resorts, including limbo dancing. At Maho Beach Hotel, Coconuts Comedy Club features local and visiting stand-up comedians.

Shopping

Hundreds of shops sell duty-free goods to tempt tourists. Head for Front Street, Philipsburg, Rue de la République and Marina Porte la Royale, Marigot, Maho Beach, and Mullet Bay.

Voltage: Dutch side: 110 volts AC; **French** side: 220 volts 60 cycles.

Getting Around

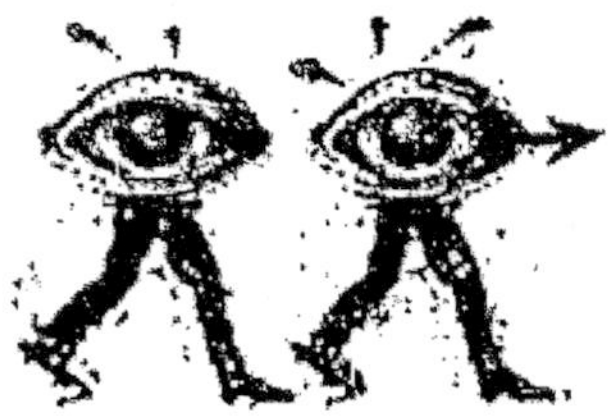

By Car

Cars drive on the right. Foreign licenses are accepted. Car hire companies operating on the island, include:
Hertz, tel: 54541.
Avis, tel: 875060.

By Taxi

Taxis are available at all of the island's ports of entry. There are no meters but there are fixed charges so check the price before you start. A good way of seeing the island is to take an island taxi tour.

By Bus

Buses travel regularly from 6am–midnight between Philipsburg and Marigot, as well as other principal routes. Ask at the tourist office for details of island tours by minibus.

Inter-Island Links

Destinations linked with St Martin by local airlines include Barbados, Trinidad and Tobago, Martinique, St Barthélemy, Anguilla, BVI, St Kitts, Curaçao, Aruba, Bonaire, St Thomas, Saba, St Eustatius, and Jamaica. Inter-island airlines include:
Winair, tel: 54210.
Air Martinque, tel: 54212.
LIAT, tel: 52403.

A ferry from Marigot serves Anguilla (7am–5pm), there is also a ferry from both Philipsburg and Marigot to St Barthélemy. *El Tigre* is a 60-ft (20-meter) catamaran running between the two islands.

Where to Stay

Choosing a Hotel

Hotels on St Martin are not cheap, especially during the peak winter season. During the summer season, many of the rates may be substantially discounted, often by 30–50 percent. Both the French and Dutch sides have small guesthouses, as well as apartments and villas, which can be rented at weekly or monthly rates.

Hotel Listings

DUTCH SIDE

Divi Little Bay Beach Resort
PO Box 961, St Maarten, NA.
Tel: 22333.
Fax: 25410.
Large resort on Little Bay. **$$$**

Maho Beach Hotel
PO Box 834, Simpson Bay, St Maarten, NA.
Tel: 52115.
Fax: 53180.
Large resort, casino, restaurants and shopping. **$$$**

La Vista Hotel
PO Box 2086, St Maarten, NA.
Tel: 43005.
Fax: 43010.
Small, personal, Antillean-style resort on Pelican Point near to the beach. **$$–$$$**

Oyster Bay Beach Resort
PO Box 239, St Maarten, NA.
Tel: 36040.
Fax: 36695.
Expanded and renovated resort located on the scenic east coast of the island adjacent to Oyster Pond Marina. **$$–$$$**

Pasanggrahan Hotel
19 Front Street, Philipsburg, NA.
Tel: 23588.
Small atmospheric colonial hotel with pool. **$–$$**

Royal Palm Hotel
PO Box 431, St Maarten, NA.
Tel: 43737.
Fax: 42965.
Two- and three-bedroom suites on Simpson Bay. **$$**

Price Guide

Price categories are based on the cost of a double room, for one night:
$ = less than $100
$$ = $100–200
$$$ = more than $200.

FRENCH SIDE

L'Habitation
Anse Marcel 97150, St Martin, FWI.
Tel: 876700.
Good facilities including a spa and a marina. **$$$**

Hevea
Grand Case 97150, St Martin, FWI.
Tel: 875685.
Intimate inn. **$–$$**

Le Mecidien
Anse Marcel, BPS81, 97106 Marigot, FWI.
Tel: 876700.
Fax: 873038.
A hotel consisting of two parts – L' Habitation and Domaine. With a casino, spa and marina. **$$$**

Royale Louisiana
Marigot 97150, St Martin, FWI.
Tel: 878651.
This hotel is conveniently situated in the heart of town. **$$**

La Samanna
Baie Longue 97150, St Martin, FWI.
Tel: 876400.
Fax: 878786.
An exclusive resort, refurbished with excellent facilities. **$$$**

Where to Eat

What to Eat

St Martin's restaurants reflect the various cultures which have come together on the island. On both sides, traditional French cooking and spicy Caribbean cuisine are available. Sometimes the two rub off on one another, as when a familiar French recipe is prepared with very un-Gallic tropical fruits. On the Dutch side, dining options include Dutch favorites such as pea soup and sausages. An unexpected dining experience is offered by restaurants serving *rijstaffel*, an Indonesian meal as huge and complex as a Javanese *gamelan.* It comes to St Martin via the Dutch, who previously counted Indonesia among their colonies. There are many restaurants on the French side, particularly in Grand Case.

Restaurant Listings

DUTCH SIDE

The Boathouse
Welfare Road, Simpson Bay.
Tel: 45409.
Seafood, steaks, and pasta in an informal nautical setting. **$$**

Chesterfields
Great Bay Marina, Philipsburg.
Tel: 23484.
Seafood and pasta overlooking the water. Popular watering hole for yachties. **$$**

Grand Café Europe
Maho Plaza.
Tel: 54455.
Grilled steaks and Dutch seafood, including fresh mussels flown in from Holland. **$$**

Ren & Stimpy's
6 Sister Modesta Road, Simpson Bay.
Tel: 52270.
Italian and Creole food, reasonably priced in this restaurant off the beaten track. **$–$$**

La Riviera
Front Street, Philipsburg.
Tel: 25725.
French and Italian cuisine. **$$**

Pasanggrahan Hotel
19 Front Street, Philipsburg.
Tel: 23588.
International cuisine in charming colonial-era beachfront hotel. **$–$$**

Saratoga
Simpson Bay Yacht Club.
Tel: 42421.
New American cuisine featured on Great Chefs series. **$$–$$$**

Wayang Doll
167 Front Street, Philipsburg.
Tel: 22687.
Indonesian food on the waterfront. **$$**

Price Guide

Price categories are based on the cost of a meal for one person, excluding drinks:
$ = less than $20
$$ = $20–30
$$$ = more than $30.

FRENCH SIDE

Bistrot Nu
Marigot.
Tel: 879709.
Locally popular restaurant serving seafood, French and Italian cooking. **$$**

The Rainbow
Grand Case.
Tel: 875580.
Caribbean-style seafood. **$$**

Le Santal
Nettle Bay Beach, near Marigot.
Tel: 875348.
Internationally renowned as one

of the best restaurants in the Caribbean. French. **$$$**

La Vie en Rose
Marigot.
Tel: 875442.
French Caribbean flavors on a balcony overlooking the harbor. **$$$**

La Brasserie de Marigot
11 Rue du Général de Gaulle, Marigot.
Tel: 879443.
French Caribbean cooking with a very French ambience including tables on the pavement. Take out also available. **$$**

Price Guide

Price categories are based on the cost of a meal for one person, excluding drinks:
$ = less than $20
$$ = $20–30
$$$ = more than $30.

Le Cottage
Grand Case.
Tel: 290330.
French Creole cuisine prepared by a French chef. Good wines. **$$$**

Outdoor Activities

Watersports

Watersports are a highlight on St Martin, and your hotel will almost certainly be able to organize diving, snorkeling, windsurfing, and sailing. Diving is mostly from boats onto wrecks. The snorkeling is superb; try Dawn Beach or Little Bay Beach. There are many boats which will take you on snorkeling trips.

12-Meter Challenge

If you fancy crewing aboard an America's Cup 12-meter craft (previous sailing experience not always necessary), then this is the place to do it. There are races between four vessels, sometimes including Dennis Connor's *Stars and Stripes.* Races take place off Philipsburg every Wednesday, lasting about three hours. Contact Bobby's Marina (tel: 43354) for more details.

Beaches

The beaches are the main attraction on St Martin, there are more than 30 dotted between the large resort hotels. Some worth trying are:
Dawn Beach, Mullet Bay and Cupecoy Beach (nude beach) on the **Dutch** side; and Baie Nettlé, Anse Marcel and Baie Orientale (with a section for nude bathing) on the **French** side.

Getting Acquainted

St Barthélemy, Saba and St Eustatius

Near St Martin, and easily accessible from it, are three smaller islands, St Barthélemy (known as St Barths), Saba, and St Eustatius (known as Statia).

St Barths is a 10-sq. mile (25 sq. km) French island, 15 miles (24 km) southeast of St Martin. Settled by Norman and Breton farmers, St Barths is said to resemble a little chunk of northwest France set in the tropical sea.

Saba is 28 miles (45 km) south of St Martin, and has no beaches at all, to speak of. There just isn't room: the highest point on this 5-sq. mile (13-sq. km) island is 2,855 ft (870 meters), giving the whole island the look of a verdant cone.

St Eustatius (Statia) is 11 sq. miles (28 sq. km) and Dutch. Saba and Statia are members of the Netherlands Antilles.

Public Holidays

St Barths: broadly the same as French St Martin (*see page 340*).
Saba and Statia: broadly the same as St Maarten (*see page 340*).

Calendar of Events

On **St Barths**, Carnival is held before Lent, with a festival in Gustavia on August 20; there are more celebrations on August 24, the day of the island's patron saint. **Saba's** Carnival is at the end of July, and **Statia's** the last two weeks of July.

Planning the Trip

Money Matters

In **St Barths**, the franc is the official currency, but US dollars are widely accepted. In **Saba** and **Statia**, the Dutch florin or guilder is the official currency, but, again, the dollar is freely used. Credit cards are rarely accepted outside hotels and dive shops. There are several banks in Gustavia, **St Barths**, some, such as the Crédit Agricole, Rue Bord de la Mer, with ATMs.

In Windwardside, **Saba**, Barclays Bank is open Monday–Friday 8.30am–12.30pm. In **Statia**, Barclays Bank, Wilhelminaweg, is open Monday–Thursday 8.30am–3.30pm, Friday 8.30am–12.30pm, and there are two other banks with similar hours.

Departure tax: St Barths 30FF, **Saba** and **Statia** US$5 to Netherlands Antilles, US$10 elsewhere. You pay only once if transferring to St Martin, and then flying home.

Tourist Offices Abroad

St Barths: see St Martin, French side (*page 341*). Website: http://www.Franceguide.com
Saba and **Statia**: see St Maarten (*page 341*).

Practical Tips

Telephone and Fax

The area code for **St Barths** is **590**; for **Saba**, **5994**; and for **Statia**, **5993**. Buy a phone card to use the public payphones on St Barths. Fax at SiBarth, Avenue Gen. de Gaulle, Gustavia.

Local Tourist Offices

St Barths: Quai de Gaulle, Gustavia. Tel: 27877.
Saba: Windwardside. Tel: 62231.
Statia: Fort Oranjestraat. Tel: 82433.

Medical Treatment

St Barths: Gustavia Hospital, tel: 276035.
Saba: Medical Center, tel: 63239.
Decompression chamber, Saba Marine Center, tel: 63295.
Statia: Queen Beatrice Hospital, tel: 82211.

Shopping

On St Barths, Gustavia and St Jean are best for tax-free luxury goods such as designer wear, perfume and quality local crafts.

Voltage: St Barths: 220 volts AC. **Saba** and **Statia:** 110 volts AC.

Saban Shopping

Saba lace, the drawn-thread work, is also known as Spanish work because it originated from Venezuela. It has been made for over 100 years here, and is on sale in shops and from private houses – any taxi driver should be able to take you to an outlet. The Saba Artisan's Foundation sells locally designed and produced clothing and fabric.

Getting Around

By Car

All valid foreign driving licenses are accepted.

In **St Barths** car rentals are available – with pick-ups at the airport. Advance reservations are particularly important on this little island. Most rental cars have standard transmissions. Rental agencies include:
Hertz, tel: 277114.
Budget, tel: 276743.

Saba has no car rentals. Taxis and tour operators will take you where you wish to go.

In **Statia** always reserve a rental car Contact:
St Eustatius Car Rental, tel: 82572.

By Taxi

Taxis are available on all three islands, for pick-ups at airports and ferry ports, and for island tours. Agree the price in advance.

Inter-Island Links

St Barths is linked by air with Puerto Rico, St Martin, St Thomas, Antigua, Anguilla, Guadeloupe, St Kitts, Barbados, and St Croix; **Saba** is linked with St Martin, St Kitts, and Statia; and **Statia** is linked with St Martin, St Kitts, and Saba. Airlines include:
Winair, tel: 276101 (St Barths); 54237 (Statia); 62255 (Saba).
● **Air Guadeloupe**, tel: 276190 (St Barths).

St Barths is served by catamarans and ferries while **Saba** is served by a motorized hydrofoil catamaran.

Where to Stay

Choosing a Hotel

There is a variety of accommodation available on the islands, although large resort hotels are still quite unusual there are villas, apartments, guest houses and classy hotels. As a general rule St Barths lives up to its reputation as a tropical haven for the wealthy, this is the place for luxurious, intimate hotels, while Saba has a selection of small comfortable inns, many offering diving packages to guests. Statia has a more limited choice with small, often family-run lodgings.

Hotel Listings

ST BARTHS

St Barths Beach Hotel
Grand Cul de Sac 97133, St Barthélemy, FWI.
Tel: 276070.
Fax: 277557.
A combination of rooms and bungalows near the sea. **$$$**

Hostellerie des Trois Forces
Vitet 97133, St Barthélemy, FWI.
Tel: 276125.
Fax: 278138.
Simple cottages with kitchenettes in a hillside setting. Superb hotel restaurant; pool. **$**

Le Toiny
Toiny 97133, St Barthélemy, FWI.
Tel: 278888.
Fax: 278930.
Small, select plantation-style hotel on a lovely hillside. **$$$**

Village St Jean
St Jean 97133, St Barthélemy, FWI.
Tel: 276139.
Fax: 277796.
Good value, on popular St Jean beach. **$–$$**

SABA

Captain's Quarters
Windwardside, NA.
Tel: 62201.
Fax: 62377.
Well-known hotel with rooms in a restored old sea captain's house. **$$**

Cranston's Antique Inn
The Bottom, Saba, NA.
Tel: 63203.
The first guesthouse on the island. Very atmospheric. **$**

Scout's Place
Windwardside, NA.
Tel: 62205.
Fax: 62388.
Simple rooms, some with shared bath, in a typical Saban house in the town center. **$**

STATIA

La Maison Sur la Plage
Zeelandia Bay, St Eustatius, NA.
Tel/Fax: 82256.
Quiet and comfortable cottages with good views of the island. **$$**

Kings Well
Oranjestad (between Upper and Lower Town).
Tel/Fax: 82538.
Small and friendly. Simply decorated rooms with kitchenettes. Some rooms have a great ocean view. **$–$$**

Price Guide

Price categories are based on the cost of a double room, for one night:
$ = less than $100
$$ = $100–200
$$$ = more than $200.

Where to Eat

Restaurant Listings

ST BARTHS

Au Port
Face à la Poste, Gustavia.
Tel: 276236.
Long-established with a nautical feel; French and Creole food. **$$$**

Eddy's
Rue du Centenaire, Gustavia.
Tel: 275417.
French and Caribbean dishes in an eclectic setting with a Far-Eastern flavor. **$$**

Price Guide

Price categories are based on the cost of a meal for one person, excluding drinks:
$ = less than $20
$$ = $20–30
$$$ = more than $30.

Eden Rock
St Jean.
Tel: 277294.
A wonderful atmosphere, overlooking the bay; now British owned and serving French and Creole dishes. **$$**

Francois Plantation
Colombier.
Tel: 277882.
Classic French cuisine and wines to match in a smart dining room. **$$$**

La Gloriette
Cul de Sac.
Tel: 277566.
Local French Creole cuisine served in a beachside setting. **$$–$$$**

Le Select
Gustavia.
An informal bar with hamburgers. Popular nightspot. **$$**

SABA

Captain's Quarters
Windwardside.
Tel: 62377.
Creole food in a relaxed verandah setting. Weekend barbecues. **$$**

Saba Chinese Restaurant
Windwardside.
Tel: 62268.
Good Chinese food, plus steaks and salads. **$–$$**

STATIA

Cool Corner
Fort Oranjestraat.
Tel: 82523.
Popular bar and Chinese restaurant; friendly service. **$**

La Maison sur la Plage
Zeelandia Bay.
Tel: 82256.
Sea views and good French wine and food. **$$–$$$**

Outdoor Activities

Diving

Saba offers superb diving, including breathtaking caves and cliffs inhabited by tropical fish and coral, carefully controlled by the Marine Park (tel: 63295) which encircles the island. Dive companies on Saba include:
Saba Deep Sea Diving Center, Fort Bay. Tel: 63347.
Sea Saba Dive Center, Windwardside. Tel: 62246.
There is a guided snorkeling trail (Edward S. Arnold Snorkel Trail) around the Marine Park.

Statia also offers wonderful diving in clear waters with the added interest of shipwrecks and the bonus of relatively few divers. Contact: **Dive Statia**, tel: 82435. Snorkelers can swim among submerged warehouses and taverns from the old port, and visit shipwrecks – some over 300 years old. **St Barths** also has excellent diving, particularly on offshore reefs and islets. Contact: **Océan Must**, tel: 276225.

Hiking

On **Saba**, you can climb up the 1,064 steps to the top of Mount Scenery. On a clear day you can see for miles. A national park is opening in 1999 offering a range of gentler trails.

On **Statia,** hikers will find a lush rainforest covering an ancient volcano (The Quill), through which flits an iridescent hummingbird unique to the island. The tourist office publishes details of trails, some of which are in poor condition.

Getting Acquainted

St Kitts and Nevis

The two-island nation of St Kitts and Nevis lies toward the northern end of the Leeward Island chain, in the vicinity of St Martin, Antigua, and Montserrat. The volcanic origin of these islands is apparent in their mountainous landscape.

Public Holidays

January 1	**New Year's Day**
January 2	**Carnival Last Lap**
March/April	
Easter	**Good Friday**
	Easter Monday
May 4	**Labor Day**
	Whit Monday
June	
(2nd Saturday)	**Queen's Birthday**
August 3	**Emancipation Day**
August 4th	**Culturama Last Lap**
September 19	**Independence Day**
December 25	**Christmas Day**
December 26	**Boxing Day**

Calendar of Events

Easter Monday:
horse racing.
Mid–late June:
St Kitts Music Festival.
July–first Monday in August:
Culturama, carnival and arts festival on Nevis.
September:
Independence celebrations.
Mid-December–early January:
Carnival.

Planning the Trip

Money Matters

The currency on both islands is the EC dollar; US dollars are also widely accepted. Banks are generally open Monday–Thursday 8am–3pm, Friday 8am–5pm; some are open Saturday 8.30am–11am. There are ATMs at several banks, including Royal Bank of Canada.

Departure Tax: There is a departure tax of EC$27 (US$10).

Tourist Offices Abroad

IN THE US

414 East 75th Street, New York, NY 10021. Tel: 212-535 1234.

IN THE UK

10 Kensington Court, London W8 5DL. Tel: 0171-376 0881.

IN CANADA

11 Yorkville Ave, Suite 508, Toronto, Ontario M4W 1L3. Tel: 416-921 7717.

WEBSITE ADDRESS

http://www.StKitts-Nevis.com

Practical Tips

Media

A free tourist paper, the *St Kitts and Nevis Visitor,* is widely available, detailing many useful addresses and local events.

While on St Kitts and Nevis, tune into ZIZ Radio, Choice FM, or VON Radio on Nevis. ZIZ is also one of two local TV stations.

Postal Services

There are two post offices, located on Bay Road in Basseterre and Main Street in Charlestown. Open 8am–3.30pm Monday to Wednesday and Friday. On Thursday and Saturday, they are open 8am–noon.

Telephone, Fax and Internet

The area code is **869**. The local telephone company Skantel, a partnership between the St Kitts and Nevis government and Cable and Wireless, has a fully digitalized network and offers numerous up-to-date services. Direct dialed international calls may be made from any telephone by dialing 1, and operator-assisted calls may be made by dialing 0. Credit card calls, fax, Internet, e-mail, and beeper services are also available through Skantel. Offices are located at:
St Kitts: Cayon St, Basseterre. Tel: 465 2219 (open 7.30am–6pm weekdays, 7.30am–1pm Saturday, and 6–8pm Sunday and public holidays).
Nevis: Main Street, Charlestown. Tel: 469 5294.

Local Tourist Offices

St Kitts: Pelican Mall, Basseterre. Tel: 465 2620.
Nevis: Main Street, Charlestown. Tel: 469 1042.

Medical Treatment

St Kitts has two hospitals, the Joseph N. France General Hospital in Basseterre (tel: 465 2551) and a small hospital in Sandy Point, toward the island's west end. The Alexandra Hospital in Government Road, Charlestown is **Nevis**'s only hospital (tel: 469 5473). There is a pharmacy in Basseterre: City Drug Store (tel: 465 2156).

Nightlife

There is one casino at the Royal St Kitts Hotel, Frigate Bay; lively local bars and the large hotels provide evening entertainment.

Shopping

For local color, don't miss the market in Basseterre (Saturday morning). For colorful clothing, look for imaginative batik prints whose fabrics are often made from locally-grown cotton. Try:
Caribelle Batik workshops in Romney Manor, St Kitts.
Kate Design for paintings, pottery and printed silk. Shops are at Rawlins Plantation, Basseterre and Charlestown.
Port Xante absorbs cruise ship visitors with its many shops, along with **Pelican Mall** in Basseterre.

Voltage: 230 volts 60 cycles.

Religious Services

The Fig Tree Church, **Nevis**, is where the banns of marriage between Nelson and Fanny were published, while St Thomas Anglican Church is the island's oldest church. Contact The Christian Council, tel: 465 2504 (St Kitts); 469 5286 (Nevis).

Getting Around

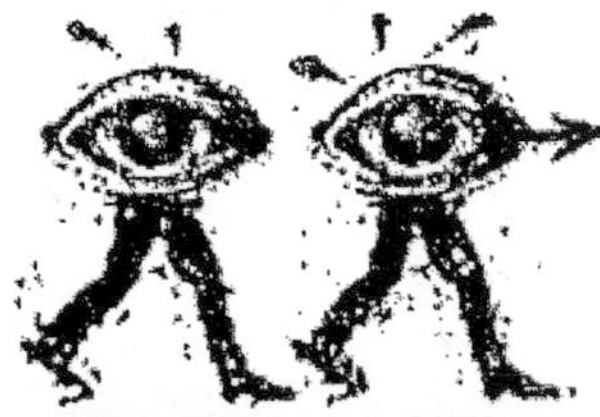

By Car

Cars drive on the left, British style. Visitors who wish to drive while on the islands must present a valid national or international license at the Traffic Department, along with a small fee. A temporary license, valid on St Kitts and Nevis, will then be issued. Branches of the Traffic Department are located at the police stations in Basseterre on Canyon Street and Charlestown on Island Road.

Saloon cars, jeeps and mini-mokes (like a beach buggy) are available for hire but should be booked well in advance especially in high season.

For more details contact:
Avis, South Independence Square, Basseterre, St Kitts. Tel: 465 6507.
Avis, Nevis. Tel: 469 1240.
You can split the rental between the two islands for the same price as hiring a car only on one island.

By Taxi

St Kitts is served by Bradshaw International Airport, from which taxis are available for the 2½-mile (4-km) trip to Basseterre – the island's major town and capital of St Kitts and Nevis. Taxis also serve the island's scattered hotels.

Travelers flying to **Nevis** land at Newcastle airport, a 7-mile (11-km) jaunt from Nevis's principal and only town, Charlestown. Once again, taxis are on hand to bring visitors to their destinations. Tariffs are fixed, but be sure to confirm the total price of your journey before starting out.

By Bus

Local people tend to use the little minibuses which service both islands. The buses are usually reliable and cheap, but they don't generally travel the general tourist routes.

Inter-Island Links

St Kitts is linked by air with many islands including Puerto Rico, Antigua, Barbados, St Martin, Anguilla, St Barths, Saba, St Eustatius, USVI, BVI, Grenada, and St Lucia.

Nevis is linked with USVI, St Barths, Anguilla, Antigua, and St Martin.

Airlines serving the routes in to and from St Kitts and Nevis include:
Winair, tel: 465-0810.
LIAT, tel: 465-2511.
Carib Aviation, tel: 465-3055.

You can travel the short distance between St Kitts and Nevis either by air taxi or by the Basseterre to Charlestown ferry, a 40-minute journey which runs daily except Thursday and Sunday.

Where to Stay

Choosing a Hotel

Hotels in St Kitts and Nevis are generally small. No hotel is permitted to be more than three floors high, so the gleaming (and impersonal) towers that have sprouted on other islands are unknown here. A number of hotels are converted plantation houses and sugar mills.

Rates vary from the peak in winter to the quieter summer season. St Kitts and Nevis also offer a number of apartments, condominiums and cottages, many for rent at weekly rates. Full details are available from the Tourist Board.

Hotel Listings

ST KITTS

Frigate Bay Beach Resort
PO Box 137, St Kitts, WI.
Tel: 465 8935.
Fax: 465 7050.
Overlooking Frigate Bay and near the golf course. All guests receive free green fees. **$$$**

The Golden Lemon
Dieppe Bay, St Kitts, WI.
Tel: 465 7260.
Fax: 465 4019.
Beautifully decorated and restored 17th-century inn and villas about 15 miles (24 km) from Basseterre. Featured in *Gourmet*, *Bon Appetit*, and Condé Nast *Traveler* magazines. **$$$**

Ocean Terrace Inn
PO Box 65, St Kitts, WI.
Tel: 465 2754.
Fax: 465 1057.
Overlooking Basseterre Bay with

splendid views of the Southeast Peninsula and Nevis. Extensively renovated. Comfortable rooms and good watersports facilities. **$$$**

Ottleys Plantation Inn
PO Box 345, St. Kitts, WI.
Tel: 465 7234.
Fax: 465 4760.
A former 18th-century sugar estate, the Great House and guest cottages are set among tropical gardens with magnificent views of both ocean and mountains. **$$$**

Price Guide

Price categories are based on the cost of a double room, for one night:
$ = less than $100
$$ = $100–200
$$$ = more than $200.

Rawlins Plantation Inn
PO Box 340, St Kitts, WI.
Tel: 465 6221.
Fax: 465 4954.
A former plantation Great House which has been converted into an elegant inn with several cottages set in tropical gardens. **$$$**

Royal St Kitts Hotel and Casino
PO Box 340, Frigate Bay, St Kitts, WI.
Tel: 465 8651.
Fax: 465 1031.
All-inclusive golf resort with a casino. It has beaches on both the Atlantic and Caribbean sides. **$$$**

Sun 'n' Sand Beach Resort
PO Box 341, St Kitts, WI.
Tel: 465 8037.
Fax: 465 6745.
Cottages and studios on the Atlantic-side beach at Frigate Bay. **$$**

NEVIS

Four Seasons Resort
PO Box 565, Nevis, WI.
Tel/Fax: 469 1112.
Deluxe resort. Villas and suites with an ocean view or a view of the Robert Trent Jones golf course. **$$$**

Golden Rock Plantation Inn
PO Box 493, Nevis, WI.
Tel: 469 3346.
Fax: 469 2113.
Romantic adventure holidays arranged at this atmospheric inn. High in the hills surrounded by cottages. **$$$**

Hermitage Plantation Inn
Fig Tree Parish, St John, Nevis, WI.
Tel: 469 3477.
Fax: 469 2481.
Historic plantation inn featuring the oldest wooden building in Nevis. **$$$**

Hurricane Cove Bungalows
Oualie Beach, Nevis, WI.
Tel/Fax: 469 9462.
Wooden bungalows perched on a bluff overlooking Oualie Beach, with views of The Narrows and St Kitts. **$$–$$$**

Montpelier Plantation Inn
St John, PO Box 474, Nevis, WI.
Tel: 469 3462.
Fax: 469 2932.
Charming Great House hotel set high in the mountains on a 60-acre (24-hectare) estate. It was ranked as No. 1 in the Condé Nast *Traveler* 1997 readers poll. **$$$**

Nisbet Plantation Beach Club
Newcastle, Nevis, WI.
Tel: 469 5325.
Fax: 469 9864.
Lovely rooms and cottages on the site of an 18th-century oceanside coconut plantation. **$$$**

Where to Eat

What to Eat

St Kitts and Nevis have many restaurants specializing in West Indian, Creole, French, Indian, and Chinese fare. In addition to the Caribbean's ubiquitous fresh seafood, perhaps the most distinctive feature of St Kitts and Nevis cuisine is the abundance of fresh vegetables from the islands' volcanic soil. Tropical produce such as breadfruit joins items such as eggplant (aubergine), sweet potatoes, okra on island plates.

Restaurant Listings

ST KITTS

Ballahoo
The Circus, Basseterre, St Kitts.
Tel: 465 4197.
West Indian seafood and fruit drinks are served in this popular meeting place with a scenic view from the balcony. **$$$**

Fisherman's Wharf
Fortlands, St Kitts.
Tel: 465 2754.
Informal dining by the sea, with a menu featuring grilled seafood. **$$$**

The Golden Lemon
Dieppe Bay, St Kitts.
Tel: 465 7260.
Acclaimed for its Continental and Caribbean dishes. Reservations required. **$$$**

Rawlins Plantation Inn
Mount Pleasant, St Kitts.
Tel: 465 6221.
Popular West Indian buffet lunch and four-course dinners. **$$–$$$**

Royal Palm Restaurant at Ottleys Plantation Inn
Ottleys, St Kitts.
Tel: 465 7234.
Innovative gourmet dining and a popular Sunday brunch in a garden setting. **$$–$$$**

NEVIS

Golden Rock Beach Restaurant
Pinney's Beach, Nevis.
Tel: 469 5346.
Known for its delicious rum punch; located in an early 19th-century stone building. **$$**

Price Guide

Price categories are based on the cost of a meal for one person, excluding drinks:
$ = less than $20
$$ = $20–30
$$$ = more than $30.

Miss June's
Jones Bay, Nevis.
Tel: 469 5330.
Home-cooked West Indian food in an intimate setting. Reservations are essential.
$$–$$$

Nisbet Plantation Beach Club
Newcastle, Nevis.
Tel: 469 5325.
Lunch and Sunday barbecue on the beach; formal dining in the Great House. **$$–$$$**

Unella's Bar and Restaurant
Charlestown, Nevis.
Tel: 469 5574.
Waterfront views. **$–$$**

Outdoor Activities

Watersports

Strong currents make swimming on the Atlantic side of the islands dangerous. Swim safely on the calmer Caribbean side.

There is excellent, unspoilt diving and snorkeling. On **St Kitts**, the places to try are:
Kenneth's Dive Center, Bay Road, Basseterre. Tel: 465 7043.
Pro-Divers, tel: 465 3223.
On **Nevis**, Oualie Beach is a good snorkeling spot and is also the base for:
Scuba Safaris, tel: 469 9518.

Hiking

Hiking is a delightful experience on both islands, with their lush rainforests and mountainous terrain. A particular thrill for the adventurous is the hike down into the crater of an old volcano on Mount Liamuiga in St Kitts. Guided hikes are available; enquire at your hotel or the local tourist office. On **Nevis**, **Eco-Tours Nevis** (tel: 469 2091) offer various options, including an Eco-Ramble.

Golf

Golfing enthusiasts are well catered for. **St Kitts** has an 18-hole championship golf course at Frigate Bay, Royal St Kitts (tel: 465 8339), and a 9-hole golf course at Golden Rock (tel: 465 8103). **Nevis** has an 18-hole course attached to the Four Seasons Resort (tel: 469 1111); non-residents are welcome to play for a fee.

Getting Acquainted

Antigua and Barbuda

Antigua and Barbuda lie in the central region of the Lesser Antilles, between St Barths, St Kitts and Nevis, Montserrat, and Guadeloupe. Together with a third island, Redonda, which is uninhabited, Antigua and Barbuda form an independent nation within the British Commonwealth. Antigua is relatively dry and flat, with the highest point, Boggy Peak at 1,330 ft (405 meters). The 62 sq. mile (161 sq. km) low-lying coral island of Barbuda is even flatter (highest elevation, 207 ft/63 meters), but in contrast to Antigua, Barbuda retains much of its forest cover. In fact, most of the island is given over to a wooded game preserve and bird sanctuary. The total population of Antigua and Barbuda is 70,000, of whom only 1,300 live on Barbuda.

Public Holidays

January 1	**New Year's Day**
January 2	**Carnival Last Lap**
March/April Easter	**Good Friday** **Easter Monday**
May (1st Monday)	**Labor Day** **Whit Monday**
June (2nd Saturday)	**Queen's birthday**
August (1st Monday and Tuesday)	**Carnival**
October (1st Monday)	**Merchants Day** (shops closed)

November 1	**Independence Day**
December 25	**Christmas Day**
December 26	**Boxing Day**

Calendar of Events

January: Men's Tennis Week – professional and amateur tournaments.
April: Women's Tennis Week – professional and amateur tournaments.
Antigua Sailing Week – a regatta with international participants held in late April.
International cricket.
July/August: Carnival – held during the week preceding the first Monday in August. Culmination of the Carnival celebrations on August Monday and Tuesday – in memory of the abolition of slavery.
October: Jazz Festival.
November: Independence Week Half Marathon in early November.

Language

The official language on Antigua is English. A colorful variation is spoken in the small villages, for example: *ah fuh me ting dat*/that belongs to me.

Planning the Trip

Money Matters

The currency is the EC dollar; US dollars are also widely accepted. Major credit cards are acceptable in most hotels and some restaurants and shops. Most of the major banks are located in High Street, St John's. Banking hours vary but are generally 8am–2pm, Monday–Thursday, 8am–4pm Friday; Bank of Antigua open 8am–noon Saturday. Several banks have ATMs which can be used outside opening hours, located at Woods Shopping Center, St John's and the Royal Bank of Canada, Market Street and High Street, St John's. There is a branch of Antigua Commercial Bank in Codrington, Barbuda. There is also a branch of American Express at Antours, Long Street, St John's.
Departure Tax: EC$30 is payable on departure.

Tourist Offices Abroad

IN THE US
610 5th Avenue, Suite 311, New York, NY 10020.
Tel: 212-541 4117.
Fax: 212-757 1607.

IN THE UK
Antigua House, 15 Thayer Street, London W1M 5LD.
Tel: 0171-486 7073.
Fax: 0171-486 1466.

IN CANADA
60 Avenue Clair East, Suite 304, Toronto, Ontario M4T 1N5.
Tel: 416-961 3085.
Fax: 416-961 7218.

Practical Tips

Media

There is only one local radio station in **Antigua**, but if your radio set has powerful receiver, you may be able to pick up signals from other islands. Most of the larger hotels have satellite TV, which is dominated by CNN and other US channels.

Postal Services

In **St John's**, the main post office is on Long Street. There is also a small post office at the international airport, and one in Codrington, **Barbuda**.

Telephone, Fax and Internet

The area code for **Antigua** and **Barbuda** is **268**. Local and long-distance calls can be made 24-hours a day from most telephones or from the offices of the Cable and Wireless telephone company on St Mary Street in St John's and the Yacht Marina Office in English Harbour, Antigua, where you can also buy telephone cards for the payphones dotted around the island, send faxes and use the Internet. There is also a 24-hour office at Wireless, near Clare Hill in northern Antigua.

Local Tourist Offices

Antigua: PO Box 363, Thames Street, St John's. Tel: 462-0480. Open 8.30am–4pm Monday–Friday, 8.30am–noon Saturday. There is also a small branch at the airport in Arrivals.

Medical Treatment

Antigua has the Holbertson Hospital, Holbertson Road, St John's. Tel: 462 0251. There is also one hospital on Barbuda, and clinics on both islands. **Pharmacies:** Woods Center, and St Mary's Street, St John's. Tel: 462 1363.

Emergency Numbers

- **General:** 999/991.
- **Police:** 462 0215.
- **Fire:** 462 0044.
- **Ambulance:** 462 0215.

Nightlife

Most resorts provide live entertainment for guests such as steel pan or reggae bands and limbo dancers. Casinos include King's Casino, Heritage Quay, (tel: 462 1727). At Shirley Heights Lookout Restaurant there is a Sunday evening barbecue and a steel band performing 3–6pm, followed by a reggae band 6–9pm. Start out early, because the road to the Heights becomes pretty congested as locals and visitors head for this popular night out. Antigua's Carnival is second in size only to Trinidad's.

Shopping

In St John's Heritage Quay and Redcliffe Quay attract cruise ship shoppers with a range of duty-free outlets and a street market. There is an art gallery exhibiting work of Caribbean artists at Harmony Hall, Brown's Bay near Freetown (tel: 462 27870).
Try the market in St John's for local produce. Antigua Black pineapple is reputed to be the sweetest in the world.

Voltage: 220 volts 60 cycles and 110 volts.

Getting Around

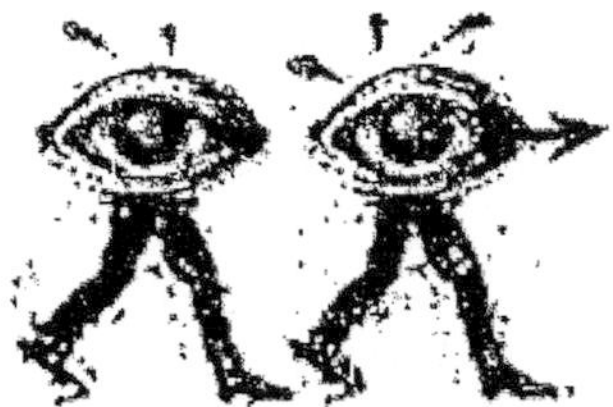

By Car

Driving is on the left, British style. Drivers should present their regular licenses, along with a small fee at a police station or car rental office in order to be issued with a local driving permit. Vehicles can be picked up at the airport, or delivered to your hotel. Agencies include:
Avis, tel: 462 2840.
Hertz, tel: 462 4114.
Dollar Rent-a-Car, tel: 462 0362.
Budget, tel: 462 3009.
On Barbuda, jeeps are available from **Williams and Thomas Car Rental**, tel: 460 0047.
Some of the roads outside St John's are narrow and potholed with no sidewalk, so beware.

By Taxi

There are plenty of taxis to meet flights at V.C. Bird International Airport, and jeeps at Barbuda's Codrington Airport. Fares are pre-set (a list is posted in Arrivals at the airport, the tourist office and hotels). Confirm the price before you start.

Inter-Island Links

Barbuda is just 10 minutes away from Antigua by air, or by ferry from St John's.

Antigua is easily accessible with direct air connections from Europe, USA and Canada and frequent links with all Caribbean islands. Airlines include:
LIAT, tel: 462 0700.
BWIA, tel: 462 1260.
Carib Aviation, tel: 462 3147.

Where to Stay

Choosing a Hotel

During the summer prices for accommodation can vary. For budget-minded travelers or long-stay visitors, Antigua has villas, guesthouses and apartments, some at weekly or monthly rates. On Barbuda there are two luxury hotels, and a few guesthouses.

Price Guide

Price categories are based on the cost of a double room, for one night:
$ = less than $100
$$ = $100–200
$$$ = more than $200.

Hotel Listings

ANTIGUA

Admiral's Inn
Nelson's Dockyard, PO Box 713, St John's, Antigua, WI.
Tel: 460 1153.
Fax: 460 1534.
Small, pretty hotel in a restored building at English Harbour. **$–$$**

Copper and Lumber Store
PO Box 184, St John's, Antigua, WI.
Tel: 460 1058.
Fax: 460 1529.
Hotel in a former warehouse directly on English Harbour. **$–$$**

Curtain Bluff Resort
Old Road, PO Box 288, St John's, Antigua, WI.
Tel: 462 8400.
Fax: 462 8409.
Exclusive hotel with all-inclusive prices and tropical garden. **$$$**

Falmouth Harbour Beach Apartments
PO Box 713, St John's, Antigua, West Indies.
Tel: 460 1027.
Fax: 460 1534.
Simple apartments near English Harbour with views of the harbor and the beach just a few minutes away. **$–$$**

Price Guide

Price categories are based on the cost of a double room, for one night:
$ = less than $100
$$ = $100–200
$$$ = more than $200.

Jolly Harbour
PO Box 1793, St John's, Antigua, WI.
Tel: 462 6166.
Fax: 462 6167.
Large complex with many leisure amenities, own yacht marina, wide range of watersports. **$$–$$$**

Murphy's Place
All Saints Road, PO Box 491, St John's, Antigua, WI.
Tel: 461 1183.
Welcoming and private. No frills rooms. **$**

Runaway Beach Club
PO Box 874, St. John's, Antigua, WI.
Tel: 462 1318.
Fax: 462 4172.
Practical holiday base directly on a sandy beach. **$$**

Spanish Main Inn,
Independence Avenue, St John's, Antigua, WI.
Tel: 462 0660.
Simple rooms above an English-style pub. **$**

BARBUDA

Coco Point Lodge
Coco Point, Barbuda, WI.
Tel: 462 3816.
Fax: 462 8334.
The first exclusive all-inclusive resort on the island, at the southern tip of the island. **$$$**

K Club
Coco Beach, Barbuda, WI.
Tel: 460 0300.
Fax: 460 0305.
Exclusive resort hotel opened in 1991 and owned by style-conscious Italians. **$$$**

Sunset View
Codrington Village, Barbuda, WI.
Tel: 460 0078.
Small, simple inn run by a local family. **$**

Asian Village

Much to the consternation of conservationists and others trying to curb insensitive overdevelopment in the Caribbean, the island of Guiana, off the northeast coast of Antigua is being transformed into a massive holiday resort to be called Asian Village. The one hundred million US dollar Malaysian investment will comprise six hotels (one with a Balinese theme), as well as apartments and town houses, a conference center, three golf courses, retail outlets and a casino. One third of the island will be developed while the rest will remain in its natural state with some enhancement, including the preservation of a mangrove swamp. Building plans have forced the departure of Welshman Taffy Bufton and his wife, the island's only inhabitants who maintained a wildlife sanctuary there. They have been rehoused on Antigua. The ground was finally broken in late April 1998 and although the project will create 4,000 much needed jobs, Antigua and the surrounding region will change irrevocably.

Where to Eat

What to Eat

There are some delicious local dishes worth trying, such as pepper-pot, conch and chicken and rice and peas. Alternatively visitors can taste some of Antigua's international cuisine, French, Italian and Vietnamese cooking are among the options.

Price Guide

Price categories are based on the cost of a meal for one person, excluding drinks:
$ = less than $20
$$ = $20–30
$$$ = more than $30.

Restaurant Listings

The Admiral's Inn
Nelson's Dockyard, PO Box 713, St John's, Antigua.
Tel: 460 10127.
This traditional hotel restaurant has West Indian cuisine. The outdoor terrace is pleasant. **$–$$**

Harmony Hall
Brown's Bay, near Freetown.
Tel: 460 4120.
A delightful lunch spot overlooking the old sugar mill and the bay; Italian dishes served on the terrace of a plantation-style house which includes an art gallery and craft shop. **$$–$$$**

Pizzas on the Quay (Big Banana Holding Co.)
Redcliffe Quay.
Tel: 462 2621.
Great pizzas and pasta. Popular at lunchtime. **$**

Boston's Restaurant
Michael's Ave, St John's.
Tel: 462 4510.
Local Antiguan cooking. **$–$$**

Brother B's
Long Street, St John's, Antigua.
Tel: 462 0616.
Seafood and local dishes. **$**

Buccaneer Cove
Dickenson Bay.
Tel: 462 2173.
Lobster a specialty; calypso on Wednesday, steel band music on Saturday, jazz on Sunday. **$$**

Calypso
Upper Redcliff Street, St John's.
Tel: 426 1965.
Good local food, with plenty of fish and seafood. **$$**

Colombo's
English Harbour.
Tel: 460 1452.
Italian cuisine, seafood. Live music on Wednesday. **$$**

The Lemon Tree
Long Street, St John's.
Tel: 462 1969.
North American atmosphere and an international menu. Evening entertainment is provided for diners. **$$–$$$**

The Lookout
Shirley Heights, Nelson's Dockyard.
Tel: 460 1785.
Elegant restaurant in a well-renovated 18th-century house. Steel pan band livens things up on Thursday and Sunday evenings. **$$–$$$**

Outdoor Activities

Birdwatching

Frigate birds, with their distinctive red throats, inflated when attracting females, can be seen on both Antigua and Barbuda. There is a Frigate Bird Sanctuary on Barbuda, across the mangrove swamps of Codrington Lagoon.

Golf

Antigua: there are golf courses at **Cedar Valley Golf Club**, tel: 462 0161 (18-hole) and the **Jolly Beach** Hotel, tel: 462 6166 (short 18-hole).
Barbuda: guests of the K Club can use the hotel's nine-hole course.

Horseback Riding

Riding tours are available at **Spring Hill Riding Club**, Rendezvous Bay, Antigua, tel: 460 2700.

Tennis

Most hotels have private tennis courts. If you require public tennis and squash courts, contact **Temo Sports**, English Harbour, tel: 460-1781.

Watersports

Many of the larger hotels employ at least one member of staff who will arrange fun and games on and in the water. A trip to Green Island for snorkeling and lunch is one recommended trip. For details of this and other oceanside jaunts contact your hotel or the **Long Bay Hotel**, tel: 463 2005.

Sailing can also be arranged through **Nicholson Yacht Charters**, tel: 460 1530, or **Sun Yacht Charters**, St John's, tel: 460 2615. If you prefer the rum 'n' sun approach, try a trip on the **Jolly Roger Pirate Ship** from Heritage Quay, St John's, tel: 462 2064.

For windsurfing, lessons and equipment, contact **Windsurf Antigua**, tel: 462 9463 or **Patrick's Windsurfing School**, Rex Halcyon Cove Hotel, Dickenson Bay, tel: 462 3094.

For a whole variety of watersports contact **Wadadli Watersports**, tel: 462 3661; and for deep-sea fishing **Lobster King**, Jolly Beach, tel: 462 4363.

DIVING

Several hotels have their own dive shops. Dive operators include:
Dive Antigua, Rex Halcyon Cove, Dickenson Bay, tel: 462 3483.
Jolly Dive, Club Antigua, tel: 462-0061.
Dockyard Divers, Nelson's Dockyard, tel: 460 1178.
Dive Runaway, Runaway Beach Club, tel: 462 2626.

Best Beaches

There is one beach for every day of the year on Antigua. Amongst the best are: Half Moon Bay, Long Bay, Galley Bay and Dark Wood Beach. On Barbuda just about any beach is recommended, try the lovely beach at Long Bay.

Getting Acquainted

Montserrat

The activity of the Soufrière Hills volcano since July 1995 means that two thirds of the island remained "out of bounds" in 1998. The remaining one third, the northern section of the island, was habitable, safe, green and friendly. For anyone interested in the extraordinary spectacle of a live volcano, Montserrat is an intriguing place to visit. The fortitude and determination of its people is also remarkable. However, normal tourist facilities are limited.

Public Holidays

January 1 **New Year's Day**
March 17 **St Patrick's Day**
Easter **Good Friday**
Easter Monday
Whit Monday
June (second Saturday) **Queen's Birthday**
August (first Monday) **August Monday**
December 25 **Christmas Day**
December 26 **Boxing Day**

Calendar of Events

Carnival is the main event: December 15–January 2.

Volcano Observatory

Mongo Hill, near St John's, is the scientific hub for volcano monitoring. The scientists welcome visitors from 1–3pm. Telephone in advance. Tel: 491 5647. Jack Boy Hill offers the best view from the north.

Planning the Trip

Money Matters

Montserrat's local currency is the EC (Eastern Caribbean) dollar; US dollars are acceptable in some places. Two banks remain: the Royal Bank of Canada, relocated to Olveston, and the Bank of Montserrat, in the old Hilton bar, above St Peter's.

Departure Tax: Check with your airline as to whether departure tax will be collected during or, at the end of your stay. Save some local currency just in case.

Good Beaches

Woodlands Beach is good for diving and for picnics. Rendezvous Beach is the island's only white sand beach. Hike there from Little Bay, once a charming black sand beach, now Montserrat's only sea access point and the potential site for a new capital.

Tourist Offices Abroad

IN THE US

Medhurst & Associates Inc.
1208 Washington Drive,
Centerport, NY 11721.
Tel: 516-425 0900.
Fax: 516-425 0903.

IN THE UK

Marketing Services Ltd
Suite 433, High Holborn House,
52–54 High Holborn, London
WC1V 6RB.
Tel: 0171-242 3131.
Fax: 0171-242 2838.

Practical Tips

Media

The local radio station, ZJB, maintains a valiant service, including twice-daily volcano reports. The weekly newspaper is the *Montserrat Reporter.*

Postal Services

The main post office was temporarily relocated to Olveston; check its current location with the tourist office.

Telephone

The area code is **664**. Cable and Wireless, now based in St John's, Antigua, has maintained an efficient telephone service. Public payphones take Eastern Caribbean dollar phonecards or coins.

Local Tourist Office

There is one tourist office on the island:

Montserrat Tourist Board, PO Box 7, Plymouth. Tel: 491 2320. Website: http://www.mrat.com

Medical Treatment

The medical facilities available on the island are severely restricted. The Glendon Hospital, Plymouth, has been relocated to St John's, Antigua. Any serious cases are transferred to neighboring islands.

Electricity

Voltage is supplied at 220 volts, 60 cycles.

Getting Around

By Car

Drive on the left, British style. The steep, now heavily used and pot-holed roads of the north were being improved in 1998. There are no current formal car hire services. A local driving license can be obtained from the police. Hitchhiking is safe and easy, but it is not recommended.

By Taxi

Taxis are available; the Tourist Board should be able to supply visitors with company names and telephone numbers.

By Bus

A public bus service (using mini-buses) serves the safe northern part of the island.

Inter-Island Links

The airport closed because of volcanic activity in June 1997. The only ways to get to and from Montserrat are by helicopter or ferry, both from Antigua.

The helicopter (a nine-seater, so book early) offers a twice-daily service (except Wednesday), taking 20 minutes. There is limited luggage space. Contact: **Montserrat Aviation Services**, tel: 491 2533.

Carib World Travel, tel: 460 6101.

Carib Aviation, Antigua. Tel: 462 3147.

The ferry (200-seater Antilles Express) operates from St John's, Antigua, twice daily Monday to Saturday.

Where to Stay and Eat

Hotels

The choice is extremely limited at present. A list of bed and breakfast accommodation, guesthouses and self-contained, self-catering flatlets attached to private homes, in the north of the island, is available from the Montserrat Tourist Board.

Restaurants

Most restaurants and snack bars in the north are small, informal places, many set up by people relocated from the south. Some are only open for breakfast and lunch, others are no more than roadside stands serving excellent rice and peas, fish, chicken and the like. **Annie Morgan's** in St John's, (open Friday and Saturday), is famous for its goat water (Montserrat's goat stew). The **Emerald Café** at Sweeney's has a more extensive menu than most.

Outdoor Activities

The diving sites of the north remain accessible. **Sea Wolf Diving School** (tel: 491 6859), caters for all levels, from beginner to assistant instructor. Snorkeling equipment is also available.

For boat trips, contact **Danny Sweeney**, tel: 491 5645.

Getting Acquainted

Guadeloupe

South of Antigua and north of Dominica, toward the center of the Lesser Antilles, lies Guadeloupe. It's on a French archipelago which also includes the islands of St Barthélemy, St Martin, Les Saintes, La Desirade, Marie Galante.

Public Holidays

January 1	**New Year's Day**
February	**Ash Wednesday**
variable	**Easter**
July 14	**Bastille Day**
July 21	**Schoelcher Day** (emancipation)
August 15	**Assumption Day**
November 1	**All Saints Day**
November 11	**Armistice Day**
November 22	**Ste Cecilia Day**
December 24	**Christmas Eve**
December 25	**Christmas Day**
December 28	**Young Saints Day**; Children's Parade
December 31	**New Year's Eve**

Calendar of Events

Carnival, in February consists of five days of jubilation, dressing up and partying in the streets. In late May is the **Fête de la Musique Traditionnelle** in Ste Anne. **Fête des Cuisinieres**, Cooks' Festival is held in August in Pointe-à-Pitre. Also in August is the **Tour de la Guadeloupe**, an international cycle race. The first Saturday in November sees the **Creole Music Festival**, also at Pointe-à-Pitre.

Planning the Trip

Money Matters

The local currency is the French franc (Ff), but US dollars (US$) are also accepted at some establishments. Most major credit cards are accepted throughout the island. There are also banks with ATMs (Automatic Teller Machines) within Guadeloupe which will allow you withdraw cash directly from your bank account or from a credit card.

Tourist Offices Abroad

IN CANADA

French Tourist Office
1981 Avenue McGill College, Suite 480, Montréal PQH 3A 2W9.
Tel: 514-844 8566.
Fax: 514-844 8901.
30 St Patrick Street, Suite 700, Toronto MST 3A3.
Tel: 416-593 4723.
Fax: 979 7587.

IN THE UK

French Tourist Office (Maison de la France)
178 Picadilly, London W1 0AL.
Tel: 0171-629 2869.
Fax: 0171-493 6594.

IN THE US

Guadeloupe Tourist Office.
Tel: (888) 448-233 56873
French Tourist Office, 610 Fifth Avenue, New York, NY 10020.
Tel: 212-757 0218.
Fax: 212-247 6468.
645 North Michigan Avenue, Suite 630, Chicago, Illinois 60611.
Tel: 312-751 7800.

Practical Tips

Media

France-Antilles is the island's daily paper. English Language publications are available from newsstands near the tourist and commercial centers. RFO (Radio France Outre-Mer) is the public broadcasting channel with a radio and TV station.

Postal Services

In Pointe-à-Pitre, post offices are located on Boulevard Hanne and Boulevard Legitimus.

Telephone and Fax

The area code is **590**. Long-distance telephone calls can be made from payphones and most hotels. Larger hotels and business organizations also have fax facilities. Telegrams, faxes, and phone calls can be made from main post offices.

Local Tourist Offices

Office du Tourisme de la Guadeloupe, 5 Square de la Banque, BP 422, 97163 Pointe-à-Pitre.
Tel: 82 09 30.
Office du Tourisme, Basse-Terre
Tel: 81 24 83.
Office Municipal de St-François
Tel: 88 48 74.

Medical Treatment

Guadeloupe is well-served by hospitals and clinics and some doctors speak English. Your hotel and the Tourist Board can help locate a doctor in an emergency.

Emergency Numbers

- **Police:** 17.
- **Fire:** 18.

Nightlife

There are two casinos on the island, in Gosier and St François. Most of the larger hotels provide live evening entertainment, usually at the weekend. Resort areas frequented by tourists also have bars and discos.

Shopping

Shoppers in Guadeloupe searching for quality local arts and crafts, perfume and designer clothing and all things French will not be disappointed. There are modern facilities at the cruise ship terminal in Pointe-à-Pitre, which has tropical gardens, restaurants and shops, there are also shops at the Centre St-John Perse and the Cora Center in Bas-du-Fort. Also worth a stop is the Marché Couvert food market, and why not take a stroll down the fashionable rue Frebault with its upmarket shops and sometimes snooty staff.

Voltage: 220 volts, 50 cycles.

Religious Services

The population of Guadeloupe is mainly Roman Catholic, but there are also groups of Seventh Day Adventists, Evangelists, Methodists and Hindus. Contact the local tourist office for advice about services and the locations of houses of worship.

Getting Around

On Arrival

Seagoing passengers arrive in Guadeloupe at centrally located Pointe-à-Pitre, which, along with Basse-Terre, is one of the island's two major towns. Air passengers touch down at the Raizet International Airport outside Pointe-à-Pitre, although some traffic passes through airports near Basse-Terre and St François.

By Taxi

At all points of entry – air and sea – taxis are available to take you to your hotel or elsewhere, but they are expensive and not all routes have pre-fixed rates. Drivers usually only speak French, so be prepared.

By Car

To rent a car for 20 days or less, your current valid license is all you will need. For longer periods, Guadeloupe requires an International Driver's Permit. Visiting drivers should have at least one year's driving experience. Pointe-à-Pitre and Raizet Airport both have car rental agencies. Mopeds are also available for hire.

Inter-Island Links

Air links with neighboring Caribbean islands are available with the following airlines:
Air Guadeloupe, tel: 21 12 90.
Air Caraibes, tel: 21 09 10
Air Saint-Martin, tel: 21 12 87.
Air Martinique, tel: 21 13 42.

Where to Stay

Choosing a Hotel

Accommodation on Guadeloupe is varied with lots of choice, from large luxury resorts to small family-run guesthouses and camp grounds. Hotels are mainly concentrated around Gosier, Grand-Terre.

Hotel Listings

GRANDE-TERRE

Auberge De La Veille Tour
Montauban, Gosier,
Guadeloupe, FWI.
Tel: 84 23 23.
Fax: 84 33 43
An authentic 18th-century windmill with 104 deluxe rooms set in a 7-acre (3 ha) tropical park overlooking the sea. **$$$**

Price Guide

Price categories are based on the cost of a double room, for one night:
$ = less than $100
$$ = $100–200
$$$ = more than $200.

Hotel La Toubana
Ste Anne, Guadeloupe, FWI.
Tel: 88 25 78.
Fax: 88 38 90.
This hotel offers spectacular vistas of the south coast and offshore island. Surrounded by lush tropical gardens, its 32 intimate cottages feature kitchenettes, terraces, and views. Amenities include a gorgeous pool, a private beach, tennis, and a popular French and creole restaurant. **$**

Les Residences Yucca
Pointes de la Verdure, Gosier,
Guadeloupe, FWI.
Tel: 90 46 46 (La Créole Beach).
Fax: 90 46 66
Part of a group under the same management as the upscale **La Créole Beach**, this popular complex features 100 spacious rooms. Boutiques, restaurants, nightlife, and casino are within easy walking distance. **$$**

BASSE-TERRE

Auberge De La Distillerie
Route de Versailles, Tabanon,
Petit Bourg, Guadeloupe, FWI.
Tel: 94 25 91.
Fax: 94 11 91.
Nestled in the foothills of Basse-Terre between pineapple fields and the rainforest, this country inn sits near the entrance to the Parc National. It has a superb creole restaurant. **$$**

Le Jardin Malanga
L'Hermitage, Trois-Rivières,
Guadeloupe, FWI.
Tel: 92 67 57.
Fax: 92 67 58.
This unique, beautifully renovated 1927 estate house and its three spacious guest houses feature lush gardens and spectacular hillside views of les Saintes. A perfect location, for exploring the famous Chutes du Carbet. **$**

Where to Eat

What to Eat

Guadeloupe's cuisine mirrors its many cultures. The local Creole specialties combine the finesse of French cuisine, the spice of African cookery, and the exoticism of East Indian and Southeast Asian recipes. Fresh seafood appears on most menus. Other specialties are: shellfish, smoked fish, stuffed land crabs, stewed conch, and a variety of curry dishes.

Guadeloupe is considered one of the true culinary capitals of the Caribbean, with some 200 restaurants recommended by the Tourist Office. Some in hotels and others in lovely settings by the sea.

Restaurant Listings

GRANDE-TERRE

Auberge De La Vieille Tour
Gosier.
Tel: 84 23 23
French and Creole specialties and a spectacular view. Open for dinner. **$$$**

Auberge Le Relax
Morne à L'eau.
Tel: 24 87 61.
Creole cuisine. **$$**

Chez Honoré
Anse à la Gourde, St François.
Tel: 88 52 19.
Creole specialties and clawless lobster. Open only at lunchtimes. **$**

Chez Prudence (Folie Plage)
Anse Bertrand.
Tel: 22 11 17.
Creole cuisine. **$–$$**

Le Relais du Moulin
Ste Anne.
Tel: 88 23 96.
Hotel restaurant serving Creole specialties. **$–$$**

BASSE-TERRE

Couleur Caraibe
Route de la Traversée des Mamelles, Pointe-Noire.
Tel: 98 89 59.
Creole cuisine. **$–$$**

Le Karacoli
Deshaies.
Tel: 28 41 17.
Creole cuisine on the beach. Open lunchtimes only. **$–$$**

Restaurant du Domaine de Severin
La Boucan, Ste Rose.
Tel: 28 34 54.
Creole cuisine. **$–$$**

Restaurant du Parc de Valombreuse
Cabout, Petit Bourg.
Tel: 95 50 50.
Creole cuisine. Open lunchtimes only. **$**

Le Ti'Racoon
Parc Zoologique – Route des Deux Mamelles, Bouillante.
Tel: 98 83 52.
French and Creole specialties. **$–$$**

La Touna
Bouillante.
Tel: 98 70 10.
Seafood and fish. Open lunchtimes only. **$**

Outdoor Activities

Excursions

Many tour companies and associations organize excursions on foot, mountain bike, boat, plane, and by coach. Contact:
Guadeloupe Decouverte, Jarry. Tel: 25 20 87.
Emeraude Guadeloupe, St Claude.
Tel: 81 98 28.
Association Des Guides Accompagnateurs De Moyenne Montagne, St Claude.
Tel: 80 24 25.

Golf

For golfing in Guadeloupe, contact **Golf International De St François**, tel: 88 41 87.

Tennis

There are several tennis clubs on Guadeloupe, including:
Ligue De Tennis, tel: 90 90 97.
Marina Tennis Club, Gosier. Tel: 90 82 91.
Centre Lamby Lambert, Gosier. Tel: 90 90 97.

Sailing

Guadeloupe possesses well-equipped marinas that answer the needs of local as well as international sailors:
Marina Du Bas-Du-Fort, Pointe-à-Pitre. Tel: 90 84 85.
Marina De St Francois, tel: 88 47 28.

You can also charter a boat for island and bay-hopping:
Socomeco, tel: 84 32 07.
Marina De Riviere-Sens, tel: 81 77 61.

Stardust Marine, Lagon Bleu, Gosier. Tel: 90 92 02.
Corail Caraibe/Caraibe Catamaran, tel: 90 91 13.
Privilege Vacances, tel: 90 71 89.

Watersports

There are many picturesque and safe bays located throughout the islands of the archipelago.

SURFING

For surfing, contact **Comité Guadeloupéen De Surf**, Ste Anne, tel: 23 10 93.

Windsurfing lessons and equipment are widely available, try:
Sport Away Ecole Natalie Simon, St-François, tel: 88 72 04.
LCS, Ste Anne, tel: 88 15 17.
UCPA, St François, tel: 88 64 80.

SCUBA DIVING

For scuba diving, contact:
Aux Aquanautes Antillais, Plage de Malandure, Bouillante. Tel: 98 87 30.
Tropical Sub, tel: 0590-28 52 67.
Plaisir Plongee Caraibe, Chez Guy and Christian, Pigeon, Bouillante. Tel: 0590-98 82 43.

Waterskiing is available from many sources, including:
AGSN Club, tel: 26 17 47.

Getting Acquainted

Dominica

Dominica is located smack in the middle of the gracefully curving Antillean chain, between Guadeloupe and Martinique. Measuring 15 miles (25 km) wide by 29 miles (46 km) long, Dominica is blessed with the sort of dramatic and breathtaking scenery that comes with mountainous terrain.

Public Holidays

January 1	**New Year's Day**
Easter	**Good Friday**
	Easter Monday
May 1	**Labor Day**
	Whit Monday
August (1st Monday)	**August Monday**
November 3	**Independence Day**
November 4	**Community Service Day**
December 25	**Christmas Day**
December 26	**Boxing Day**

Calendar of Events

Carnival: Monday and Tuesday preceding Ash Wednesday.
Creole Day: October (national costume is worn).

Planning the Trip

Money Matters

The currency is the EC dollar, although US dollars are acceptable in some places. Banking hours are usually Monday–Thursday 8am–3pm, Friday 8am–5pm. Barclays, the Royal Bank of Canada, and the Bank of Nova Scotia are the main commercial banks, all with branches in Roseau. There are several ATMs, including one at the Royal Bank of Canada, Bay Street.
Departure Tax: All visitors who remain in Dominica for more than 24 hours will need to pay a departure tax of EC$30.

TIPPING

A 10 percent service charge will be added to your bill in most restaurants.

Tipping for taxis etc is not required, but is welcome, while airport porters may expect to be tipped.

Tourist Offices Abroad

IN THE US

Dominica Tourist Office, 10 East 21st Street, Suite 600, New York, NY 10010.
Tel: 212-475 7543.

IN THE UK

Dominica High Commission, 1 Collingham Gardens, London SW5 OHW.
Tel: 0171-835 1937.

Website address
http://www.dominica.dm

Practical Tips

Media

There are two local radio stations – DBS and Kairi Radio – and four local weekly newspapers: the *Independent*, the *Mirror*, the *Chronicle*, and the *Tropical Star*.

Postal Service

The main post office is at the Bay Front, Roseau (open 8am–4pm Monday–Friday).

Telephone

The area code is **767**. Cable and Wireless provides the telecommunications service at Mercury House, Hanover Street, Roseau. Phonecards are available from Cable and Wireless and some shops and hotels.

Local Tourist Office

Old Market Square, Roseau (open 8am–6pm Monday–Friday, 9am–1pm Saturday).

Medical Treatment

Princess Margaret Hospital Roseau, tel: 448 2231; there is also a small hospital in Marigot.
Pharmacy: Jolly's, 37 Great George Street, Roseau, tel: 448 3388.

EMERGENCY NUMBER
Police, fire or ambulance: **999**.

Shopping

Look for quality crafts in the Carib territory and in Roseau center.
voltage: 220 volts AC 50 cycles.

Getting Around

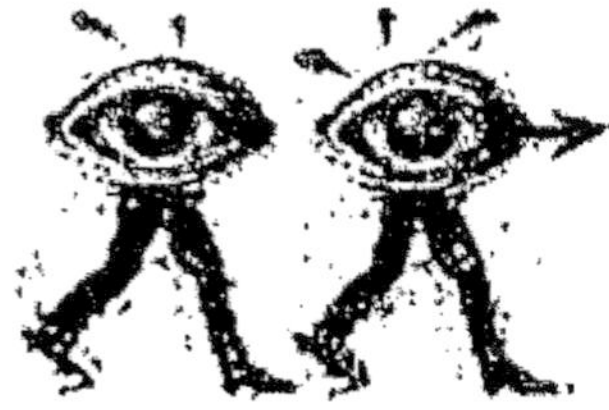

By Car

Driving is on the left-hand side, British style. The speed limit in built-up areas is 20 mph (32 kph). Elsewhere there is no limit. Roads in Dominica are characteristically twisting and narrow, with steep gradients. Road surfaces vary from excellent to pot-holed.

There are various car rental companies in and around Roseau. You need a national or international driver's license and a local visitor's permit. The latter is available from the police traffic department (High Street, Roseau), from the police station or airport, or from your car rental company. Car hire companies include:
Avis, tel: 448 2481.
Budget, tel: 449 2080.

Cars can be picked up at and returned to the airport.

Hitchhiking is possible, but there is usually little traffic in country areas.

By Taxi

Dominica's airport is located near Marigot, on the island's northeast coast. Taxis are available there to take travelers on the long but scenic drive to Roseau, the capital, where many hotels and guesthouses are located.

There are numerous taxi services. On fixed routes the fares are set by the government. Otherwise, settle on a price before you start your journey. Taxis do not cruise the streets and are sometimes difficult to find at night. See the telephone directory or enquire at the tourist office for taxi telephone numbers, or ask your hotel or restaurant to order one.

By Bus

Minibuses are the local form of public transport, from early in the morning to nightfall. They run mainly to and from Roseau. There are no fixed timetables; buses leave when they are full (in Roseau there are various departure points depending on the destination). There are frequent services to villages around Roseau, but making a round trip in one day from Roseau to more remote communities can be a problem. Coming into Roseau in the early morning from towns such as Plymouth or Marigot, and returning at lunchtime or in the afternoon is easier.

Inter-Island Links

There are no direct flights from Europe to Dominica. Connections with Dominica are made with the regional airline, LIAT, from neighboring Caribbean islands, including Antigua, Guadeloupe, and Martinique. American Eagle flies daily from San Juan, Puerto Rico (with connections to North America). The main airport is Melville Hall Airport. Helenair (from St Lucia) and Guadeloupe Air occasionally also use the smaller Canefield Airport, close to Roseau.
Contact numbers:
LIAT, tel: 448 2421.
American Eagle, tel: 445 7204.
Air Guadeloupe, tel: 448 2181.

An efficient ferry service connects Dominica with Guadeloupe (to the north) and Martinique and St Lucia (to the south). It departs from Roseau almost daily. For tickets and information, contact:
Caribbean Express: upstairs in the Whitchurch Center, Roseau. Tel: 448 2181.

Where to Stay

Choosing a Hotel

This selection of hotels offers a range of quality and price in different parts of the island. However, most accommodation is concentrated around Roseau.

Hotel Listings

Anchorage Hotel
PO Box 34, Roseau, Dominica, WI.
Tel: 448 2638.
Fax: 448 5680.
Long-established, family-run hotel, just south of Roseau. **$$**

Cherry Lodge Guesthouse
20 Kennedy Avenue, Roseau, Dominica, WI.
Tel: 448 2366.
Traditional building, with wooden verandah. **$**

D'Auchamps Cottage
PO Box 1889, Roseau, Dominica, WI.
Tel: 448 3346.
Self-catering in a lovely old estate, with delightful garden trails. Near Trafalgar Village. **$$**

Evergreen Hotel
PO Box 309, Roseau, Dominica, WI.
Tel: 448 3288.
Fax: 448 6800.
A family-run hotel on the seafront south of Roseau. **$$**

Floral Gardens
PO Box 192, Concord Village, Dominica, WI.
Tel: 445 7636.
Fax: 445 7333.
One of the few hotels/guest-houses in the northeast. **$$**

Fort Young Hotel
PO Box 519, Roseau, Dominica, WI.
Tel: 448 5000.
Fax: 448 5006.
Dominica's smartest hotel, overlooking the sea, with mainly a business clientèle. Swimming pool; pleasant atmosphere. **$$$**

Papillote Wilderness Retreat
PO Box 2287, Roseau, Dominica, WI.
Tel: 448 2287.
Fax: 448 2285.
Small secluded inn in the rain-forest, with an acclaimed garden. Natural hot-water pools. Close to Trafalgar Falls. **$$**

Petit Coulibri Cottages
PO Box 131, Roseau, Dominica, WI.
Tel/Fax: 446 3150.
Charming, wood and stone loft cottages, in the south, with views across to Martinique. **$$$**

Price Guide

Price categories are based on the cost of a double room, for one night:
$ = less than $100
$$ = $100–200
$$$ = more than $200.

Roxy's Mountain Lodge
PO Box 265, Roseau, Dominica, WI.
Tel: 448 4854.
Family-run guesthouse in the mountain village of Laudat, the starting point for the walk to the Boiling Lake. Popular with back-packers. **$**

Zandoli Inn
PO Box 2099, Roseau, Dominica, WI.
Tel: 446 3361.
Fax: 446 3344.
On the south coast, this new hotel is perched over the Martinique Channel. Delightful design and color schemes, surrounded by a developing arboretum. Plunge pool. **$$–$$$**

Where to Eat

What to Eat

Apart from the hotels and restaurants listed below, all of which serve Creole food using home-grown products, there are many little snack bars all over the place that may (or may not) produce some excellent meals. If you enjoy local Caribbean food, try them. Fresh fruit juices (made with tamarind, guava, sorrel, grapefruit, and so on) are one of the delights of Dominican cuisine, along with specialties such as mountain chicken (a large frog endemic to Dominica); crab backs and *titiri* (fritters made of tiny fish). Other more "down-home" Dominican dishes include saltfish, ground provisions (*dasheen*, yam, sweet potato, cous-cous etc), *callaloo* (young shoots of the *dasheen*) soup. Fruit and vegetables are plentiful: visit the market to see the wonderful range of produce.

Restaurant Listings

Callaloo
King George V Street, Roseau.
Tel: 448 3386.
Upstairs verandah. **$$**

Floral Gardens
Floral Gardens Hotel, Concord.
Tel: 445 7636.
On the banks of the Pagua River. **$$**

La Guiyave
15 Cork Street, Roseau.
Tel: 448 2930.
Lunches only are served on a pleasant verandah overlooking the street. **$$**

La Robe Creole
3 Victoria Street, Roseau.
Tel: 448 2896.
The capital's smartest restaurant with a delicious variety of dishes. **$$$**

The Mousehole
Victoria Street, Roseau.
Snack bar serving lunchtime *rotis*, codfish, and bakes and other local specialties. Adjoining La Robe Creole. **$**

Mango's Bar and Restaurant
Bay Street, Portsmouth.
Tel: 445 3099.
Moderately priced Creole cooking in a yellow and white cottage. **$$**

Price Guide

Price categories are based on the cost of a meal for one person, excluding drinks:
$ = less than $20
$$ = $20–30
$$$ = more than $30.

Papillote Wilderness Retreat
Trafalgar Falls Road.
Tel: 448 2287.
Lovely restaurant overlooking the valley, near the famous Falls. Reservations essential. **$$**

Pearl's Cuisine
King George V Street, Roseau.
Tel: 448 8707.
Hearty helpings; there is also a take away service. **$$**

Olive Lander's
Atkinson.
On the edge of the Carib Territory. Order in advance. **$**

Outdoor Activities

Diving

Skin Diver Magazine wrote that Dominica is "...the undisputed diving capital of the Eastern Caribbean as well as one of the most unusual locations." Features include steep 1000-ft (300-meter) drop-offs, hot springs, pinnacles, and walls. All can be found close to the shore. Dive sites are concentrated along the west coast. There are also **Whale-watching** trips organized by dive shops.

The dive operators offer a variety of packages for both beginners and experienced divers, and also provide accommodation. An annual **Dive Fest** takes place in July, which features diving, kayaking, swimming, fishing, snorkeling, sunset cruises, and other water activities and competitions.

Approved dive operators, who all welcome beginners and also provide snorkeling equipment, include:
Anchorage Dive Center, PO Box 34, Roseau. Tel: 448 2638. Fax: 448 5680.
Cabrits Dive Center, Picard Estate, Portsmouth. Tel: 445 3010. Fax: 445 3011.
Dive Castaways, PO Box 5, Roseau. Tel: 449 6244. Fax: 449 6246.
Dive Dominica, PO Box 2253, Roseau. Tel: 448 2188. Fax: 448 6088.
East Carib Dive, PO Box 375, Roseau. Tel: 449 6575. Fax: 449 6603.
Nature Island Dive, PO Box 2354, Roseau. Tel: 449 8181. Fax: 449 8182.

Good Beaches

The best black sand beaches along the west coast are Castaways, Picard Beach, Douglas Bay, Batalie, and Toucarie. All are safe for swimming. The few white sand beaches (safe inside the coral reef, although watch out for currents) are along the north coast, at Woodford Hill, Turtle Point, and Pointe Baptiste. The sweeping bays on the Atlantic coast are enticing but dangerous.

Horseback Riding

Contact **Greenwood Stables**, Soufrière, tel: 448 7245.

Tennis

Play at the **Castaway Hotel**, St Joseph, and there are courts at the private **Dominica Club**.

Hiking

Hiking in the rainforest in the interior of Dominica is a magnificent experience. Do not ever go hiking alone, always go with a local tour guide. Established tour operators, with good reputations, include:
Ken's Hinterland Adventure Tours and Taxi Service, Khatts. Tel: 448 4850. Fax: 448 8486.
Antours, tel:448 4850. Fax: 448 6088.
Your guesthouse will also recommend reliable guides for either hiking or day tours. Young men from Laudat will offer their services (cheaper than the more established guides) for the arduous hike to the Boiling Lake; take your chances, but many are well-informed. To see the parrots at Syndicate, contact the Forestry Division in the Botanical Gardens, Roseau, tel: 448 2401.

Getting Acquainted

Martinique

Located south of the Tropic of Cancer, Martinique, a French overseas *département*, is a 420-sq mile (1,050-sq km) island belonging to the Windward Islands group in the Lesser Antilles.

Public Holidays

January 1	**New Year's Day**
February	**Carnival** (5 days of jubilation)
Easter	**Easter Sunday**
	Easter Monday
May 22	**Slavery Abolition Day**
July 14	**Bastille Day**
July 21	**Schoelcher Day**
August 15	**Assumption Day**
November 1	**All Saints Day**
November 11	**Armistice Day**
December 25	**Christmas Day**

Calendar of Events

March: International Sailing Week (Fort de France Yacht Club); Foire Exposition (Stade de Dillon Fort de France).
March: Pro-Am Golf Tournament
April: Aqua Festival (Festival of the Sea); Convergences (encounter of the inhabitants of the various "Mornes" or hills belonging to the town of Ajoupa Brouillon); Martinique Tourism Expo: Caribbean Tourism Trade Fair.
May 1–30: Mai of Saint Pierre (festivities in commemoration of the eruption of the Pelee volcano); Caribbean Theatre Festival (organized by National Cultural Centre, CMAC).
June: Jazz at the Leyritz Plantation Estate (Cultural Centre Joseph Zephir, tel: 0596 78 94 67).
July: Fort de France Cultural Festival; International bicycle race; Crayfish Festival in Ajoupa Brouillon.
August: Yawl sailing race around the Island.
October: Pan-Caribbean Golf Tournament.
November: Biennial International Jazz Festival or the International guitar festival (alternate years). Organized by National Cultural Centre (CMAC).
December: Tourism exhibition organized by the regional tourism bureau; Rum Festival, Musée du Rhum, St James Distillery.

Carnival

During the five days of Carnival each day has a special costume theme.
Saturday and Sunday: Free dress.
Monday: Burlesque weddings.
Tuesday: Red devils.
Ash Wednesday: Black and white dress for the funeral of his majesty "Vaval", a huge effigy which people burn in the Bay of Fort-de-France at dusk.

Planning the Trip

Money Matters

The local currency on Martinique is the French franc (Ff), but US dollars (US$) are also accepted at some of the establishments frequented by tourists. Most major credit cards are accepted throughout the island. There are also banks with ATMs.

Tourist Offices Abroad

IN CANADA

Martinique Tourist Office,
2159 rue Mackay, Montreal, Quebec H3G 2J2.
Tel: 514-844 8566.
Fax: 514-844 8901.

Maison de la France,
1981 Ave. McGill College, Suite 490, Montreal PQ 3A2 2W9.
Tel: 514-288 4264.
Fax: 514-845 4868

IN THE UK

Maison de la France,
178 Picadilly, London W1V OAL.
Tel: 0171-629 2869.
Fax: 0171-493 6594.

IN THE US

Martinique Promotion Bureau,
444 Madison Avenue, 16th Floor, New York, NY 10022.
Tel: 212-838 7800.
Fax: 212-838 7855.
Email: Martinique@nyo.com

Website address
http://www.martinique.org

Practical Tips

Media

The daily newspaper is the *France-Antilles. Martinique Info* is a free tourist publication and *Ti Gourmet* lists island eateries. Radio France Outre-Mer (RFO) broadcasts on the radio and TV.

Postal Services

There are post offices in all of the main towns. Hotels, tabacs and other shops also sell stamps.

Telephone and Fax

The area code for Martinique is **596**. Direct-dialed telephone calls can be made from public payphones and hotels. The larger hotels and businesses also have fax facilities. Telegrams, faxes, and phones calls can be made from post offices.

Local Tourist Offices

76 rue Lazare Carnot, 97200 Fort-de-France. Tel: 60 27 73. Fax: 60 27 95.
Maison du Tourism Vert, 9 Boulevard du General de Gaulle, 97200 Fort-de-France.
Tel: 63 18 54. Fax: 70 17 61.

Medical Treatment

There are 18 hospitals and clinics. The best is **La Meynard** in Fort-de-France, many speak English. Dental care is also available.
Medical Emergencies:
SAMU, Hospital Pierre Zobda Quitman (La Meynard), Lamentin. Tel: 75 15 15.

Getting Around

On Arrival

Travelers arriving in Martinique by boat will dock near Fort-de-France, the island's principal town. Air passengers touch down at Lamentin, the airport at Fort-de-France, where both taxis and rental cars are available.

By Car

To rent a car for 20 days or less, your current valid license is all you will need. For longer periods, Martinique requires an international driver's permit. Visiting drivers should have at least one year's driving experience.

Taxis are relatively expensive.

Inter-Island Links

Airlines connecting Martinique to Antigua, Barbados, Dominica, Grenada, Guadeloupe, Puerto Rico, St Lucia, St Martin, St Vincent and Trinidad include:
Air Caraibe, tel: 51 17 27.
Air Saint-Martin, tel: 51 57 03.
Jet Aviation Service, tel: 51 57 03.
Ferries link Martinique to Dominica, Guadeloupe and St Lucia. Contact:
Caribbean Express Des Iles, tel: 63 12 11.

Good Beaches

The best beaches are in the north of the island. In general Atlantic coast swimming is dangerous: Look out for the sign: BAIGNADE DANGEREUSE.

Where to Stay

Choosing a Hotel

Martinique has a wide selection of accommodation to choose from. From vast, upscale resort hotels, the charming, smaller places which form the Relais Créoles group of hotels, to apartments and guesthouses.

Hotel Listings

NORTHERN MARTINIQUE

Bel Air Village
Bourg, 97226 Morne Vert, Martinique, FWI.
Tel: 55 52 94.
Fax: 55 52 97.
A building of four rooms and 12 apartments five minutes from the beach. Recommended for nature lovers. **$–$$**

Brin d'Amour
97220 Trinité, Martinique, FWI.
Tel: 58 53 45.
Fax: 57 45 82.
Creole house and cottages in a large tropical garden. **$–$$**

Habitation Lagrange
97225 Marigot, Martinique, FWI.
Tel: 53 60 60.
Fax: 53 50 58.
Excellent facilities for all the family. **$**

Hotel Baie du Gallion
Pres qu'île de la Caravelle Tartane, 97220 Trinité, Martinique, FWI.
Tel: 58 65 30.
Fax: 58 25 76.
On Caravelle peninsula near numerous bays and coves.**$–$$**

Marouba Club
Le Coin, 97221 Carbet, Martinique, FWI.
Tel: 78 00 21.
Fax: 78 05 65.
Situated in a tropical park on the edge of a beautiful volcanic sand beach. Excellent facilities and activities. **$$–$$$**

Leyritz Plantation
Bourg, 97218 Basse Pointe, Martinique, FWI.
Tel: 78 53 92
Fax:78 92 44
This 18th-century sugar plantation has been restored to charming Creole style. Creole cuisine. **$–$$**

Price Guide

Price categories are based on the cost of a double room, for one night:
$ = less than $100
$$ = $100–200
$$$ = more than $200.

La Sikri Auberge
97214 Lorrain, Martinique, FWI.
Tel: 53 81 00.
Fax: 53 78 73.
Families are welcome in this verdant natural setting. **$**

CENTRAL MARTINIQUE

Batelière
97233 Schoelcher, Martinique, FWI.
Tel: 61 49 49.
Fax: 61 62 29.
Whether you're on holiday or on a business trip, this hotel offers a fine atmosphere for rest and leisure. **$$**

La Malmaison
7 rue de la Liberté, 97200 Fort-de-France, Martinique, FWI.
Tel: 63 90 85.
Fax: 60 03 93.
Pleasant rooms overlooking the Savannah Park garden, and good service. **$$**

SOUTHERN MARTINIQUE

Auberge La Matadore
Anse Mitan, 97229 Les Trois-Ilets, Martinique, FWI.
Tel: 66 05 36.
Fax: 66 07 45.
Located near the marina, this large hotel has comfortable rooms and is renowned for its Creole and French cuisine. **$**

La Dunette
Bourg, 97227 Ste Anne, Martinique, FWI.
Tel: 76 73 90.
Fax: 76 76 05.
Located not far from the prettiest beach on the island, La Dunette overlooks the Diamond Rock. **$**

Fregate Bleu
Quartier Fregate, 97240 François, Martinique, FWI.
Tel: 54 54 66.
Fax: 54 78 48.
Panoramic view of the Atlantic and the islets of François. **$**

Le Manoir de Beauregard
Route des Salines, 97227 Ste Anne, Martinique, FWI.
Tel: 76 73 40.
Fax: 76 93 24.
A splendid 18th-century creole house. **$–$$**

Village du Diamant
Dizac, 97223 Le Diamant, Martinique, FWI.
Tel: 76 41 89.
Fax: 63 53 32.
On one of the most beautiful beaches and a few minutes from the picturesque town of Le Diamant. **$–$$**

Nightlife

Martinique buzzes with life in the evening from casinos and floor shows to discos and bars. Visitors can also choose to listen to the local zouk, jazz or classical music.

Where to Eat

What to Eat

Part of Martinique's French feeling is its celebration of good food. Familiar French dishes are given an unfamiliar twist by the use of tropical fruits, vegetables, and seafood. In addition to French-inspired cooking, visitors will also find plenty of spicy West-Indian specialties. Restaurant hours are usually from noon–3pm and 7–10pm. Most restaurants accept major credit cards.

Price Guide

Price categories are based on the cost of a meal for one person, excluding drinks:
$ = less than $20
$$ = $20–30
$$$ = more than $30.

Restaurant Listings

Auberge de la Sikri
Quartier Etoile, Lorrain.
Tel: 53 81 00.
Creole food served every day from noon except Sunday. **$$**

Le Balaou
Route des Salines, Hammeau de Beauregard-Sainte-Anne.
Tel: 76 75 75.
Open every day for delicious Creole cuisine. **$$**

La Belle Epoque
97, route de Didier, Fort-de-France.
Tel: 64 41 19.
Serves French and Creole food. Closed Saturday noon and Sunday. **$$**

Creole Food

A few examples:
Crabes Farcis: stuffed crabshell with a spicy crab-based stuffing.
Blaff de Poissons ou crustaces (poached fish or shellfish): the ingredients are poached in highly-flavored water containing thyme, parsley, laurel, local chives, and pimento.
Feroce: a mixture made from crushed avocado, codfish, cassava flour with a touch of hot pepper pimento.
Try a "Ti-Punch" aperitif before a meal and a dark rum afterwards.

La Datcha
Plage du Coin, Carbet.
Tel: 78 04 45.
Open every day except Sunday evening. Its specialty is *langoustes dans le vivier* (claw-less lobster). A traditional orchestra plays every Saturday evening. **$$–$$$**

Le Don de la Mer
Bourg de Tartane, Trinité.
Tel: 58 26 85.
Open every day for fish and seafood specialties. **$$**

Le Fromager
Route de Fond Denis, St Pierre.
Tel: 76 19 07.
Serves Creole specialties. **$$**

Le Lagon Bleu
Pont de Plaisance, Marin.
Tel: 74 80 10.
A French, Creole and seafood restaurant. **$$**

Le Marayeur
Pointe des Negres, Fort-de-France.
Tel: 70 19 18.
Try Creole and seafood specialties here. **$$**

Outdoor Activities

Watersports

Popular areas for watersports include Tartane (Trinité), Robert, Schoelcher, and St Pierre. In the south, scuba diving, water skiing, jet skiing, surfing and windsurfing, sailing and canoeing are all available. Contact:
Agi Cat Club, Immeuble Sarde N55, Pointe du Bout, 97229 Les Trois-Ilets. Tel: 66 03 01. Fax: 66 03 24.
Ship Shop, Carenantilles – Ancienne Usine du Marin, 97290 Marin. Tel: 74 70 08. Fax: 74 78 22.
Ursulet Laurent, 97231 Le Robert. Tel: 65 18 18. Fax: 65 00 46.

Diving

Atout Plongée, 46, Plateau Roy, 97233 Schoelcher. Tel: 70 29 33. Fax: 61 21 42.
Club Mediteranée Les Boucanniers, 97227 Ste Anne. Tel: 76 76 74. Fax: 76 72 02.
Mondia Sub Sarl, Pointe la Chery, 97223 Diamant. Tel/Fax: 76 25 80.
Tropical Sub Plongée, La Guinguette, BP 10 Quartier Mouillage, 97250 St Pierre. Tel: 78 38 03. Fax: 52 46 82.

Golf

Martinique Golf and Country Club, 97229 Les Trois-Ilets. Tel: 68 32 81. Fax: 68 38 97.

Tennis

Ligue Régional de Tennis: Petit Manoir, Lamentin. Tel: 51 08 00.

Getting Acquainted

St Lucia

St Lucia lies at the southern end of the Lesser Antilles between Martinique and St Vincent. The island has been independent since 1979, and has a population of some 150,000. The island is 27 miles (43 km) long and 14 miles (22 km) wide. It is volcanic in origin, as can be seen from its hot sulfur springs, mountainous terrain, fertile soil, and the famous peaks of the Pitons.

Public Holidays

January 1–2	**New Year's Celebrations**
February 22	**Independence Day**
March/April	**Easter**
	Good Friday
May 1	**Labour Day**
August 1	**Emancipation Day**
August 30	**Feast of St Rose de Lima**
October 17	**Feast of La Marguérite**
December 13	**National Day**
December 25	**Christmas Day**
December 26	**Boxing Day**

Calendar of Events

February: Carnival (the two days leading up to Ash Wednesday).
April: Festival of Comedy.
May: St Lucia Jazz Festival.
October: Thanksgiving Day; St Lucia Bill Fishing Tournament; Jounnen Kweyol Entenasyonnal (International Creole Day).

Planning the Trip

Money Matters

The currency is the EC dollar, although US dollars are also acceptable in most places. There are foreign exchange facilities in Castries, the National Commercial Bank (NCB) also has a branch at Hewanorra International Airport, open 12.30pm until the last flight leaves.

Departure Tax: All visitors are required to pay EC$27 when leaving the island.

Tourist Offices Abroad

IN CANADA

130 Spadina Avenue, Suite 703
Toronto, Ontario M3V 2L4.
Tel: 416-703 0141
Fax: 416-703 0181

IN THE UK

St Lucia Tourist Board, 421a Finchley Road, London NW3 6HJ.
Tel: 0171-431 3675.
Fax: 0171-431 7920.

IN THE US

St Lucia Tourist Board, 800 Second Ave., Suite 400J, New York 10017.
Tel: 212-867 2951/2950.
Fax: 212-867 2795.

Website address:
http://www.interknowledge.com/st-lucia

Practical Tips

Media

St Lucia's popular newspaper *The Voice* is published three times a week, while *The Star*, the *Crusader*, the *Vanguard*, the *Mirror* and *One Caribbean* are island weeklies.

The hotel and restaurant association produces a half-yearly magazine called *Visions*. Distributed via many hotels, the guide includes restaurant reports and information about coming events.

There are two television channels, Channel 4 and DBS, St Lucia also receives a variety of programs from the USA. Three radio stations, Radio St Lucia, Radio 100 and Radio Caribbean International, broadcast local news and music.

Postal Services

The post office in Castries is in Bridge Street, while most towns have a small post office. In general opening hours are 8.30am–4.30pm Monday–Friday. Some hotels sell stamps and have a limited postal service for guests.

Telephone and Fax

The dialing code for St Lucia is **758**. Long-distance calls can be made and faxes sent from most hotels. However, the service provided at the Cable and Wireless offices (Bridge Street, Castries) is more reliable and cheaper. You can also buy phonecards for public payphones there.

Local Tourist Office

St Lucia Tourist Board: PO Box 221, Pointe Seraphine, Castries. Tel: 452 5968/452 4094.
Fax: 453 1121.
Email: SLUTOUR@candw.lc

Medical Treatment

There is a large hospital, the **Victoria Hospital** (tel: 453 7059), in Castries. There are also several smaller medical facilities in: Soufrière (tel: 459 7258/5001), Dennery (tel: 453 3310) and St Jude's Vieux Fort (tel: 454 6041).

There are a few pharmacies in Castries including one on Gros Islet Highway and another in Gablewoods Shopping Mall.

Emergency Numbers

- **Emergencies:** 999/911.

Shopping

Pointe Seraphine is a modern shopping complex convenient for the cruise ship crowd. It has a selection of duty-free goods including perfume and designer-wear and locally-made arts and crafts. Bustling Castries Market is worth a look, if only to see the tropical fresh fruit and vegetables and St Lucian handicrafts. Gablewoods Mall is open 6 days a week, 9am–9pm.

Voltage: 220 volts, 50 cycles AC and 110 volts, 60 cycles.

Nightlife

Friday night is the time to "Jump-up" at Gros Islet's regular street party. This event, with its loud music and aromatic food stalls is popular with locals and tourists. Most of the hotels provide live entertainment for guests. There are also some nightclubs and bars in Castries and Rodney Bay.

Getting Around

By Taxi

Taxis are available at Hewanorra International Airport in the south and Vigie Airport, near Castries. Most hotels lie in the northwest of the island; so if you land at Hewanorra, you can expect a long, albeit picturesque, journey. Always agree the fare before starting your journey.

By Car

Drive on the left. Visiting drivers must obtain a temporary driving permit, valid for three months, by presenting a current driving license at the police station (Bridge Street, Castries), or car rental company, with a small fee of around EC$20. Car rentals:
Avis, tel: 451 6976.
Budget, tel: 452 0233.
Cool Breeze Jeep-Car Rental, tel: 454 7898.
Hertz, tel: 452 0680.

By Bus

Traveling on the bus in St Lucia is cheap and it can be fun. Minibuses run to and from the main towns throughout the day, but are less reliable at night.

Inter-Island Links

LIAT flights from Vigie Airport connect St Lucia to islands including Antigua, Dominica, Grenada, Barbados, St Kitts and Nevis, St Vincent and Trinidad. There is also a high-speed catamaran service, Caribbean Express, to Martinique, Guadeloupe and Dominica.

Where to Stay

Choosing a Hotel

St Lucia has a wide choice of accommodation, from vast all-inclusive resorts and luxury hotels, to intimate inns and guesthouses.

Hotel Listings

Anse Chastanet
PO Box 700, Soufrière, St Lucia, WI.
Tel/Fax: 459 7700.
Comfortable hotel in a romantic location. Situated on a picturesque hillside directly above a dark grey palm-fringed beach. Comprehensive diving facilities. **$$$**

Price Guide

Price categories are based on the cost of a double room, for one night:
$ = less than $100
$$ = $100–200
$$$ = more than $200.

Glencastle Resort
PO Box 143, Castries, St Lucia, WI.
Tel: 450 0833.
Fax: 450 0837.
Small, attractive resort in the hills above Rodney Bay. **$**

Green Parrot Inn
Castries, The Morne, St Lucia, WI.
Tel: 452 3399.
Fax: 453 2272.
Comfortable rooms in a practical hotel situated about 3 miles (5 km) outside the main town of Castries. **$–$$**

Hummingbird Beach Resort
PO Box 280, Soufrière, St Lucia, WI.
Tel: 459 7232.
Fax: 459 7033.
Friendly little beach hotel with attractively furnished rooms. **$$–$$$**

The Islander Hotel
PO Box 907, Gros Islet, Reduit Beach, St Lucia, WI.
Tel: 452 0255.
Fax: 452 0958.
Practical hotel near the beach. Friendly service. **$$**

Jalousie Hilton Resort & Spa
PO Box 251, Soufrière, St Lucia, WI.
Tel: 459 7666
Fax: 459 7667
Luxury hotel in the Pitons, with sports facilities and its own helicopter pad. **$$$**

Marigot Bay Resort
PO Box 101, Marigot Bay, St Lucia, WI.
Tel: 451 4356.
Fax: 451 4353.
Dependable little hotel complex in an idyllic location. **$$–$$$**

Royal St Lucian
PO Box 977, Gros Islet, Reduit Beach, St Lucia, WI.
Tel: 452 9999.
Fax: 452 9639.
Luxury resort with lots of amenities including a spa. **$$$**

The Still Plantation & Beach Resort
PO Box 246, Soufrière, St Lucia, WI.
Tel: 459 7224.
Fax: 459 7301.
Generously sized studios on the lovely beach at Soufrière. **$–$$**

Fox Grove Inn
Mon Repos Post Office, Micoud, St Lucia, WI.
Tel/Fax: 454 0271.
Pretty 12-room hotel on the Atlantic coast, well away from the bustle. Ideal for nature-loving holiday-makers. **$**

Where to Eat

What to Eat

The specialties of St Lucia include pumpkin soup and soufflé, flying fish, *poile dudon* (a chicken dish), pepperpot, green fig (banana) and saltfish, conch and *tablette* (a sweetmeat made of coconut).

Restaurant Listings

Capone's
Rodney Bay.
Tel: 452 0284.
Italian cuisine with a Caribbean accent. Inexpensive take-out available. **$$–$$$**

The Charthouse
Rodney Bay.
Tel: 452 8115.
Crayfish and steaks from the grill, served on the waterfront. **$$–$$$**

Chez Paul (Formerly Rain)
next to Derek Walcott Square, Castries.
Tel: 451 3111.
Sophisticated French-Creole cuisine, sometimes with an Asian influence. **$$–$$$**

Coal Pot
Vigie Marina, Castries.
Tel: 452 6811.
International and Caribbean specialties from a French chef. **$$**

Dasheene Restaurant and Bar
Soufrière, Ladera Resort.
Tel: 459 7323.
Sophisticated blend of international and Creole cuisine. Dining with a wonderful mountainside view. **$$–$$$**

Ginger Lily
Rodney Bay.
Tel: 452 8303.
Varied Chinese cuisine. **$–$$**

The Great House Restaurant
Cap Estate.
Tel: 450 0450.
French-Creole specialties in an elegant plantation house. **$$$**

Jimmie's
Vigie Cove, Castries.
Tel: 452 5142.
Delicious West Indian cuisine. Fish specialties. **$$–$$$**

The Lime Restaurant
Rodney Bay.
Tel: 452 8351.
Three establishments under one roof. Thai-Indian tandoori cuisine in the "Oriental", grilled steaks and fish in "Mariners", and coffee, cake and ice cream in the "Quarterdeck". Live music on Monday. **$–$$**

Price Guide

Price categories are based on the cost of a meal for one person, excluding drinks:
$ = less than $20
$$ = $20–30
$$$ = more than $30.

The Marina Steakhouse
Rodney Bay, Gros Islet Highway.
Tel: 452 9800.
Steaks and fish. Live music on Friday evening. **$$–$$$**

Peppino's Pizza
Bridge Street, Castries.
Tel: 452 3942.
Pizza, pasta, and burgers. **$**

Outdoor Activities

Watersports

There many places offering watersports on the island from sailing, surfing and waterskiing to diving and deep-sea fishing.

SAILING

Visitors can choose a yacht or boat charter, crewed or bareboat, and sail to nearby islands. Most charter companies are based in Marigot Bay and Rodney Bay. For more details contact:
Moorings St Lucia, Marigot Bay. Tel: 451 4357.
Sun Sail Stevens, Rodney Bay. Tel: 452 8648.

FISHING

For deep-sea fishing, contact:
Reel Affair, tel: 452 5117.
Captain Mike, tel: 452 7044.

DIVING

For diving and snorkeling, try:
Anse Chastanet Dive Centre, tel: 459 1354.

Horseback Riding

Visitors can tour the island on horseback, along the beaches or through St Lucia's lush countryside. Contact:
International Riding Stables, Gros Islet, tel: 452 8139.
Trims Riding School, Cas en Bas, tel: 452 8273.

Golf

There are two courses on the island, a public one at the Cap Estate (tel: 450 8523) and a private one at the Sandals St Lucia Resort (tel: 452 3081).

Getting Acquainted

St Vincent and the Grenadines

At the bottom of the Antillean curve, near St Lucia, Barbados, and Grenada, is an 18 by 11-mile (30 by 18-km) island, with a chain of 32 islets to the south. This is St Vincent and the Grenadines. St Vincent – the large island – is mountainous, with volcanic ridges rising to over 4,000 ft (1,200 meters). The Grenadines – varying in size from 7 sq. miles (18 sq. km) to mere dots in the ocean – have terrain both mountainous and flat, surrounded by glistening sand and clear waters.

Public Holidays

January 1	**New Year's Day**
January 22	**St Vincent and the Grenadines Day**
March/April Easter	**Good Friday**
	Easter Monday
	Whit Monday
July 7	**Caricom Day**
July (early)	**Carnival Tuesday**
August (1st Monday)	**August Monday**
October 27	**Independence Day**
December 25	**Christmas Day**
December 26	**Boxing Day**

Calendar of Events

Easter: Bequia Regatta, boat races and festivities on Bequia; Easterval, a weekend of music, culture and boat races on Union Island.
July: Carnival.
Late July/early August: Canouan Yacht Races and festivities.
Late November: Petit St Vincent Yacht Races and evening festivities.
December 16–24: Nine Mornings parades and dances in the days leading up to Christmas.

Island Events

"Vincy Mas", St Vincent's Carnival, is held during the first two weeks of July. Twelve days of calypso and steel pan music culminate in a vibrant, colorful, costumed party. Over the Easter weekend the Bequia Regatta attracts locals and visitors alike who all congregate to show off both their sailing skills and their ability to "party hearty".

Planning the Trip

Money Matters

The currency is the EC dollar. It is tied to the US dollar. US dollars can be used in most places, and major credit cards are acceptable in most hotels, restaurants, and car rental agencies, but check first. In restaurants and hotels the standard service charge is 10 percent. Where no service charge has been added, a tip of 10 percent is appreciated.

Major international banks with local branches include Barclays in Kingstown (tel: 456 1706), another branch in Bequia, and CIBC in Kingstown (tel: 457 2873).

Departure Tax: There is a departure tax of EC$20.

Tourist Offices Abroad

IN THE UK

10 Kensington Court, London W8 5DL. Tel: 0171-937 6570.

IN THE US

801 Second Avenue, New York, NY 10017. Tel 212-687 4981.

IN CANADA

Suite 504, 1000 University Avenue, Toronto, Ontario M5J 1V6. Tel: 416-924 5796.

Website address:
http://www.vincy.com/

Practical Tips

Media

The Vincentian and *The News* are the islands two newspapers. The tourist board distributes two free magazines packed with information for visitors: *Discover St Vincent & The Grenadines* and the *Escape Tourist Guide*.

Postal Services

The post office in Kingstown is on Halifax Street. The opening hours are 8.30am–3pm Monday–Friday, 8.30–11.30am Saturday.

Telephone, Fax and Telex

The area code is **784**. The most dependable way to place long-distance calls, telegrams, and telexes is to go to a Cable and Wireless office in Kingstown, you'll find it on Halifax Street. There are other branches elsewhere on St Vincent. If your hotel isn't near a Cable and Wireless office, your hotel may be able to handle some of your communication needs.

Local Tourist Offices

The main office is:
St Vincent and Grenadines Department of Tourism, Finance Complex, Bay Street, Kingstown, St Vincent. Tel: 457 1502.
There are also branches at the E. T. Joshua Airport, tel: 458 4685; on Bequia, tel: 458 3286 and Union Island, tel: 458 3286.

Medical Treatment

There are four hospitals on St Vincent: two in Kingstown (one with a dental clinic), one in Georgetown, and another in Chateaubelair. There is also a medical facility on Bequia. Clinics are also located on the other smaller islands of the Grenadines.

Useful Numbers

Emergency police, fire, ambulance: 999.
Kingstown General Hospital: 456 1185.
Bequia Hospital: 458 3294.

Shopping

St Vincent and Bequia are good places to find colorful batiks and lots of locally made art and crafts, such as straw baskets and wood carvings.

Voltage: 220 volts, 50 cycles.

Good Beaches

Throughout the islands of the Grenadines there are a multitude of exceptional white sand beaches, often tucked away in scenic, secluded bays. Most of the beaches on St Vincent are of the black sand, volcanic type, though these can still be very beautiful. There are a number of light sand beaches in the area of Villa. As with many other Caribbean islands, swimming on the Windward Atlantic coast is not recommended. Windwhipped waves and craggy rocks make for excellent viewing, but can endanger the swimmer. All of St Vincent's beaches are public. If the route to a beach leads over private land, though, make sure you ask the owner before crossing.

Getting Around

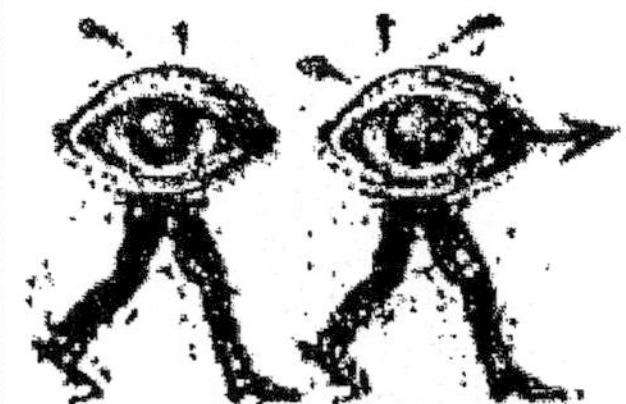

By Car

Driving is on the left, British style. You will need an international license, or failing that, for a moderate fee you can purchase a local license at the Police Station in Bay Street, Kingstown, or the Licensing Authority in Halifax Street.
Rental companies include:
Hertz, Kingstown. Tel: 456 1743.
Unico Rentals, Arnos Vale Airport. Tel: 456 5744.

By Taxi

Flights arrive at St Vincent's E.T. Joshua Airport, where there are plenty of taxis to take you to your destination. Taxis and minibuses are also available on Bequia and Union Island. There are fixed tariffs for journeys; but check the price before you start.

By Bus

Local buses on St Vincent and the Grenadines tend to be both busy and noisy, but they are also cheap and run reasonably frequently.

Island Tours

There are different ways to tour the island of St Vincent and Bequia too. Contact:
Fantasea Tours, tel: 457 4477.
Baleine Tours, tel: 457 4089.
Sailors Bicycle Tours, tel: 457 1712.
Sam's Taxi Tours, tel: 456 4338.

Inter-Island Links

St Vincent is linked by air with other Caribbean islands including Barbados, Trinidad, St Lucia, Martinique, and Grenada. Petit St Vincent, Palm Island and exclusive Mustique, all private islands, are also accessible with permission.

Short trips throughout the islands of the Grenadines – Bequia, Union Island, Canouan and Mayreau – are readily available and usually very enjoyable. Generally speaking, boat trips tend to be the best option as they are usually easy and more economical. There are a number of inexpensive ferries and a mail boat that ply the local waters each week. Schedules can be erratic, so check carefully for departure times, the local tourist office can help plan the trip; also contact:

Admiralty Transport: Port Elizabeth, Bequia. Tel: 458 3348.

If you prefer to island-hop by air, the following airlines have services:

LIAT, tel: 457 1821.
SVG Air, tel: 456 5610.
Mustique Airways, tel: 458 4380.

Where to Stay

Choosing a Hotel

Apart from St Vincent and Bequia three islands are given over entirely to upscale holiday resort developments: Young Island, just 200 yds (183 meters) off St Vincent's shore, and Palm Island and Petit St Vincent in the Grenadines.

Hotel Listings

ST VINCENT

Beachcombers Villa
PO Box 126, Villa, St Vincent, WI.
Tel: 458 4283.
Fax: 458 4385.
Individual, small cottages pleasantly sited on the beach at Villa. **$$**

Cobblestone Inn
PO Box 867, Upper Bay Street, Kingstown, St Vincent, WI.
Tel: 456 1937.
Fax: 456 1938.
Housed in an early 19th-century arrowroot warehouse, this quiet town hotel has two restaurants, including one on the roof. **$$**

Haddon Hotel
McKies Hill, PO Box 144, Kingstown, St Vincent, WI.
Tel: 456 1897.
Fax: 456 2726.
In town, 10 minutes' drive from the beach, with air-conditioned rooms with TV and tennis. **$**

Sunset Shores
PO Box 849, Villa, St Vincent, WI.
Tel: 458 4411.
Fax: 457 4800.
On the beach, with pool and air-conditioned rooms. A 10-minute drive from Kingstown. **$$**

Umbrella Beach Hotel
Villa, St Vincent, WI.
Tel: 458 4561.
Fax: 457 4930.
Basic but clean and quaint accommodation on the beach opposite Young Island. **$**

Young Island Resort
PO Box 211, St Vincent, WI.
Tel: 458 4826.
Fax: 457 4567.
Exclusive, luxurious resort situated on its own small private island. **$$$**

Price Guide

Price categories are based on the cost of a double room, for one night:
$ = less than $100
$$ = $100–200
$$$ = more than $200.

BEQUIA

Bequia Beach Club
Friendship Bay, Bequia, St Vincent and the Grenadines, WI.
Tel: 458 3248.
Fax: 458 3689.
Small hotel with watersports facilities. **$$**

Frangipani
Bequia, St Vincent and the Grenadines, WI.
Tel: 458 3255.
Fax: 458 3824.
Simple accommodation in a seafaring setting, housed in an old chandlery. The rooms are tastefully decorated and the hotel bar is a popular place to stop for a drink. **$–$$**

Gingerbread Apartments
PO Box 1, Bequia, St Vincent and the Grenadines, WI.
Tel: 458 3300.
Fax: 458 3907.
One-room apartments with kitchen and bathroom. Restaurant, bar, and friendly owners. **$$**

OTHER GRENADINES ISLANDS

Canouan Beach Hotel
PO Box 530, Kingstown, St Vincent and the Grenadines, WI.
Tel: 458 8888.
Fax: 458 8875.
Luxury accommodation on the beach on Canouan in cottages and rooms in the main building.
$$$

Firefly Guesthouse
PO Box 340, Kingstown, St Vincent and the Grenadines, WI.
Tel: 456 3514.
Tiny informal, but elegant hotel, in a lovely position on Mustique. Book well in advance. **$$$**

Palm Island Beach Club
Palm Island, St Vincent and the Grenadines, WI.
Tel: 458 8824.
Fax: 458 8804.
All-inclusive type of resort on a private island surrounded by white sand beach. Watersports, sailing. **$$$**

Petit St Vincent (PSV)
Petit St Vincent, St Vincent and the Grenadines, WI.
Tel: 458 8801.
Fax: 458 8428.
A delightful resort hideaway where peace and privacy are the order of the day. **$$$**

Where to Eat

What to Eat

Spicy West Indian cuisine predominates with continental and American fare also available. A wide variety of exotic fruits and vegetables, along with an abundance of succulent lobster and other fresh seafood, enrich St Vincent's cooking. Try something unusual – barbecued goat or fresh shark, for example.

Restaurant Listings

ST VINCENT

Beachcomber Bar and Restaurant
Villa Beach.
Tel: 458 4283.
Casual ambience with good simple food and open-air dining on the beach. **$–$$**

Bounty
Egmont Street, Kingstown.
Tel: 456 1776.
Snacks and sandwiches at the place where locals go for their lunch. **$**

Price Guide

Price categories are based on the cost of a meal for one person, excluding drinks:
$ = less than $20
$$ = $20–30
$$$ = more than $30.

Cobblestone Inn
Upper Bay Street, Kingstown.
Tel: 456 1937.
Rooftop restaurant serving West Indian food and hamburgers. **$$**

Dolphins
Villa Beach.
Tel: 457 4337.
Local paintings on display. **$$**

French Restaurant
Villa Beach.
Tel: 458 4972.
Classic French cuisine with a West Indian twist. Popular with visitors. **$$$**

Juliette's
Middle Street, Kingstown.
Tel: 457 1645.
Simple food in town. **$**

BEQUIA

Whalebone Inn
Port Elizabeth.
Tel: 458 3233.
West Indian food with an emphasis on seafood, in an atmospheric setting. **$$**

Daphne's
Port Elizabeth.
Tel: 458 3271.
Creole meals to eat in or take away. **$**

MUSTIQUE

Basil's Bar
Britannia Bay.
Tel: 458 4621.
Famous bar built over the water and a haunt of the rich and famous. Good seafood dishes.
$$$

Outdoor Activities

Diving

With abundant coral reefs and excellent visibility, the Grenadines offer first-rate diving conditions. Divers will find a wide range of sponges, corals, fish, exciting marine life, and a number of sunken wrecks. Divers of all levels can be accommodated.

Dive operators in St Vincent and the Grenadines include:
Dive St Vincent, PO Box 864. Tel: 457 4928.
Bequia Dive Resort, Friendship Bay. Tel: 458 3248.
Dive Canouan, Tamarind Beach Hotel. Tel: 458 8851.
Dive Mustique, Cotton House Hotel. Tel: 458 4777.
Grenadines Dive, Union Island. Tel: 458 8138.

Sailing

The following companies can organize bareboat sailing or a yacht with a crew:
Barefoot Yacht Charters, PO Box 39, St Vincent. Tel: 456 9526.
Caribbean Sailing Yachts, PO Box 133, St Vincent. Tel: 458 4308.
ATM Yachts, Union Island. Tel: 458 8581.
Passion Day Charters, Bequia. Tel: 458 3884.

Watersports

For other watersports, contact:
Mariners Watersports, PO Box 639, St Vincent. Tel: 458 4228.
Mustique Watersports, Mustique Company. Tel: 456 4777.

Getting Acquainted

Grenada

Grenada is the most southerly of the Windward Islands, lying toward the bottom of the Lesser Antilles chain. The island is volcanic and mountainous, the highest point, Mount St Catherine, reaching 2,755 ft (840 meters). Two other, smaller, islands are dependent territories: Carriacou and Petit Martinique.

Public Holidays

January 1	**New Year's Day**
February 7	**Independence Day**
March/April Easter	**Good Friday** **Easter Monday**
May 1	**Labor Day**
June	**Corpus Christi**
August (1st Monday/Tuesday)	**Emancipation Days**
August	**Carnival**
October 25	**Thanksgiving**
December 25	**Christmas Day**
December 26	**Boxing Day**

Calendar of Events

January: The Spice Island Fishing Tournament is held at the end of the month.
June: Fisherman's Birthday is celebrated in Gouyave at the end of the month.
August: The first weekend is the Carriacou Regatta; the 2nd weekend in August is Carnival time in Grenada.

Planning the Trip

Money Matters

The currency is the East Caribbean (EC) dollar. US dollars are also widely accepted in the island. Banks are open from 8am–2pm Monday–Thursday, 8am–5pm on Friday. They close for lunch 1pm–2.30pm. Most banks are in St George's, but there are branches in Grenville, Gouyave, Sauteurs, and Carriacou.
Departure Tax: There is a departure tax of EC$35 (EC$17.50 for children between 5 and 12) payable at the airport. Infants are not subject to this tax.

Tourist Offices Abroad

IN CANADA

Grenada Tourism Office, 439 University Avenue, Ontario M5G 1Y8. Tel: 416-595 1339.

IN THE UK

Grenada Tourism Office, 1 Collingham Gardens, Earls Court, London SW5 0HW. Tel: 0171-370 5164.

IN THE US

Grenada Tourism Office, 820 Second Avenue, Suite 900D, New York, NY 10017. Tel: 212-687 9554.

Website address:
http://www.interknowlege.com/grenada

Practical Tips

Media

Weekly newspapers include *Grenadian Voice*, the *Informer*, and *Grenada Guardian*, dealing with local politics and scandal. US papers are available in hotel shops and at Sea Change bookstore on the Carenage. There are four local radio stations and two TV stations, and satellite TV is widespread. Cable TV is being installed.

Postal Services

The main post office is on Lagoon Road (south of Carenage), St George's (open 8am–3.30pm Monday–Thursday, 8am–4.30pm Friday). Some villages have sub-post offices.

Telephone and Fax

The area code is **473**. International calls, faxes, and telexes can be made from the Cable and Wireless offices on the Carenage (open 7am–7pm Mon–Sat, 4pm–6pm Sun). Grenada has direct-dial services and credit card calls can be made to Europe and North America via AT&T.

Local Tourist Office

Grenada Board of Tourism: The Carenage, St George's. Tel: 440 2279.

Medical Treatment

There is a general hospital in St George's (tel: 440 2051), and smaller hospitals can be found in both Mirabeau (east coast) and Carriacou. Ask at your hotel for a recommended doctor or dentist.

Emergency Number

Police, fire, ambulance: 911.

Shopping

Among the better craft and souvenir shops in St George's is **Yellow Poui Art Gallery** (Cross Street). Local specialties include batik and screen-printed items, jewelry, and attractive spice baskets. Spices and oils are available from **Arawak Island factory** (Upper Belmont Road, tel: 440 4577).

Voltage: 220/240 volts, AC 50 cycles.

Good Beaches

Some of the best are conveniently close to St George's: Grand Anse, Morne Rouge, and Lance aux Epines. Less popular and wilder (beware of the currents) are Levera and La Sagesse.

Getting Around

By Car

Driving is on the left. Roads are sometimes in poor condition, especially in the mountains. Drivers must be over 21 and have a valid license as well as a local permit (available from the central police station). There is a good choice of rental firms, but cars are sometimes difficult to obtain, particularly in high season and during Carnival. Hire companies include:

Avis, tel: 440 3936.
Budget, tel: 440 2778.
McIntyre Bros Ltd, tel: 440 2044.
Tropicana Rentals, tel: 444 8849.
Y&R Rentals, tel: 444 4448.

In Carriacou

Martin Bullen, tel: 443 7204.

By Taxi

Taxis are available at the airport, the Carenage, and outside most hotels. They are not metered and there are no fixed charges, so it is advisable to establish the fare with the driver before setting off. Taxi-drivers can normally be hired by the hour or day for sightseeing tours of the island. Allow most of a day for a tour of Grenada.

By Bus

There are bus services around the coastal roads to St George's, but Grenada's buses are normally very crowded and travel much too fast for many visitors' comfort.

By Bicycle

Bicycles can be hired from **Ride Grenada** (tel: 444 1157). The island's mountainous terrain, tropical climate, and sometimes erratic road conditions should be borne in mind if visitors plan to tour the island on two wheels.

Inter-Island Links

LIAT and Airlines of Carriacou connect Grenada with Carriacou (6–8 flights daily). LIAT also provides services to all Eastern Caribbean destinations.
LIAT, tel: 440 2796.
Airlines of Carriacou, tel: 440 2898.

Carriacou can also be reached by schooners, most of which depart in the morning from the Carenage, returning the following day. The journey takes about four hours; refreshments are available accompanied by very loud music. Check with your hotel for sailing times and fares.

Where to Stay

Choosing a Hotel

Most of Grenada's more expensive hotels are dotted around the southern tip of the island, especially along the Grand Anse beach. Guesthouses tend to be fairly rudimentary (as reflected in their prices), and there are also plenty of holiday apartments, designed for self-catering. Detailed information and price lists are available from Grenada Board of Tourism.

Hotel Listings

Blue Horizons Cottage Hotel
PO Box 41, St George's, Grenada, WI.
Tel: 444 4316.
Fax: 444 2815.
Cottage-style buildings scattered around attractive grounds, with one of the island's best restaurants, La Belle Creole, attached. Residents are entitled to use the beachside facilities of Spice Island Resort. **$$**

The Calabash
PO Box 382, St George's, Grenada, WI.
Tel: 444 4334.
The most prestigious hotel in Grenada set in beautiful gardens of calabash (gourd) trees just outside St George's at L'Anse aux Epines. All the suites have balconies and several have their own private pools. **$$$**

Coyaba Beach Resort
PO Box 336, Grand Anse, St George's, Grenada, WI.
Tel: 444 4129.
Fax: 444 4808.
An attractive setting next to Grand Anse beach. Relatively small in comparison to the less intimate all-inclusives, but with a good range of facilities including watersports and a pool bar. **$$**

Rex Grenadian
PO Box 893, Point Salines, St George's, Grenada, WI.
Tel: 444 3333.
Fax: 444 1111.
Grenada's biggest hotel, only a few years old it has two beaches and four restaurants as well as 212 rooms. Plenty of amenities, but perhaps lacking in intimacy. **$$**

La Sagesse Nature Centre
PO Box 44, St George's, Grenada, WI.
Tel: 444 6458.
Fax: 444 6458.
Located in St David's, well away from the tourist strip, this is a charmingly informal and small guesthouse, situated on a spectacular beach. Good food and a relaxed atmosphere in its beachside restaurant. It is some distance from St George's. **$**

Price Guide

Price categories are based on the cost of a double room, for one night:
$ = less than $100
$$ = $100–200
$$$ = more than $200.

La Source
PO Box 852, Pointe Salines, St George's, Grenada, WI.
Tel: 444 2556.
Fax: 444 2561.
All-inclusive beach resort spa, with an emphasis on sports and fitness facilities. Services range from scuba diving to a salt loofah rub. **$$$**

Spice Island Beach Resort
PO Box 6, Grand Anse, St George's, Grenada, WI.
Tel: 444-4258.
Fax: 444-4807.
Beautiful beach location, some rooms with private pool. All-inclusive terms available. Ideal for watersports and swimming, but not for visitors on a tight budget. **$$$**

St Anne's Guesthouse
Paddock, St George's, Grenada, WI.
Tel: 440 2717.
Inexpensive and very friendly, a no-frills guesthouse in a pleasant suburban area. Excellent food on request, but don't expect air conditioning or a pool. **$**

CARRIACOU

Silver Beach Resort
Hillsborough, Carriacou, WI.
Tel: 443 7337.
Fax: 443 7165.
Small and relaxed hotel, situated on an idyllic grey sandy beach. Self-catering is an option or you can eat in the very good restaurant that specializes in seafood. **$**

Carriacou Regatta

The climax of Grenada's yachting year is the Carriacou Regatta, now a huge festival that involves not only local boats and boat-building skills, but parties, parades and much jollity. It is essential to book accommodation well in advance.

Where to Eat

What to Eat

Grenada's mixed colonial past has endowed the island with an interesting mix of British and French influences. Inevitably, the emphasis tends to be on seafood, but there are many local delicacies worth sampling. Callaloo soup (made from dasheen leaves, rather like spinach) is excellent, as are traditional pepperpot (a stew of almost every possible ingredient) and *lambi* (conch). Exotic game sometimes appears on tourist menus, although some may prefer not to experiment with armadillo, iguana, or manicou. Spices, especially nutmeg, are another favorite, delicious in rum punches.

Restaurant Listings

Coconut Beach
Grand Anse.
Tel: 444 4644.
Excellent French-Creole cooking with occasional live music in a beachside setting. **$$**

Price Guide

Price categories are based on the cost of a meal for one person, excluding drinks:
$ = less than $20
$$ = $20–30
$$$ = more than $30.

Mamma's
Lagoon Road.
Tel: 440-1459.
A culinary experience, the menu features iguana and other esoteric dishes. Not cheap and the service is sometimes less than perfect, but the meal is usually memorable. **$$**

Morne Fendue Plantation House
St Patrick's.
Tel: 442 9330.
One of Grenada's institutions and a small piece of history. Serves lunch only. It is essential to reserve ahead. **$$**

Nutmeg
Carenage, St George's.
Tel: 440 2539.
A great place for lunch, overlooking the town's harbor and serving simple food and deservedly famous rum punches. **$**

Southwinds
Grand Anse.
Tel: 444 4310.
Upmarket seafood restaurant, situated on a hill with lovely sea views. **$$–$$$**

Tropicana
Lagoon Road.
Tel: 440-1586.
Popular with locals, this restaurant has a covered patio and offers large portions of Chinese as well as local food. Barbecues at weekends and plenty of loud music. **$**

Outdoor Activities

Diving

Grenada and Carriacou offer a good range of diving sites, including the wreck of the *Bianca C*, which sank in 1961 outside St George's, and some spectacular reefs. Grand Anse beach has dive companies, as does Carriacou. Contact:
Dive Grenada, tel: 444 1092.
Scuba World, tel: 444 3333.
Carriacou Silver Diving, tel: 443 7882.

Watersports

Windsurfing and waterskiing facilities are available on Grand Anse beach. The Secret Harbour Hotel hires snorkeling equipment and also organizes windsurfing, yacht charters, and speedboat outings. Grenada has marinas and sheltered harbors. Contact:
Grenada Yacht Services, tel: 440 2508.
Spice Island Marina, tel: 444 4257.
Moorings' Club, tel: 444 4439.

FISHING

Grenada Yacht Services (tel: 440 2508) can organize deep-sea fishing expeditions.

Tennis

The larger hotels have tennis courts and allow non-residents to hire facilities. There is a public court at Grand Anse.

Horseback Riding

Contact **The Horseman** (tel: 440 5368) for lessons or trail riding.

Getting Acquainted

Barbados

Barbados lies 100 miles (160 km) east of the Antillean curve, at about the same latitude as St Vincent. This 21 by 14-mile (33 by 22-km) coral limestone island is divided into 11 parishes and has a population of 260,000, enjoying one of the Caribbean's highest standards of living.

Public Holidays

January 1	**New Year's Day**
January 21	**Errol Barrow Day**
March/April	
Easter	**Good Friday**
	Easter Monday
May 1	**Labor Day**
	Whit Monday
August (1st Monday)	**Kadooment Day**
October (1st Monday)	**United Nations Day**
November 30	**Independence Day**
December 25	**Christmas Day**
December 26	**Boxing Day**

Calendar of Events

January: Windsurfing championships; jazz festival; the regional cricket series.
February: The Holetown Festival.
Easter: Holder's Opera Season.
April: Oistins Fish Festival; Congaline street festival.
May: Gospelfest; Celtic Festival.
June: The Mount Gay International Regatta.
July: Crop Over festival begins.
November: Sir Garfield Sobers Seniors Cricket Festival; the Independence Classic Surfing Championship; the NIFCA (National Independence Festival of Creative Arts) cultural events.
December: Run Barbados, the island's marathon; the United Insurance Barbados Golf Open.

Celebrations

The highlight of Barbados's cultural year is the Crop Over Festival celebrating the end of the sugar cane harvest, which starts on the first Saturday of July and continues for 5 weeks. Top calypso and soca artistes compete in the Pic-o-de-Crop contest, and there is a lot of dancing and parading through the streets ending with Kadooment Day on the first Monday in August, when everyone dresses up in Carnival costumes and the festivities reach their climax.

Planning the Trip

Money Matters

The currency is the Barbados dollar at BDS$2 for US$1. US dollars are also widely accepted and goods are often labeled with a price in US dollars, so check which currency is being quoted before making a transaction. It is not permitted to export BDS dollars.

Money can be changed at banks and hotel reception desks. Travelers' checks in US dollars and all major credit cards (Visa, MasterCard, and American Express) are widely accepted.

Automatic Teller Machines (ATMs) are available in most banks around the island. Banks are open from 8am–2pm Monday–Thursday; 8am–1pm, 3–5pm Friday.

VAT at 15 percent is added to most goods and services, so always check to see whether or not the price includes VAT. The rate is 7.5 percent on hotel accommodation.

Restaurants and hotels usually add a 10 percent service charge, but it is normal to add another 5 percent as a tip. It is also usual to tip porters BDS$1 per item of luggage and room maids BDS$1 per night of your stay.

Departure Tax: A departure tax of BDS$25 per person is to be paid at the airport on departure for stays of over 24 hours. Some tour companies arrange this tax to be included as part of the price of the package.

Tourist Offices Abroad

IN CANADA

5160 Yonge Street, Suite 1800, North York, Ontario M2N GL19. Tel: 416-512 6569. Fax: 416-512 6581.

IN THE UK

263 Tottenham Court Road, London W1P 9AA. Tel: 0171-636 9448. Fax: 0171-637 1496.

IN THE US

New York: 800 2nd Avenue, New York, NY 10017. Tel: 212-986 6516/800-221 9831 (toll free in US). Fax: 212-573 9850.
Los Angeles: 3440 Wilshire Boulevard, Suite 1215, Los Angeles, California 90010. Tel: 213-380 2198. Fax: 213-384 2763.

Website addresses:

www.fleethouse.com/barbados/
www.prideofbarbados.com/

Weddings in Barbados

To get married in Barbados, apply for a marriage license at the Ministry of Home Affairs in the General Post Office Building, Cheapside, Bridgetown (tel: 431 7600). You need to provide your passport or birth certificate, and proof of divorce if you have been married before. No residential qualification or blood test is required. The license costs BDS$100 plus BDS$25 stamp fee. Many of the larger hotels will plan the formalities and arrange the wedding as part of a package.

Practical Tips

Media

Daily local newspapers are the *Advocate* and the *Nation*. Overseas newspapers are also available in shops and hotels. Two newspapers for visitors are the *Visitor* (weekly) and *Sun Seeker* (bi-monthly). *Ins & Outs of Barbados* and *Barbados in a Nutshell* are free publications placed in every accommodation.

CBC-TV is the state-owned station; satellite TV is available at most hotels. There are seven radio stations.

Postal Services

The main post office is in Cheapside, Bridgetown (open 8am–5pm Monday–Friday). Each parish has its own post office and stamps can also be bought in bookshops and hotels.

Telephone

The area code is **246**. It is simple to phone abroad with a phonecard from a public payphone. Cards to the value of BDS $10–BDS$60 are available from hotels and local stores. Calls from hotels are generally more expensive.

Local Tourist Offices

The main tourist office is at Harbour Road, Bridgetown (tel: 427 2623; fax: 426 4080). There are also offices at the **airport** (tel: 428 0937) and **cruise terminal** (tel: 426 1718). An information kiosk is at **Cave Shepherd** department store, Broad Street, Bridgetown.

Medical Treatment

The excellent **Queen Elizabeth Hospital**, Martinsdale Road, Bridgetown (tel: 436 6450), runs a 24-hour accident and emergency department. A decompression chamber for divers is also available at the **Barbados Defence Force Headquarters**. Ask at your hotel if you need a doctor or dentist.

Emergency Numbers

- **Police:** 112.
- **Fire:** 113.
- **Ambulance:** 115.

Voltage

Electricity is supplied throughout the island at 110V AC, 50 cycles. Adapters for shavers and hairdryers are available in hotels.

Shopping

Duty-free shopping is available at many shops throughout the island. To make a duty-free purchase, you must present your immigration slip (given to you when you arrive), or your passport and ticket.

In **Bridgetown** the main shopping area is along Broad Street in Da Costas Mall and Cave Shepherd department store. At **Medford Mahogany Village**, Barbarees Hill, you can watch skilful carpenters working with mahogany before you buy.

In **Hastings and Worthing** Chattel House Village, St Lawrence Gap, has a variety of shops selling souvenirs and local crafts. Quayside Center, Hastings Plaza, and Sandy Bank have a wide selection of clothing and souvenirs.

Holetown has a selection of interesting shops in Sunset Crest shopping plaza, with local crafts, swimwear and jewelry in the Chattel Village. Portobello Exhibition, Batts Rock Road (tel: 424 1687) sells colorful art.

Getting Around

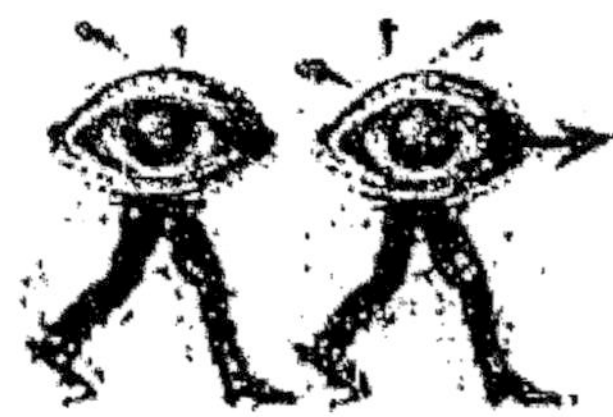

By Car

Driving is on the left, and by Caribbean standards the roads are good, although driving at night can be difficult on narrow unlit country roads. So leave plenty of time to reach your destination. The maximum speed limit outside urban areas is 50 mph (80 kph). Bajan rush hour is from 7.30–8.30am and 4.30pm–5.30pm.

Visitors' driver's licenses are available from the airport, many car hire companies, and most police stations. To obtain one you must present your own driver's license and BDS$10.

The following car hire companies offer a wide choice of cars, including mini mokes (beach buggy-style vehicles), free pick up and delivery to and from your accommodation, and free road maps. They accept Visa, American Express, and MasterCard:

Auto Rentals, tel: 428 9830; fax: 420 6844.
Sunny Isle Motors, tel: 435 7979; fax: 435 9277; e-mail: sunisle@caribsurf.com
Corbin's Car Rentals, tel: 427 9531; fax: 427 7975; e-mail: corbin's@ndl.net
National Car Rental, tel: 426 0603; fax: 429 8147; e-mail: edwards@caribsurf.com
Coconut Car Rentals, tel: 437 0297; fax: 228 9820; e-mail: coconut@caribsurf.com

By Taxi

Taxis are always in plentiful supply at the international airport, hotels and in town. Make sure you agree the fare before beginning your journey. Enquire at the airport or the hotel reception for the official rates.

Inter-Island Links

There are frequent flights and boat trips to nearby islands such as St Vincent and the Grenadines, St Lucia, and Grenada. For details, contact:
Grenadine Tours: Hastings Plaza. Tel: 435 8451.
Caribbean Safari Tours: Ship Inn, St Lawrence Gap. Tel: 427 5100.
Windward Lines: Hincks Street, Bridgetown. Tel: 431 0449.
Trans Island Air (TIA): Grantley Adams Airport. Tel: 418 1654. Fax: 428 0916.
LIAT: Grantley Adams Airport. Tel: 428 0986.

Island Tours

Tours of Barbados can be taken with:
Island Safari, tel: 432 5337; fax: 422 1966.
Custom Tours, tel: 425 0099; fax: 425 0100.
VIP Tour Services, tel: 429 4617.
Bajan tours, tel/fax: 437 9389.
Bajan Helicopters, tel: 431 0069; fax: 431 0086.

Where to Stay

Choosing a Hotel

Most of Barbados's expensive hotels line the west coast, or Platinum coast, as it is known, and the cheaper ones are generally located along the southeast coast. A few elegant, old, atmospheric hotels are also dotted around the south and east coasts. Renting a villa or an apartment is a good alternative to an hotel, especially as many of them come with maid service. Several local agents provide a range of villas and apartments to rent, such as:

Ronald Stoute and Sons: Sam Lord's Castle, St Philip. Tel: 423 6800.

Alleyne: Aguilar and Altman, St James. Tel: 432 0840.

Bajan Services: St Peter. Tel: 422 2618.

Hotel Listings

WEST COAST

Cobblers Cove
Road View, St Peter, Barbados, WI.
Tel: 422 2291.
Fax: 422 1460.
Elegant luxurious hotel built around a country house on a lovely white sand beach. Friendly staff. Suites with ocean or garden view. **$$$**

Colony Club
Porters, St James, Barbados, WI.
Tel: 422 2335.
Fax: 422 0667.
Informal elegance, with tropical gardens, watersports, and fitness center included in the price. **$$$**

Coral Reef Club
Holetown, Barbados, WI.
Tel: 422 2372.
Fax: 422 1726.
Luxury accommodation including cottages set in beautiful gardens. **$$$**

SOUTH COAST

Casuarina Beach Club
Dover, Christ Church, Barbados, WI.
Tel: 428 3600.
Fax: 428 1970.
Beach hotel in a beautiful palm garden. **$$**

Sandy Beach
Worthing, Christ Church, Barbados, WI.
Tel: 435 8000.
Fax: 435 8053.
Pretty pink and blue hotel on a wide sandy beach. **$$**

Price Guide

Price categories are based on the cost of a double room, for one night:
$ = less than $100
$$ = $100–200
$$$ = more than $200.

Silver Sands
Christ Church, Barbados, WI.
Tel: 428 6001.
Fax: 428 3758.
Off the beaten track, with basic rooms and apartments; good windsurfing. **$$**

SOUTHEAST AND EAST COAST

Atlantis Hotel
Bathsheba, St Joseph, Barbados, WI.
Tel: 433 9445.
Right on the Atlantic coast, but quite run-down looking and basic. Superb local food. **$**

Crane Beach
St Philip, Barbados, WI.
Tel: 423 6220.
Fax: 423 5343.
A traditional hotel beautifully situated on top of a cliff. **$$$**

Divi Southwinds Beach Resort
St Lawrence Gap, Christ Church, Barbados, WI.
Tel: 428 7181.
Fax:428 4674.
Luxury complex close to lively nightlife. **$$$**

Edgewater Inn
Bathsheba, St Joseph, Barbados, WI.
Tel: 433 9900.
Fax: 433 9902.
Perched on a cliff overlooking the Atlantic Ocean. Some rooms with ocean views. **$**

Inn on the Beach
Holetown, St James, Barbados, WI.
Tel: 432 0385.
Fax: 432 2440.
Air-conditioned apartments overlooking the beach. **$$**

Kingsley Club
Cattlewash, St Joseph, Barbados, WI.
Tel: 433 9422.
Fax: 433 9226.
Looks across to miles of beach and rough sea. Multi-million dollar refurbishment planned. **$$**

Sam Lord's Castle
Long Bay, St Philip, Barbados, WI.
Extensive complex with the pirate's castle at its heart. Beautiful beach that never gets crowded. **$$$**

Where to Eat

What to Eat

Barbados has restaurants featuring everything from traditional Bajan cuisine to Chinese, Italian, and American fast food. Most hotels and beach bars serve up flying fish cutters (breaded flying fish in a bun) for lunch. Other specialties are dolphin (*dorado*), red snapper, hot saltfish cakes, pickled breadfruit and pepperpot, often accompanied by rice and peas, macaroni pie, plantain, sweet potato, or yam. Among the usual fast food chains, look out for the *roti* shop – serving a savory pocket of curried chicken, prawn, beef, or potato.

Restaurant Listings

BRIDGETOWN AND WEST COAST

Brown Sugar
Aquatic Gap, Bay Street.
Tel: 426 7684.
Bajan and Caribbean specialties in the surroundings of a traditional-style home. **$$$**

The Cliff
St James.
Tel: 432 1922.
Stunning cliff top setting matches the quality of the food cooked by a prize-winning chef. **$$$**

Mango's
Speightstown.
Tel: 422 0704.
Overlooking the sea. Seafood is their specialty, especially grilled lobster. **$$**

Mullins Beach Bar
Mullins Beach, St Peter.
Tel: 422 1878.
Bajan food served on a cool verandah on the beach. Lively atmosphere. **$–$$**

Olive's Bar and Bistro
2nd Street, Holetown.
Tel: 432 2112.
Unpretentious food with a Caribbean and Mediterranean flavor. **$$**

Waterfront Cafe
The Careenage, Bridgetown.
Tel: 427 0093.
Traditional Bajan specialties and Creole cooking served up to the sound of live music. **$$**

SOUTH COAST

Carib Beach Bar
Sandy Beach, Christ Church.
Tel: 435 8540.
Fish and beach barbecues, popular with the locals. **$$**

Price Guide

Price categories are based on the cost of a meal for one person, excluding drinks:
$ = less than $20
$$ = $20–30
$$$ = more than $30.

Champers
Hastings.
Tel: 435 6644.
Dine to the sound of the ocean in this atmospheric seaside restaurant. **$$**

Pisces Restaurant
St Lawrence Gap, Christ Church.
Tel: 435 6564.
Local fresh fish and seafood specialties on the water's edge. **$$$**

The Roti Hut
Worthing Main Road.
Tel: 435 7362.
A simple eatery with the largest selection of *rotis* on the island. **$**

Shakey's Pizza
Hastings Main Road.
Tel: 435 7777.
Excellent pizza and take away. **$**

SOUTHEAST AND EAST

Crane Beach
St Philip.
Tel: 423 6220.
Good value Bajan buffet lunch at this elegant hotel on Sunday. **$$**

Edgewater Hotel
Bathsheba.
Tel: 433 9900.
Noted for its Sunday Bajan buffets. **$$**

Kingsley Club
Cattlewash.
Tel: 433 9422.
Excellent fish menu and tasty sandwiches at lunchtimes. **$$**

Nightlife

Nightclubs and Live Music

Barbados is packed with lively places to go at night, especially on the south coast:

The Boatyard, Bay Street, Bridgetown. Tel: 436 2622. Live bands every evening except Monday and Wednesday.

Harbour Lights, Bay Street, Bridgetown. Tel: 436 7225. An open-air nightclub on the beach. top live bands at weekends.

After Dark, Gateways, St Lawrence Gap. Tel: 435 6547. Three discos in one. Local spot.

The Casbah, Baku Beach. Tel: 432 2258. Sophisticated nightclub on the west coast.

The Ship Inn, St Lawrence Gap. Tel: 435 6961. Top local bands, seven nights a week.

The Waterfront Cafe, The Careenage, Bridgetown. Tel: 427 0093. Live music every night with jazz on Thursday, Friday and Saturday.

1627 And All That, in the courtyard of the Barbados Museum. Tel: 428 1627. Folkloric historical musical show with dinner included on Sunday and Thursday.

Tropical Spectacular, Plantation Restaurant and Garden Theatre, St Lawrence Gap. Tel: 428 5048. Glittering extravaganza dinner show, featuring the music and dances of the Caribbean on Wednesday and Friday.

Outdoor Activities

Watersports

Most watersports are available at the hotels along the west and south coasts.

DIVING

There are several interesting shipwrecks to explore and there is excellent visibility for divers and snorkelers. Several experienced and reputable dive operators offer certification courses for all levels from beginners to advanced instructors:
Coral Isle Divers, tel: 432 0931.
West Side Scuba Centre, tel: 432 2558.
Hightide Watersports, tel: 432 0931/228 3322.
For supplies and repairs contact:
Hazell's Waterworld, Boatyard Complex, Bay Street, Bridgetown. Tel: 228 6734, or at Sandy Bank, Hastings. Tel: 426 4043.
Atlantis Adventures, tel: 436 8929. Offers diving in a submarine.

SAILING

Mount Gay Regatta is the highlight of the yachting season in May or June. Small sailing boats, such as a Sunfish or Hobie Cat, can be rented by the hour along the south coast beaches and the west coast. Sailing trips around the island can be taken to include lunch, snorkeling, or a moonlight cruise. The following companies offer private charters:
Tiami Catamaran Sailing Cruises, tel: 427 7245.
Limbo Lady, tel: 420 5418.
Cool Runnings, tel: 436 0911.

Fishing

Fish for wahoo, dolphin (dorado), barracuda, tuna, and marlin in well-equipped boats with experienced crew. Half-day or full-day charters are available with snacks, lunch and drinks provided. Some crews will even cook your fish for you straight out of the sea. Contact:
Blue Marlin and Idyll Time, tel: 436 4322/435 6669.
Billfisher II, tel: 431 0741.
Cannon Charters, tel: 424 6107.

SURFING

Body surfing is good along the southeast coast and you can rent boards on the beach at Crane Beach Hotel. The best surfing around the island is in an area known as the Soup Bowl at Bathsheba on the Atlantic Coast, but beware of the strong currents.
Contact: the **Barbados Surfing Association** at Coconut Court Hotel, Hastings, Christ Church, tel: 427 1655 for more details.

WINDSURFING

There is excellent windsurfing to be had at the southernmost point of the island at Silver Sands and Silver Rock.
Contact: the **Windsurfing Association** at Silver Rock Hotel, Silver Sands, Christ Church, tel: 428 2866.

Good Beaches

On the calm, Caribbean west coast, are golden sand beaches with a wide selection of watersports, they include: Heywoods Beach (north of Speightstown), Mullins Beach, with a beach bar, Church Point by the Colony Club Hotel, Paynes Bay, and Fitts Village.

Tennis

Many of the larger hotels have their own tennis courts and will allow non-residents to hire facilities. It is advisable to reserve a court in advance.

Horseback Riding and Hiking

Caribbean International Riding Center provides beautiful trail rides with picnics and includes horses suitable for disabled riders (tel: 422 7433).
Highland Outdoor Tours offer scenic safari hikes and horse riding in the Scotland district (tel: 438 8069).

Every Sunday at 6am and 3.30pm, the **Barbados National Trust** guides a walk around different parts of the island – and it's free. Tel: 426 2421 for details and meeting points.

Golf

Barbados has four beautiful courses with championship 18-hole courses at Sandy Lane and Royal Westmoreland, although you can only play at the Royal Westmoreland if you are staying at a hotel which has an access agreement:
Sandy Lane Golf Club, tel: 432 4563.
Royal Westmoreland, tel: 422 4653.
Rockley Resort (nine holes), tel: 435 4873.
Almond Beach Village (nine holes), tel: 422 4900.

Getting Acquainted

Trinidad and Tobago

The most southerly Caribbean island, Trinidad lies 12 miles (20 km) off the coast of Venezuela. With an area of 1,864 sq. miles (4,660 sq. km), it is the largest island described in this book. Together with Tobago, which lies 21 miles (34 km) to the northeast, Trinidad forms an independent nation within the British Commonwealth. The main island, which is almost rectangular in shape, rises to its highest point at Cerro del Aripo (3,080 ft/ 930 meters).

Tobago, which is considerably smaller than Trinidad and covered with lush vegetation, has a number of beautiful beaches. Its highest point, which lies in the north of the island, is 1,890 ft (570 meters).

Public Holidays

January 1	New Year's Day
March/April	
Easter	Good Friday Easter Monday Indian Arrival Day
June 19	Labor Day
August 1	Discovery/ Emancipation Day
August 31	Independence Day
September 24	Republic Day
December 25	Christmas Day
December 26	Boxing Day

Calendar of Events

Hosay, the Muslim winter festival with processions, music and dance is held in February/ March. Originally a Muslim celebration for the dead, it has developed into a colorful occasion with parades, music and dancing.
Phagwa – Hindu New Year – is celebrated at the time of the March full moon.
Carnival in Trinidad and Tobago reaches a climax on the Monday and Tuesday before Ash Wednesday, and although not an official public holiday, everything is closed.
On the Tuesday after Easter is the goat race, **Buccoo**, an important social occasion in Tobago.
June is the month of **Eid-ul-Fitr**, the Islamic New Year festival which also marks the end of Ramadan.
At the end of June, the **Heritage Festival** recalls the cultural legacy of the African slaves. Concerts and displays of traditional dancing are held in many villages.
Divali, the Hindu Festival of Lights is held in October/ November in honor of the goddess Lakshmi. On this day, hundreds of tiny lights are lit by Hindus all over Trinidad and Tobago.

Planning the Trip

Money Matters

The Trinidad and Tobago (TT$) dollar is the main currency on both islands. Most hotels, restaurants and shops accept major credit cards.

The First Citizens Bank has a convenient foreign exchange booth at Piarco Airport (tel: 669 2489).

Tourist Offices Abroad

IN CANADA

The RMR Group Inc., Taurus House, 512 Duplex Avenue, Toronto M4R 2E3.
Tel: 416-485 8724.
Fax: 416-485 8256.

IN THE UK

Morris Kevan International Ltd., International House, 47 Chase Side, Enfield, Middlesex EN2 6NB.
Tel: 0181-367 3752.
Fax: 0181-367 9949.

IN THE US

Sales Marketing And Reservations Tourism Services (SMARTS), 7000 Blvd. East, Guttenberg, New Jersey 07093.
Tel: 201-662 3403.
Fax: 201-869 7628.
Travel Trade Hotline, tel: 1-800 748 4224 (toll-free in the US).

Website Addresses

www.VisitTNT.com
www.tidco.co.tt

Practical Tips

Media

RADIO

There are 10 radio stations on Trinidad. The most popular are *Radio Trinidad*, *Music Radio*, and *Radio Tempo*. There are also four television channels – two broadcast by the state-run Trinidad and Tobago Television (TTT) and two private channels (CNN TV-6 and AVM Television) which mostly show news, Indian romantic films, and music videos. Some hotels also have satellite TV.

NEWSPAPERS

Two daily papers are published in Port of Spain: the *Trinidad Guardian* and the *Trinidad Express*. The weekly paper on Tobago, the *Tobago News*, reports mainly local events.

Telephone and Fax

The dialing code for Trinidad and Tobago is **868**. A phonecard is recommended for long-distance calls, some of which have to be made through the operator. Telegrams and faxes can be sent from hotels or post offices.

Local Tourist Office

IN TRINIDAD

TIDCO (Tourism and Industrial Development Company of Trinidad and Tobago Limited), 10–14 Phillips Street, Port of Spain.
Tel: 623 6022/1932/4.
Fax: 623 3848.
Information office, Piarco. Tel: 669 5196.

IN TOBAGO

TIDCO, Unit 12, IDC Mall, Sangster's Hill, Scarborough.
Tel: 639 4333.
Fax: 639 4514.
Information office, Crown Point Airport. Tel: 639 0509.

Medical Treatment

There are two modern hospitals on **Trinidad**: the Mount Hope Medical Complex near Port of Spain (tel: 623 2951) and the Adventist Hospital, Western Main Road, Port of Spain (tel: 622 1191).

On **Tobago** there is a hospital in Scarborough (tel: 639 2551).

Emergency Numbers

Police: 999.
Fire and Ambulance: 990.

Nightlife

Trinidad has lots to do in the evening, and it really comes alive during Carnival when the island vibrates with steel pan and calypso music and the accompanying parties and wild street parades. Some of the large hotels provide live music and entertainment for guests and there is a selection of bars and nightclubs where visitors can dance the night away.

Shopping

The Normandie Hotel has a well-stocked, modern shopping mall where visitors can buy locally made batik prints, T-shirts and other art and crafts, and a variety of other goods. There is also interesting shopping in the mall on Charlotte Street and on St Ann's Road. For a good selection of local calypso and soca music try Rhyner's Record shop on Prince Street, Port of Spain.

Voltage: 110 AC, 60 cycles; 220 AC, 60 cycles.

Getting Around

By Car

Visitors wishing to rent a car must be at least 21 years old and in possession of a valid driving license. Traffic drives on the left in Trinidad and Tobago. Car rental companies:

Amar Rentals Ltd.
Prince Charles Street, San Fernando
Tel: 657 6089/7272.
Fax: 657 6084.

Executive Limousine Service
Tragarete Road, Port of Spain.
Tel: 625 1170/2624.
Fax: 623 4304.

Motorbike Rentals:

Baird's Rentals Ltd.
Crown Point and Scarborough, Tobago.
Tel: 639 2528.
Fax: 639 4126.

By Taxi and Bus

Taxis are available for hire at central points. There are also buses running between the larger towns on the island. Some taxis follow set routes and minibus-taxis provide additional transport.

Inter-Island Links

Apart from Saturday, there is a ferry service between the two islands. The crossing from Port of Spain to Scarborough takes about 6 hours. Air Caribbean also runs a service linking the two islands. The journey takes 20 minutes and there are 13 flights every day.

Where to Stay

Choosing a Hotel

The two islands can offer a range of accommodation to suit every budget, from international hotel chains to simple private establishments. For most visitors, Trinidad is the island to party, while Tobago is an ideal place to relax.

Hotel Listings

TRINIDAD

Alicia's House
7 Coblentz Gardens, St Ann's, Port of Spain.
Tel: 623 2802.
Fax: 623 8560.
Attractive guesthouse in a residential suburb. **$–$$**

Asa Wright Nature Centre and Lodge
Blanchisseuse Road, Arima.
Tel: 667 4655.
Fax: 667 0493.
Inn for nature lovers in an isolated location in the Northern Range. Full board only. **$$$**

Price Guide

Price categories are based on the cost of a double room, for one night:
$ = less than $100
$$ = $100–200
$$$ = more than $200.

Blanchisseuse Beach Resort,
Blanchisseuse.
Tel: 628 3731.
Fax: 628 3737.
Small guesthouse on the beach. **$–$$**

La Calypso
46 French Street, Woodbrook.
Tel: 622 4077.
Fax: 623 8560.
Friendly guesthouse with good service. **$**

Holiday Inn
Wrightson Road, Port of Spain.
Tel: 625 3361.
Fax: 625 4166.
Modern, comfortable city hotel directly by the harbor, with good views from the restaurant. **$$$**

Johnson's
16 Buller Street, Woodbrook, Port of Spain.
Tel: 628 7553.
Friendly bed-and-breakfast accommodation, central location and relatively quiet. **$–$$**

Kapok
16 Cotton Hill, Port of Spain.
Tel: 622 6441.
Fax: 622 9677.
Dependable city hotel with two renowned restaurants. **$$$**

The Normandie Hotel
10 Nook Avenue, St Ann's, Port of Spain.
Tel/Fax: 624 1181.
Practical, impersonal and fairly quiet. **$$**

Schultzi's
35 Fitts Street, Port of Spain.
Tel: 622 7521.
Simple family guesthouse in a central location with a kitchen for self-caterers. **$**

Trinidad Hilton
Lady Young Road, St Ann's, Port of Spain.
Tel: 624 3211.
Fax: 624 4485.
Far and away the best: central location, plenty of amenities and live shows in the evening. **$$$**

TOBAGO

Arnos Vale Hotel
Plymouth.
Tel: 639 2881.
Fax: 639 4629.
Picturesque, quiet location surrounded by luxuriant vegetation. Small beach. The breakfast buffet is a rendezvous for exotic birds. **$$$**

Blue Waters Inn
Batteaux Bay, Speyside.
Tel: 660 4341.
Fax: 660 5195.
Comfortable hotel favored by divers in a remote location on the northwest coast.**$$–$$$**

Coco Reef Hotel
Coconut Beach, Crown Point.
Tel: 639 8571.
Fax: 639 8574.
New 5-star hotel with a small beach and tastefully decorated rooms. Popular with German visitors. **$$$**

Price Guide

Price categories are based on the cost of a double room, for one night:
$ = less than $100
$$ = $100–200
$$$ = more than $200.

Le Grand Courlan
Grafton Beach, Black Rock.
Tel: 639 9667.
Fax: 639 0030.
New, rather impersonal luxury hotel with its own spa and numerous sports facilities. **$$$**

Kariwak Village
Crown Point.
Tel: 639 8442.
Fax: 639 8441.
Small village of simple, round huts in a lovely tropical garden. A short walk to the beach and live entertainment at the weekend. **$$$**

Mount Irvine Bay Hotel and Golf Club
PO Box 222.
Tel: 639 8871.
Fax: 639 8800.
Discreet and elegant hotel with a British air. Golf course surrounded by palm trees on the site of an old sugar mill. **$$$**

Richmond Great House
Belle Garden.
Tel/Fax: 660 4467.
Accommodation in an old plantation house on a hill above Windward Road. Airy, quiet rooms. **$$–$$$**

Turtle Beach Hotel
Great Courland Bay.
Tel: 639 2851.
Fax: 639 4629.
Pleasant holiday hotel on a beautiful wide beach. Mostly English clientele. **$$**

Where to Eat

What to Eat

On no other island will you find such a colorful mix of nationalities as on Trinidad and Tobago. The culinary traditions of the African, Indian, Chinese, and French settlers who were some of the original residents have contributed to the wide variety of the cuisine on both islands. The various specialties are mostly prepared from fresh seafood, tropical fruit, and vegetables. The price of a meal is relatively high, but with a little care you can still keep within a limited budget.

Restaurant Listings

TRINIDAD

La Fantaisie
The Normandie, Port of Spain.
Tel: 624 1181.
Creole-style nouvelle cuisine. **$$$**

Hong Kong City
86A Tragarete Road, Port of Spain.
Tel: 622 3949.
Chinese specialties with a Creole twist. **$**

Monsoon
72 Tragarete Road, Port of Spain.
Tel: 628 7684.
Excellent Indian cuisine plus take aways. **$**

Schultzi's Eaterie
5 Edward Street, Port of Spain.
Tel: 627 7906.
Friendly snack bar with typical West Indian dishes and sandwiches. **$**

Surf Country Inn
Blanchisseuse.
Tel: 669 2475.
International and West Indian cuisine with wonderful north coast views from the verandah. Popular with locals on Sunday. **$–$$**

Tiki Village
Kapok Hotel, Port of Spain.
Tel: 622 6441.
Polynesian cuisine, with fish and seafood specialties. **$**

Timberline
North Coast Road, Maracas.
Tel: 638 2263.
Fine Creole specialties. **$$**

TOBAGO

Black Rock Café
Black Rock.
Tel: 639 7625.
Pretty verandah restaurant with local dishes, steaks and seafood. **$–$$**

Price Guide

Price categories are based on the cost of a meal for one person, excluding drinks:
$ = less than $20
$$ = $20–30
$$$ = more than $30.

Bonkers
Storebay Local Road, Crown Point.
Tel: 639 7173.
Comfortable restaurant with dependable local dishes and the best cocktails on the island. **$–$$**

Jemma's Seaview Kitchen,
Speyside.
Tel: 660 4066.
Top-rate island cuisine, served in a cheerful tree house by the sea. **$**

Miss Jean
Storebay Beach Facilities.
Simple, inexpensive and well seasoned dishes. **$**

Old Donkey Cart House
Bacolet Street, Scarborough.
Tel: 639 3551.
Wooden house with playfully romantic decor. International and Caribbean cuisine; well-stocked wine cellar. **$$**

Rouselle's Seafood Restaurant
Bacolet Street, Scarborough.
Tel: 639 4738.
Frequently recommended establishment with a well-deserved reputation and typical island cuisine.**$$–$$$**

Seahorse Inn
Old Grafton Road.
Tel: 639 0686.
Idyllic situation with wonderful sea views. **$**

Outdoor Activities

Birdwatching

Although Carnival attracts many people to Trinidad, the island and its sister Tobago have much more to offer visitors. The beautiful landscape, rich with vegetation, is home to more than 400 species of bird and over 600 butterfly species, making it a haven for birdwatchers and nature lovers. The islands also have many wildlife sanctuaries and nature reserves. The most popular include:
Asa Wright Nature Centre and Lodge, Arima, tel: 667 4655; fax: 667 0493.
Caroni Bird Sanctuary, Caroni, tel. 645 1305.
Little Tobago, an island off Speyside in Northeast Tobago.

Hiking

Walking is a good way to explore the islands and see the fabulous flora and fauna. Always travel with an experienced guide. For more details contact:
The Forestry Division, Long Circular Road, Port of Spain. Tel; 622 4521; 622 7476.
Trinidad and Tobago Field Naturalists' Club, The Secretary. 1 Errol Park Road, St Ann's. Tel; 625 3386; 645 2132 (evenings and weekends).
Chaguaramas Development Authority Guided Tours, tel: 634 4227/4364.
Pioneer Journeys, Pat Turpin, Man-O-War Bay Cottages, Charlotteville. Tel: 660 4327.

Watersports

DIVING

The best diving and snorkelling can be found among the exciting reefs around Tobago and its neighboring islands. Dive operators on the island work with beginners and experienced divers. For more details contact:
Man Friday Diving, Charlotteville, tel/fax: 660 4676.
Dive Tobago, Pigeon Point, tel: 639 0202; fax: 639 2727.

Game Fishing

The colorful sea life and clear waters off Trinidad and Tobago are ideal for fishing. In the north coast of Trinidad anglers can find wahoo and sailfish, and off Tobago one can hook tuna, dolphin (dorado) and even a marlin. There is also an annual Caribbean International Game Fish Tournament. For more information on where to fish and details of boat charters contact: **Trinidad and Tobago Game Fishing Association**, tel: 624 5304.

Tennis

The **Trinidad Hilton** in Port of Spain and **Mount Irvine Bay Hotel** in Tobago have tennis courts. There are also public courts on Upper Frederick Street, Port of Spain, tel: 623 1121.

Getting Acquainted

ABC Islands

Aruba, **Bonaire**, and **Curaçao** are the most westerly of the Lesser Antilles and are flat and dry, with an average annual rainfall of only 20 inches (50 cm). One can discover the many species of cactus that grow here, and also the strange Watapana (or Divi-Divi) tree, whose top always inclines to the southwest in line with the prevailing northeast trade winds.

Politically, the ABC Islands, together with St Maarten, St Eustatius, and Saba, belong to the Netherlands Antilles and are thus a part of the Kingdom of the Netherlands. Aruba has a special status within the group.

Public Holidays

January 1	New Year's Day
March 18	Aruba Day
Easter	Good Friday
	Easter Monday
April 30	Coronation Day
	Queen's Birthday
May 1	Labor Day
	Whit Monday
July 2	Curaçao Flag Day
September 6	Bonaire Day
December 25	Christmas Day
December 26	Boxing Day

Calendar of Events

January: **Carnival** on Curaçao.
February: **Carnival** on Bonaire.
March: **International Sailing Regatta**, Curaçao.
October: **Annual Sailing Regatta**, Bonaire.
Variable: **International Theatre Festival**, Aruba.

Planning the Trip

Money Matters

The main currency on Aruba is the Aruban florin (Af), while Bonaire and Curaçao use the Netherlands Antilles florin (NAf), also known as the Netherlands Antilles guilder.
US dollars are widely accepted in tourist areas on all three islands.

Tourist Offices Abroad

ARUBA

In Canada

Aruba Tourism Authority,
86 Bloor St. West, Ste. 204,
Toronto, ONT. M5S 1M5.
Tel: 416-975 1950.
Fax: 416-975 1947.
E-mail: ata.canada@toaruba.com

In the US

Aruba Tourism Authority,
1000 Harbor Blvd.,
Weehawken, NJ 07087.
Tel: 201-330 0800.
Fax: 201-330 8757.
E-mail:
ata.newjersey@toaruba.com

Aruba Tourism Authority,
1 Financial Plaza, Suite 136,
Ft. Lauderdale, FL 33394.
Tel: 954-767 6477.
Fax: 954-767 0432.
E-mail: ata.florida@toaruba.com

Website Address:

www.aruba.com

BONAIRE

In Canada

Tel: 1-800-826 6247 (toll-free in Canada only).

In Europe

Interreps B.V.,
Visseringlaan 24,
2288 ER Rijswijk, The Netherlands.
Tel: 31-70 395 4444.
Fax: 31-70 336 8333.
Email:
interrep@interrep.demon.nl

In the US

Adams Unlimited,
10 Rockefeller Plaza, Suite 900,
New York, NY 10020.
Tel: 212-956 5912.
Fax: 212-956 5913.

Website Address:

www.interknowledge.com/bonaire

CURAÇAO

In Europe

Curaçao Tourist Bureau Europe,
Vastland 82-84,
3011 BP Rotterdam, Holland.
Tel: 31-10 414 2639.
E-mail: ctbenl@wirehub.nl

In the US

The Curaçao Tourist Board
475 Park Avenue, Suite 2000
New York, NY 10016.
Tel: 212-683 7660.
Fax: 212-683 9337.
E-mail: curacao@ix.netcom.com

The Curaçao Tourist Board,
330 Biscayne Boulevard,
Miami, FL 33132.
Tel: 305-374 5811.
Fax: 305-374 6741.

Website Addresses:

www.curacao-tourism.com
www.curacao.com

Practical Tips

Media

There are several radio stations on the ABC Islands. *Trans World Radio* (Medium Wave 800 KHZ) and *Radio Paradise* (FM 103,1) broadcast regularly in English. Aruba's television station, *Tele Aruba* on Channel 13, broadcasts local and American programs. In Curaçao and Bonaire you can receive *Tele Curaçao* on Channel 6 and 8 and *Flamingo TV* on Channel 11. Most hotels have satellite TV.

Postal Services

The main post offices are in the center of Oranjestad, Willemstad, and Kralendijk.

Telephone and Fax

The telephone code for **Aruba** is 29 78; for **Bonaire** 59 97; and for **Curaçao** 59 99. Local and long-distance calls can be made from hotels or from the telephone offices in or near the post offices, or from the offices of Setel, Setar, and Telbo, from where faxes and telegrams can also be sent.

Local Tourist Offices

Aruba: Aruba Tourism Authority, 172 L.G. Smith Boulevard, Oranjestad. Tel: 82 37 77. Fax: 83 47 02.
Bonaire: Bonaire Tourist Board, Kaya Simón Bolivar 12, Kralendijk. Tel: 83 22. Fax: 84 08.
Curaçao: Tourism Development Bureau, PO Box 8266, Pietermaai 19, Willemstad, Tel: 461 6000. Fax: 461 2305.

Medical Treatment

On Aruba and Curaçao you will find modern hospitals which correspond to European standards as well as good doctors in private practice.
Medical facilities on Bonaire are also reasonable.
Decompression chambers for divers are available on all three islands.

Emergency Numbers

Aruba: 11 100.
Bonaire: 11.
Curaçao: Police and Fire: 114; Ambulance: 112; Tourist Safety Service: 63 79 11.

Nightlife

Aruba has upscale restaurants, nightclubs and bars with live music and 11 glitzy casinos, while Bonaire more laid back, but this island has a few lively bars and nightclubs too.
Curaçao has sophisticated dining and casinos, open for gambling until the wee hours. Visitors can dance to local merengue music at nightclubs and bars or enjoy the evening entertainment in the hotels.

Shopping

The ABC islands have a range of tax-free shopping outlets. While Bonaire shopping is limited, Oranjestad in Aruba is a shoppers paradise with designer wear, perfume and local art, but it can be busy when a cruise ship docks. Sometimes shops are open seven days a week here.

but Curaçao offers great tax-free purchases and several shopping malls and interesting boutiques to explore.

Voltage: Aruba: 110 AC, 60 cycles; Bonaire: 127 AC, 50 cycles and 120 AC, 50 cycles; Curaçao: 110–130 AC, 50 cycles.

Getting Around

By Car

International car rental firms have offices at the airport as well as in many hotels. Those wishing to rent a car must be 21 years of age and in possession of a valid national driving license. For more information on car rentals contact:
Budget Rent A Car, Aruba, tel: 82 86 00.
Topless Rent A Car, Aruba, tel: 87 52 36; 87 12 96.
Dollar Rent A Car, Bonaire, tel: 8888; 5588; fax: 7788.
Avis, Curaçao, tel: 461 1255; fax: 461 5253.
Budget, Curaçao, tel: 868 3466; fax: 868 0644.

By Taxi

Taxis are available for hire at the airport, cruise terminals, and other central locations. In addition, on Aruba and Curaçao public transport is provided by buses and taxis following fixed routes. Always agree the fare before beginning a taxi journey.

Inter-Island Links

ALM runs scheduled flights between the three islands several times a day. In Bonaire they land at Flamingo Airport and Queen Beatrix International Airport in Aruba. ALM and **Air Aruba** link the ABC Islands to North America and Puerto Rico.

Where to Stay

Choosing a Hotel

High season in the Netherlands Antilles is from mid-December to mid-April. Prices are somewhat lower in summer. Apart from the hotels there are numerous guesthouses and apartments, which are usually considerably cheaper (albeit more modest) than the hotels. The relevant tourist office can supply details. Some accommodation is only available for rent on a weekly or monthly basis.

Hotel Listings

ARUBA

Amsterdam Manor
252 J.E. Irausquin Boulevard, Palm Beach.
Tel: 714 92.
Fax: 714 63.
Elegant family hotel in the style of a Dutch canal house. Across from the beach. **$$**

Best Western Manchebo Beach Resort
55 J.E. Irausquin Boulevard, Palm Beach.
Tel: 307 80.
Fax: 336 67.
Down-to-earth middle-class hotel on a white-sand beach. International clientele. **$$$**

Best Western Talk of the Town
55 L.G. Smith Boulevard, Eagle Beach.
Tel: 233 80.
Fax: 203 27.
Situated on the edge of Oranjestad, with a good restaurant and discotheque.
$–$$

Bucuti Beach Resort
55B L.G. Smith Boulevard, Eagle Beach.
Tel: 361 41.
Fax: 252 72.
Medium-sized, family-style hotel complex in a top location; popular with Europeans.
$$–$$$

Coconut Inn
Noord 31.
Tel: 662 88.
Fax: 654 33.
Friendly bed-and-breakfast establishment with comfortable rooms for self-caterers. **$–$$**

Hyatt Regency
85 J.E. Irausquin Boulevard, Palm Beach.
Tel: 612 34.
Fax: 654 78.
Luxurious mini Las Vegas by the beach. Casino, aquatic fun park, an artificial ruined castle, and expensive boutiques. **$$$**

Sonesta Seaport Village
Oranjestad.
Tel: 83 56 00.
Spacious, slightly impersonal luxury hotel directly by the harbor, with its own bathing island and marina. **$$$**

Price Guide

Price categories are based on the cost of a double room, for one night:
$ = less than $100
$$ = $100–200
$$$ = more than $200.

BONAIRE

Captain Don's Habitat
Kaya Gobernador N. Debrot 103, Kralendijk.
Tel: 82 90.
Fax: 82 40.
Hotel built on a coral reef with a famous diving station; very small beach. **$$$**

Carib Inn
Boulevard J.A. Abraham 46, Kralendijk.
Tel: 88 19.
Fax: 52 95.
Small family-owned hotel, ideal for divers. **$**

Price Guide

Price categories are based on the cost of a double room, for one night:
$ = less than $100
$$ = $100–200
$$$ = more than $200.

Divi Flamingo Beach Resort,
J.A. Abraham Blvd 40, Kralendijk.
Tel: 82 85.
Fax: 82 38.
The oldest hotel on the island. **$$$**

Harbour Village Beach Resort
Kaya Gobernador N. Debrot 71, Kralendijk.
Tel: 75 00.
Fax: 75 07.
Luxury resort with first-class water sports facilities. **$$$**

Sand Dollar Condominiums
Kaya Gobernador N. Debrot 79, Kralendijk.
Tel: 87 38.
Fax: 87 60.
Apartment hotel with American management. **$$–$$**

Sorobon Beach Resort
Lac Bay
Tel: 80 80.
Fax: 88 46.
Small beach hotel in a remote location; relaxed atmosphere. **$$**

CURAÇAO

Avila Beach Hotel
Penstraat 130, Willemstad.
Tel: 461 4377.
Fax: 461 1493.
Tastefully extended former governor's residence with antique furniture and colonial flair. **$$**

Buona-Sera-Inn
Kaya Godett 104, Pietermaai.
Tel: 461 8286.
Fax: 461 8344.
Simple family-run guesthouse in a renovated colonial residence. **$**

Habitat Curaçao
Coral Estate, Rif Saint Marie.
Tel: 864 0800.
Fax: 864 8464.
Colorful complex with practical cottages and suites for divers.

Park Hotel
Frederikstraat 84, Willemstad.
Tel: 62 31 12.
Friendly lodging in Otrabanda. **$**

Porto Paseo
Rouvilleweg 47, Willemstad.
Tel: 62 78 78.
Fax: 62 79 69.
Attractive beach hotel. **$$**

Princess Beach and Casino
M.L. King Boulevard 8.
Tel: 36 78 88.
Fax: 61 40 03.
Elegant beach hotel, the social hub of the island. **$$$**

Sheraton Curaçao Caribbean
John F. Kennedy Boulevard, Piscaderbaai.
Tel: 62 50 00.
Fax: 62 58 46.
Large American-style resort. Attractive beachside location. **$$**

Sonesta Beach Resort and Casino
John F. Kennedy Boulevard, Piscaderbaai.
Tel: 736 8800.
Fax: 462 7502.
Pleasant luxury hotel with Dutch-Caribbean architecture. Sandy beach and perfect service. **$$$**

Where to Eat

What to Eat

Thanks to its colorful history, the cuisine of the ABC Islands is varied and cosmopolitan. On all three islands you will find Indonesian, Chinese, French, Spanish, and Italian restaurants. The specialties include a large number of seafood dishes. Aruba and Curaçao also have mobile restaurants in which local snacks like *pastechi* and *krokets* are prepared, and which operate until the small hours.

Restaurant Listings

ARUBA

Boonoonoonoos
Wilhelminastraat 18A, Oranjestad.
Tel: 83 18 88.
Prize-winning gourmet restaurant with imaginative dishes based on local specialties. **$$$**

Price Guide

Price categories are based on the cost of a meal for one person, excluding drinks:
$ = less than $20
$$ = $20–30
$$$ = more than $30.

Charlie's Bar
San Nicolas.
Tel: 84 50 86.
A refreshingly chaotic pub with unique flair and good, unpretentious food. **$$$**

Chez Mathilde
Havenstraat 23, Oranjestad.
Tel: 34 968.
French cuisine in an attractively

renovated house dating from the 19th century. **$$$**

Jo-Ann
Mahuma 5b, Oranjestad.
Tel: 82 03 44.
Small, comfortable restaurant with hearty portions and friendly service. **$$**

Papiamento
Washington 61, Oranjestad.
Tel: 245 44.
European and local cuisine in an old villa. **$$$**

BONAIRE

Den Laman
Kaya Gob. N. Debrot, Kralendijk.
Tel: 89 55.
Specializes in fine seafood. **$$$**

Zeesicht
Kaya N.J.E. Craane 12, Kralendijk.
Tel: 84 34.
Lovely terrace by the harbor. Good fish dishes. **$$$**

CURAÇAO

Belle Terrace
Hotel Avila Beach, Penstraat 130, Willemstad.
Tel: 61 43 77.
Scandinavian and local dishes in an elegant setting. **$$–$$$**

Bistro Le Clochard
Riffort, Otrabanda.
Tel: 62 56 66.
Gourmet cuisine with French-Swiss accents. Delightful location on the Sint Anabaai.

De Taveerne
Landhuis Groot Davelaar.
Tel: 737 0669.
Elegant restaurant in a historic building. **$$$**

Jaanchie's
Westpunt.
Tel: 864 0126.
A congenial garden restaurant, which is famous for its fish soup amongst other seafood specialties. **$**

Outdoor Activities

Diving

The Tourist Offices provide informative brochures listing the diving grounds and schools. **Dive Curaçao** is particularly good.

The waters around Bonaire are designated as an official marine park, diving in the clear waters off the island is a real experience with its coral reefs and colorful marine life. It is an ideal destination for underwater photographers.

Try the following dive operators:
Aruba: Aruba Pro Dive, Oranjestad, tel: 82 55 20; fax: 83 77 23.
Bonaire: Sand Dollar Dive and Photo, Kralendijk, tel: 52 52; fax: 87 60.
Curaçao: Underwater Curaçao, Willemstad, tel:461 8100.

Watersports

The ocean off the ABC Islands draws visitors seeking a variety of water activities and sports from windsurfing and fishing to snorkelling and sailing. The sea is often crystal clear and shallow near the coastline and the coral reefs and rich fish population can offer hours of fun. Most of the large hotels have watersports or the local tourist office can recommend boat charters.

Birdwatching

Bonaire is a favorite of birdwatchers. The island is home to 170 species of birds mainly clustered around Goto Lake, Pekelmeer, Cai and Dos Pos. Look out for the flamingo, Bonaire's national symbol.

Hiking

The best way of studying the islands' remarkable flora and fauna is to walk, drive, or ride through the National Parks. The coastline can be explored from the water by taking a cruise on one of the well-equipped pleasure boats.

Mountain Biking

The flat, but rugged terrain of the ABC Islands is ideal for biking. It is a good way of discovering the land, wildlife and reaching some of the more secluded beaches. Bonaire is the site of a challenging triathlon in November. It includes a cycle route, a swim and run. For details of mountain bike rentals and tours contact:
Pablito Big Rental, Oranjestad, tel: 87 86 55.
Discover Bonaire, tel: 5252.

Golf

There are several well-maintained courses including: **Tierra del Sol**, an 18-hole golf course in the north west of Aruba. The **Aruba Golf Club** has an interesting 9-hole course and the **Curaçao Golf Club** in Emmastad is open to members and non-members.

ART & PHOTO CREDITS

Monty Alexander 62
Herve Amiard 74
Tony Arruza 30, 264, 272
Junia Browne 24
William Clark, Courtesy of Jamaica National Library 35
Edith Crocker 243
Courtesy of Barbados Museum & Historical Society 32, 40
Courtesy of Jamaica National Library 29, 31
Courtesy of St. James Beach Hotel 45
Mitch Epstein 58, 10/11, 60/61, 78/79, 80/81, 121, 124/125, 133, 136/137, 141, 142, 144/145, 146, 152/53, 157, 156, 159, 160/161, 172, 171, 169, 167, 56/57, 176, 180, 192/193, 194, 199, 204/205, 216/217, 218, 223, 226, 228/229, 255, 277
Antoine Ferreo, Courtesy of Balmain Antiques 22/23, 26
Brigitte Geh 184, 200, 202
Glyn Genin 201T, 222T
A. M. Gross 185
N. H. P. A. Dan'el Heuclin 225
Edmond Van Hooricle 55, 59, 118, 139, 143, 190, 235, 246, 248, 279, 287, 290/291, 296, 297, 299, 300, 301, 305
Pierre Husseno 72
Volkmar E. Janicke 119,126, 130, 131, 132, 177, 209, 234, 237, 245, 249, 250/251, 285, 289, 236T, 280T
Gerold Jung 201
Catherine Karnow 25, 54, 252
Bob Krist 2/3, 8/9, 47, 52, 53, 70, 73, 82/83, 84, 88/89, 90, 91, 94, 96T, 97, 98T, 99, 100, 106T, 108, 111, 112T, 113, 122, 127, 129, 134, 135, 206, 207, 211, 213, 230, 231, 236, 238, 256, 257, 295, 303, 304, 307, 312, 232T
F. W. Lane/FLPA 212
David Lyons 19, 219, 221, 222, 224
William Miller, Courtesy of Jamaica National Library 28
Jenny Palmer 168, 173
Pascalito 63
Richard T. Nowitz 6/7, 50, 274/275, 276, 288, 278T
Christine Rettenmeier 4/5, 292, 294
Rex Features 142T, 191
Martin Rosefeldt 18, 43, 44, 60, 65, 75, 94T, 132T, 198, 200T, 264T, 266T, 267T, 268, 269, 270, 270T
Wolfgang Rossig 142, 134T, 298T, 309, 310T, 311T
Elizabeth Saft, Courtesy of New York Public Library 33, 38, 39, 41
Terraqua 21, 138, 168T, 242, 296T
C. Tilt, Courtesy of Jamaica National Library 33
Associated Press/Topham 188
Topham Picturepoint 186/187
Topham Picture Source 19, 42, 66, 64, 189
Gertraud M. Trox 36/37, 108T, 109, 112, 123, 147, 148T, 149, 154, 155, 158T, 162, 166, 174/175, 178T, 179, 181, 182, 183, 203, 210, 210T 227,
Marc Vorsatz 240/241, 247, 249
Bill Wassman 17, 49, 51, 68/69, 133T, 158, 258/259, 260, 261, 265, 266, 265T, 267, 271, 273, 302, 304T
Amanda Weil 98, 95, 96, 101, 104, 105
Solvin Zankl 93T, 148

Cartographic Editor **Zoë Goodwin**
Production **Stuart A. Everitt**
Design Consultants
Carlotta Junger & Graham Mitchener
Picture Research **Hilary Genin**

Picture Spreads

Pages 76/77
Top row from left to right: Bob Krist, David Lyons, Martin Rosefeldt, Bill Wassman
Center row: Volkmar E. Janicke, Gertraud M. Trox, Martin Rosefeldt
Bottom row: Richard Nowitz, Martin Rosefeldt, Martin Rosefeldt

Pages 114/115
Top row from left to right: Martin Rosefeldt, Marc Vorsatz, Gertraud M. Trox, Bill Wassman
Center row: David Lyons, Marc Vorsatz, Bob Krist
Bottom row: Bob Krist, Gertraud M. Trox, Martin Rosefeldt, Bill Wassman

Pages 150/151
All pictures by Terraqua except top row left by Martin Rosefeldt

Pages 214/215
Top row from left to right: Gertraud M. Trox, Terraqua, Bob Krist, A. M. Gross
Center row: A. M. Gross, A. M. Gross, Martin Rosefeldt
Bottom row: Bob Krist, Martin Rosefeldt, A. M. Gross, Bob Krist

Pages 282/283
Top row from left to right: Terraqua, Marc Vorsatz, Marc Vorsatz, Terraqua
Center row: Bill Wassman, Marc Vorsatz
Bottom row: Martin Rosefeldt, Marc Vorsatz, Marc Vorsatz, Terraqua

Map Production Polyglott Kartographie

Index

Numbers in italics refer to photographs

a

t